T0388584

Finance for Sustainable Development in Africa

Although a number of selected African countries have made efforts to implement various financial sector reforms, many countries have not fully implemented the requisite reforms required for sustainable development. Instead, they have focused mainly on bank-based financial reforms, thereby neglecting market-based financial reforms. This study provides a one-stop shop for understanding the history and evolution of the financial sector in Africa with a special focus on the sub-Saharan region where the financial system in many countries is still at a relatively nascent stage. The analysis is extensive and robust, and starts from financial repression to financial liberalisation (both internal and external), and its role in sustainable development and poverty alleviation.

The book covers a range of important research issues pertaining to financial development in selected African countries, including interest rate reforms; the dynamics of bank-based and market-based financial development; the role of the informal financial sector in sustainable development; the finance-growth nexus; bank-based versus market-based financial sectors in Africa; financial development and information and communication technology; and financial development and gender equality, among other topics. The book also considers the relationship between the COVID-19 global pandemic and financial development, and concludes by presenting a forecast of the future trends of financial and sustainable development on the African continent in general and sub-Saharan Africa in particular. The chapters are authored by prominent scholars and researchers in the field of finance and banking, applied econometrics and development economics, with a deep understanding and knowledge of financial development and the local situations in African countries.

The book provides crucial reference material for academics, researchers, policymakers and students of all levels and is a must-read for anyone wishing to understand the nature of finance and sustainable development in Africa in relation to the rest of the world. This book covers African countries, but with more emphasis on the sub-Saharan African region where the financial systems in many of the countries are still relatively underdeveloped.

Nicholas Mbaya Odhiambo is a Professor and Head of the Macroeconomic Policy Analysis (MPA) Research Programme at the University of South Africa (UNISA). He is also a Fellow of the African Academy of Sciences (AAS).

Erasmus Larbi Owusu is a Market and Economics Researcher and a Data Science Consultant. He is the Founder and the Chief Executive Officer (CEO) of SumsureIQ, a full service market research agency and data science consultancy working for clients across various African countries.

Simplice Anutechia Asongu is a Distinguished Visiting Professor at the University of Johannesburg in South Africa, Lead Economist and Director of the African Governance and Development Institute (Yaoundé, Cameroon) and Lead Economist and Director of the European Xtramile Centre of African Studies (Liège, Belgium).

Routledge Studies in Development Economics

For more information about this series, please visit: www.routledge.com/Routledge-Studies-in-Development-Economics/book-series/SE0266

Finance for Sustainable Development in Africa

Evolution, Impact and Policy Implications

Edited by
Nicholas Mbaya Odhiambo,
Erasmus Larbi Owusu, and
Simplice Anutechia Asongu

Routledge
Taylor & Francis Group

LONDON AND NEW YORK

First published 2023
by Routledge
4 Park Square, Milton Park, Abingdon, Oxon OX14 4RN

and by Routledge
605 Third Avenue, New York, NY 10158

Routledge is an imprint of the Taylor & Francis Group, an informa business

British Library Cataloguing-in-Publication Data
A catalogue record for this book is available from the British Library

ISBN: 978-1-032-10377-8 (hbk)
ISBN: 978-1-032-10379-2 (pbk)
ISBN: 978-1-003-21504-2 (ebk)

DOI: 10.4324/9781003215042

Typeset in Bembo
by codeMantra

Contents

4 Interest Rate Reforms in African Countries 43

ERASMUS LARBI OWUSU

5 Financial Determinants of Informal Financial Development in African Countries 58

SIMPLICE ANUTECHIA ASONGU, VALENTINE B. SOUMTANG AND
OFEH M. EDOH

6 Finance–Growth Nexus: A Review of Afrocentric Literature 76

NICHOLAS MBAYA ODHIAMBO

17 Financial Institutions, Poverty and Severity of Poverty in African Countries

SIMPLICE ANUTECHIA ASONGU, VALENTINE B. SOUMTANG AND
OFEH M. EDOH

Figures

Tables

Contributors

Joshua Yindenaba Abor is a Professor of Finance at the University of Ghana Business School. He has contributed to the financial economics literature, mainly in the areas of banking and finance, monetary policy, development finance, financial market development, FinTech innovation and financial inclusion, SME finance, private sector development, corporate finance and governance, international finance and trade, and international financial flows and growth.

Bosede Ngozi Adeleye is a Lecturer in the Department of Accountancy, Finance and Economics and Lincoln International Business School (LIBS) at the University of Lincoln, UK. Before joining the University of Lincoln, she was a lecturer in the Department of Economics and Development Studies at Covenant University, Nigeria. She received her BSc in Economics from Ogun State University in 1994. Then she earned an MSc in Banking and Finance from Bayero University, Kano, Nigeria in 1999 and a second MSc in International Economics from the University of Sussex, UK in 2014. She graduated with a PhD in Economics from Covenant University in 2018.

Elikplimi Komla Agbloyor is an Associate Professor in Finance at the University of Ghana Business School. He received his PhD in Finance from the University of Ghana in November 2012. He is currently an affiliate member of the Association of Chartered Certified Accountants (ACCA). He is a Certified Financial Risk Manager of Global Association of Risk Professionals (GARP). His research interests include artificial intelligence and machine learning, banking, corporate governance, cross-border mergers and acquisitions, financial inclusion, economic growth and development, financial development, institutions, international capital flows (FDI, portfolio flows and debt flows) and remittances.

Joshua Akanyonge is currently a Senior Lecturer with over nine years teaching undergraduate and postgraduate degree courses. He has developed the love for teaching and research in the accounting and finance disciplines. His research interests include financial intermediation (bank finance and performance); corporate finance; SME development and financing; and management accounting research. He earned his Diploma in Basic Education from the University of Cape Coast, Ghana, his BBA from the International University (IU) of Applied Sciences, Germany, his MSc in Economics & Business Administration from the University of Vaasa, Finland and his PhD in Management (Costing & Financial Management) from Central University of Nicaragua.

Anthony Enisan Akinlo is a Professor in Economics at the Obafemi Awolowo University, Ile-Ife, Nigeria. He is currently on leave as Vice Chancellor at the Redeemer's University, Ede, Nigeria. He received his BSc, MSc and PhD in Economics from the Obafemi Awolowo University, Ile-Ife in 1985, 1988 and 2005, respectively. He has published over 160 articles in many reputable economic journals. He specializes in the areas of economic reforms and growth. He has supervised 30 PhD theses and served as consultant to many international organizations.

Olumuyiwa Tolulope Apanisile is a Lecturer at the Obafemi Awolowo University, Ile-Ife. He received his BSc in Economics from the Faculty of Social Sciences, Obafemi Awolowo University, Ile-Ife in 2007. Then, he earned an MSc in Economics from the Obafemi Awolowo University, Ile-Ife in 2012. He graduated with a PhD in Economics from the Obafemi Awolowo University, Ile-Ife in 2016.

Anutechia Simplice Asongu is a Distinguished Visiting Professor at the University of Johannesburg in South Africa. He is also Lead Economist and Director of the African Governance and Development Institute (Yaoundé, Cameroon) and Lead Economist and Director of the European Xtramile Centre of African Studies (Liège, Belgium).

Valentine B. Soumtang is an Assistant Lecturer and Researcher at the University of Yaounde II-Soa in Cameroon since January 2021. She graduated from this University where she obtained her Bachelor's degree in Monetary, Financial and Banking Economics in 2011. She then obtained her MSc in Research in Monetary and Banking Macroeconomics in 2014, before graduating with a PhD in Monetary, Financial and Banking Economics from the same University in January 2021.

Carolyn Chisadza is a Senior Lecturer in the Economics Department at the University of Pretoria, South Africa. Carolyn received her BCom (Hons) in Economics from the Department of Economics, University of Pretoria, in 2009. Then she earned her MCom in Economics from the University of Pretoria in 2012. Carolyn graduated with a PhD in Economics from the University of Pretoria in 2017.

Matthew Clance is an Associate Professor in the Department of Economics at the University of Pretoria and a Fellow at Pan-African Scientific Council. Matthew received his BS in Economics from Georgia College &

State University in 2004. He then received his MA and PhD in economics from Clemson University in 2009 and 2012, respectively.

Ofeh M. Edoh is a PhD candidate in Development Economics at the University of Yaoundé II. Before joining the University of Yaoundé II, she was a Master's student at the University of Dschang. She received her BSc in Money, Banking and Finance from the Faculty of Economics and Management, University of Dschang, Cameroon in 2019. Then she earned an MSc in Public Economics and Human Resource Management from the University of Dschang in 2021. She is presently a PhD candidate in Development Economics at the University of Yaoundé II, Cameroon.

Rangan Gupta is a Professor in Economics at the University of Pretoria, South Africa. He received his BSc in Economics from the Department of Economics, Ramakrishna Mission Residential (R.K.M.R.) College, Narendrapur, University of Calcutta, India in 1997. Then he earned an MSc in Economics from the University of Calcutta, India in 1999. He graduated with a PhD in Economics from the University of Connecticut, USA in 2005.

Agyapomaa Gyeke–Dako holds PhD and MSc in Economics from the School of Economics, University of Nottingham (UK) and BA in Economics with Geography from the University of Ghana. She is currently a Senior Lecturer in Economics at the University of Ghana Business. Prior to her joining the University of Ghana Business School, she worked with Durham Business School (UK) for three years. She has also served as the Country Programme Manager of the Bloomberg Media Initiative Africa, Financial Journalism Training Programme. She has special interests in Micro, Small and Medium Enterprises (MSME) Development, Monetary and Financial Economics, Economic Growth and Development, Corporate Governance and Gender Diversity.

Mercy T. Musakwa is a Research Fellow at the University of South Africa. She received her BSc in Economics from the University of Zimbabwe, in 2000. Then she earned her MSc in Economics from the same university in 2002. She graduated with a PhD in Economics from the University of South Africa in 2018.

Nicholas Ngepah holds a PhD in Economics from the University of Cape Town, South Africa. Currently, he is a Professor of Economics at the School of Economics, University of Johannesburg. His research interests are development economics; energy economics; health economics; and poverty, inequality and growth. He has published papers in various journals, including *African Development Review, Environmental Science & Pollution Research, Quality & Quantity, Economic Research-Ekonomska Istraživanja, Peace Economics, Peace Science and Public Policy* and *International Economic Journal*, among others.

Sheilla Nyasha is a Research Fellow at the University of South Africa (UNISA). She received her BSc in Economics from the Faculty of Social Studies, University of Zimbabwe, in 2005. Then she earned an MSc in Economics from the same university in 2007. She graduated with a DCom in Economics from UNISA in 2015.

William Obeng-Amponsah is a Lecturer in Mathematics, Statistics and Finance at the Regent University College of Science and Technology (RUCST). He received his BSc (Hons) in Mathematics and Statistics (Combined major) from the Faculty of Mathematical Sciences, University of Ghana, Legon, in Ghana. Then he earned an MSc in Quantitative Finance from the University of Westminster in London, UK. He graduated with a PhD in Management Science and Engineering from the Wuhan University of Technology in China.

Nicholas Mbaya Odhiambo is a Professor and Head of the Macroeconomic Policy Analysis (MPA) Research Programme at the University of South (UNISA). Before joining UNISA in 2006, we worked as Head of Department / Programme Coordinator in the Department of Economics at the University of Fort Hare. He received his BA (Hons) degree from the Faculty of Arts and Social Science, Egerton University (Kenya) in 1993. Then he earned an MA (Economics) degree from the University of Dar es Salaam in 1999. He graduated with a PhD in Economics from the University of Stellenbosch in 2004.

Nathanael Ojong is an Assistant Professor of International Development Studies and Deputy Director of the Harriet Tubman Institute for Research on Africa and its Diasporas at York University in Canada. He holds an MA in Development Management from the University of Westminster in England and PhD in Development Studies from the Graduate Institute of International and Development Studies in Switzerland.

Erasmus Larbi Owusu is a Market and an Economic Researcher and the founder and CEO of SumsureIQ Ltd, a full range research consultancy service company headquartered in Accra, Ghana. Before that he was a Director and Head of Data Science and Analytics at Nielsen for African Countries, Benelux, Germany and Greece. He received his MSc (Hons) degree from the Faculty of Economics and Statistics, Odessa State Economic University, Ukraine, in 1993. Then he earned an MPhil (Development Economics) degree from the University of Cambridge, UK in 1997. He graduated with a PhD in Economics from the University of South Africa (UNISA), South Africa in 2012. Erasmus has special interest in sustainable economic development, banking and financial sector development.

Charles Shaaba Saba is a Research Fellow in the School of Economics, University of Johannesburg, South Africa. He holds a PhD degree in Economics from the University of Johannesburg. He taught development economics and analysis of economic data. He has published papers in various journals, including *Telecommunications Policy, Quality & Quantity, Economic Research-Ekonomska Istraživanja, Peace Economics, Peace Science and Public Policy* and *International Economic Journal,* among others.

Talknice Saungweme is a Lecturer in Economics at Great Zimbabwe University and a Research Fellow at the University of South Africa. He received his BSc and MSc in Economics from the Faculty of Business Management Sciences and Economics, University of Zimbabwe, in 2005 and 2007, respectively. He graduated with a PhD in Economics from the University of South Africa in 2020. His research works over the years have centred mostly on development issues in sub-Saharan African countries.

Magdalene Kasyoka Wilson is a Senior Lecturer in the School of Economics College of Business and Economics at the University of Johannesburg. Before joining the University of Johannesburg, Magdalene was a Lecturer in the Department of Economics and Economic History at Rhodes University in South Africa. She received her BA (Hons) from the University of Nairobi, Kenya. Then she earned a MA (Econs) from the University of Botswana. Magdalene graduated with a PhD in Economics from the University of Johannesburg in South Africa. Magdalene is currently involved in teaching undergraduate econometrics and postgraduate international trade and policy issues and has published in various peer-reviewed international journals. Her research interest is in international finance, international trade and macroeconomics.

Tendai Zawaira is a Postdoctoral Research Fellow in the Economics Department at the University of Pretoria, South Africa. Tendai received her BCom (Hons) in Economics from Midlands State University (Zimbabwe) in 2010. Then she earned her MCom in Economics from Midlands State University (Zimbabwe) in 2014. Tendai graduated with a PhD in Economics from the University of Pretoria in 2021.

1 Introduction

Erasmus Larbi Owusu and Nicholas Mbaya Odhiambo

This book provides a one-stop shop for understanding the history and evolution of the financial sector in Africa with a special focus on sub-Saharan African region from financial repression to financial liberalisation, and its role in sustainable development and poverty alleviation. The content of the book is multifaceted and covers a wide range of topics, including (i) interest rate reforms; (ii) the dynamics of bank-based and market-based financial development; (iii) the role of the informal financial sector in sustainable development; (iv) finance-growth nexus; (v) financial development and poverty alleviation; (vi) financial development and information and communication technology (ICT) in Africa; (vii) financial development and remittance inflows to Africa; (viii) microfinance, small and medium enterprises (SMEs) and economic development; and (ix) financial development and gender equality, among other topics.

It is structured in parts that logically follow one another to give a comprehensive understanding of finance for sustainable development in Africa, which encompasses the evolution of financial sector reforms, the state of financial sector development, and the role of the financial sector in gender equality and the informal sector of the economy. The chapters are authored by prominent scholars and researchers in the field of finance and banking, applied econometrics and development economics with a deep understanding and knowledge of financial development and the local situations in selected African countries. It is a must-read for anyone wishing to understand the nature of finance and sustainable development in Africa in general and SSA region in particular in relation to the rest of the world. It will be a crucial reference material for academics, researchers, policymakers and students of all levels who are interested in understanding finance for sustainable development in selected African countries.

1.1 Significance of the Book

This book is about the historical and contemporary review of finance for sustainable development in selected African countries, as well as finance in the informal sectors, and the use of mobile money to alleviate poverty. It also looks at financial development and remittance across selected African countries.

DOI: 10.4324/9781003215042-1

It is a research-oriented book in the sense that each chapter is a product of research on the subject matter. It, therefore, endeavours to forecast future trends of financial and sustainable development on the African continent. It is the first book of its kind to provide comprehensive and holistic coverage of financial dynamics in Africa with a clear focus on sustainable development. To our knowledge, no book on this topic brings together the history, evolution, financial repression, financial liberalisation, mobile money (ICT), remittance, finance in the informal sector and finance as a tool for gender equality in Africa to alleviate poverty on the continent. The book is well integrated and provides an insightful understanding of the role of the financial sector in sustainable development in Africa.

This scholarly book is anticipated to be used as part of study material in the fields of economic and management sciences, finance, development economics and applied econometrics across all universities and colleges in Africa and beyond. It is also anticipated to be a crucial reference book on financial sector development and sustainable economic growth. Topics related to the dynamics of financial sector development and its impact on economic growth and sustainable development are widely taught in several economic and management science–related subjects in every university across the world.

1.2 Structure and Outline of the Book

In Chapter 2, the evolution of financial sector reforms in Africa is examined further. Specifically, it investigates the timing, sequence and effects of the reforms on the performance of the African financial sector. To achieve this objective, the financial sector policies and development pre-, during and post-liberalisation periods are assessed. It is found that despite the financial sector reforms, the sector performed below expectation as the problems of low efficiency, low liquidity and sensitive institutional problems noticed in the sector before liberalisation have not been resolved.

Chapter 3 presents an overview of some key financial sector reforms that have been implemented in a number countries in sub-Saharan Africa since the onset of the new orthodoxy of financial liberalisation in the 1980s. The chapter also explores trends of some financial sector indicators in selected countries since the 1990s. In order to evaluate financial sector development in African countries, both bank-based and market-based financial sector indicators have been explored. Some of the financial sector indicators that have been reviewed in this chapter include interest rate spreads, financial deepening, bank asset concentration and stock market development. The selection of countries used in the analysis is mainly based on the availability of data for the various indicators and sample period.

Chapter 4 proffers useful perspicacity on some specific challenges of the role of interest rate regimes in selected African countries, namely development and macroeconomic performance. It presents an overview of interest rate and financial reform policies. It outlines the evolution of interest rates and the financial sector across the continent over the past two decades. It also evaluates the overall performance of interest rate reforms, as well as the speed and the sequencing thereof.

Chapter 5 provides a review of previous studies on the causal link between financial development and economic growth in selected African countries. It explores all existing theories underpinning the causal relationship between financial development and economic growth in a stepwise fashion. Although prior attempts have been made to conduct this survey, the bulk of the previous studies applied a universal approach to the literature review. Put slightly differently, most of the literature reviews of previous studies were global in nature and did not focus on African countries.

Chapter 6 uses a multidimensional approach to interrogate the relationship between stock market development and economic growth in Africa using unbalanced panel data from 16 African countries during the period 2010−2017. The results of the study show that using an aggregated sample does not convey the true relationship between the stock market and growth in Africa. However, disaggregation of data into income groups visibly shows that, for the most part, the stock market development has a significant and positive impact on economic growth.

In Chapter 7, the relationship between stock market, banking sector development and economic growth is examined in five selected African countries during the period 1993−2019. Three interaction terms between three proxies of stock market and bank-based financial development proxy are used, thereby estimating three models. Two estimators, namely the fully modified ordinary least squares (FMOLS) and dynamic ordinary least squares (DOLS), are used for each model, thereby resulting in six estimations. Furthermore, a wide range of panel data techniques is employed, namely (i) four cross-sectional dependence tests; (ii) first- and second-generation panel unit root tests; and (iii) panel co-integration tests, to examine this linkage.

Chapter 8 focuses on the relationship between microfinance sustainability, social performance and economic development in selected African countries. The chapter finds no relationship between various measures of MFI sustainability, social performance and economic development. However, in terms of MFI financial/profitability indicators, it finds that the provision of deposit and lending services by MFIs promotes or drives economic development. A further drill-down finds that indicators of MFI social performance, such as the number of active borrowers, the average loan size and the percentage of female borrowers, are significantly related to economic development in high-income selected African countries. The number of active borrowers and the percentage of female borrowers are positively associated with economic development, while the average loan size is negatively related to economic development, suggesting that when MFIs focus on their core mission of lending to the poor, they promote economic development in high-income countries. The study also found the provision of subsidies to be positively related to economic development in low-income African countries.

In Chapter 9, the impact of remittance inflows on financial development is analysed in five selected African countries, namely Cote d'Ivoire, Ghana, Kenya, Nigeria and South Africa. A wide range of financial development proxies covering the period from 2000 to 2017 is used to examine this linkage. In total, six proxies are used, including three proxies for bank-based financial development and another three proxies for stock market development. Several modern econometric techniques are used to examine this linkage in a stepwise fashion. The techniques used include the cross-sectional dependence test, first- and second-generation unit root tests, first- and second-generation co-integration tests, and the dynamic ordinary least squares (DOLS) and fully modified ordinary least squares (FMOLS) dynamic models.

In Chapter 10, the association between financial inclusion and gender inequality in African countries is examined. The chapter found that generally, most individuals in sub-Saharan Africa rely on informal sources of finance, such as savings at a savings club and borrowing from family and friends compared to formal financial sources. Moreover, women are more likely to turn to informal sources compared to men.

Chapter 11 is aimed at providing an understanding of SMEs' access to financing in selected African countries, with particular interest in establishing whether there are similarities and differences in the determinants of SMEs' access to finance across other regions of the world. For robustness, case studies of financial developments and SMEs in Ghana, Nigeria, South Africa, Morocco and Tanzania are presented in this chapter. It is posited that although selected African countries have made progress, including the modernisation and expansion of banking systems and financial accessibility, there are still major weaknesses, such as low domestic savings mobilisation, underdevelopment of their capital markets and insufficient credit to key sectors of the economy for inclusive and sustainable economic growth.

In Chapter 12, the causal linkage between financial development and economic growth is explored in 24 African economies from 1980 to 2017. A variety of modern panel data techniques are employed, namely (i) four cross-sectional dependence tests; (ii) first- and second-generation panel unit root tests; (iii) panel co-integration tests; and (iv) heterogeneous non-causality tests. Four proxies of financial development are incorporated in the analysis, notably bank deposits as a share of GDP (BDGDP), deposit bank assets as a share of GDP (DBAGDP), liquid liabilities as a share of GDP (LLGDP), and private credit by deposit money banks as a share of GDP (PCRDBGDP). The selected countries are also decomposed into low-income (LICs) and middle-income (MICs) groups to be able to determine whether the nexus between financial development and economic growth is influenced by the countries' levels of income.

Chapter 13 is aimed at examining the impact of bank-based financial development on economic growth in 26 African countries during the period 2013–2017. Four indicators of bank-based financial development are used, namely liquid liabilities, deposit money bank assets, private credit to deposit money banks and other financial institutions, and bank deposits, thereby leading to four separate specifications for each growth model. In addition, an array of control variables, namely interest rate, inflation, regulation and trade, was also employed. The generalised method of moments (GMM) techniques are used in the study to examine this linkage.

In Chapter 14, the nexus between ICT diffusion and financial development is empirically examined in 45 African countries over the period 2000–2018. Unlike some of the previous studies, the recently developed panel VAR in the generalised method of moments (GMM) estimation technique is used to examine this linkage.

Chapter 15 is aimed at assessing financial determinants of informal financial sector development in 48 sub-Saharan African countries during the period 1995–2017. Quantile regression methods are used as an empirical strategy, which enables the determinants throughout the conditional distribution of informal sector development dynamics to be assessed. The following financial determinants affect informal financial development differently in terms of magnitude and sign, namely bank overhead costs; net Internet margin; bank concentration; return on equity; bank cost-to-income ratio; financial stability; loans from non-resident banks; offshore bank deposits; and remittances. A plethora of perspectives are presented, among others, U-Shape, S-Shape and positive or negative thresholds. Not only is a practical way provided by which to assess the incidence of financial determinants on informal financial sector development, but also financial instruments by which informal financial development can be curbed.

Chapter 16 examines how the COVID-19 pandemic has affected financial development and financial inclusion in African countries. The study provides both broad perspectives and country-specific frameworks based on selected country case studies. Some emphasis is placed on the achievement of sustainable development goals (SDGs) that are related to financial inclusion. The study aims to understand what immediate challenges the COVID-19 pandemic has represented to the economies and societies, on the one hand, and, on the other, the effect of COVID-19 on the interconnected financial systems in terms of consequences of the pandemic. The relevance of the study builds on the importance of these insights in helping both scholars and policymakers to understand how the effect of the pandemic on the financial system and by extension, the global economy can be mitigated for more financial inclusion.

Chapter 17 explores how financial institution dynamics have affected poverty and its severity in 42 African countries during the period 1980–2019. To make the study more policy-relevant, three financial development indicators are used, namely financial institution depth, financial institution access and financial institution efficiency. A quantile regression approach is adopted as an empirical strategy to assess how financial institution dynamics affect poverty and the severity of poverty throughout the conditional distribution of poverty and the severity of poverty.

Part I

Historical Evolution of Finance in Africa

2 The Evolution of Financial Sector Reforms in African Countries

Anthony Enisan Akinlo and Olumuyiwa Tolulope Apanisile

2.1 Introduction

The importance of the financial sector cannot be overemphasized in an economy. The sector contributes to the growth and development of an economy through financial intermediation. Financial intermediation is the process of transferring resources/funds from sector/agents with surplus resources/funds to sector/agents with deficit resources/funds through the financial sector. This process enables different sectors of the economy to grow at the same pace while contributing significantly to the growth process of the country. It is worthy of note that the banking sector is not the only institution in the financial sector. However, it is more pronounced than other sectors in the financial system because it is the major stakeholder. The financial sector also comprises other stakeholders that do not accept deposits and give out loans. Also, there are money and capital markets where the short-term and long-term loans are raised through the use of bonds, stocks, etc. The two markets, with the bank institutions that support them, constitute an important segment of the sector. However, the slow pace of the growth of the financial sector in Africa has been attributed to the failure of African countries to develop and attract more capital. According to Omoruyi (1991), the pace of growth experienced in the sector underscores its relevance to the development of an economy.

The extant literature identified financial crises as one of the factors inhibiting the financial sector from performing its developmental role. From 1997 to date, the world economy has experienced four major global financial crises. These include the financial crisis that emanated in Asia in 1997, the Argentina financial crisis of 2001, the global financial crisis of 2007, and the Russian crisis of 2014. The period of crises was characterized by sharp practices that marred and weakened the performance of the sector, leading to a lull in macroeconomic activities. African countries were greatly affected by these crises due to their level of integration into the world economy.

These adverse conditions gave rise to different reforms in the face of the financial crisis that bewildered the financial sector in Africa. These reforms are sets of programmes implemented to boost and regulate activities of the

DOI: 10.4324/9781003215042-3

financial sector to transform the sector and remove barriers to growth and development. Due to the importance of the financial sector in the growth and development of any economy, restructuring in the sector will affect other sectors of the economy, thereby bringing huge transformation to the economy and its citizenry. The trading activity within the capital market is an integral part of the financial system, even in developed economies. These reforms often evolve as a result of finding solutions to the problems posed by technological progress and other financial crises. The market for long-term loans underwent various programmes to aid its performance. Undoubtedly, the developmental programmes carried out in the sector have enhanced the development of the sector and the economy as a whole. The trading activities in the market for long-term loans and the financial system play a critical role in the development and growth of the economy. Reforms are essential for the better performance of the financial market because it opens the sector into new approaches, methods, services, and institutions.

Policies embedded in the financial reforms, in response to the series of financial crises, include financial liberalization, liberalization of interest rates, credit ceiling removal, and privatization. Others are the restructuring of banks owned by the states, promotion of measures that enhance the growth of financial markets, effective bank supervisory and regulation, and recapitalization of deposit-taking banks that led to mergers and acquisitions in some countries within Africa. The primary reasons for this reform are to reposition and deepen the financial sector to meet up with the global best practices, build resistance against external shocks, and contribute significantly to the growth and development of the region. The new policies aim to prevent the sector from being exposed to external shocks, protect the sector from the underground economy, and improve the sector's performance. This is evidenced in the recent banking sector reforms in Africa including creating barriers for universal banking, reducing the number of years the managing directors and the chief executive officer of banks spent in the office in some countries within the continent, and the creation of an agency that is responsible for rescuing ailing banks.

Given that the financial sector reforms in Africa were an attempt to overturn the negative effects of the repressive policies in the continent, the approach of individual country to achieving this objective differed. For instance, in Nigeria, there was a merger and acquisition among banks due to an increase in their capital base from two billion naira to 25 billion naira. This recapitalization reduced the number of banks from 89 to 24. In addition, Ghana and Tanzania removed lending restrictions, which led to market determination of interest rates. This action improved financial intermediation, thereby providing incentives to investors and in turn increased productivity. Furthermore, while Botswana, Kenya, Malawi, and Zambia adopted a step-by-step approach to the implementation of financial liberalization by executing different measures at different times, other countries such as Cote d'Ivoire, The Gambia, Mali, Uganda, and Zimbabwe executed several liberalization measures in the same year. Basically, the study aimed at explaining the evolution of reforms in the continent and examines the consequence of the newly introduced set of programmes on the performance of the sector in Africa and drew lessons from it.

Apart from this introduction, the study examines different financial sector policies and development in Africa before liberalization in Section 2.2. In Section 2.3, the study examines the relationship between financial liberalization and financial crisis. Section 2.4 discusses financial restructuring that takes place after the financial crisis in the region. Lastly, various lessons from the history of the financial crisis and reforms in Africa are enumerated.

2.2 Financial Sector Policies and Development before Liberalization in Africa

Most African economies were liberalized between the 1970s and 1980s. Before liberalization, African economies were characterized by a repressed financial system. African economies during these periods were characterized by policies such as direct control of interest rates in the economy, credit rationing, lack of a well-developed money market and market for the securities, and the banking system that is underdeveloped and highly regulated. In addition, the financial repression comprised government participation in the developmental process, state-instituted developmental programmes, concentration on programmes meant for indigent people that felt neglected, and promotion of bribery and corruption among those in power. The financial system, before liberalization, became a channel through which loans were allocated below the prevailing rates in the market, financial instruments and public funds were used for private and personal purposes, and other public resources were transferred to favour units of the economy. Furthermore, banks owned by states were also used to allocate credit to the preferred sectors of the economy. Prudential regulation was sacrificed on the altar of favouritism, thereby reducing the cost of credits given to the selected few; this was done deliberately to enhance the distribution of income within the countries of the region.

Repressed finance was seen as a means through which resources and funds were moved from depositors that were paid low interest to borrowers in the public and the private sectors that were favoured by the government and as a result received credit at low interest rate. The low interest rate charged on loans resulted in greater demand for credit beyond its supply. Government, therefore, resulted in controlling the outflows of capital. This was done, not to protect the domestic savings, but rather to reduce capital flight, correct low interest rate policy, and control macroeconomic instability. The control of capital was seen as a means of dealing with erring stakeholders whose actions encourage mismanagement (Hanson, 1994). The structures of the African financial system during this period led to misallocation of credit, financial distress, entry barrier for new participants into the industry, and inefficiency that wasted savings and impaired growth prospects. To further examine the effect of the pre-liberalization financial sector policies on the growth and development of Africa, we divided the continent into three groups: Eastern and Southern Africa, Western and Central Africa, and the sub-Saharan Africa. We investigated the performance of the financial sector using the ratios of domestic credit to the private sector (% of GDP) and the banks' credit to the private sector (% of GDP) as proxies for determining their performance.

Figure 2.1 shows how well the financial sector performed its financial intermediation role in Africa between 1965 and 1985. As shown in Figure 2.1, the amount of credit made available to private sectors, each year, in all three regions is below 50%. The highest value recorded was 44.85% in Eastern and Southern Africa in the year 1984. Overall, this analysis shows that the repressed financial policies restricted the flow of credit, thereby hindering the growth and development process during the pre-liberalization period. On a regional basis, the eastern and southern regions recorded the highest performance when compared to the other two regions considered in the study.

Furthermore, Figure 2.2 presents the performance of commercial banks as critical stakeholders in the African financial system. This is done by examining the amount of domestic credit made available between 1965 and 1985. This period represents the pre-liberalization period in Africa. It can be inferred from Figure 2.2 that the amount of credit provided to the private sector by the bank, as a percentage of GDP, is less than 40%. This result is consistent in all three regions under investigation. Overall, the financial sector policies implemented before liberalization in Africa limit the growth and development of the region.

Several studies in the literature have identified what led to the liberalization of the financial sector in Africa. They are poor results of the repressed financial system adopted, high costs of the repressed system, and pressures from globalization. It has been argued in the literature that during the period

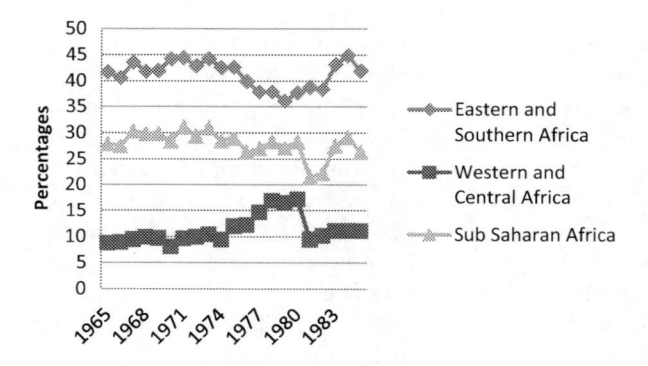

Figure 2.1 Trend in domestic credit to the private sector in Africa.

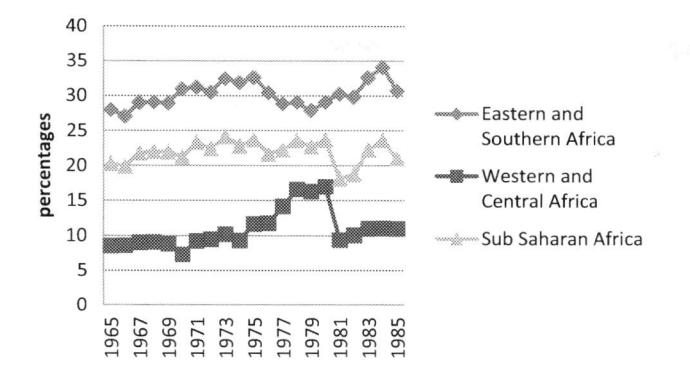

Figure 2.2 Banks' credit to the private sector between 1965 and 1985.

of a repressed financial system, limited mobilization and lack of efficiency in the distribution of credit retarded output. Reduced cost of capital weakened banks' ability to attract deposits, thereby reducing the volume of bank deposits in the region. Capital flight also defiled all control measures put in place as an increased number of cases were recorded. There were cases of underground dealings in the economy that spur wastages (McKinnon, 1973; Shaw, 1973; Dooley et al., 1986). It was also discovered that the overall situation of the region worsened during the period as the distribution of income was aggravated by the financial repression, high inflation induced subsidy for the directed credits obtained from a bank, and there was increased government borrowing.

Moreover, the implemented financial guideline was highly expensive. The period required frequent review of the existing financial structure to accommodate new developments. It also required the payment of state and development banks' debt by the government. The political environment was tensed up, and there were cases of corruption. Approved loans became bad debt in the economy because commercial banks financed businesses without prospects, investors ran away from obtaining loans due to the high cost of capital, and borrowers see credit obtained from state-owned banks as bailouts. In addition, financial intermediaries continued to accumulate bad debts until the period of high inflation when the value of money is wiped out and depositors' claims are eroded. Due to the non-monitoring of the financial system, the recorded losses were oblivion in the economy and to the government that owned them. The prevailing economic condition assisted the financial system, majorly the commercial banks, to hide their financial problems. The liberalization of the financial system revealed the cost of the repressed system.

Lastly, the developmental pressure is another essential impetus for financial liberalization in Africa. Between the 1970s and 1980s, the repression of the financial system experienced intense pressure from trade liberalization and openness of the economy. The financial liberalization reduced the barriers to capital flight that form the basis for the supply of low-interest deposits. Initially, barriers placed on the flow of capital seem adequate; however, in the long run, strategies were developed to subvert them. Therefore, stakeholders have more access to the recently developed strategies as the economy is liberalized.

2.3 Financial Liberalization and Financial Crisis

The financial sector policies implemented in Africa, before liberalization, described the financial sector in the region as the channel through which funds are mobilized from one sector to another. This implies financial sector is limited to the movement of funds in the economy without performing any other role. This definition is relatively too narrow and does not capture the intermediary action of the sector in its entirety. In an economy characterized by uncertainty, the role of the financial sector should involve the allocation and sharing of risk, in addition to the mobilization of funds and credit allocation, among the players in the market. All these could be achieved in a liberalized financial system. Essentially, a liberalized financial system produces a healthy and efficient financial sector that contributes significantly to the growth and development of an economy.

Given the performance of the African financial system, Mckinnon (1973) and Shaw (1973) proposed the liberalization of the African financial system for better performance and contribution to the growth and development process. They contended that finance is critical for growth and development. They further argued that the best way of ensuring an efficient financial sector is through the liberalization of the financial system. Based on the importance of financial liberalization to the achievement of growth and development, and coupled with the poor performance of the African economy during the period of repressed economy, the region liberalized its financial sector to contribute significantly to economic growth. The main objective of this exercise is to achieve economic growth that would lead to development through financial development. South Africa was the first country to liberalize its financial sector in 1980. Other countries liberalized their financial sectors between the 1980s and 1990s.

Fowowe (2011) classified the effects of financial liberalization on the African economies into three categories: savings, investment, and economic growth. According to the study, the liberalization of the financial sector encourages savings through the flexibility of interest rates, granting more bank licenses, and prudential banking regulations. As savings increase in the economy, investment also increases, thereby resulting in increased growth. Figures 2.3 and 2.4 show the domestic credit to the private sector (% of GDP) and the domestic credit to the private sector by banks (% of GDP) during and after liberalization. Figure 2.3 shows that liberalizing the financial sector improved the credit allocation in Africa between the periods under

Figure 2.3 Trend in domestic credit to the private sector in Africa.

Figure 2.4 Banks' credit to the private sector between 1986 and 2020.

investigation. The value of credit increased from 40% during the period of repressed policy to 105% during the liberalization policy period in Eastern and Southern Africa. The case is the same for Western and Central Africa and the entire sub-Saharan Africa.

In the same way, the domestic to the private sector by banks, as a percentage of GDP increased for all the regions under consideration. This implies efficiency in the commercial banks arising from liberalization.

However, despite the advantages of financial liberalization, the results are below expectation. Sensitive institutional problems remain critical in Africa. Given the recent reforms carried out in the financial sector, the sector in

Africa setup is still faced with the problem of low efficiency, low liquidity, and less capital. More importantly, Africa has not been able to attract foreign investors that flew to developing countries given the increase in the interest of world investors since the early 90s. The available data revealed that the total private capital flows exceeded the flow of official development assistance. This trend became noticeable in the 1980s and it continued in the same direction. However, the reverse is the case in Africa as the development assistance is greater than the inflow of private capital. Also, the comparative analysis showed that the flow of total aggregate development assistance fell in the same year that the total private capital flows increased to other developing countries.

In addition, the policy was accompanied by financial instability, which eventually led to financial crises. Several authors have identified six main causes of financial crises in the literature. They are increased capital mobility, sudden shifts to safe and liquid assets, management failures to evaluate and control risk-taking in the financial institution, institutional weaknesses, the extent of integration into the world economy, and weak capital regulation and supervision (Angkinand, Sawangngoenyuang, and Wihlborg, 2010; Allen and Giovannetti, 2011). Furthermore, Alawode and Ikhide (1997) argued that financial liberalization in Africa led to the financial crisis because policymakers did not understand the concept of financial liberalization. Financial liberalization was taken to be the mere removal of all existing controls on financial institutions without paying attention to prudential regulations and controls, which are vital components of the programme. Another reason attributed to this fact by the same authors is that the timing, sequencing, and speed of financial reforms are not appropriate in Africa.

Concerning the timing, the authors argued that financial liberalization should come after achieving macroeconomic stability and real sector freedom. This could be achieved by substantially reducing the size of fiscal deficits and monetary growth rates to dampen inflationary expectations. If government deficits remain large, liberalization-induced increases in interest rates would swell debt service payments and further expand the fiscal deficits. Also, since many regulations imposed on the financial sector are designed to raise revenue and finance fiscal deficits, it would be ill-advised to dismantle controls without first erecting a viable tax collection system (see McKinnon, 1991; Gibson and Tsakalotos, 1991; Alawode and Ikhide, 1997). Such action will help to compensate for the revenue lost from abandoning taxes on the financial sector and ensure non-inflationary government deficits in the post-liberalization period. In a situation where macroeconomic stability proves challenging to attain before financial liberalization, then strong regulation and supervision will be vital for successful liberalization. This condition was absent during the financial liberalization process in Africa.

Another critical factor that led to the financial crises in Africa is the sequencing of the financial reforms. By sequencing, we mean the chronological order through which financial reforms were implemented. The first step in sequencing is the restructuring of the financial system. This implies liquidating the distressed financial institutions. Any attempts to liberalize without restructuring would hinder weak banks from effectively competing within the sector and reduce the overall efficiency of the sector. It is, therefore, important that weak institutions be strengthened and hopeless ones dissolved before full-scale liberalization begins. The next step in the sequencing of the financial sector is to introduce market-based weapons of monetary control while retaining direct credit controls. This exercise would secure an alternative way of controlling liquidity before the eventual removal of direct credit controls. The argument is that the removal of credit control before the introduction of the market-based instruments will lead to a loss of monetary control with adverse consequences for macroeconomic stability. Lastly, the removal of direct controls on interest rates and credit ceilings marks the conclusion of the sequencing of financial liberalization. With macroeconomic stability and strong bank supervision erected, abolishing barriers to credit enhanced commercial banks' ability to pool credits and give out credit in a financially stable economy. When the use of market instruments has failed to produce the expected result, barriers to credit could be left alone, as the system adjusts to the new regimented setting.

Furthermore, on the issue of the speed of financial reforms, Alawode and Ikhide (1997) sound a note of warning on the pace at which the financial sector is liberalized. For a successful financial reform, all controls must not be completely removed. According to them, a big-bang approach should not be employed. This is because financial institutions and other stakeholders are used to operating in an environment where government intervention and controls prevail, and therefore, there is a need for the introduction of programmes that allow every stakeholder to familiarize themselves with the new dispensation. Banks that are owned and supervised by the government experienced inefficiency. Therefore, introducing them into a liberalized and competitive setting is dangerous. Hence, governments should avoid a hurried and abrupt removal of existing controls. In particular, the abolition of barriers to the cost of capital should be spontaneous but rather taken one after the other. The removal of ceilings on credit should also be phased over time. Financial liberalization has greater chances of success if spread out over a long period, allowing the financial sector enough time to adapt.

To examine the impact of financial crises on the African economy, we look at the GDP per capita (constant 2010 US$) as a measure of development. Figure 2.5 presents the graphical illustration. GDP per capita measures output per head in Africa after financial liberalization. The diagram shows an upward trend during the period of liberalization. This trend implies financial liberalization improves the living standard of people in the region. However, during the period of the financial crisis in the region, the living condition of people dropped, signifying a negative impact. Besides, the irregular movement of the trend shows instability in the economic performance of the region. This suggests that the region is not insulated against shocks. The

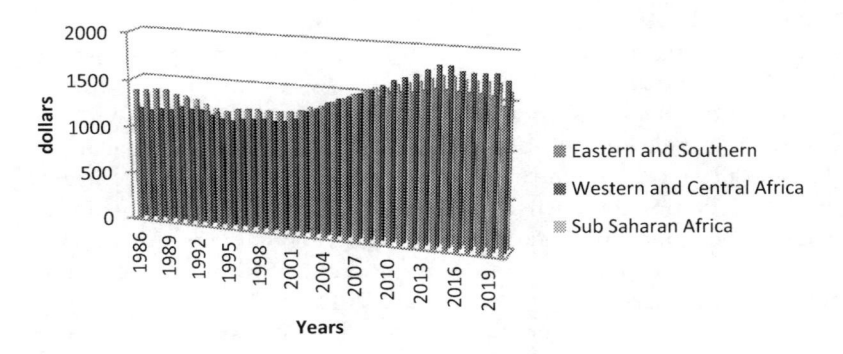

Figure 2.5 Trend in GDP per capita in Africa.

emergence of any shock, whether external or internal, has a significant effect on the economy.

2.4 Financial Restructuring after Crisis

The financial problems experienced in Africa generated controversy on the appropriate policy to be adopted. This is because the usual stabilization policy that involves the use of the monetary and fiscal policy was only effective for excess demand and deficit account reduction. However, policy to resolve the financial sector crisis and its attendant complications generated a more complex problem without a ready-made solution. Given the specific bank's problem, the recommended solution is to provide capital for the ailing banks at an increased rate of interest and provide cover for depositors with small capital. It was found out that banks were faced with complex problems as owners of distressed banks resulted in risky plans (De Juan, 2002).

Furthermore, the nature of the problems identified in a commercial bank signifies the existence of multiple problems in the financial system. To this end, the closure of a bank without duly compensating the bank's depositors will have a chain effect on other banks within the system. Such effects include siphoning the depositor's money by the owners of the bank. Because the existing problem noticed in a bank in the region is general to all the banks within the financial system, the system is faced with liquidity problem. The liquidity problem generates a more serious problem within the system that defies any standard solution. The government, therefore, was faced with a dilemma. The first option is either to rescue the ailing banks and generate more crises in the system or support the system by giving bailout and cause instability that will affect the achievement of macroeconomic objectives (World Bank, 2000). There is also an issue of by how much should government intervene in the crisis so as not to expose the economy to external shocks. This decision affects local investors and commercial banks if the policy persists. However, government intervention in the form of bailout is favourable to local borrowers but puts more pressure on the exchange rate, thereby affecting investors that deal in foreign currency. It has been observed that the use of country's external reserve is more appropriate in implementing this policy. However, the external reserve is finite; therefore, continuous depletion of the reserve may expose the economy to currency attack.

The failure of the financial liberalization reforms in insulating the African economies from financial crises led to several restructuring efforts in the region. These were designed to protect the financial sector against internal and external shocks. The restructuring aimed at consolidating the steps taken during the financial liberalization so that the development in the financial sector could aid the achievement of economic growth that would translate to development. The financial restructuring package includes improving the macroeconomic stability, strengthening the regulation and supervision of banks, improving the regulatory frameworks, developing the non-bank sector, and sustaining the reforms, and increasing competition.

Senbet and Otchere (2005) identified an increase in the establishment of stock exchanges as one of the restructurings after the financial crises. According to them, the number of stock exchange markets in Africa has increased to 29. This number represents 38 nations' capital markets. The increase in the number of stock exchange markets has prompted the establishment of regional markets. As of 2020, there are two regional stock exchange markets in Africa. The first one is located in Abidjan, while the second one is located in Libreville. The Abidjan stock exchange serves Benin, Burkina Faso, Guinea Bissau, Ivory Coast, Mali, Niger, Senegal, and Togo. The second stock exchange market serves Central Africa Republic, Chad, Democratic Republic of Congo, Equatorial Guinea, and Gabon. Currently, the Johannesburg Stock Exchange is the largest on the continent. This is followed by the Nigerian Stock Exchange, Namibian Stock Exchange, Zimbabwe Stock Exchange, and the Casablanca Stock Exchange.

The stock market is said to enhance the development of any economy. It serves as a bridge that connects the level of savings in the economy with the level of investment. The stock market transforms the savings surplus in an economy into medium- and long-term investments. The consensus in the literature is that the liquidity of the stock market, over the years, spurs growth in the long run, among developing countries. In the absence of a stock market with adequate capital, engaging in long-term investment that is profitable will not be possible because investors are reluctant to tie down their investment for a long period of time.

Contrastingly, stock market with adequate capital enables investors to quickly raise enough funds by providing the avenue to sell their shares. Hence, having a well-functioning and stable financial system is a requirement for economic growth. An important segment of the financial sector that is growth-enhancing is the stock market. In recent times, a widespread and increasing growth and development has been noticed in the region's stock market. Not minding the size, structure, and the state of the market, the presence and prospect of the market are needed for viable activities in the economy. Stock market is an avenue for raising equity and finance for investment by potential investors. This function presents stock market as the engine of growth for economic activities (Alajekwu and Achugbu, 2012; Anigbogu and Nduka, 2014).

Stock market performance is seen as a good measure of a country's strength in achieving economic growth (Henry and Olabanji, 2013). Therefore, the index of an active stock market is a useful tool for measuring the rate of change in general level of economic activities. Another important function of a stock market is that it provides the channel for the formation and effective allocation of capital. It is also seen as an important avenue for raising the needed fund for businesses in the long run. The market stimulates savings for the sectors of the economy with surplus, thereby pooling funds for further investment and more returns for investors (Henry and Olabanji, 2013).

2.5 Conclusion

There are several lessons to be learned in the evolution of financial sector reforms in Africa. It was very glaring that the liberalization of the financial sector is a necessary but not sufficient condition for the development of the financial sector. By implication, financial liberalization could not be implemented in isolation. For the continent to reap the benefits of liberalization, the macroeconomic environment must be stable. Achieving macroeconomic stability is vital before and after the implementation of financial liberalization. Furthermore, strong institutional quality is a requisite for reaping the benefits of financial liberalization. Most countries in the continent have weak institutions, which serve as a bane to the effectiveness of the reforms. Other factors that are important to achieving the objectives of financial liberalization are improving access to banking services, improved regulation and supervision in the financial sector, and the development of technological know-how to compete in the world market.

It was also observed that the liberalization of the financial sector that does not consider the socio-economic environment of Africa will fail. The implementation of extensive reforms, carried out by most economies of Africa, has failed to achieve the stated objectives because they did not consider the socio-economic settings of the region. Such reforms are faced with problems such as demonetization of the rural sector, exposure of the financial market to shocks, inadequate capital for active sectors of the economy, and emergence of private-owned banks that are monopolistic in nature. In addition, the financial sector reforms were graced with shocks to the financial sector and crises in the banking sector. These occurred as a result of wrong interpretation of the business environment that led to putting the cart before the horse in implementing the reform. Markets in the short run were characterized with imperfection and inadequacy. This notwithstanding, the market serves as the channel through which policy operates. It, therefore, became imperative for the government to implement policies that will enhance the development of the financial sector over the period of transition. This involves spreading the financial aid to the less privileged areas and sectors in the economy. In addition, a step-by-step approach to the development of the sector should be developed and handed over to the private sector with close monitoring. Efforts should be geared towards establishing private–public partnership in providing developmental capital for economic agents and units in the economy. Such programmes will grow to become a fully developed private sector initiative as the structure of the distribution within the system improves.

The region is also characterized by a lesser access to capital. This is evident in the number of households (below 20%) that have credit access in the region. It was also observed that the region contained communities that were sparsely populated and linked with poor infrastructures. More importantly, majority of the population are low-income earners. This implies there is urgent need for development programmes that will facilitate financial inclusion for the benefits of households and micro, small, and medium enterprises (MSMEs). Access to long-term financial services should also be prioritized. It can be concluded that though financial reforms have contributed immensely to achieving a stable financial system in Africa, however, much more is required for achieving economic diversification and inclusive growth.

References

Alajekwu, U. B. and Achugbu, A. A. (2012). The Role of Stock Market Development on Economic Growth in Nigeria: A Time Series Analysis. *African Research Review*, 6(24): 51–70.

Alawode, A. A. and Ikhide, S. I. (1997). Why Should Financial Liberalisation Induce Financial Crisis? *Savings and Development*, 21(3): 261–274.

Allen, F. and Giovannetti, G. (2011). The Effects of the Financial Crisis on Sub-Saharan Africa. *Review of Development Finance*, 1(1): 1–27.

Angkinand, A. P., Sawangngoenyuang, W. and Wihlborg, C. (2010). Financial Liberalization and Banking Crises: A Cross-Country Analysis. *International Review of Finance*, 10: 263–292. DOI: 10.1111/j.1468-2443.2010.01114.x.

Anigbogu, U. E. and Nduka, E. K. (2014). Stock Market Performance and Economic Growth: Evidence from Nigeria Employing Vector Error Correction Model Framework. *The Economics and Finance Letters*, 1(4): 90–103.

De Juan, A. (2002). From Good Bankers to Bad Bankers. In G. Caprio, P. Honohan, and D. Vittas, eds., *Financial Sector Policy for Developing Countries—A Reader*. Oxford: Oxford University Press, pp. 19–30.

Dooley, M., Helkie, W., Tyron, R. and Underwood, J. (1986). An Analysis of External Debt Positions of Eight Countries through 1990. *Journal of Development Economics*, 21(2): 283–318.

Fowowe, B. (2011). Financial Liberalization in Sub-Saharan Africa: What Do We Know? *Journal of Economic Surveys*. DOI: 10.1111/j.1467-6419.2011.00689.x.

Gibson, H. and Tsakalotos, E. (1991). European Monetary Union and Macroeconomic Policy in Southern Policy: The case of Positive Integration. *Journal of Public Policy*, 11(3): 249–273.

Hanson, J. (1994). An Open Capital Account: A Brief Survey of the Issues and Results. In G. Caprio, I. Atiyas, and J. Hanson, eds., *Financial Reform: Theory and Experience*. Cambridge: Cambridge University Press, pp. 1–31.

Henry, O. and Olabanji, E. (2013). Stock Market Performance and Sustainable Economic Growth in Nigeria: A Boinds Testing Co-Integration Approach. *Journal of Sustainable Development*, 6(8): 84–92.

McKinnon, R. (1991). Financial Control in the Transition from Classical Socialism to a Market Economy. *Journal of Economic Perspectives*, 5(4): 107–122.

McKinnon, R. (1973). *Money and Capital in Economic Development*. Washington, DC: The Brookings Institution.

Omoruyi, S. E. (1991). The Financial Sector in Africa; Overview and Reforms in Economic Adjustment Programmes. *Central Bank of Nigeria Economic and Financial Review*, 29(2): 110–124.

Senbet, L. W. and Otchere, I. (2005). Financial Sector Reforms in Africa. Perspectives on Issues and Policies. Prepared for the Annual World Bank Conference on Development Economics (ABCDE), Dakar, Senegal, January 2005.

Shaw, E. (1973). *Financial Deepening in Economic Development*. New York: Oxford University Press.

World Bank (2000). The World Bank annual report 2000: Annual review and summary financial information (English). Washington, D.C.: World Bank Group. http://documents. worldbank.org/curated/en/931281468741326669/Annual-review-and-summary-financial-information.

3 Financial Reforms and Financial Development in Africa

Evidence from Selected SSA Countries

Magdalene Kasyoka Wilson and
Nicholas Mbaya Odhiambo

3.1 Introduction

The debate on the role of finance in facilitating economic growth and enhancing sustainable development has attracted a plethora of both theoretical and empirical literature since the 18th century. In the theoretical strand, various dominant theories have emerged regarding the efficacy of financial development in fostering growth and development in developing countries. Before the orthodoxy of financial liberalisation, the dominant policy that prevailed in many countries was the financial repression policy, which involved government administrative and quantitative controls such as (i) interest rate ceilings, which were artificially kept below the market clearing rates; (ii) fixed exchange rates and quantitative foreign exchange controls; (iii) selective and discriminatory credit controls; and (iv) high cash reserve ratios, which were imposed on financial institutions, among others. In its purest form, the policy of financial repression gave the government the mandate to influence the control of the financial sector by (i) determining who receives and provides credit and at what price; (ii) determining which financial institutions are permitted to participate in the financial sector and how they should operate; (iii) owning financial intermediaries; and iv) exercising quantitative controls over the movement of international capital (see Williamson & Mahar, 1998; Odhiambo, 2004).

Although this policy has been challenged by some economists, it was somewhat supported by the Keynesian theory of interest rate, which tends to be in favour of a prior investment rather than a prior savings approach. According to the Keynesian school, low interest rate policy tends to bolster investment and income as it reduces the cost of borrowing, which ultimately leads to an increase in savings. Simply put, low interest rates encourage total savings by encouraging investment (see Odhiambo, 2004). Another argument in support of the financial policy is based on the Keynesian stance, which tends to give prominence to the role of government in economic growth and development. According to the Keynesian school of thought, governments should endeavour to influence economies from time to time through increased spending in order to stimulate demand, especially during recession.

DOI: 10.4324/9781003215042-4

In 1973, Ronald Mackinnon and Edward Shaw vehemently challenged the conventional wisdom of low interest rates and other financial controls in their separate theses. According to McKinnon (1973) and Shaw (1973), the policy of financial repression affects the development of an economy negatively in several ways. First, when a financial sector is repressed, savings vehicles are not well developed as the returns on savings are likely to be either negative or unstable. Second, in the face of financial repression, financial intermediaries cannot allocate savings that they have collected efficiently among high-yield competing uses. Third, when financial repression predominates, potential investors are discouraged from investing since financial repression policies reduce returns on investment. The argument advanced by McKinnon-Shaw (1973) is that although a decrease in interest rate may lead to an increase in demand for investment, at extremely low interest rate the desired level of savings will be too low; hence, demand for loanable funds will exceed its supply. And when this happened, the low interest rate policy may result in a decrease in savings, investment and economic growth. Moreover, given the high inflation rates experienced by some developing countries, the low interest rates administered under a financial repression regime may result in a negative real interest rate, which may further discourage savings. The McKinnon-Shaw (1973) hypothesis, therefore, gave rise to the new ortho-doxy known as "financial liberalisation." As opposed to financial repression, financial liberalisation allows the financial market to determine who grants and gets credit and at what price. A full financial liberalisation in its purest form involves six main dimensions, namely (i) deregulation of all interest rates; (ii) elimination of credit controls by the government; (iii) free entry (exit) into (out of) the banking sector; (iv) commercial banks autonomy; (v) private ownership of banks; and (vi) liberalisation of international capital flows (Odhiambo, 2011).

According to pro-financial liberalisation economists, the advantages of financial liberalisation include, among others, (i) a more varied intermedi-ation between savers and borrowers; and (ii) a freer flow of money from financial intermediaries to projects with high rates of return. In addition, under financial liberalisation, the "invisible hand" is expected to match the supply and demand for funds accurately and efficiently. In this way, finan-cial liberalisation leads to an increase in savings and the efficiency in which financial resources are allocated, thereby leading to an increase in economic growth. Overall, financial liberalisation has been found by some studies to foster development and increase long-run growth (Levine, 1997; Detragiache & Demirgüç-Kunt, 1998). Other studies have also found that financial liber-alisation can enable developing countries to stimulate their domestic savings and economic growth, and reduce excessive dependence on their foreign capital flows (Detragiache & Demirgüç-Kunt, 1998).

Although the policy of financial liberalisation has been implemented by many African countries, in some countries, the policy caused more harm than good due to the way it was implemented. Indeed, previous studies have shown that the policy of financial liberalisation, just as other reform policies, may not yield the desired benefits if the requisite timing, sequencing and pace are not adhered to (Gibson & Tsakalotos, 1994; Noland, 1996; Fry, 1997; Detragiache & Demirgüç-Kunt, 1998). Unfortunately, some developing countries hurriedly implemented the policy of financial liberalisation without necessarily observing its preconditions. For example, some countries implemented external financial reforms before implementing domestic financial reforms, thereby exposing their markets to external shocks. Other countries did not put in place the necessary structural reforms within some sectors of their economies to support the liberalisation of their financial sectors. Yet, it has been proven that countries with inadequate regulatory and supervisory frameworks, macroeconomic imbalances or whose financial institutions are insolvent may run into some serious problems if they liberalise interest rates too rapidly or too early, which might force them to re-introduce interest controls (see Mehran & Laurens, 1997).[1]

Although there is no one-size-fits-all approach to financial liberalisation for all countries, there are some general principles that tend to apply universally to many countries, which could mitigate the negative effects of financial liberalisation in an economy. First, countries should consider pursuing domestic financial liberalisation before proceeding with the implementation of external liberalisation. Second, it is critical to distinguish between (i) deposit and loan transactions; and (ii) wholesale and retail transactions. Ideally, the liberalisation of whole interest rates should take the lead, followed by lending rates and then deposit rates. Third, countries should ensure that financial liberalisation is accompanied by a strong and credible stabilisation programme in order to (i) stimulate the private sector; and (ii) ensure that there is a system of prudential controls over the financial sector. Fourth, although financial liberalisation is a necessary condition for economic growth, it is not advisable to abandon all the aspects of financial repression in its totality since such a move may result in extremely high interest rates, which may be equally damaging. Instead, the country should consider some mild and friendly interventions in the form of financial restraints, which have been found to be necessary in keeping interest rates below market rates at least in the short run (see Odhiambo, 2004). Indeed, studies have shown that, even if free financial markets are the ultimate goal, owing to the existence of market failures, some mild and market-friendly government controls need to be maintained in order to ensure the stability in the overall financial sector of the economy (Fry, 1997; Odhiambo, 2004).

The objectives of this chapter are, first, to provide an overview of some of the key financial sector reforms that have been implemented in some sub-Saharan African countries since the onset of the new orthodoxy of financial liberalisation in the 1980s. Some of the countries included in this analysis are South Africa and Mauritius, which were among the first sub-Saharan African countries to implement financial reforms in the 1980s. Other countries included in the analysis are Botswana, Burkina Faso, Cabo Verde,

Cameroon, Chad, Democratic Republic of Congo, Eswatini, Equatorial Guinea, Gambia, Ghana, Guinea Bissau, Kenya, Madagascar, Malawi, Mali, Mozambique, Namibia, Niger, Senegal, Seychelles, Tanzania, Togo, Uganda, Zambia and Zimbabwe.

Second, the chapter discusses some of the bank-based and market-based financial reforms that have been implemented in the studied countries since the onset of financial liberalisation in the 1980s. This is followed by the trends and patterns of financial development in the studied countries. Some of the trends discussed include interest rate spreads, financial deepening and widening, bank concentration and stock market development.

3.2 Financial Reforms in Sub-Saharan Africa

After independence, most countries in sub-Saharan Africa focused on the provision of credit, which was viewed as important for economic growth. In order to take control of credit systems, many governments nationalised banks, which led to the misallocation of resources (Gelbard & Leite, 1999). For example, subsidised credit was directed to certain sectors of the economy and credit controls were used (Fowowe, 2011; Odhiambo, 2011). Interest rates were regulated by governments, which set high lending and low deposit rates, resulting in wide interest rate spreads.

The interventionist policies of the 1980s did not bear much fruit in terms of economic growth and development. By mid-1980s, some countries embarked on financial reforms, most of which came as part of the recommendations of the International Monetary Fund (IMF) and the World Bank's structural adjustment programmes. The reforms include monetary policy–based reforms such as liberalisation of interest rates and exchange rates, reduction in reserve requirements, removal of credit constraints, reforms on the structure of banking and security/stock markets and the proper management of capital controls (Gelbard & Leite, 1999; Reinhart & Tokatlidis, 2003).

The financial reforms were aimed at mobilising savings for investment, following the debates in the 1970s on financial repression, started by McKinnon (1973) and Shaw (1973). Financial liberalisation is the process of allowing market forces to determine the price of credit and its allocation (Odhiambo, 2011). Interest rate liberalisation is central to financial reforms, with the idea being that when interest rates are determined by the market, their increase stimulates higher savings which would, in turn, make more credit available for investment. The removal of credit constraints, for example, by lowering reserve requirements would increase borrowing, resulting in higher investment, consumption and economic growth (Reinhart & Tokatlidis, 2003). Increasing the number of banks by granting more licences would increase competition in the industry leading to better provision of services. The outcome of financial liberalisation is to generate higher output leading to economic growth in countries that previously suffered from financial repression.

African countries have now had more than three decades of experience with financial sector reforms − with different outcomes. We observe some of the changes in financial institutions and markets in Section 3.3. Some countries, for example, South Africa and Mauritius, were among the first to implement financial reforms in the 1980s, while other countries such as Kenya, Mozambique and Madagascar began implementation in the 1990s. When we classify reforms into domestic and external, most countries implemented interest rate and credit reforms in the late 1990s, but other countries have been slow to liberalise the capital account (Reinhart & Tokatlidis, 2003). With regard to the sequencing of financial reforms, most sub-Saharan African countries first implemented internal financial reforms before embarking on external financial reforms.

Countries adopted different speeds of implementation of their financial reforms. Fowowe (2011:85) reports that Ghana, Gambia, Senegal and Madagascar adopted a rapid approach, whereas countries such as Mauritius, Kenya, Cameroon and Zimbabwe used a more gradual approach. Some countries implemented deep reforms, both domestic and external, while others had shallow reforms (Reinhart & Tokatlidis, 2003), that is, implemented the bare minimum. For instance, countries such as Ghana, South Africa, Mauritius and Senegal went for a full liberalisation approach, whereas Cameroon and Malawi chose partial liberalisation of financial reforms (Fowowe, 2011:85).

South Africa is an interesting case study because it was among the first countries to implement financial reforms. South Africa's interest rate and credit controls were removed in 1980, and bank liquidity ratios were reduced substantially thereafter in the early- to mid-1980s. In 1985, capital controls were increased owing to capital flight. In 1995, the dual exchange rate systems in South Africa were unified and a managed float was implemented. However, capital controls remained in place while exchange rate controls were kept until 1995 (Odhiambo, 2011).

With regard to market-based reforms, compared to the 1980s, more countries initiated securities markets. Jefferis Smith (2005:55) note that by 2003, only 12 formal markets were being monitored by the S&P's emerging markets database. These include South Africa, Kenya, Nigeria and Zimbabwe, Botswana, Ghana, Mauritius, Tanzania, Swaziland,[2] Zambia, Malawi and Uganda. Apart from establishing new stock markets, the financial reforms undertaken by African countries also improved the efficiency of already existing stock markets, for example, in Kenya and South Africa (Jefferis & Smith, 2005). Furthermore, privatisation programmes undertaken in African countries involved listing of shares, which further boosted the stock markets. Restrictions of participation by foreign investors in stock markets were also eased, and liberalisation of current and capital accounts enabled more participation by investors (Jefferis & Smith, 2005).

3.3 Trends and Patterns of Financial Development in Sub-Saharan Africa

Researchers and policymakers are interested in the effect of financial reforms on financial systems and development. However, the measurement of financial development has been a challenge for researchers. As a result, various indicators of financial development have been used in empirical work. These include monetary aggregates, stock market indicators and institutional indicators (Ndikumana, 2001). However, Gelbard & Leite (1999) have discussed extensively the limitations of using some of the indicators, such as monetary. aggregates. The authors argue that a thorough assessment of the financial system should include six indices that characterise financial systems. The key finding from Gelbard & Leite's (1999) study is that significant financial development occurred during the period between 1987 and 1997, which is the period when financial reforms were implemented in most sub-Saharan African countries.

In parts 1–4 of this section, we present trends of financial development indicators in selected sub-Saharan African countries using the more traditional measures of financial development, as reported in the literature. Section 3.3.1 presents interest rate spreads. Section 3.3.2 focuses on financial deepening. Section 3.3.3 looks at bank concentration. Section 3.3.4 looks at stock market development. In Section 3.3.5, we present the more broad-based indices of financial development in sub-Saharan Africa compiled by the IMF.

3.3.1 Interest Rate Spreads in Sub-Saharan Africa

Trends of interest rate spreads are discussed for selected countries in sub-Saharan Africa.[3] The selection of countries is mainly determined by the availability of data from 1990 to 2020 – the period of financial liberalisation. The selected countries are placed into two groups, for analysis.

The left pane of Figure 3.1 depicts trends for Botswana (BWA), South Africa (ZAF) and Mauritius (MUS). Interest rate spreads for Botswana rose from about 1.76% in 1990, reaching a peak at 7.87% in 2008 during the 2008 financial crisis, and have declined since then to 4.29% in 2020. South Africa's interest rate spread starts at 2.14% in 1990 and peaks at 5.68% in 1999. Since 2000, the interest rate spread in South Africa has shown more or less a downward trend reaching 2.83% in 2020. Notably, the interest rate spread in Mauritius increased throughout the 1990s, reaching a peak of 13.79% in 2005 before a sharp decline that bottomed out at 0.53% in 2010 and then gradually increased to 5.5% in 2020.

The second group of selected countries includes Nigeria (NGA), Kenya (KEN) and Zambia (ZMB), as shown on the right panel of Figure 3.1. A sharp increase in interest rate spreads is observed in Kenya and Zambia in the early 1990s after the implementation of interest rate reforms. The spread

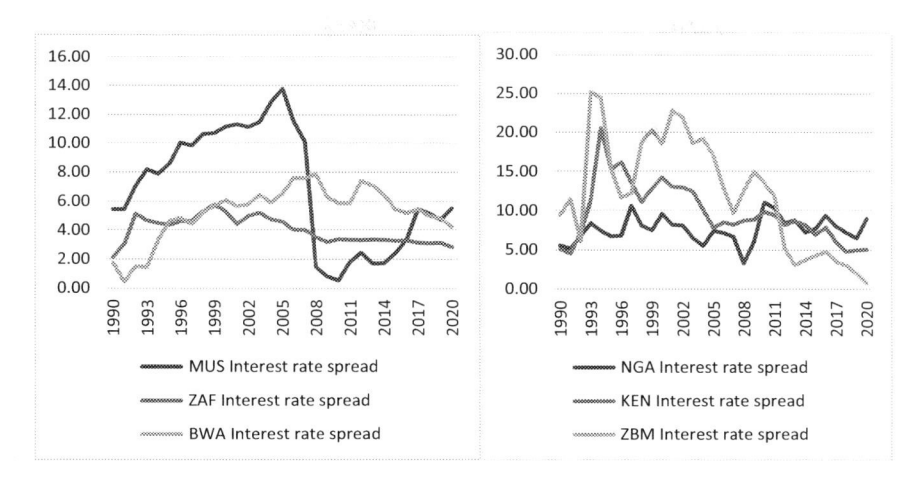

Figure 3.1 Interest rate spreads for Botswana, Mauritius and South Africa, and for Kenya, Nigeria and Zambia. Authors' computations based on data from the World Bank (World Development Indicators, 2021a).

in interest rates went up by almost 15% in the two countries to 25.17% in Zambia in 1993 and 20.52% in Kenya in 1994. However, interest rate spread in Nigeria remained below 11.07% during the period from 1990 to 2020. For Kenya, interest rate spreads declined to 16.2% in 1996, followed by a gradual decrease thereafter to 5.03% in 2020. Zambia's interest rate spreads also increased between 1996 and 2001 with a peak of almost 23% in 2001, and then a gradual decline thereafter to 0.76% in 2020.

Therefore, we can conclude that for the six selected countries, there was a general increase in interest rate spreads in the 1990s after the implementation of financial reforms. The period of the 2000s exhibits a mixed picture, with a decline in interest spreads in most countries, for example, in Kenya and South Africa, and an increase in interest rate spreads in a few countries. However, during the decade of 2011–2020 interest rate spreads for many countries show a general downward trend. The selection of countries used in the analysis is mainly determined by the availability of data for the sample period.

3.3.2 Financial Deepening in Sub-Saharan Africa

Two indicators of financial depth for the banking sector were used in order to discuss trends in financial sector development in sub-Saharan Africa. The chosen indicators of financial depth are, first, the ratio of liquid liabilities to GDP, which is the broadest measure of financial depth in the banking sector (Beck, Demirgüç-Kunt, & Levine, 2000, 2009); and second, private sector credit by money banks as a percentage of GDP. Ten-year averages are shown starting from 1991 to 2020 for 38 sub-Saharan African countries, based on the availability of data. The descriptive statistics are shown in Appendices 3.1 and 3.2.

Countries that are considered to have sizeable financial systems as measured by the ratio of liquid liabilities to GDP of above 40 (Ndikumana, 2001) have risen from only four countries (Mauritius, Seychelles, Cabo Verde and South Africa) during the period from 1991 to 2000 to ten countries during the most recent decade 2011–2020. The additional countries include Botswana, Guinea-Bissau, Kenya, Mozambique, Namibia and Togo. It is to be noted that Mauritius and South Africa were among the first countries to implement financial reforms, and their approach was gradual and full liberalisation (Fowowe, 2011:85), hence have better outcomes in terms of financial depth. Botswana and Kenya also adopted a more gradual approach but with partial liberalisation. Countries with a ratio of liquidities to GDP below 20 have decreased from 24 in 1991–2000 to only five countries during the decade 2011–2020. The increase in the number of countries with wider financial systems indicates that many countries have improved and widened their financial systems during the financial liberalisation period. However, the decrease in the depth of financial institutions in some SSA countries, for example, South Africa, could be associated with the movement from a bank-based to a more market-based financial system that has also been observed in developed countries.

When the second measure of financial depth – private sector credit by money banks as a percentage of GDP (Beck et al., 2000) – is considered, it is found that only four countries had a ratio above 20 in the 1991–2000 period. These countries are South Africa, Mauritius, Namibia and Cabo Verde. During the 2001–2010 decade, this number increased to seven countries, with the following additional countries: Kenya, Seychelles and Botswana. The most recent decade of 2011–2020 has seen this number increase to 13 countries, with the following additional countries: Togo, Senegal, Mozambique, Burkina Faso, Mali and Eswatini. According to Fowowe (2011), Senegal started financial liberalisation as early as 1980 with bank deregulation and restructuring, but implemented interest rate reforms in 1989 with other reforms following afterwards. Countries with a ratio of private sector credit by money banks as a percentage of GDP that is below 5 has decreased from ten countries in 1991–2000 to seven countries during the first decade of the century, to zero in the 2011–2020 period.

The increase in the number of countries with a higher ratio of financial depth (with the use of the two indicators) shows an increase in financial development in sub-Saharan Africa, which could be associated with the continued improvement of financial systems and deeper implementation of financial reforms. Countries that adopted deep reforms and a gradual approach to financial liberalisation seem to have benefited the most from financial reforms, whereas countries that had a rapid liberalisation approach with deep reforms took some time to uplift the financial systems.

3.3.3 Banking Concentration in Sub-Saharan Africa

It is well known that finance facilitates economic growth and that the banking system is the main source of finance for developing countries. In this section, the trends of indicators of banking sector development are analysed from 2000 to 2020 for a selection of sub-Saharan African countries.[4] The time period and selection of countries are subject to availability of data on the measures of bank concentration.

Bank concentration refers to assets of the largest banks as a share of assets of all commercial banks (Beck et al., 2000:601). Two measures of bank concentration are used: first, three-bank concentration ratio, which is "assets of three largest banks as a share of assets of all commercial banks" (Beck et al., 2000:601); and second, five-bank concentration ratio, which is based on assets of the five largest banks. A high bank concentration ratio indicates lack of competition in the commercial banking sector.

Trends of three- and five-bank concentration ratios are presented for the period 2000–2020 for countries that had available data, as indicated earlier. Based on the selection of sub-Saharan countries, Figure 3.2 shows bank concentration indicators for South Africa, Mauritius, Botswana and Nigeria.

South Africa's three-bank concentration ratio was 86.98 in 2000, rose to 99.54 in 2004, declined to 77.28 in 2006 and remained more or less the same until 2014. There is a sharp increase in the bank concentration ratio from 2015 onwards to 99.88. South Africa's five-bank concentration ratio was 94.84 in 2000, decreased slightly to 91.46 in 2001 but rose 100% from 2004 onwards until 2020. Hence, even though South Africa is regarded as having the most developed financial system in sub-Saharan Africa, the banking sector is relatively dominated by a few banks, as shown by the bank concentration ratios.

Botswana's three-bank concentration ratio started at 96.56 in 2000 and declined to 64.69 in 2014 before rising to 97.37 in 2019. The country's five-bank concentration started at 100% in 2000, decreased to 89.78 in 2014 and rose back to 100% from 2015 onwards. Mauritius started with a three-bank concentration ratio of 91.25 in 2000, which gradually declined to 45.54 in 2014 but increased to 68.21 by 2020. The five-bank concentration ratio in Mauritius was 98.55 in 2000, decreased to 66.27 by 2014 but rose again to 88.83 in 2020.

Nigeria's three- and five-bank concentration ratios of 27.45 and 36.93, respectively, in 2000, as shown in Figure 3.2, indicate much competition in the banking sector. However, the three- and five-bank concentration ratio increased from 36.11 and 51.49, respectively, in 2004 to 84.72 and 100%, respectively, in 2010. The ratios decreased to 40 and 60, respectively, from 2012 to 2014 but rose sharply to 78.11 and 97.32 in 2015. The three-bank concentration ratio reached a peak of 91.62 in 2018, while the five-bank concentration ratio stayed above 97 from 2015 onwards.

For the selected group of countries and sample period, Figure 3.3 shows bank concentration indicators for Côte d'Ivoire, Senegal and Kenya. A

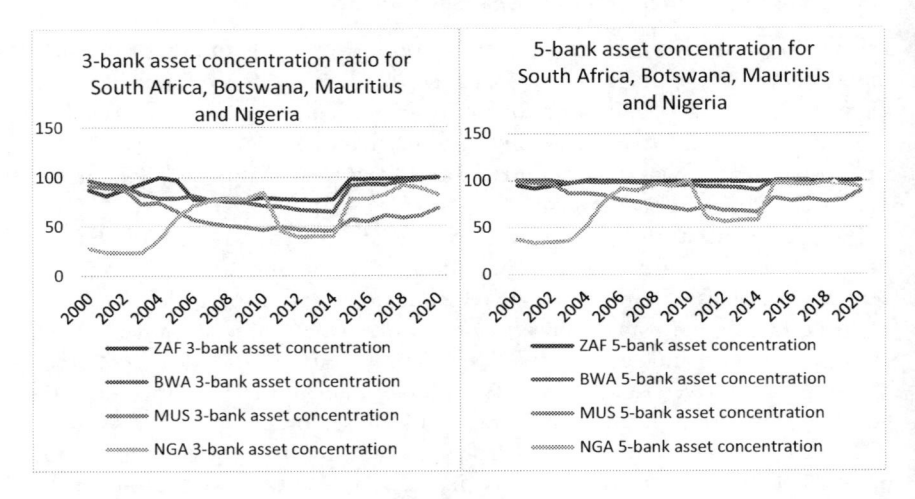

Figure 3.2 Bank asset concentration ratio for South Africa, Botswana, Mauritius and Nigeria. Authors' computations based on data from the World Bank (Global Financial Development Database, 2021b).

decrease in the three-bank concentration ratio in Côte d'Ivoire from 77.21 in 2000 to 50.06 in 2020 indicates a gradual increase in bank competition during the study period. Côte d'Ivoire embarked on bank de-nationalisation and restructuring in 1989 (Fowowe, 2011) which seems to have improved competition in the banking system as indicated by the significant reduction in three-bank concentration ratio. For Senegal, three-bank concentration ratios also declined from 66.66 in 2000 to 43.72 in 2019. The five-bank concentration ratios have also decreased from 90.75 and 91.96 in 2000 for Côte d'Ivoire and Senegal, to 74.64 and 60.30 in 2020, respectively. This general decrease in the five-bank concentration ratios for Côte d'Ivoire and Senegal during the period from 2000 to 2020 also indicates more competition in the banking sector during the period of financial reforms. Senegal started financial liberalisation measures with bank de-nationalisation and restructuring in 1981 (Fowowe, 2011) and seems to have reduced its bank concentration over time.

Kenya's three-bank concentration also decreased from 64.97 in 2000 to 33.48 in 2014. However, the ratio doubled between 2014 and 2016 from 33.48 to 71.16 owing to mergers in the banking sector. The five-bank concentration ratio for Kenya was 76.96 in 2000, which increased to 85.69 in 2020, with an upward shift observed in 2014 from 48.65 to 83.33 in 2016.

In summary, the indicators of bank concentration show that during the study period 1990−2020, some countries (for example, South Africa and Botswana) had a high average bank concentration ratio. In some countries, the average bank concentration ratio has declined over time (for example, Côte d'Ivoire and Senegal), while other countries (for example, Nigeria and

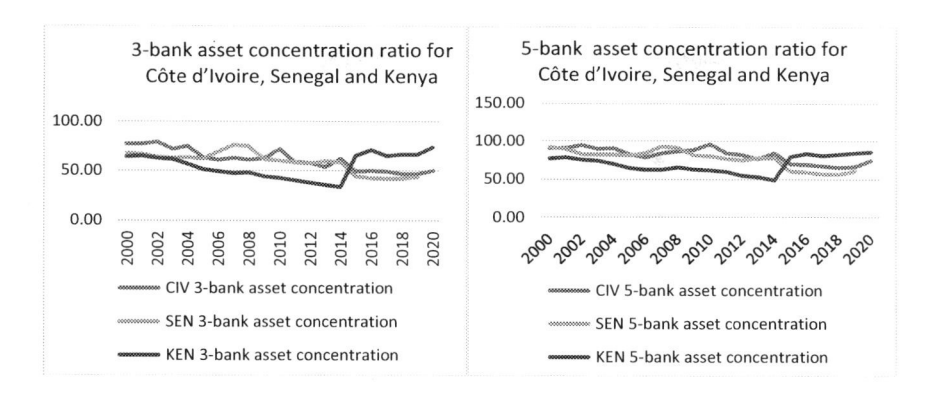

Figure 3.3 Bank asset concentration ratio for Côte d'Ivoire, Senegal and Kenya. Authors' computations based on data from the World Bank (Global Financial Development Database, 2021b).

Kenya) started with a low concentration ratio, which has increased during the last decade owing to bank mergers. The selection of countries for analysis was limited by the availability of data on the measures of bank concentration.

3.3.4 Stock Market Development in Sub-Saharan Africa

3.3.4.1 Indicators of Depth and Efficiency of Stock Markets

South Africa is considered to have a well-established and relatively sophisticated financial market. South Africa has the largest domestic stock market in sub-Saharan Africa with a market capitalisation of 348.28 relative to GDP in 2020, as shown in Figure 3.4. Johannesburg Securities Exchange has grown from 149.02 in 1991 to averages of 157.34, 205.76 and 273.76 in the last three decades. The stock market efficiency, as measured by stock market value traded, has more than tripled during the period from 1991 to 2020 from 22.76 in the period 1991–2001, to 82.99 in the period 2011–2020. When stock market efficiency is considered in terms of market turnover ratio, it is observed that in the period 1991–2000, the ratio was 14.74, which increased to 26.21 in the period 2001–2010, and 30.09 in the period 2011–2020. Levine and Zervos (1998) have argued that it is the liquidity or efficiency of financial markets that matters more for economic growth than the size or depth of financial markets.

The Mauritius stock market capitalisation as a percentage of GDP was 56.44 in 2020, as shown in Figure 3.4. The average for the period from 1993 to 2001 is 33.02 and that for the period from 2011 to 2020 is 65.62; hence, the stock market depth has almost doubled during the period from 1993 to 2020. However, both measures of stock market efficiency – that is, value traded and market turnover ratio – are at 3.19 and 4.87, respectively, relative to GDP during the most recent decade (from 2011 to 2020).

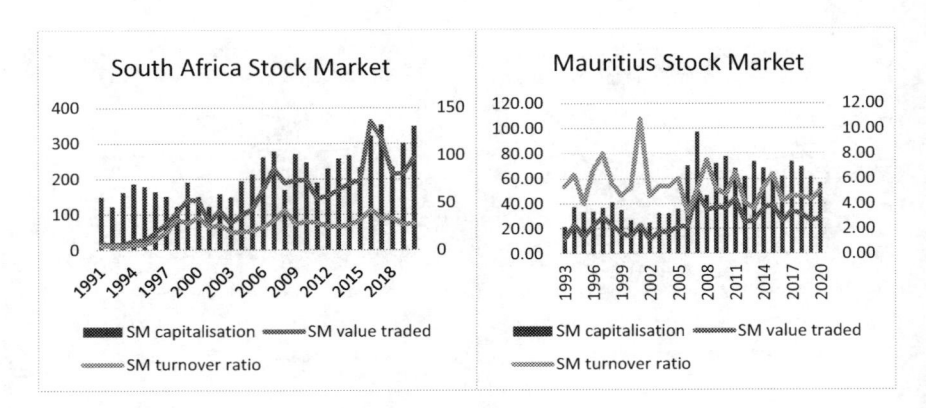

Figure 3.4 Stock market indices for South Africa and Mauritius. Authors' computations based on data from the World Bank (Global Financial Development Database, 2021b).

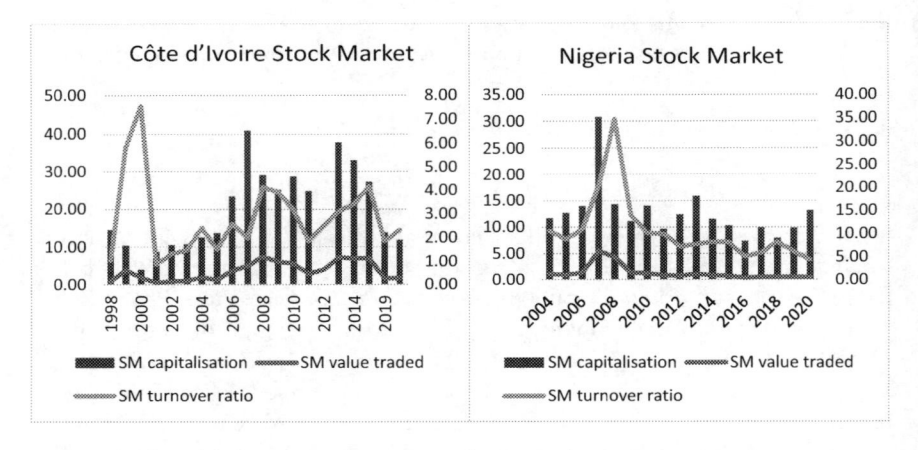

Figure 3.5 Stock market indices for Côte d'Ivoire and Nigeria. Authors' computations based on data from the World Bank (Global Financial Development Database, 2021b).

Côte d'Ivoire represents a regional stock market known as *Régionale des Valeurs Mobilières SA*, which serves eight Francophone West African countries[5] sharing a common currency, the CFA franc. For the period from 1998 to 2020, the average stock market capitalisation ratio was 20, and stock market liquidity was 2.87 using stock market turnover ratio, and 0.58 using stocks traded-to-GDP ratio (Figure 3.5).

The average stock market capitalisation ratio for the period from 2004 to 2020 for Nigeria is 12.7, with stock market efficiency as measured by

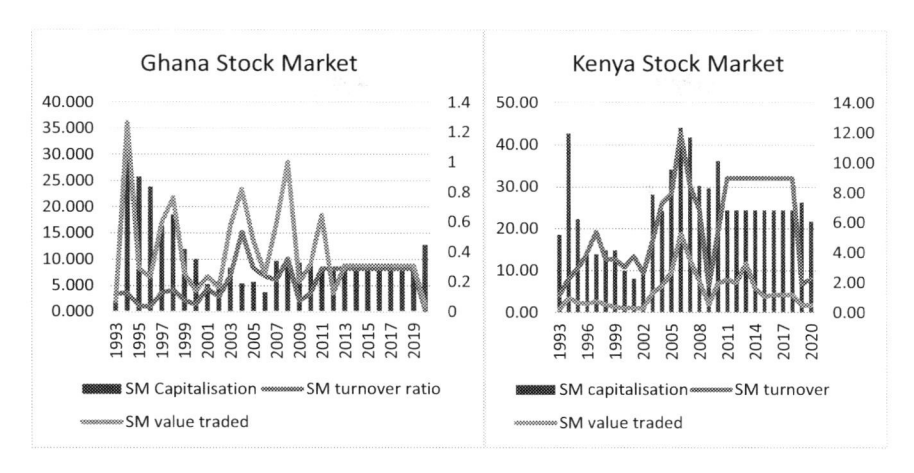

Figure 3.6 Stock market indices for Ghana and Kenya. Authors' computations based on data from the World Bank Global (Financial Development Database, 2021b) and the Federal Reserve Bank of St. Louis.

stock market turnover ratio of 10.63, and stock market value added is 0.47 (Figure 3.5).

The average stock market capitalisation ratio for the period from 1993 to 2020 for Ghana and Kenya is 10.69 and 24.33, respectively (Figure 3.6). The average stock market turnover ratio and average value traded for Ghana are 5.74 and 0.4, respectively. For Kenya, the average turnover ratio is 5.81, and the average value traded is 1.39. It is notable that for both countries, market capitalisation and turnover ratios remained approximately the same from 2011 to 2019, whereas for Ghana, the value traded ratio stayed at 0.307 from 2013 to 2019.

3.3.5 Indices of Financial Development in Sub-Saharan Africa

> Financial development is defined as a combination of depth (size and liquidity of markets), access (ability of individuals to access financial services), and efficiency (ability of institutions to provide financial services at low cost and with sustainable revenues, and the level of activity of capital markets).
>
> (Sahay, Čihák, N'Diaye, & Barajas, 2015)

In this section, the average indices of financial development (FD indexes) constructed by Sahay et al. (2015) at the IMF are presented. The FD indexes are broad-based measures of financial development, which incorporate both banking and non-banking institutions. The indices give a snapshot picture of the development of the financial sector during the post-reform period for selected sub-Saharan African countries.[6]

Figure 3.7 shows the overall average of financial development index for eight selected sub-Saharan African countries. Based on the average index reported in Figure 3.7, South Africa and Mauritius have the highest overall average financial development index of 0.5 and 0.36, respectively. Nigeria's average financial development index for the period from 1990 to 2019 is 0.19, while that of Kenya is 0.15, Côte d'Ivoire is 0.14 and Ghana is 0.11.

When the overall financial development index is disaggregated into financial institutions (FI) and financial markets (FM), it is found that financial institutions in sub-Saharan Africa are relatively more developed than financial markets. South Africa has the highest average for both financial institutions and financial markets, with indexes of 0.6 and 0.37, respectively, for the period from 1990 to 2019. The average score for Mauritius for the period from 1990 to 2019 is 0.44 for financial institutions, and 0.27 for financial markets, respectively. The average financial institution index for Kenya is 0.23, while the average financial market index for Nigeria is 0.19.

When the average indexes are unpacked for financial institutions in terms of financial depth, financial access and financial efficiency, as shown in Figure 3.8, it is found that the selected countries perform best on the efficiency of financial institutions compared to other indicators. The average score is above 0.4 for the selected countries during the period 1990–2019. With regard to the depth of the financial institutions, and for the selected countries in sub-Saharan Africa, the highest average scores were recorded in South Africa, Mauritius and Kenya. For access to financial institutions, the highest average scores were recorded in Mauritius, South Africa, Nigeria and Kenya from 1990 to 2019. Turning to financial markets in terms of depth, efficiency and access, it is observed that South Africa leads with two indicators, with an average score of 0.56 on financial market depth and 0.28 for financial market

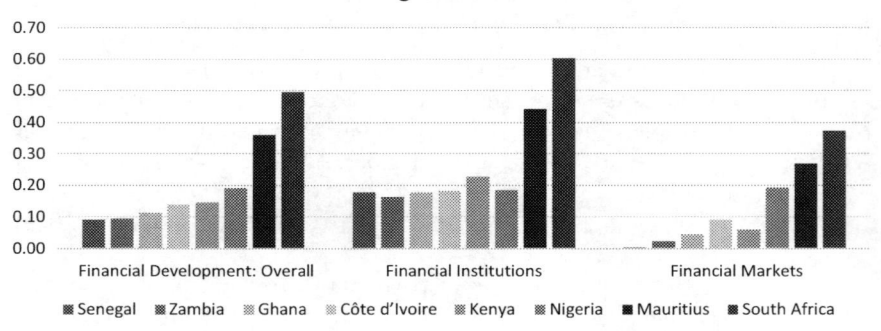

Figure 3.7 Financial development indices: averages for 1990–2019 for selected sub-Saharan African countries. Authors' computations based on data from the International Monetary Fund (Financial Development Index Database, 2021).

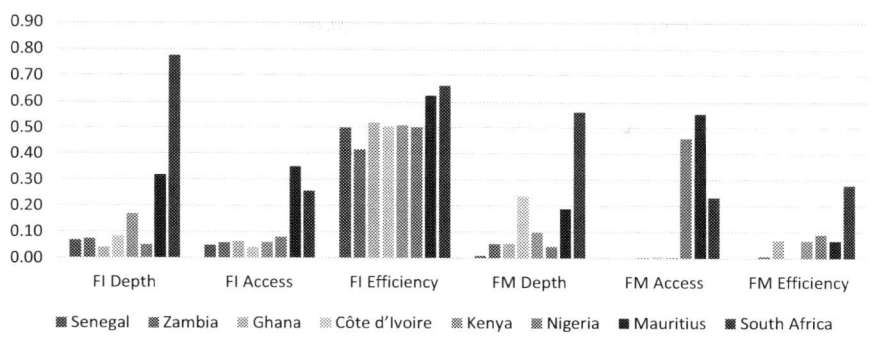

Figure 3.8 Financial institutions and financial markets – depth, efficiency and access in selected sub-Saharan African countries. Authors' computations based on data from the International Monetary Fund (Financial Development Index Database, 2021).

efficiency for the period from 1990 to 2019. The other selected sub-Saharan countries with high financial market depth scores are Côte d'Ivoire, Mauritius and Kenya. The selected countries with a relatively high average for financial market efficiency scores during the period from 1990 to 2019 are Nigeria, Mauritius, Kenya and Ghana. On financial market access, and for the selected countries in sub-Saharan Africa, the countries with the highest average scores are Mauritius, Nigeria and South Africa for the period from 1990 to 2019.

3.4 Conclusion

This chapter has given an overview of financial reforms and financial development in sub-Saharan African countries for the period 1990–2020. The chapter includes some of the early reformers, such as South Africa and Mauritius. Financial reforms of countries such as Ghana, Gambia, Senegal and Madagascar have been described to be rapid in the main, while countries such as Mauritius, Kenya, Cameroon and Zimbabwe used a more gradual approach. While this study has found that financial reforms have been somewhat too slow in some sub-Saharan African countries, we caution against rapid financial liberalisation, which is not accompanied by macroeconomic stability. We also caution against the *laissez-faire* approach to financial liberalisation since the conditions necessary for such a policy are still unattainable in many sub-Saharan African countries. Moreover, given the imperfect nature of the financial systems in many developing countries, partly owing to information asymmetry, leaving the financial sector to be controlled exclusively by invisible hands could be just as detrimental as financial repression. The financial sector in sub-Saharan Africa could be described as being in a nascent developing stage and is primarily dominated by financial institutions – banks and other financial intermediaries. Financial institutions have done well in terms of efficiency, with the following countries showing high scores: South Africa, Mauritius, Ghana, Kenya, Nigeria, Côte d'Ivoire and Senegal. Overall, countries with the most developed financial sectors in the region include South Africa, Mauritius, Nigeria, Kenya, Côte d'Ivoire and Ghana. However, the market-based financial sector is still underdeveloped in many countries and, at times, almost non-existent in some countries.

With regard to indicators of financial development, there was a general increase in interest rate spreads in the 1990s after the implementation of financial reforms, but the period of the 2000s exhibits a mixed picture, with a decline in interest spreads in most countries and an increase in interest rates in some countries. However, interest rate spreads show a general downward trend for the selected countries during the most recent decade from 2011 to 2020. With the use of two indicators of financial depth, an increase is observed in the number of countries with wider financial systems, which indicates that many countries have improved their financial systems during the financial liberalisation period.

The indicators of bank concentration show that, during the study period 1990–2020, some countries (for example, South Africa and Botswana) had a high average bank concentration ratio. In some countries, the average bank concentration ratio has declined over time (for example, Côte d'Ivoire and Senegal), while other countries (for example, Nigeria and Kenya) started with a low concentration ratio, which has increased during the last decade owing to bank mergers.

Although financial markets in many sub-Saharan African countries are still in their nascent stage, the region boasts of South Africa's Johannesburg Securities Exchange (JSE), which is ranked number 17 in the world in 2022, with a market capitalisation of US$1,356,590.81 million. The JSE has continued to grow in size, and stock market efficiency has more than doubled since 1991. Stock markets in other countries such as Mauritius, Côte d'Ivoire, Kenya, Ghana and Nigeria have continued to grow in size, but stock market liquidity has remained low. The region also boasts of a vibrant mobile money technology, which has played a key role in accommodating the unbanked consumers in the region. The mobile money in Africa started in Kenya in 2007 when Safaricom launched its peer-to-peer money transfer M-PESA solution. Indeed, M-PESA currently remains the most successful mobile money transfer service globally and has played a significant role in reducing the cost of transactions. To date, M-PESA has 30 million active users in Kenya and is active in six African countries.

Notes

1 See also Odhiambo (2004).
2 Swaziland has recently been renamed as Eswatini.
3 Botswana, South Africa, Mauritius, Kenya, Nigeria and Zambia.
4 South Africa, Mauritius, Nigeria, Botswana, Kenya, Côte d'Ivoire and Senegal.
5 Benin, Burkina Faso, Guinea-Bissau, Côte d'Ivoire, Mali, Niger, Senegal and Togo.
6 Côte d'Ivoire, Ghana, Kenya, Nigeria, Mauritius, Senegal, South Africa and Zambia.

References

Beck, T., Demirgüç-Kunt, A., & Levine, R. (2000). A new database on the structure and development of the financial sector. *The World Bank Economic Review, 14*(3), 597–605.

Beck, T., Demirgüç-Kunt, A., & Levine, R. (2009). Financial institutions and markets across countries and over time-data and analysis. *World Bank policy research working paper,* (4943).

Detragiache, M. E., & Demirgüç-Kunt, A. (1998). *Financial liberalization and financial fragility.* Washington D.C.: International Monetary Fund.

Fowowe, B. (2011). Financial sector reforms and private investment in sub-Saharan Africa n countries. *Journal of Economic Development, 36*(3), 79.

Fry, M. J. (1997). In favour of financial liberalisation. *The Economic Journal, 107*(442), 754–770.

Gelbard, M. E., & Leite, M. S. P. (1999). *Measuring financial development in sub-Saharan Africa.* International Monetary Fund.

Gibson, H., & Tsakalotos, E. (1994). The scope and limits of financial liberalisation in developing countries: A critical survey. *The Journal of Development Studies, 30*(3), 578–628.

International Monetary Fund. (2021). *Financial Development Index Database.* Washington D.C.: IMF.

Jefferis, K., & Smith, G. (2005). The changing efficiency of African stock markets. *South African Journal of Economics, 73*(1), 54–67.

Levine, R. (1997). Financial development and economic growth: Views and agenda. *Journal of Economic Literature, 35*(2), 688–726.

Levine, R., & Zervos, S. (1998). Capital control liberalization and stock market development. *World Development, 26*(7), 1169–1183.

Mehran, H., & Laurens, B. (1997). Interest rates: An approach to liberalization. *Finance and Development, 34,* 33–37.

McKinnon, R. (1973). *Money and capital in economic development.* The Brookings Institute, Washington, DC.

Ndikumana, L. (2001). Financial markets and economic development in Africa. Political Economy Research Institute, University of Massachusetts Amherst, Working Paper Series, Number 17. Available at: https://papers.ssrn.com/sol3/papers.cfm?abstract_id=333321.

Noland, M. (1996), Financial sector liberalisation in Africa in the framework of economic reform programmes. Institute of International Economics, APEC Working Paper 14.

Odhiambo, N. M. (2004). *Financial liberalization and economic growth in sub-Saharan African countries: Dilemmas and prospects.* Doctoral dissertation, Stellenbosch University, Stellenbosch.

Odhiambo, N. M. (2011). *The impact of financial liberalization in developing countries: Experiences from four SADC countries.* Organization for Social Science Research in Eastern Africa.

Reinhart, C. M., & Tokatlidis, I. (2003). Financial liberalisation: The African experience. *Journal of African Economies, 12*(suppl_2), ii53–ii88.

Sahay, R., Čihák, M., N'Diaye, P., & Barajas, A. (2015). *Rethinking financial deepening: Stability and growth in emerging markets.* International Monetary Fund Staff Discussion Note.

Shaw, E. S. (1973). *Financial deepening in economic development.* New York: Oxford University Press, xii + 260.

Williamson, J., & Mahar, M. (1998). *A survey of financial liberalization* (No. 211). Princeton University International Economics.

World Bank. (2021a). *World Development Indicators 2021.* Washington D.C.: The World Bank.

World Bank. (2021b). *Global Financial Development Database.* Washington D.C.: The World Bank.

Appendices

Appendix 3.1 Financial Sector Reforms in Sub-
Saharan Africa

Country	Internal	External
Benin	1989	1996
Botswana	1991	1995
Burkina Faso	1989	1996
Cameroon	1990	1996
Central Afr. Rep.	1990	1996
Chad	1990	1996
Congo, Rep.	1990	1996
Côte d'Ivoire	1989	1996
Gabon	1990	1996
Gambia	1986	1988
Ghana	1988	1994
Guinea–Bissau	1989	1996
Kenya	1991	1993
Madagascar	1994	1996
Malawi	1988	1995
Mali	1989	1996
Mauritania	1990	1995
Mauritius	1981	1993
Mozambique	1994	1994
Namibia	1991	1995
Niger	1989	1996
Nigeria	1987-91,1995	1995
Senegal	1989	1996
South Africa	1980	1983
Tanzania	1991	1996
Togo	1989	1996
Uganda	1988	1990
Zambia	1992	1994
Zimbabwe	1991	1994

Source: Adopted from Reinhart and Tokatlidis (2003).

Appendix 3.2 Financial Depth in Sub-Saharan African Countries from 1991 to 2020

Country	Liquid Liabilities			Private Credit by Banks		
	1991–2000	2001–2010	2011–2020	1991–2000	2001–2010	2011–2020
Angola	21.07	19.93	32.92	2.94	9.00	17.93
Benin	18.01	20.85	28.85	6.44	11.49	16.56
Botswana	24.20	39.54	42.96	12.72	22.18	32.03
Burkina Faso	19.05	20.14	34.08	8.62	13.96	24.76
Burundi	18.76	24.20	28.39	13.09	16.48	18.16
Cabo Verde	54.48	72.35	97.90	21.25	45.05	63.01
Cameroon	13.93	17.18	20.26	9.33	8.79	14.00
Chad	11.11	9.88	14.72	3.86	3.11	7.89
Comoros	12.58	15.29	25.59	6.55	5.82	14.05
Congo, Dem. Rep.	3.42	6.15	13.14	0.73	1.98	5.71
Congo, Rep.	14.45	15.83	26.43	8.61	3.25	12.57
Côte d'Ivoire	18.05	18.88	28.82	15.15	10.46	16.58
Equatorial Guinea	9.09	7.48	12.90	8.35	3.47	10.71
Eswatini	22.24	20.13	27.36	15.34	16.40	20.86
Gambia, The	11.27	23.35	36.96	4.32	7.34	8.39
Ghana	9.49	16.24	25.29	3.18	8.04	12.18
Guinea	7.00	14.95	24.40	2.96	2.97	8.80
Guinea-Bissau	7.12	19.41	40.86	1.99	2.52	11.58
Kenya	29.81	35.34	42.57	18.69	23.80	34.06
Lesotho	33.12	31.39	34.43	17.44	9.69	18.58
Madagascar	20.24	19.58	22.33	10.13	8.60	11.76
Mali	17.62	24.46	28.58	10.37	15.72	22.47
Mauritius	74.37	92.14	112.57	46.82	71.62	94.87
Mozambique	18.81	24.68	46.64	10.08	12.48	25.58
Namibia	35.00	44.09	55.57	37.04	47.83	53.05
Niger	9.94	11.23	17.91	5.03	6.16	10.82
Nigeria	12.93	16.58	24.41	7.40	12.27	11.86
Rwanda	15.70	15.31	20.25	7.55	10.36	19.93
Senegal	17.47	26.38	37.21	14.90	17.30	26.94
Seychelles	69.12	85.56	74.19	11.59	23.64	28.85
Sierra Leone	8.84	16.47	22.88	1.89	4.14	5.65
South Africa	50.94	42.75	43.97	60.47	69.32	67.27
Sudan	19.58	15.93	24.44	4.19	7.69	9.08
Tanzania	19.86	19.13	21.88	6.68	8.27	12.99
Togo	22.55	29.84	50.60	16.43	15.99	33.87
Uganda	9.48	14.25	13.94	3.58	6.97	11.65

Source: Authors' computations based on data from the World Bank (Global Financial Development Database 2021b).

4 Interest Rate Reforms in African Countries

Erasmus Larbi Owusu

4.1 Introduction

Interest rate can be defined as the reward or income on equity or opportunity cost of deferring current consumption into the future (Uchendu, 1993). This definition clearly demonstrates that interest rate is a concept that can have a myriad of meanings depending on the perspective in which it is viewed. Interest rate can therefore be seen as an indistinct concept, a position affirmed by the availability of multitude types of interest rates, for example, country base rate, savings rate, discount rate, lending rate, bond rate and Treasury bill rate. Apart from this, interest rate can also be considered in two lenses, as nominal or real. These types try to cater for the moderating influence of inflation on rates. Thus, nominal rates embody the monetary effects, while the real rates allow for inflation on the nominal interest rate.

Economists have generally recognised that external factors and market imperfections may cause governments around the world to intervene in operations of the domestic financial markets. In most African countries, the financial sector can be widely characterised as being either emerging and/or to some extent oligopolistic (limited completion). It is therefore not startling to observe that central government intervention in these financial sectors is immanent. The question then is not whether policy interventions in this sector should be stopped or curtailed at all but rather how these policy intervention reforms have impacts on the financial systems or sectors of these countries.

It is therefore imperative that rational criteria are designed as alternatives to which the authorities and policymakers are able to determine the level and fabric of interest rates in the fledgling and imperfect financial markets of many African countries. No single criterion is the panacea. However, there are many policy options on which they could base their policy decisions. These policy decisions hinge on the immediate and ultimate objectives of the financial market and the current phase of the financial system, the development of the economy and its relationship to other economies in Africa and the rest of the world. In situations where there are multiple criteria to design

DOI: 10.4324/9781003215042-5

the policy interventions, the weight to be allocated to each of these criteria becomes also important. Notwithstanding such difficulties, it is still critical to search for a set of frameworks that would promote the establishment of interest rate levels that would be conformable with the macroeconomic objectives of the economy.

In this chapter, the role of interest rate reforms in economic development in selected African countries is examined. It will also explore the experiences of various countries with the liberalisation of the interest rate, on a case study basis. In this chapter, we will consider the evolution of interest rate reforms in selected African countries, as well as their performances over the last two decades and in future. The chapter will also focus on the speed and the sequencing of interest reforms in selected African countries. For this purpose, the countries have been chosen to provide varying conventional and policy groundwork so that the discussion on interest rate policy reforms should assume a sufficiently general tone across the continent. The countries are Nigeria, Ghana and Cote d'Ivoire (from the CFA franc zone) from the West Africa region; Kenya from the East Africa region; South Africa and Tanzania from the Southern African Development Community (SADC) countries; Ethiopia from the horn of Africa; and Egypt from North Africa. These countries account for over 75% of economic activities (by gross domestic product (GDP)) on the continent.

The chapter is organised in the succeeding order. In Section 4.2 of the chapter, the characteristics of the financial systems in selected African countries are described. Section 4.3 discusses the interest rate policies pursued in those countries in the last two decades. Section 4.4 contains case examples of the sequencing of relevant interest rates and financial sector reforms in the selected countries. The last section contains the conclusions of the chapter.

4.2 Characteristics of the Financial System in African Countries

Although the foundation, the degree of sophistication and private participation of the financial systems vary considerably among the selected countries, some basic characteristics are common to most of them. For example, except for South Africa and Nigeria, public-owned financial institutions have a varying degree of importance in the financial systems. This is true even in countries such as Cote d'Ivoire, Ghana, Kenya and Tanzania, where some privatisation policies have been implemented in the last two decades to Egypt where the public-owned section is quite significant, that is, over 55% of deposit money banks, to Ethiopia where a significant majority, over 80%, of the financial sector is public-owned. Another common characteristic of the financial systems in the selected countries is the foreign participation in the deposit money banks. This tends to be negligible in Ethiopia, to some extent in Nigeria and South Africa, and to significant and very significant in Ghana, Tanzania, Cote d'Ivoire, Kenya and Egypt.

The financial systems in these countries have developed and evolved with major improvements in efficiency in the last two decades. However, there are some countries where, typically, it is made up of few deposit money banks, some merchant banks, some development banks, some savings and deposit institutions, some rural banks (particularly in Ghana), some postal banks (South Africa), some microfinance, and Mobil Money and Internet banking institutions. The most prevalent is mobile money (MoMo). Mobile money is new mobile phone technology that allows individuals and businesses to receive, store and spend money using their mobile phones. It is sometimes referred to as a "mobile wallet". There are more than 150 different mobile money services across African countries. Mobile money is also available across Asia and Latin America. Mobile money has become a popular alternative to both cash and banks since it is easy to use and secure and can be used anywhere there is a mobile phone signal.

Furthermore, except for Cote d'Ivoire, all the other selected countries have their independent central bank, independent financial market and independent currency. Cote d'Ivoire on the contrary shares a currency with seven other West African countries. It is therefore heavily influenced by the policies of the West African Economic and Monetary Union (WAEMU), which serves as its central bank (Owusu, 2012). In the last two decades, the central banks have established independent Monetary Policy Committees (MPC), which are mandated to set the country base rates (CBR) against the central government inflation targets. Thus, the financial systems in African countries can be described in a gist as central bank, government and foreign-dominated except to a lower extent in Nigeria and South Africa.

Moreover, in all the selected countries and across African countries, there is a certain amount of currency substitution in the financial sector. Currency substitution is when a country uses a foreign currency instead of, or in addition to, the domestic currency, primarily due to the greater sturdiness of that foreign currency. These can be in the form of foreign currency bank accounts or the usage of physical currency in business transactions. Currency substitution is also known as dollarisation when the US dollar (USD) is the currency that is being used as a substitute. However, the extent of currency substitution in each country differs. This has a significant impact on the interest and exchange rate policies in the countries.

An additional key feature in the financial markets in African countries is the borrowing requirements of the public sector with comparatively low financial savings and financial deepening. Irrespective of the political system and the stage of economic development, as well as the financial sophistication, tends to be by far, the public sector is the major borrower in the financial sector with low domestic savings. Claims on central government including loans to central government institutions' net of deposits have declined in most African countries but comparatively still high and exceeded 50% of total credit extended by the banking system in Egypt in the last decade. In the previous decade, from 2001 to 2010, claims on central government exceeded 20% on average in Egypt, Ethiopia and South Africa (Table 4.1).

Although the large credits to the central government in these countries are a direct consequence of the large percentage of public investment in total investment (Table 4.2), a significant portion of these funds also goes to finance current budget deficits. Except for Kenya and South Africa, the ratio of central government investment in gross domestic investment exceeds 25% on average in the last two decades with the ratio reducing to below 20% on average in Nigeria in the last decade.

Domestic savings in general on average have been relatively low across all the countries (Table 4.3). Domestic savings in Africa is relatively low mostly below 25% of GDP on average in the last two decades. Nigeria, however, recorded savings of over 30% on GDP on average between 2001 and 2010 but declined to 20% on average in the last decade. Tanzania and Ghana on the contrary increase their domestic savings on average by about 6% points and

Table 4.1 Selected African countries: claims on central government, 2001–2020 (% of GDP, average per decade)

Country	2001–2010	2011–2020
Cote d'Ivoire	5.0	7.8
Egypt, Arab Rep.	30.5	51.5
Ethiopia	22.1	a
Ghana	12.3	11.5
Kenya	8.4	8.8
Nigeria	b	2.9
Tanzania	0.6	3.6
South Africa	23.7	17.4

Source: World Development Indicator.
a   Data not available.
b   Claim is negative (deposits exceeded loans).

Table 4.2 Selected African countries: ratio of government investments to total investments, 2001–2020 (average per decade)

Country	2001–2010	2011–2020
Cote d'Ivoire	28.3%	28.7%
Egypt, Arab Rep.	46.1%	48.8%
Ethiopia	39.0%[a]	37.8%
Ghana	30.0%	24.0%[a]
Kenya	18.0%[a]	19.0%[a]
Nigeria	25.0%[a]	18.0%[a]
Tanzania	27.6%	28.6%
South Africa	15.6%	14.5%

Source: World Development Indicator.
a   Estimation by Author from IMF World Economic Outlook and World Development Indicator.

Table 4.3 Selected African countries: gross domestic savings, 2001–2020 (% of GDP, average per decade)

Country	2001–2010	2011–2020
Cote d'Ivoire	18.6	22.2
Egypt, Arab Rep.	15.0	7.0
Ethiopia	a	20.6
Ghana	3.9	14.2
Kenya	7.3	6.2
Nigeria	32.3	20.4
Tanzania	23.2	29.0
South Africa	20.0	19.2

Source: World Development Indicator.
a Data not available.

Table 4.4 Selected African countries: ratio of financial savings to gross domestic product, 2001–2020 (% of GDP, average per decade)

Country	2001–2010	2011–2020
Cote d'Ivoire	24.0	32.1
Egypt, Arab Rep.	90.7	80.8
Ethiopia	41.4	a
Ghana	29.6	27.0
Kenya	37.4	40.0
Nigeria	16.7	24.4
Tanzania	20.3	21.9
South Africa	69.1	73.7

Source: World Development Indicator.
a Data not available.

10% points respectively. One interesting observation is the drop in domestic savings in Egypt by over 50% on average in the last decade compared to the previous.

Finally, data on financial savings, defined as the ratio of broad money (M2) to GDP, are provided in Table 4.4.

The average ratio of financial savings to gross domestic product (GDP) varied across African countries. Except for Egypt and South Africa where the ratio is over 60% over the last two decades, the ratios are mostly below 40% over the last two decades in the other countries. This suggests relatively low financial deepening[1] in most African countries.

4.3 Interest Rate Policies in African Countries in the Last Two Decades

Low-interest rate policies implemented by many emerging markets and across many countries in Africa are implicitly intended to be connected to three main deliberations: firstly, the desire to increase the investment levels in the country; secondly, the desire to improve the efficient allocation of sectorial investment; and thirdly, the desire to keep inflationary pressures low. Before we analyse the interest rate structures established as a result of the numerous interest rate policies followed by African countries over the last two decades, we will examine some of the theoretical foundations.

In the literature, McKinnon (1973) and Shaw (1973) posit that low–interest rates do not necessarily stimulate investment and economic growth. They are of the view that if real interest rates are reduced below market equilibrium levels, investment demand will increase; however, actual investment will decrease. Because at low levels of interest rates, there will be insufficient savings to finance these investments.

Furthermore, they are of the view that demand in excess of investment will require that competing investors for financial resources will be in favour of borrowing at the reduced or the prevailing interest rate. In countries where there exist rationing and control over lending rates, it is perfectly unlikely that financial intermediaries will choose to provide funds in accordance with a ranking of rates of return on investment. In addition, factors such as the capacity to provide collateral, political influence and other affiliations are likely to play a significant role in the credit allocation decisions. Consequently, a low–interest rate policy will not only impede investment but will also reduce the mean rate of return on investment to levels outside the optimal attainable rate.

In many African countries, the attempts to improve credit allocation were very important considerations behind the interest rate policies (Table 4.5). This is because, in most African countries, a significant percentage of the credit extended to the private sector by the financial intermediaries goes to the import businesses, while only a tiny proportion are used to finance the domestic expansion of the real productive sector of the market. Historically, the desire to change the credit allocation to benefit the real productive sectors of the economy has had the repercussion of the introduction of targeted credit controls in many African countries in the past. However, in the last two decades, these restrictive barriers have been dismantled for the reasons of the implementation of interest rate reform policies.

According to Johnson (1975) and Khatkhate and Delano (1978), the implementation of these policies will lead to the reduction in loan interest rates offered to the preferred sectors; however, in general, these have tended to put more pressure on average lending rates pushing it downwards and sometimes leading it into negative real rate levels. Furthermore, the central banks provided special financing incentives to the deposit money banks such that lowered lending rates were favoured, which led to the creation of money by money deposit banks and therefore inflationary pressures. In addition, lending rates in many African countries were kept stable for lengthened periods, and hence, most real lending rates were reduced below the optimum levels by an increase in prices. Thus, the use of interest rate differentials to support financial resource allocation was strong and positive. However, expansive application of this policy framework is not advisable, especially, because of the difficulties devised by the interchangeability of money in ensuring that the financial resources are used for the purpose they were originally intended for (Owusu, 2012).

The desire to keep inflationary pressures low is mentioned in many cases as a defence for low-interest rate policies as the cost of interest rate reforms. There is no doubt that there will be immediate cost implications involved in interest rate reforms. However, the possible inflationary impact of interest rate reform seems to have been overestimated in some countries. This means that an increase in interest rates directly affects the real economy and it is probably going to be little, and even this little increase is not expected to be completely passed on to the final consumers. Moreover, an increase in interest rates is probably going to minimise the amassing or stockpiling of goods, which was ubiquitous across Africa leading to an increase in aggregate supply. Finally, the medium-run consequence of an interest rate increase will no doubt be a curtailment in inflation, since it will tend to dampen or reduce aggregate demand to the same level as aggregate supply by extinguishing the excess investment demand. In most of the selected countries, there has not been any major interest rate policy change after the initial interest rate reforms. However, there have been some minor amendments to correct distortions in the reform policies in some countries in the last two decades.

A typical example is Kenya, where despite the non-positive impact of the various interest rate controls enforced after independence in 1963 for 20 years, the Kenyan government progressively transitioned to a market economy in the early 1990s. They have implemented an interest rate capping policy through the amended law setting interest rates [the Banking (Amendment) Act, 2016]. This law came into force on 14 September 2016 capping bounds on lending and deposit rates. The law prescribes the upper limit of lending rate at no more than 4% above the based rate of the Kenyan Central Bank and the lower limit of interest rate given on a deposit held in interest-earning accounts with financial intermediaries to at least 70% of the same rate (see Owusu (2012) for similar policy guidelines). As per the Central Bank of Kenya (CBK) Act, Section 36(4) and the central bank set the bank rate (CBK, 2018).

Kenya has seen some impact on the financial sector as a result of its law. According to the Central Bank of Kenya (CBK, 2018), from the commencement of the interest rate setting law in September 2016, the number of credit facilities offered by the financial intermediaries has declined considerably between October 2016 and June 2017, thereby leading to rising average loan size, by 36.7% over the period. The rising value of loan facilities as against the reduced number of loans indicates lower access to small borrowers and larger loans to more traditional firms and central government. Additionally, further to the interest rate caps, financial intermediaries are now generating more of their income from non–interest-bearing asset sources. Thus, the share on non-interest income was about 12.4% as at September 2016, but it has now increased gradually to about 15.2% as at June 2017. The transfer to non-interest income has been seen across all the categories of financial inter-mediaries (Central Bank of Kenya (CBK), 2018).

Finally, the interest rate cap is affecting the sectoral allocation of credit and hence reducing economic growth. This is supported by the fact that as of September 2016, Medium and Small Manufacturing Enterprises (MSMEs) accounted for about 28.4% of GDP. However, in 2017, the real GDP growth of the MSMEs declined by 1.4% points. As a result, overall real GDP growth was expected to reduce by 0.40% points.

Another example is South Africa. Here, the financial sector is of particular interest due to the dismantling of the Apartheid regime in 1994. After the Apartheid regime, South Africa gained a significant increase in confidence from investors both domestically and internationally. This put the spotlight on financial sector reforms to take cognisant of the increased attention, and these multitudes of reforms also led to financial sector reforms. The financial reform policy had a major impact on the financial deepening of the econ-omy, as more once-excluded households and businesses were exposed to the growing formal financial sector (Muyambiri and Odhiambo, 2014). Some of the interest rate reforms in South Africa in the last two decades are as follows.

Thus, in November 2012, the authorities started with the publication of the Banks (Amendment) Bill. This was intended to amend the existing Banks Act, 1990, as follows: (i) to re-define certain expressions in the sector; (ii) to improve certain definitions and make it flexible; (iii) to align certain provisions with their practical application; (iv) to refresh and improve references to leg-islation and institutions; (v) to widen the bank naming convention to include representative offices; (vi) to make it clear and indicate that a contravention of the Financial Intelligence Centre Act, 2001, is a reason for suspension or can-cellation of bank's registration; (vii) to make the Banks Act, 1990, compatible with the Companies Act, 2008; and (viii) to comply and streamline financial activity requirements on the basis of the Basel Committee of Banking Super-vision effective on January 2013 (Muyambiri & Odhiambo, 2014).

4.4 Sequencing of Interest Rate Reform Policies in African Countries

This section presents the speed and sequencing of the implementation of the policy of interest rate reforms in the selected African countries in the last two decades. African countries, as in many other developing countries, export revenue depends significantly on a single commercial commodity, have faced several challenges after the implementation of interest rate reform policies. Some of these challenges could be due to the speed and sequencing of the policy reforms. Besides gradual increasing and high-interest rates, other chal-lenges that they have experienced related to volatile and unstable savings, investment and financial deepening trends universally drop in the applica-tion of sectoral allocation of credit policies; in some cases, very low to low economic growth rate in relation to financial depth; the relatively increase and widespread in relation to lending and deposit rates; as well as increasingly foreign currency deposits in the domestic universal banks have become a feature (Owusu, 2012; Owusu and Odhiambo, 2016).

Most economists have reasonable and justifiable concerns about financial sector reform sequencing. This is because there is always a danger that policymakers and policy implementers would use sequencing arguments to avoid the enforcement and the implementation of policy framework to which they are not fully committed and these could have adverse consequences. According to McKinnon (1991), there are two macroeconomic requirements for a successful implementation of interest rate reform policies. The first of such policy is the fiscal control policy framework, and the second one is the control over universal domestic banks for monetary policy reasons. He argues that since interest rate reforms involve the removal of many regulations, it is crucial and necessary that other sources of revenue must first be found; thus, there is a need to develop and improve the means of collection taxes before embarking on interest rate and financial sector policy reforms. Below are case examples of the interest rate and financial sector reform sequencing in Nigeria, South Africa and Ghana (Tables 4.5, 4.6 and 4.7).

Table 4.5 Sequencing of interest rate and financial reforms in Nigeria

Year	Policy Reform:
1986	• Establishment of two foreign exchange markets • Complete removal of interest rate controls • Liberalisation of bank licensing • Unification of foreign exchange markets
1988	• Establishment of foreign exchange bureaus • Relaxation of bank portfolio restrictions • Establishment of the Nigerian Deposit Insurance Corporation
1989	• Permission to pay interest on demand deposits by banks • Introduction of auction markets for government securities • Upward review of the capital adequacy standards • Prohibition of credit based on foreign exchange deposits extended
1990	• Upward adjustment of risk-weighted capital standard introduced and banks' required paid-up capital • Introduction of uniform accounting standards for banks • Introduction of stabilisation securities to mop up excess liquidity
1991	• Embargo on the issuance of bank licensing • Authorisation given to the Central Bank of Nigeria to regulate and supervise all financial intermediaries
1992	• Removal of interest rate controls once again • Beginning the process of the privatisation of government-owned banks • Commencement of the capital market deregulations • Re-organisation of the foreign exchange markets • Credit controls abolished
1993	• Introduction of indirect monetary instruments • Restructuring on five commercial banks

(Continued)

Table 4.5 (Continued)

Year	Policy Reform:
1994	• Re-imposition of interest and exchange rate controls
1995	• Modifications of interest rate control policies
	• Abolition of Exchange Rate Control Act, 1962
	• Liberalisation of the foreign exchange rate and financial markets.
	• Removal of the restrictions on foreign transfers and remittances
2003	• Establishment of the Monetary Policy Committee by the Central Bank of Nigeria
2004	• Announcement of the recapitalisation of banks by the Central Bank of Nigeria
	• Central bank increases the minimum financial intermediaries' paid-up capital.
2005	• Central Bank of Nigeria introduced a new microfinancing policy framework.
	• Establishment of the Monetary Policy Implementation Committee (MPIC) at the 192nd meeting of the Monetary Policy Committee (MPC) on 25 October 2005. At inception, the membership of the Committee included the Deputy Governor (Economic Policy) as the Chairman, the Directors of Research and Statistics and Banking Operations Departments.
2006	• Start of recapitalisation exercise
2007	• The passage of the new Central Bank of Nigeria Act (2007) into law by the National Assembly to reconstitute the Monetary Policy Committee (MPC). This was to facilitate the attainment of the objective of price stability and to support the economic policy of the federal government.

Source: Adopted from Ikhide and Alawode (1994); Owusu (2012) and author's Investigations.

Table 4.6 Sequencing of interest rate and financial reforms in South Africa

Year	Policy Reform:
1994	• The South African Reserve Bank (SARB) became a contributor to the Basel Bank Supervision standards.
	• SARB became a signatory to the Core Principles for Effective Banking Supervision of 1987.
	• Liberalisation of the South African financial sector. The number of foreign banks permitted to establish offices rose. And it has risen from 31 to 46 by 2004.
1996	• Foreign financial institutions to follow tighter requirements in order to register in the country. This was embodied in the Government Gazette No. 17115 of 1996.
1998	• Introduction of a third system of monetary accommodation from March 1998.
	• Appointment of 12 banking institutions to represent the central as government in the bond markets. The order to liquidate the Islamic Bank Limited was given.
	• Considerable depreciation of the South African Rand (thus, about 28% in nominal terms against the US dollar from April to August 1998), prompting a monetary policy response that resulted in short-term rates soaring 7 percentage points.

Year	Policy Reform:
1999	• The Fidelity Bank Limited was put under curatorship by the authorities. • Establishment of the Monetary Policy Committee (MPC). Adoption of the inflation-targeting policy framework for monetary policy in South Africa. The 14-member MPC meets seven times a year. The first meeting was on 13 October 1999.
2000	• Introduction of inflation-targeting policy framework was by Government Gazette No. 21936 of 28 December 2000.
2001	• Depreciation of the South African Rand by 21% in nominal terms against the US dollar between September and December 2001.
2002	• Introduction of an inflation-targeting strategy, in an attempt to bring consumer prices under control.
2004	• Order given for Regal Treasury Private Bank Limited liquidation.
2007	• Rennies Bank Limited changes name to Bidvest Bank Limited.
2008	• Amendment of the Banks Act on 1 January 2008, in order to comply with the requirements and principles of the Basel II framework.
2009	• Cancellations of two bank registrations: Commerzbank Aktiengesellschaft and Meeg Bank Limited.
2010	• The South African Postbank Limited Act, 2010. • The registration of the Imperial Bank Limited and other banks was cancelled.
2011	• Cancellation of the registration of the Royal Bank of Scotland NV.
2012	• The Parliament passed the South African Postbank Limited Act, 2010. This was published in the Government Gazette No. 33835. • Banks Act. "The November – Banks Amendment Bill published". This is in order to amend the Banks Act, 1990. • Cancelation on the registration of the Credit Agricole Corporate and Investment Bank – South Africa Branches from January 2013.

Source: Adopted from Muyambiri and Odhiambo (2014) and author's investigations.

Table 4.7 Sequencing of interest rate and financial policy reforms in Ghana

Year	Policy Reform:
1982	• The domestic currency, the CEDI, was demonetisation. Thus, there is 30% reduction of total quantity of money in circulation.
1983	• Establishment of multiple windows to determine the exchange rate.
1986	• Established a two-window system of trading to determine exchange rates.
1987	• Abolition of the two-window system for the determination of exchange rate and combining them to form a unified window system. • Creation of a consolidated Discount House. • The lower and the upper limits of deposit rate regime abolished. However, the rates on lending were unchanged.
1988	• Bank of Ghana abolished the minimum lending rates which the universal banks are allowed to charge.

(Continued)

Table 4.7 (Continued)

Year	Policy Reform:
1989	• The banking law (PNDCL 225) was passed.
	• Liberalisation of interest rates. Financial intermediaries and institutions were allowed to determining the lending and savings rates.
	• Establishment of the capital markets in Ghana.
1990	• Establishment of a fledgling inter-bank market.
	• The 20% mandatory requirement for the financial intermediaries and institutions to lend to the agricultural sector was fully removed.
	• Operations started by the Ghana Stock Exchange (GSE).
1991	• Full liberalisation of interest rates.
	• Money markets formalised.
	• Security Discount Company (SDC) was set up.
1992	• Full liberalisation of the exchange rate determination process.
	• The revised Bank of Ghana Law (PNDCL 291) banking was passed.
	• The independence of the central bank, the Bank of Ghana, was established.
1993	• The Bank of Ghana Financial Institutions (Non-Banking) Law (PNDCL 328) was passed.
	• Partial liberalisation of the capital account to allow limited participation of foreign investors in the capital market.
1995	• Rehabilitated and privatisation of unused banks' assets.
	• Public banks were privatised to allow public participation.
2002	• Establishment of the Monetary Policy Committee (MPC) by Bank of Ghana Act, 2002 (Act 612), Section 27.
	• The policy framework of the MPC is for the initiation of proposals for the formulation of the monetary policies of the central bank, as well as providing the statistical data and advice necessary for the formulation of monetary policies.
2006	• Full liberalisation of the capital account.
	• Removal of the restrictions on foreign investors in the capital market.
	• The secondary reserve requirement for banks was abolished.
	• Allowance of banks to expand credit into other sectors in the economy not specified in their license but using their old license for such activities.
	• Financial deepening measures implemented in the financial system in Ghana, the Exchange Control Act, 1961, were replaced by the Foreign Exchange Act (Act 723) in December 2006.
2007	• Redenomination of the local currency by removing four zeros from the prevailing equivalent amounts.
	• The Bank of Ghana officially adopted an inflation-targeting (IT) policy framework underpinned with a flexible exchange rate regime. The framework is designed to ensure price stability over the medium term.
	• Establishment of various policies by the Bank of Ghana in the areas of institutional, accountability and operational structures to support the implementation.

Year	Policy Reform:	
2008	• Introduction of the E–ZWICH platform. In line with making the economy cashless, a National payment system known as the "E–ZWICH".	
	• The purpose of the E–ZWICH was to establish a common platform for all payment transactions in Ghana and also allow banks that did not have a platform to be able to join that common platform at a relatively low cost.	
2018	• Raising Ghana minimum capital requirements.	
	• Universal banks were given until December 2018 by the Bank of Ghana to meet a new minimum capital requirement of GHS400m ($86.4m), which replaces the previous level of GHS120m ($25.9m). While the effects of the change have yet to be fully felt, it has the potential to significantly alter the structure of the industry.	

Source: Adopted from Owusu (2012) and author's investigations.

4.5 Conclusion

We can conclude from the above discussion and preceding facts that the interest rate and financial reform policies implemented in African countries and most cases with the assistance of IMF and the World Bank starting from 1989 with the specific aim of liberalising the financial sectors so as to eliminate or drop its preferential discount rate, leaving banks' interest rate to be determined by each member country, have had mixed results based on available research.

Based on the analysed characteristic of the financial system in African countries from the selected countries, we find that the large credits to the policymakers in these countries are a direct consequence of the large percentage of public investment in total investment. That domestic savings on average have been relatively low across all the countries and some improvement in financial savings, defined as the ratio of broad money (M2) to GDP. Likewise, the average ratio of financial savings to gross domestic product (GDP) has also seen minor improvements across African countries.

Owusu (2012) also finds that the interest rates have reduced significantly across African countries since the financial sector reform policies were implemented and this has had positive impacts. Thus, there has been an increase in foreign capital flow seen across many African countries, there has been some positive improvement in the reserve position of most of the countries, many African countries have seen stability but decreasing financial savings, and they have prevented the falling financial deepening and resource mobilisation to some degree. These policies have also reduced the interest rate spread as a result of stabilising the lending and deposit rates in some of the countries.

Nevertheless, the reform policies have brought with it many interconnected challenges that need addressing by the policymakers. These challenges include, among others, a drastic increase in the rate of imports and a reduction of credits to the real productive sectors of the economy with the outcome that the share of private sector credits in the total credits has not improved as expected after the implementation of the policy. Some of the main reasons underpinning these challenges could be lack of effective completion in the financial sectors, in addition to lack of competition among the financial intermediaries as well as other factors such as information asymmetry regarding loan and credit terms available at other banks coupled with high operational cost could explain some of this. There is also the potential for distortion resulting from the sequence of the implementation of the policy reforms. Potential solutions to these challenges would be that the central banks in conjunction with the central government with support from the deposit money banks and other financial intermediaries mount a public education campaign on banking and financial issues, as well as microfinance and other forms of formal financial sectors.

Note

1 Note that currency substitution or dollarisation may have an impact on the level of financial deepening depending on the valuation of the foreign currencies.

References

Central Bank of Kenya. (2018). The Impact of Interest Rate Capping on the Economy of Kenya: Highlights, Draft Comments, *Central Bank of Kenya*, 2018.

Ikhide, S. I. and Alawode, A.A. (1994). Financial Sector Reforms, Macroeconomic Instability and the Order of Economic Liberalisation: The Evidence from Nigeria, African Economic Research Consortium (AERC) Final Report.

Johnson, O.E.G. (1975). Direct Credit Controls in a Development Context: The Case of African Countries, in *Government Credit Allocation: Where Do We Go from Here?* (ed. G. Benston), pp. 151–80. San Francisco, CA: Institute for Contemporary Studies.

Khatkhate, D.R and Delano P. (1978). Operation of Selective Credit Policies in Less Developed Countries: Certain Critical Issues, *World Development*, Vol. 6, pp. 979–990.

McKinnon, R.I. (1973). *Money and Capital in Economic Development*, Washington, DC.

McKinnon, R.I. (1991). *The Order of Economic Liberalisation*, New York: John Hopkins University Press.

Muyambiri, B and Odhiambo, N.M. (2014). A Chronological Analysis of Monetary Policy and the Financial System in South Africa, *Public and Municipal Finance*, Vol. 3(2), pp. 19–29.

Odhiambo, N.M. (2009). Interest Rate Reforms, Financial Deepening and Economic Growth in Kenya: An Empirical Investigation, *Journal of Developing Areas (JDA)*, Vol. 43(1), pp. 295–313.

Owusu, E.L. (2012). Financial Liberalisation and Sustainable Economic Growth in ECOWAS Countries. Department of Economics, Doctorate Thesis, *University*

of South Africa (UNISA), Pretoria, South Africa. http://www.worldcat.org/title/
financial-liberalisation-and-sustainable-economic-growth-in-ecowas-countries/
oclc/830810863&referer=brief_results

Owusu, E.L and Odhiambo, N.M. (2016). Interest Rate Liberalisation in West
African Countries: Challenges and Implications, *Ekonomski Pregled*, Vol. 67(6),
pp. 557–580. http://www.hde.hr/autori1_en.aspx?Podrucje=613

Shaw, E.S. (1973). *Financial Deepening in Economic Development*, New York: Oxford
University Press.

Uchendu, O. (1993). Interest Rate Policy, Savings and Investment in Nigeria, *Central
Bank of Nigeria (CBN) Quarterly Review*, Vol. 31(1), pp. 34–52.

World Bank. (2020). *World Development Indicators, Various Issues to 2020.*
Washington, DC.

Further Reading

Asefa, T. (2016). Financial Sector Liberalization in Ethiopia: Resistance, Justifica-
tion and Its Credibility, *Journal for Studies in Management and Planning*, Vol. 2(4),
pp. 231–250. http://edupediapublications.org/journals/index.php/JSMaP/

Efobi, U.R and Asonglu, S. (2018). *Financing Sustainable Development in Africa*, London: Palgrave Macmillan.

Kapadia. S.R. (2011). Egypt's Financial Liberalisation: Why Didn't It Do What It
Said It Would on the Box? *Graduate School of Development Studies, International Institute of Social Studies (ISSS)*, The Hague, The Netherlands, November 2011.

Odhiambo, N.M. (2002). Financial Sector Reforms, Savings and Economic Development in Kenya, *Savings and Development Supplement, African Review of Money Finance
and Banking*, Economics and Trade Development and Technology, pp. 5–22.

Odhiambo, N.M. (2008), Interest Rate Reforms, Financial Depth and Savings in
Tanzania: A Dynamic Linkage, *Savings and Development*, Vol. 32(2), pp. 141–158.

Owusu, E.L and Odhiambo, N.M. (2013). Financial Liberalization and Economic
Growth in Ivory Coast: An Empirical Investigation, *Investment Management and
Financial Innovation,* Vol. 10(4), pp. 171–180. http://businessperspectives.org/
component/option,com_journals/task,issue/id,251/jid,4/Itemid,74/

5 Financial Determinants of Informal Financial Development in African Countries

Simplice Anutechia Asongu, Valentine B. Soumtang and Ofeh M. Edoh

5.1 Introduction

This study is motivated by two main strands in the scholarly and policy literature, notably: the role of informal finance in the economy and gaps in the literature. The two points are expanded in turn. First, the informal financial sector still represents a substantial part of the financial system in Africa, not least, because most of the adult population does not yet have bank accounts in formal financial institutions and by extension, recourse to informal financial mechanisms in borrowing and savings (Klapper & Singer, 2015; Tchamyou *et al.*, 2019). Moreover, according to Aryeetey (2008), many analysts and scholars understand informal finance as an effect of a formal financial system that is inadequate, and therefore, reforms in the financial sectors are expected to engender a decline in the influence of the informal financial sector. According to the author, "transformation of the informal financial sector can take place if it is driven by a need to increase access to the resources of the formal financial sector" (Aryeetey, 2008, p. 6). Building on this narrative, the purpose of this study is to assess formal financial sector determinants of the informal financial sector, not least, because of the need to fill an apparent gap in the attendant literature.

Second, as substantiated or critically engaged in Section 5.2, the corresponding formal and informal finance literature has not focused on the problem statement being considered in this study. Moreover, in this study, the concepts of informal financial development and financial informalization are conceived, defined and measured building on disentanglement of the financial system in order to articulate the formal, semi-formal, informal and non-formal financial sectors. Informal financial development is understood as the progress of the informal financial sector relative to other economic sectors, while financial sector informalization is defined as the progress of the informal financial sector to the detriment of the formal and semi-formal financial sectors (Asongu, 2015). Hence, the study also provides a practical way by which to assess the incidence of indicators of the formal financial system on the informal financial sector.

DOI: 10.4324/9781003215042-6

The rest of the study is organized as follows: The literature review is covered in Section 5.2, while the data and methodology are discussed in Section 5.3. The empirical results are provided in Section 5.4, while Section 5.5 concludes with future research directions.

5.2 Review of the Literature

Financial development is recognized in the literature as a factor of development because of its effects in terms of faster growth and better allocative efficiency. To this end, works have most often focused on formal finance. However, the development gap that exists between different countries can be justified by the existence and role played by informal financial systems in some countries (Ullah, 2019). Indeed, the economic system of several developing countries is heavily dominated by an informal financial system due to their institutional specificities. To this effect, Steel *et al.* (1997) explain that there are two main reasons that can justify the existence of the informal sector. First, excessive state intervention leads to underdeveloped financial systems. Second, formal banks are faced with costly procedures and problematic management, which contributes to poor access to credit; this in turn contributes to a sharp rise in informal finance. In relation to this aspect, studies on informal finance focus on the different theories behind this concept, its different determinants and its effects in general.

Initially, with regard to the theoretical background, several works have dwelt on the existence of informal finance. In particular, according to the financial repression hypothesis, Mckinnon (1973) and Shaw (1973)[1] state that the existence of large informal financial sectors is due to repressive financial systems. In other words, when the state sets interest rate ceilings and allocates credit, a large part of the population is excluded from using formal credit services. As a result, this part of the population has no choice but to turn to informal means of accessing credit, such as family, friends, relatives and tontines. Following this work, the structuralist school (Taylor, 1979; Van Wijnbergen, 1983) argues that credit market failures create gaps in the formal financial system. This encourages individuals to move from the formal to the informal financial system, hence the existence of informal credit markets alongside formal credit institutions. So according to them, the importance of informal finance in developing countries is explained by the structural weaknesses of formal finance.

On the contrary, the institutionalist school argues that informal finance gets its legitimacy from the institutional constraints faced by the formal institutions operating in some areas. According to Bagachwa (1995, 1996), these constraints include the lack of appropriate mechanisms to deal with financial risk management, contract enforcement and loan selection and monitoring. As a result, formal institutions are likely to serve only those clients who present minimal risk and cost to them. Other clients will have to turn to informal sources to meet their financial service needs. Another strand of the literature explains that imperfect information and costly contract enforcement lead to market failures and thus fragmentation of the credit market. Informal finance is based on relationships, and reputation and information asymmetries between informal lenders and their borrowers are less important. The loan application process is lighter, and the collateral required is easier to satisfy (Allen *et al.*, 2010). Thus, agency theory suggests that adverse selection or reluctance of lenders to lend to firms can be perceived as risky borrowing by lenders. In such a case, especially for small- and medium-sized enterprises (SMEs), access to capital may be limited. Moral hazard is another problem that lenders face due to asymmetric information (Tchamyou & Asongu, 2017a; Asongu & Odhiambo, 2018; Tchamyou, 2019). This can further compound the lack of access to capital for SMEs in banks (Allen *et al.*, 2019).

Second, with regard to the different determinants, the literature distinguishes economic determinants and institutional determinants. Related to economic determinants, Deng *et al.* (2019) study data based on a series of national surveys of Chinese enterprises between 2006 and 2012. They show that corporate social capital plays an important role in informal finance. They also demonstrate that it is positively correlated with their ability to obtain informal finance. And this effect is more pronounced in situations of financial crisis, when social trust in general is weakened. Similarly, Sekyi *et al.* (2019) examine access to informal credit among farmers in rural Ghana. They show that age is a key determinant. Rural farm households' decision to access informal credit is negatively correlated with individual age and education. Indeed, the authors suggest that informal lenders may view older farmers as high-risk clients for fear that they will die.

Also, an educated farmer can conceptualize credit information, assimilate this information and better understand the credit system. However, they instead show that factors such as farm size, multicrop production, non-farm business equipment and group membership positively influence rural farm households' decision to access informal credit. Subsequently, work by Zins and Weill (2016) shows that in Kenya, being a woman increases the propensity to engage in informal savings as African women use informal finance more than formal. In the same vein, Sile and Bett (2015) determine that gender, as well as the sector of activity, is an important factor for informal finance. This is because women in rural areas resort to informal finance because they do not have tangible collateral to finance domestic expenses due to cultural restrictions on property ownership. This is because there are few formal institutions in rural areas, low awareness and low income in rural areas.

Furthermore, income is also an important determinant. Instead, the authors show that increasing income enhances the choice of using informal finance. These authors also point out that the level of education significantly influences the choice of informal finance. Individuals with primary education or no education all use informal systems for savings and credit, while those with higher education at secondary level do not use informal loans. The study shows that the age of an individual significantly affects his choice of informal finance. The majority of informal finance users are young (under 35 years old). This is because young people do not have the security required by formal financial institutions for credit services. So they turn to informal finance.

Also, Campero and Kaiser (2013) study the knowledge and use of formal and informal credit sources in Mexico. They use an ensemble training model and selection correction. They find that household size positively affects knowledge and use of informal credit sources. Also, a study conducted in Nigeria investigated the determinants of credit demand and supply in informal credit markets (Nto *et al.*, 2011). It does a double least squares analysis and shows that farm income, profit and education determine the demand for informal credit.

In terms of institutional determinants, some authors such as An and Lin (2021) study the impact of legal origin on informal finance between 2005 and 2019. They find that places with a common law origin have better informal financial development than those with a civil law tradition. Also, the work of Cao *et al.* (2019) employs the ordinary least squares (OLS) method for the period 2003 and 2013 on Chinese non-state and listed firms. They show that religion increases trade credit which is one of the main instruments of informal finance. They rely on Buddhism, Taoism and Christianity.

Finally, the literature has focused on the different effects of informal finance on economic development in general. To this end, Goodland *et al.* (1999) showed that informal financial enterprises contribute to the equitable distribution and use of local resources, especially incoming commodities. This is because the credit obtained has been used to finance income-generating activities that yield higher returns than the loan contracted, thus ensuring economic stability. This ensures economic stability. Some works have also shown that loans provided by the rotating savings credit association increase the income of individuals and stimulate asset building (Zaman, 1999). They also improve the economic situation of subsistence farmers through easy access to financing for adequate storage facilities to protect their agricultural products from seasonal price fluctuations.

It is also noted that in China, informal finance provides four times more access to credit than formal finance. The informal sector represents a major source of finance for traders and farmers who systematically provide socio-economic development (Tsai, 2004). Similarly, Ghazala (2006) finds positive effects of informal financial institutions such as microcredit programmes on the welfare of the people. He finds that microcredit reduces poverty through microfinance and savings societies. Also, microcredit increases women's empowerment, and improves savings and purchase of agricultural inputs and easy access to loans with significantly reduced interest rates. Ngutor *et al.* (2013) also find that the informal financial institutions that exist in Adikpo reduce poverty through easy access to credit. In the same vein, Sekyi *et al.* (2019) also argue that access to informal credit significantly promotes agricultural productivity. Specifically, they find that farmers with access to informal credit were able to achieve 48.42 kg/ha more yield than their counterparts without access to informal credit.

5.3 Data and Methodology

5.3.1 Data

The study used data for the period 1995–2017 from 48 countries in sub-Saharan Africa.[2] The indicators selected for the study are from the Financial Development and Structure Database (FDSD) of the World Bank. Accordingly, the number of countries and corresponding periodicity are motivated by constraints in the availability of data at the time of the study. As apparent in Table 5.1 and consistent with recent literature (Asongu, 2015; Tchamyou *et al.*, 2019), the financial sector formalization and informalization variables are derived from the FDSD of the World Bank. Given the information disclosed in Table 5.1, the financial formalization indicator reflects how the formal financial sector is being enhanced at the expense of the informal financial sector, while financial informalization denotes the development of the informal financial sector to the detriment of the formal financial sector. The context of the financial system underpinning the financial sector development propositions is presented in Table 5.2.

Given the motivation of this study, which is to assess the financial determinants of the informal financial sector, only Propositions 3 and 7, respectively, for informal financial sector development and financial sector informalization, are used in the study. The financial determinants are selected from the FDSD. Accordingly, all variables that have convenient degrees of freedom for the period 1995–2017 are selected, namely, bank overhead costs to total assets; net internet margin; bank concentration; return on equity; bank cost-to-income ratio; financial stability; loans from non-resident banks; offshore bank deposits; and remittances. Given that the study is focused on assessing determinants of informal financial development, we cannot a priori establish the signs of the financial indicators.

The definitions and sources of variables are provided in Appendix 5.1, while the summary statistics is disclosed in Appendix 5.2. Appendix 5.3 provides the correlation matrix, which informs the study on concerns about multicollinearity. Accordingly, concerns about multicollinearity affect the estimated signs of determinants and, by extension, could misplace policy implications (Asongu *et al.*, 2020, 2021).

5.3.2 Methodology

Given the nature of the problem statement, which is to assess determinants of informal financial development throughout the conditional distribution of informal financial development dynamics, a quantile regression approach is adopted, consistent with the literature that has adopted a similar approach to assess a similar problem statement for alternative outcomes such as governance standards, notably, Billger and Goel (2009) and Asongu (2013). Accordingly, the employment of the QR technique enables the study to assess how

Table 5.1 Summary of financial sector formalization and informalization variables

Panel A: GDP-Based Financial Development Indicators

Propositions	Name(s)	Formula	Elucidation
Proposition 1	Formal financial development	Bank deposits/GDP	Bank deposits[3] here refer to demand, time and savings deposits in deposit money banks.
Proposition 2	Semi-formal financial development	(Financial deposits − Bank deposits)/ GDP	Financial deposits[4] are demand, time and savings deposits in deposit money banks and other financial institutions.
Proposition 3	Informal financial development	(Money Supply − Financial deposits)/GDP	
Proposition 4	Informal and semi-formal financial development	(Money Supply − Bank deposits)/ GDP	

Panel B: Measures of Financial Sector Importance

Proposition 5	Financial intermediary formalization	Bank deposits/ Money Supply (M2)	From 'informal and semi-formal' to *formal* financial development (formalization).[5]
Proposition 6	Financial intermediary 'semi-formalization'	(Financial deposits − Bank deposits)/ Money Supply	From 'informal and formal' to *semi-formal* financial development (semi-formalization).[6]
Proposition 7	Financial intermediary 'informalization'	(Money Supply − Financial deposits)/ Money Supply	From 'formal and semi-formal' to *informal* financial development (Informalization).[7]
Proposition 8	Financial intermediary 'semi-formalization and informalization'	(Money Supply − Bank Deposits)/ Money Supply	Formal to '*informal and semi-formal*' financial development: (Semi-formalization and informalization)[8]

Source: Asongu (2015).
N.B: Propositions 5, 6 and 7 add up to unity (one) arithmetically spelling out the underlying assumption of sector importance. Hence, when their time series properties are considered in empirical analysis, the evolution of one sector is to the detriment of other sectors and vice versa.

Table 5.2 Segments of the financial system by degree of formality in paper's context

Paper's Context			Tiers	Definitions	Institutions	Principal Clients
Formal financial system	IMF definition of financial system from International Financial Statistics (IFS)	Formal financial sector (deposit banks)	Formal banks	Licensed by central bank	Commercial and development banks	Large businesses, government
Semi-formal and informal financial systems		Semi-formal financial sector (other financial institutions)	Specialized non-bank financial institutions		Rural banks, post banks, savings and loan companies, deposit-taking microfinance banks	Large rural enterprises, salaried workers, small and medium enterprises
			Other non-bank financial institutions	Legally registered but not licensed as financial institution by central bank and government	Credit unions, microfinance NGOs	Microenterprises, entrepreneurial poor
	Missing component in IFS definition	Informal financial sector	Informal banks	Not legally registered at national level (though may be linked to a registered association)	Savings collectors, savings and credit associations, money lenders	Self-employed poor

Source: Asongu and Acha-Anyi (2017).

the considered financial determinants affect informal financial development dynamics when initial levels of attendant informal financial development dynamics are taken into account. Hence, in line with the attendant literature, the technique is appropriate when low, intermediate and high levels of the corresponding informal financial development dynamics are considered, notably, Koenker and Hallock (2001), Tchamyou and Asongu, (2017b) and Boateng *et al.* (2018).

It is also important to note that compared to the OLS technique that assumes the presence of normally distributed error terms, the QR approach is not contingent on residuals that are normally distributed. Moreover, in QR, the parameter estimates are obtained at multiple points of the conditional distribution of the outcome variable (Koenker & Bassett, 1978). Accordingly, the θth quantile estimator of informal financial development is obtained by solving for the following optimization problem in Equation (5.1), which is disclosed without subscripts for simplicity and ease of presentation.

$$\min_{\beta \in R^k} \left[\sum_{i \in \{i: yi \geq xi'\beta\}} \theta \left| yi - xi'\beta \right| + \sum_{i \in \{i: yi < xi'\beta\}} (1-\theta) \left| yi - xi'\beta \right| \right], \tag{5.1}$$

where $\theta \in (0,1)$. Compared to OLS, which is fundamentally focused on minimizing the sum of squared residuals, the QR approach, for multiple quantiles, focused on minimizing the weighted sum of absolute deviations for various quantiles such as the 25th or 75th (with $\theta = 0.25$ or 0.75, respectively) by weighing approximately the residuals. The conditional quantile of informal financial development yi given xi is:

$$Q_Y \left(\frac{\theta}{xi} \right) = xi'\beta\theta \tag{5.2}$$

where for each θth specific quantile, unique slope parameters are computed. This formulation is analogous to $E(y / x) = xi'\beta$ in the OLS slope where parameters are examined exclusively at the mean of the conditional distribution of informal financial development. For the model in Eq. (5.2), the dependent variable yi is the informal financial sector development indicator, while xi contains a constant term, bank overhead costs to total assets; net internet margin; bank concentration; return on equity; bank cost-to-income ratio; financial stability; loans from non-resident banks; offshore bank deposits; and remittances.

5.4 Empirical Results

The empirical results are disclosed in this section in Tables 5.3 and 5.4, respectively, focusing on informal financial sector development (Proposition 3) and financial sector informalization (Proposition 7). It is worthwhile to note that compared to the OLS results, the QR findings are different in terms of signs and magnitude of signs, which is further evidence that the adoption of the QR approach is worthwhile, not least, because responses of the considered determinants are contingent on the initial levels of informal financial development. The findings reported in Tables 5.3 and 5.4 are discussed in terms of four main perspectives: (i) U–Shape, (ii) S–Shape and (iii) positive or negative thresholds with increasing or decreasing tendencies, respectively, and (iv) estimates that do not fall in any of the first three categories.

It is relevant to note that consistent with complementary threshold literature (Asongu, 2014, 2017); the notion of threshold based on QR is assessed in the light of how the estimates respond to the outcome variable throughout the conditional distribution of the outcome variable. For instance, if an estimate consistently increases throughout the conditional distribution of the outcome variable, the notion of positive threshold is used, and in the same vein, if an estimate consistently decreases throughout the conditional distribution of the outcome variable, the notion of negative threshold is employed to describe the tendency. As for a U–Shape tendency, the magnitude of the estimate first decreases as initial levels of the outcome variable increase before eventually increasing in top quantiles of the outcome variable. With respect to an S–Shape, the corresponding magnitude either increases, decreases and then increases, or decreases, increases and then decreases throughout the conditional distribution of the outcome variable.

The following findings can be established for Table 5.3 on the nexus between financial development and informal financial sector development: (i) net interest margin decreases informal financial development with a negative threshold from the 25th to the 90th quantile; (ii) financial stability and life insurance penetration exert a negative effect with a U–Shape tendency; (iii) non–life insurance and offshore bank deposits have a positive effect with an S–Shape tendency; (iv) remittances and return on equity (bank cost-to-income ratio) have (has) a positive (negative) impact, though not throughout the conditional distribution of informal financial sector development; and (v) the incidence of loans from non–resident banks is negative in the 25th quantile and positive in the 75th quantile.

The following findings are apparent in Table 5.4 related to finance and financial sector informalization (Proposition 7): (i) bank concentration has a positive effect with a positive tendency from the median to the highest quantile, while life insurance has a negative effect with a negative threshold; (ii) the effects of bank-to-income ratio, financial stability, non–life insurance and loans for non–resident banks are predominantly negative in the bottom quantile, while the impact of return on equity and remittances are positive in the bottom and top quantiles, though not throughout the conditional distribution; and (iii) the positive effect of overhead cost is exclusively significant in the top quantiles of financial sector informalization.

Table 5.3 Finance and informal financial sector development (Proposition 3)

	OLS	Q.10	Q.25	Q.50	Q.75	Q.90
Dependent Variable: Informal Financial Sector Development (Proposition 3)						
Constant	**14.499*** ** **(0.001)**	**7.349*** **(0.050)**	**8.396** ** **(0.034)**	**11.158*** ** **(0.008)**	**22.776*** ** **(0.000)**	**22.628*** ** **(0.000)**
Overhead	0.175 (0.423)	−0.271 (0.293)	−0.086 (0.751)	−0.085 (0.767)	0.133 (0.647)	0.490 (0.100)
Net interest margin	**−0.718*** ** **(0.000)**	−0.173 (0.389)	**−0.409*** **(0.054)**	**−0.440*** **(0.051)**	**−0.810*** ** **(0.001)**	**−1.021*** ** **(0.000)**
Bank concentration	0.015 (0.465)	0.019 (0.397)	0.014 (0.558)	0.004 (0.847)	0.018 (0.477)	−0.001 (0.959)
Return on equity	**0.079** ** **(0.043)**	0.052 (0.104)	**0.066*** **(0.052)**	**0.072** ** **(0.047)**	0.021 (0.574)	0.061 (0.103)
Bank cost-to-income ratio	**−0.134*** ** **(0.006)**	−0.019 (0.674)	−0.025 (0.599)	−0.043 (0.393)	**−0.125** ** **(0.019)**	**−0.108** ** **(0.042)**
Financial stability	0.197 (0.164)	**−0.162** ** **(0.023)**	**−0.142*** **(0.056)**	−0.036 (0.648)	**−0.319*** ** **(0.000)**	**−0.321*** ** **(0.000)**
Life insurance	**−8.818*** ** **(0.000)**	**−11.027*** ** **(0.000)**	**−10.471*** ** **(0.000)**	**−6.106*** ** **(0.000)**	**−3.606*** ** **(0.000)**	**−3.825*** ** **(0.000)**
Non-life insurance	**7.796*** ** **(0.005)**	**3.095** ** **(0.038)**	**8.060*** ** **(0.000)**	**6.750*** ** **(0.000)**	**5.824*** ** **(0.001)**	**11.048*** ** **(0.000)**
Loans from Non-resident Banks	−0.074 (0.532)	−0.041 (0.494)	**−0.152** ** **(0.018)**	0.006 (0.929)	**0.189*** ** **(0.007)**	0.093 (0.184)
Offshore bank deposits.	**0.007*** ** **(0.003)**	**0.012*** ** **(0.000)**	**0.008** ** **(0.017)**	**0.009** ** **(0.047)**	**0.006*** **(0.080)**	0.002 (0.491)
Remittances	**0.432*** ** **(0.002)**	**0.342*** ** **(0.006)**	**0.264** ** **(0.044)**	0.120 (0.387)	**0.263*** **(0.067)**	0.191 (0.182)
R^2/pseudo-R^2	0.747	0.735	0.482	0.242	0.182	0.248
Fisher	**28.59*** **					
Observations	489	489	489	489	489	489

*, ** and ***: Significance levels of 10%, 5% and 1%, respectively. OLS: ordinary least squares. R^2 for OLS and pseudo-R^2 for quantile regression. Lower quantiles (e.g., *Q* 0.1) signify nations where informal financial sector development is least.

Table 5.4 Finance and financial sector informalization (Proposition 7)

	OLS	Q.10	Q.25	Q.50	Q.75	Q.90
	Dependent Variable: Financial Sector Informalization (Proposition 7)					
Constant	**0.421*****	**0.406****	**0.447*****	**0.382*****	**0.432*****	**0.405*****
	(0.000)	**(0.011)**	**(0.000)**	**(0.000)**	**(0.000)**	**(0.000)**
Overhead	**0.013****	0.011	0.003	−0.0007	**0.025*****	**0.025*****
	(0.018)	(0.274)	(0.637)	(0.906)	**(0.001)**	**(0.000)**
Net interest margin	−0.001	−0.004	0.002	0.004	−0.005	**−0.008****
	(0.773)	(0.570)	(0.576)	(0.362)	(0.315)	**(0.038)**
Bank concentration	**0.002*****	**0.002****	0.0004	**0.001****	**0.002*****	**0.003*****
	(0.000)	**(0.019)**	(0.458)	**(0.021)**	**(0.000)**	**(0.000)**
Return on equity	**0.001***	0.002	**0.001****	**0.002*****	0.001	**0.001****
	(0.053)	(0.117)	**(0.028)**	**(0.006)**	(0.178)	**(0.029)**
Bank cost-to-income ratio	**−0.003*****	**−0.003****	**−0.002***	−0.0004	−0.002	−0.0009
	(0.000)	**(0.044)**	**(0.068)**	(0.710)	(0.101)	(0.294)
Financial stability	0.005	**−0.005***	**−0.003****	−0.002	−0.003	**−0.007*****
	(0.129)	**(0.056)**	(0.035)	(0.166)	(0.102)	**(0.000)**
Life insurance	**−0.184*****	**−0.247*****	**−0.243*****	**−0.136*****	**−0.084*****	**−0.063*****
	(0.000)	**(0.000)**	(0.000)	(0.000)	(0.000)	**(0.000)**
Non-life insurance	−0.059	**−0.137****	0.049	−0.037	−0.069	**−0.056***
	(0.348)	**(0.031)**	(0.211)	(0.326)	(0.111)	**(0.050)**
Loans from non-resident banks	**−0.004***	0.001	**−0.002***	−0.002	−0.001	−0.0003
	(0.077)	(0.516)	**(0.091)**	(0.157)	(0.424)	(0.793)
Offshore bank deposits.	**0.0001****	0.0001	0.0001	0.0001	0.00006	2.49e−06
	(0.012)	(0.203)	(0.128)	(0.175)	(0.510)	(0.969)
Remittances	**0.009***	**0.010***	0.001	−0.002	**0.006***	**0.008*****
	(0.050)	**(0.057)**	(0.639)	(0.427)	**(0.078)**	**(0.001)**
R^2/pseudo-R^2	0.792	0.722	0.522	0.344	0.291	0.342
Fisher	**31.27*****					
Observations	488	488	488	488	488	488

*, ** and ***: Significance levels of 10%, 5% and 1%, respectively. OLS: ordinary least squares. R^2 for OLS and pseudo-R^2 for quantile regression. Lower quantiles (e.g., Q 0.1) signify nations where financial sector informalization is least.

5.5 Conclusion and Future Research Direction

The purpose of this study has been to examine trends of informal financial development in Africa over the past decades by assessing how financial determinants have affected the informal financial sector. Particularly, the concepts of informal financial development and financial informalization have been conceived, defined and measured building on disentanglement of the financial system in order to articulate the formal, semi-formal, informal and non-formal financial sectors. Informal financial development is understood as the progress of the informal financial sector relative to other economic sectors, while financial sector informalization is defined as the progress of the informal financial sector to the detriment of the formal and semi-formal financial sectors.

The empirical evidence is based quantile regression approaches with data from 48 countries in sub-Saharan Africa for the period 1995–2017. The multitudes of financial determinants as reported are discussed in terms of many perspectives, *inter alia*: U-Shape, S-Shape and positive or negative thresholds. The study not only provides a practical way by which to assess the incidence of financial determinants on informal financial sector development, but also provides financial instruments by which informal financial development can be curbed.

Future studies can improve the extant literature by employing alternative estimation techniques and financial instruments to assess which financial determinants boost the informal financial sector and, by extension, which can be employed to decrease the influence of the sector in the economy. Moreover, the study could be replicated within the remit of the formal financial sector, notably, by assessing how financial determinants affect formal financial sector development (i.e., Proposition 1) and financial sector formalization (Proposition 5).

Notes

1 These authors implemented the theory of financial liberalization being the free access to financial services by the people without the intervention of the state as a solution to financial repression.
2 The 48 countries are as follows: "Angola; Benin; Botswana; Burkina Faso; Burundi; Cabo Verde; Cameroon; Central African Republic; Chad; Comoros; Congo Democratic Republic; Congo Republic; Côte d'Ivoire; Equatorial Guinea; Eritrea; Eswatini; Ethiopia; Gabon; Gambia, The; Ghana; Guinea; Guinea-Bissau; Kenya; Lesotho; Liberia; Madagascar; Malawi; Mali; Mauritania; Mauritius; Mozambique; Namibia; Niger; Nigeria; Rwanda; Senegal ; Seychelles; Sierra Leone ; Somalia ; South Africa; South Sudan; Sudan; São Tomé and Principe; Tanzania; Togo; Uganda; Zambia and Zimbabwe".
3 Lines 24 and 25 of the International Financial Statistics (October 2008).
4 Lines 24, 25 and 45 of the International Financial Statistics (2008).
5 "Accordingly, in undeveloped countries money supply is not equal to liquid liabilities or bank deposits. While in undeveloped countries, bank deposits as a ratio of money supply is less than one, in developed countries this ratio is almost

equal to 1. This indicator appreciates the degree by which money in circulation is absorbed by the banking system. Here we define 'financial formalization' as the propensity of the formal banking system to absorb money in circulation." (Asongu, 2015, p. 432).

6 "This indicator measures the rate at which the semi-formal financial sector is evolving at the expense of formal and informal sectors." (Asongu, 2015, p. 432).

7 "This proposition appreciates the degree by which the informal financial sector is developing to the detriment of formal and semi-formal sectors." (Asongu, 2015, p. 432).

8 "The proposition measures the deterioration of the formal banking sector in the interest of other financial sectors (informal and semi-formal). From common sense, propositions 5 and 8 should be almost perfectly antagonistic, meaning the former (formal financial development at the cost of other financial sectors) and the latter (formal sector deterioration) should almost display a perfectly negative degree of substitution or correlation" (Asongu, 2015, p. 432).

References

Allen F., Chakrabarti R., De S., Qian J., & Qian M. (2010). "Law, institutions and finance in China and India", in *Emerging Giants. China and India in the World Economy*, ed. by OU Press, Eichengreen, Barry and Gupta, Poonam and Kumar, Rajiv, pp. 125–184.

Allen F., Qian M., & Xie J., (2019). "Understanding informal financing", *Journal of Financial Intermediation*, *39*(July), pp. 19–33.

An J., & Lin C. (2021). "Legal origins and informal financial development", *SSRN 3862205.*

Aryeetey, E. (2008). *Informal finance to formal finance in sub-Saharan Africa: Lessons from linkage efforts*, Institute of Statistical, Social and Economic Research University of Ghana, Accra.

Asongu S. A. (2013). "Fighting corruption in Africa: Do existing corruption–control levels matter?", *International Journal of Development Issues*, *12*(1), pp. 36–52.

Asongu S. A. (2014). "Financial development dynamic thresholds of financial globalization: Evidence from Africa", *Journal of Economic Studies*, *41*(2), pp. 166–195.

Asongu S. A. (2015). "Liberalisation and financial sector competition: A critical contribution to the empirics with an African assessment", *South African Journal of Economics*, *83*(3), pp. 425–451.

Asongu S. A., (2017). "Assessing marginal, threshold, and net effects of financial globalisation on financial development in Africa", *Journal of Multinational Financial Management*, *40*(June), pp. 103–114.

Asongu S. A. & Acha-Anyi P. N. (2017). "ICT, conflicts in financial intermediation and financial access: Evidence of synergy and threshold effects", *Netnomics*, *18*(2–3), pp. 131–168.

Asongu S. A., Biekpe, N. & Cassimon, D. (2020). "Understanding the greater diffusion of mobile money innovations in Africa", *Telecommunications Policy*, *44*(8), 102000.

Asongu S. A., Biekpe N., & Cassimon D. (2021). "On the diffusion of mobile phone innovations for financial inclusion", *Technology in Society*, *65*(May), 101542.

Asongu S. A., & Odhiambo N. M. (2018). "Information asymmetry, financialization, and financial access", *International Finance*, *21*(3), pp. 297–315.

Bagachwa M. S. D. (1995). "Financial integration and development in Sub-Saharan Africa: A study of informal finance in Tanzania", *ODI Working Paper, 1.* https://agris.fao.org/agris-search/search.do?recordID=GB9617756   (Accessed: 23/11/2021).

Bagachwa M. S. D. (1996). "Financial linkage and development in sub-Saharan Africa: A study of formal finance in Tanzania", *Working Paper 87*, Overseas Development Institute, London.

Billger S. M., & Goel R. K. (2009). "Do existing corruption levels matter in controlling corruption? Cross-country quantile regression estimates", *Journal of Development Economics, 90*(2), pp. 299–305.

Boateng A., Asongu S. A., Akamavi R., & Tchamyou V. S. (2018). "Information asymmetry and market power in the African Banking Industry", *Journal of Multinational Financial Management, 44*(March), pp. 69–83.

Campero A., & Kaiser K. (2013). "Access to credit: Awareness and use of formal and informal credit institutions", *Working Papers,* 07. https://www.econstor.eu/handle/10419/83717 (Accessed: 23/11/2021).

Cao C., Chan K. C., Hou W., & Jia F. (2019). "Does religion matter to informal finance? Evidence from trade credit in China", *Regional Studies, 53*(10), pp. 1410–1420.

Deng L., Jiang P., Li S. & Liao M. (2019). "Social capital and access to informal finance-evidence from Chinese private firms", *Accounting and Finance, 59*(5), pp. 2767–2815.

Ghazala M. (2006). "Rural, informal and micro-finance: Sustainable rural and urban development", *worldbank, org./B8COGHMQXL.*

Goodland A., Onumah G., Amadi J. & Griffith G. (1999). *Rural finance.* Natural Resources Institute. Series No. 1, London.

Klapper L., & Singer D. (2015). "The role of informal financial services in Africa", *Journal of African Economies, 24*(Sup. 1), pp. i12–i31.

Koenker R., & Bassett Jr. G. (1978). "Regression quantiles", *Econometrica, 46*(1), pp. 33–50.

Koenker R., & Hallock F.K. (2001). "Quantile regression", *Journal of Economic Perspectives, 15*(4), pp. 143–156.

McKinnon R. I. (1973). *Money and capital in economic development,* Brookings Institution, Washington, DC.

Nto P. O. O., Mbanasor J. A., & Nwaru J. C. (2011). "Analysis of risk among agribusiness enterprises investment in Abia State, Nigeria", *Journal of Economics and International Finance, 3*(3), pp. 187–197.

Sekyi S., Domanban P. B., & Honya G. K. (2019). "The impact of informal credit on rural agricultural productivity in the savannah ecological zone of Ghana", *African Journal of Economic and Management Studies, 11*(2), pp. 301–315.

Shaw E. S. (1973). *Financial deepening in economic development,* Oxford University Press, New York.

Sile I. C., & Bett J. (2015). "Determinants of informal finance use in Kenya", *Research Journal of Finance and Accounting, 6*(21), pp. 6–19.

Steel W., Aryeetey E., Hettige H., & Nissanke M. (1997). "Informal financial markets under liberalization in four African countries", *World Development, 25*(5), pp. 817–830.

Taylor J. A. (1979). "The consultative council on local government finance-a critical analysis of its origins and development", *Local Government Studies, 5*(3), pp. 7–36.

Tchamyou V. S. (2019). "The role of information sharing in modulating the effect of financial access on inequality", *Journal of African Business*, *20*(3), pp. 317–338.

Tchamyou V. S., & Asongu S. A. (2017a). "Information sharing and financial sector development in Africa", *Journal of African Business*, *18*(1), pp. 24–49.

Tchamyou V. S., & Asongu S. A. (2017b). "Conditional market timing in the mutual fund industry", *Research in International Business and Finance*, *42*(December), pp. 1355–1366.

Tchamyou V.S., Erreygers G., & Cassimon D. (2019). "Inequality, ICT and financial access in Africa", *Technological Forecasting and Social Change*, *139*(February), pp. 169–184.

Tsai K. S. (2004). "Imperfect substitutes: The local political economy of informal finance and microfinance in rural China and India", *World Development*, *32*(9), pp. 1487–1507.

Tsai L. L. (2002). "Cadres, temple and lineage institutions, and governance in rural China", *The China Journal*, *48*, pp. 1–27.

Ullah B. (2019). "Firm innovation in transition economies: The role of formal versus informal finance", *Journal of Multinational Financial Management*, *50*, pp. 58–75.

Van Wijnbergen S. (1983). "Credit policy, inflation and growth in a financially repressed economy", *Journal of Development Economics*, *13*(1–2), pp. 45–65.

Zaman H. (1999). "Assessing the impact of micro-credit on poverty and vulnerability in Bangladesh: A case study of BRAC", *Mimeo*, World Bank, Washington, DC.

Zins A., & Weill L. (2016). "The determinants of financial inclusion in Africa", *Review of Development Finance*, *6*(1), pp. 46–57.

Appendices

Appendix 5.1 Definitions and Sources of Variables

Variables	Definitions	Sources
Informal financial development	Proportion of money supply circulating outside the financial system as percentage of GDP: (Money Supply − Financial deposits)/GDP. (Proportion 3)	FDSD (World Bank), Asongu (2015)
Financial intermediary 'informalization'	From 'formal and semi-formal' to informal financial development (Informalization). "This proposition appreciates the degree by which the informal financial sector is developing to the detriment of formal and semi-formal sectors" (Asongu, 2015, p. 432). (Proposition 7)	FDSD (World Bank), Asongu (2015)
Overhead	Bank overhead costs to total assets (%). Accounting value of a bank's overhead costs as a share of its total assets.	FDSD (World Bank)
Net interest margin	Net interest margin (%). Accounting value of bank's net interest revenue as a share of its interest-bearing (total earning) assets.	FDSD (World Bank)
Bank concentration	Bank concentration (%). Assets of three largest banks as a share of assets of all commercial banks.	FDSD (World Bank)
Return on equity	Bank return on equity. Average return on assets (net income/ total equity)	FDSD (World Bank)
Bank cost-to-income ratio	Bank cost-to-income ratio (%). Total costs as a share of total income of all commercial banks.	FDSD (World Bank)

(Continued)

Appendix 5.1 (Continued)

Variables	Definitions	Sources
Financial stability	Bank Z-score. Z-score is estimated as (ROA+equity/assets)/sd(ROA); sd(ROA) is the standard deviation of ROA.	FDSD (World Bank)
Life insurance	Life insurance premium volume as a share of GDP.	FDSD (World Bank)
Non-life insurance	Non-life insurance premium volume as a share of GDP.	FDSD (World Bank)
Loans from Non-resident banks.	Loans from non-resident banks (AMT outstanding) to GDP (%).Offshore bank loans relative to GDP.	FDSD (World Bank)
Offshore bank deposits.	Offshore bank deposits to domestic bank deposits (%)	FDSD (World Bank)
Remittances	Net remittance inflows as a share of GDP.	FDSD (World Bank)

GDP: gross domestic product. GNI: gross national income. GCIP: Global Consumption and Income Project.

Appendix 5.2 Summary Statistics

	Mean	SD	Min	Max	Obs
Informal financial development	10.442	69.737	−972.204	571.732	1,104
Financial intermediary 'informalization'	0.323	1.405	−22.622	0.954	1,020
Overhead	6.161	4.587	0.001	89.423	868
Net interest margin	7.526	6.435	0.0001	114.248	855
Bank concentration	77.367	18.641	22.280	100.000	707
Return on equity	21.120	20.216	−93.620	161.923	869
Bank cost-to-income ratio	59.628	18.584	19.895	218.087	875
Financial stability	10.975	7.050	0.566	96.680	893
Life insurance	0.835	2.182	0.0004	15.380	733
Non-life insurance	0.798	0.923	0.003	14.722	778
Loan from non-resident banks	59.248	402.779	0.000	5198.04	916
Offshore bank deposits	101.378	332.937	1.68e−06	5467.123	1,016
Remittances	3.853	8.517	0.000	108.403	876

SD: standard deviation. Min: minimum. Max: maximum.

Appendix 5.3 Correlation Matrix (uniform sample size: 488)

	Prop3	Prop7	Overhead	NIM	B.Conc	ROE	Costinc	Zscore	LifeI	NlifeI	LNRB	OSBD	Remit
Prop3	1.000												
Prop7	0.949	1.000											
Overhead	0.132	0.256	1.000										
NIM	0.152	0.292	0.619	1.000									
B.Conc	0.016	0.071	−0.060	−0.071	1.000								
ROE	0.090	0.138	0.045	0.355	0.203	1.000							
Costinc	−0.011	0.036	0.480	−0.032	−0.034	−0.370	1.000						
Zscore	−0.216	−0.253	−0.212	−0.210	−0.111	−0.208	−0.068	1.000					
LifeI	−0.836	−0.875	−0.281	−0.288	0.013	−0.062	−0.118	0.327	1.000				
NlifeI	−0.560	−0.707	−0.305	−0.295	−0.016	−0.073	−0.220	0.276	0.783	1.000			
LNRB	−0.099	−0.201	−0.155	−0.176	0.123	−0.082	−0.079	0.158	0.170	0.338	1.000		
OSBD	0.148	0.090	−0.095	−0.018	0.140	0.047	−0.193	−0.021	−0.065	0.119	0.174	1.000	
Remit	0.162	0.131	−0.022	−0.085	0.022	−0.076	0.164	−0.001	−0.106	−0.032	−0.002	−0.040	1.000

Prop3: informal financial sector development. Prop7: financial sector informalization. Overhead: bank overhead costs to total assets (%). NIM: net internet margin. B.Conc: bank concentration (%). ROE: return on equity. Costinc: bank cost-to-income ratio (%). Zscore: financial stability. LNRB: loans from non-resident banks. OSBD: offshore bank deposits. Remit: remittances.

6 Finance–Growth Nexus

A Review of Afrocentric Literature

Nicholas Mbaya Odhiambo

6.1 Introduction

Although many studies have found the link between financial development and economic growth to be undeniable, the nature of the relationship between these two important macroeconomic variables has not been fully understood to date from either the theoretical or empirical fronts. The origin of the finance–growth nexus debate can be traced as far back as to Schumpeter (1911) who argued that finance is dominant in promoting economic growth. This was followed by studies, such as those by Gurley and Shaw (1955), who argued that economic development is likely to be hindered if self-finance and direct finance are made accessible without involvement of the financial intermediaries. The important role that the financial sector plays in economic growth and development was later popularised by the financial liberalisation policy of McKinnon (1973) and Shaw (1973). Both authors, in their seminal works, cautioned developing countries against the pursuance of financial repression policies. These include low- or administered interest rates, concessional credit practices, and selective credit control, amongst others. According to McKinnon-Shaw (1973), financial repression policies do not only lead to low savings, but also result in inefficient allocation of resources, disintermediation in the banking system, and segmentation of financial markets (Khan & Hasan, 1998). Indeed, the McKinnon–Shaw financial liberalisation policy was so persuasive that it even influenced the thinking of international organisations like the World Bank and the International Monetary Fund (IMF) (see Odhiambo, 2004). The gist of the McKinnon–Shaw theory was that low (or negative) real interest rates simply deter savings, which negatively affects the availability of investable funds, thereby leading to a decrease in investment and economic growth (see Khan & Hasan, 1998; Odhiambo, 2004). In particular, McKinnon's complementarity hypothesis became too popular because of its amenability to empirical investigation. According to McKinnon's (1973) complementarity hypothesis, the more attractive the process of accumulating money through an attractive positive interest rate, the greater the incentive for economic agents to invest in developing countries. This is mainly because in developing countries, the

DOI: 10.4324/9781003215042-7

investible (loanable) funds are scarce; hence, many potential investors are obliged first to accumulate money balances in the form of savings before they can invest. Moreover, since the investment expenditure is lumpier than the consumption expenditure, the aggregate demand for money is likely to increase as the proportion of investment in total expenditure increases (see McKinnon, 1973; Fry, 1978, 1982; Arrieta, 1988; Clarke, 1996).

Although the hypotheses of both McKinnon (1973) and Shaw (1973) are based on 'prior-savings', as opposed to the Keynesian's 'prior-investment' as the necessary condition for growth, they differ in terms of the transmission through which interest rates affect savings, investment, and economic growth (see also Fry, 1978, 1988; Gibson & Tsakalotos, 1994). As opposed to McKinnon (1973), Shaw's (1973) approach is based on a 'debt-intermediation' view, which he pioneered and popularised in the 1950s (Gurley & Shaw, 1960).[1] Recent studies have also found that by channelling investible funds (savings) to productive uses, financial systems can serve a vital role in economic development (see Lee, 2001). Consequently, the more developed a financial sector is, the more efficient it will in allocating investable funds to productive borrowers. This positive link between finance and economic development has also been supported by Levine (1997).

Although some previous have attempted to conduct a review of the previous empirical studies on the relationship between finance and growth, the bulk of the previous studies applied a universal approach to literature review. Indeed, most of the literature reviews of previous studies were global in nature and did not focus on Africa in general, and sub-Saharan Africa in particular. To our knowledge, this could be one of the first papers of its kind to provide a detailed survey on previous empirical literature on the causal link between finance and growth with a clear focus on the African countries.

The remainder of this chapter is organised as follows. Section 6.2 gives an overview of the debate between the finance-led growth and growth-led finance hypotheses, from a theoretical front. Section 6.3 delves into the Afrocentric empirical literature review on the finance–growth nexus, including the supply-leading, demand-following, and bidirectional causality responses. Section 6.4 concludes the study.

6.2 Finance–Growth Nexus Debate

One critical question that has remained unresolved in the empirical literature is whether policymakers should first pursue financial development in order to spur growth, or economic growth in order to spur financial development, or whether they should pursue both macroeconomic variables simultaneously. Put slightly differently, between the financial sector and the real sector of the economy, which one leads and which one lags in the process of sustainable development? The quest to answer this critical question has led to three views in the literature. The first view, which has attracted a great deal of literature over the past decades, is the so-called 'supply-leading response', which argues that finance is important for economic growth and therefore leads to real sector development. In other words, the supply-leading response argues that the financial sector precedes and spurs growth in the real sector of the economy by directing scarce funds from small savers to large investors according to the relative rate of return (see also Jung, 1986). The supply-leading response entails the creation of financial system institutions as well as the supply of their financial services in advance of their demand (see also Odhiambo, 2004). Apart from transferring resources from the traditional sector of the economy to the modern sector, the supply-leading response also stimulates an entrepreneurial response in the modern sector of the economy (Patrick, 1966). According to Patrick (1966), this occurs owing to the availability of the supply-leading funds, which enables entrepreneurs to 'think big' (Patrick, 1966:176). According to Patrick (1966), the supply-leading response is likely to play a more significant role at the beginning of the growth process. The supply-leading response has been widely supported by studies such as those of Crichton and De Silva (1989), King and Levine (1993), De Gregoria and Guidotti (1995), Levine (1997), and Levine and Zervos (1998), amongst others.

The second view that has recently attracted a plethora of empirical investigation is the so-called 'demand-following response'. The 'demand-following' response may be defined as the process during which the growth of modern financial institutions and their related financial services respond to the demand for such services by investors or savers in the real sector of the economy (see Patrick, 1966). Hence, the proponents of this view argue that it is the real sector of the economy that drives financial sector growth and that the demand for financial services depends largely on the growth of the real sector of the economy. In other words, the more rapid the real sector grows, the higher the demand for external funds and other financial services, which ultimately increases financial intermediation (see Odhiambo, 2004). One of the earliest advocates of the demand-following response is Robinson (1952), who argues that it is economic growth, which drives the growth of the financial services sector; and that where there is growth, finance will always follow. According to Robinson (1952), finance simply follows the growth of the economy owing to more demand for financial services (see also Nyasha and Odhiambo, 2014). Hence, an increase in the demand for financial services is likely to lead to further financial sector growth as the real sector of the economy grows.[2] This view has also been supported by other studies, such as those by Gurley and Shaw (1967), and by Goldsmith (1969).

As opposed to the supply-leading, the demand-following response is more pronounced at the later stages of real sector development. According to Patrick's hypothesis, the causal link between finance and growth is likely to change during the course of real sector development. Finance is only able to stimulate the real sector development before a sustained modern real sector development takes place; however, as the modern growth takes place, the supply-leading response becomes less important as the demand-following phenomenon becomes more dominant (Patrick, 1966).

In between these two extreme views, there is a third view, i.e., the middle-ground view, which argues that both finance and real sector development are mutually reinforcing; hence, they Granger-cause each other. This view contends that the link between finance and growth is neither exclusively demand-following nor supply-leading, but rather a bidirectional one. Although this view has not attracted a contentious debate as the supply-leading and demand-following responses, it has received support from a number of empirical studies in recent years.

Despite the aforementioned views that maintain that there is causality between finance and real sector growth, at least in one direction, there is a fourth view known as the 'neutrality view', which argues that there is no distinct causal relationship between these two macroeconomic variables. According to the neutrality view, the financial sector and real sector development are independent; hence, any causal relationship between them is purely mechanical. Although this view has not been supported widely by many studies, it is currently gaining momentum on the empirical front. Some of the empirical studies that have found some support for this view include those by Nyasha and Odhiambo (2015) for the case of South Africa during the period 1980–2012 when bank-based finance was used as a proxy for finance; Nyasha and Odhiambo (2018) in the case of Kenya, South Africa, and the USA when bank-based finance was used a proxy for financial development; Odhiambo et al. (2019) for the case of English-speaking SSA countries when finance is proxied by deposit money bank assets; and more recently, Opoku et al. (2019) for the most part of their analysis. In the next section, we provide an extensive review of some of the previous empirical studies on the causal link between finance and growth based on the first three dominant views using data from SSA countries.

6.3 Empirical Literature Review

6.3.1 The Supply-Leading Response

The empirical studies from African countries that have found some support for the supply-leading response include studies such as those by Ghali (1999), Agbetsiafa (2004), Ghirmay (2004), Odhiambo (2007), Chukwu and Agu (2009), Odhiambo (2009), Akinlo and Egbetunde (2010), Ogwumike and Salisu (2012), Odhiambo (2013), Menyah et al. (2014), Phiri (2015), Nyasha et al. (2017), Olayungbo and Quadri (2019), Odhiambo and Nyasha (2020), Olorogun et al. (2020), and Yakubu et al. (2021) amongst others. Ghali (1999), when assessing the causal link between finance and growth in Tunisia using annual time-series data, found results that suggest that finance could be an engine of real sector growth. Agbetsiafa (2004), while using the ECM-based Granger causality to examine the causality between finance and growth in a sample of eight emerging SSA economies, found one-way causality from finance to growth in six countries. Ghirmay (2004), when examining the link between finance and growth in 13 SSA countries, found that finance plays a significant causal role in economic growth in eight of the studied countries. Odhiambo (2007) in an attempt to investigate the supply-leading versus the demand-following responses using data from three SSA countries found a supply-leading response to be dominant in Tanzania. Chukwu and Agu (2009) also found evidence of the supply-leading hypothesis in Nigeria when loan and bank deposit liabilities were used to measure the level of financial development. Likewise, Odhiambo (2009a) had similar findings in the case of Zambia while using a trivariate Granger causality model. While re-examining the causal link between finance and growth using data from ten SSA countries, Akinlo and Egbetunde (2010) found finance to Granger-cause growth in Central African Republic, Congo Republic, Gabon, and Nigeria. Ogwumike and Salisu (2012), in examining the link between finance and growth in Nigeria using a VAR–Granger causality test, also found support for the supply-leading response. In another study aimed at investigating the causal link between finance and growth in Botswana, Odhiambo (2013) found that there is a unidirectional causal flow from finance to growth when the domestic credit to the private sector (DCPS) was used as a proxy for financial sector development. Menyah et al. (2014) found similar results in three out of 21 African countries when using a panel bootstrapped approach to Granger causality. Phiri (2015), while examining the asymmetric causal link between finance and economic growth in South Africa, found inter alia that banking activity Granger-causes economic growth. While evaluating the causal linkage between finance and growth in Ethiopia, Nyasha et al. (2017) found that banks Granger-cause growth in the long run. Olayungbo and Quadri (2019), while examining the link between remittances, financial development, and growth in 20 SSA countries, found that finance Granger-causes growth. While using an array of financial development proxies to examine the causal link between finance and growth in Uganda using an ARDL approach, Odhiambo and Nyasha (2020) found that there is a distinct causal flow from finance to growth when finance is measured by liquid liabilities and bank deposits. Olorogun et al. (2020), while revisiting the nexus between FDI, financial sector development, and growth in Nigeria inter alia, found financial sector development be a good predictor for sustainable economic growth in Nigeria. Yakubu et al. (2021), while examining the link between finance, trade, political stability, and growth in Egypt, found amongst other things that finance Granger-causes growth in the short run. Table 6.1 gives a summary of some of the previous studies done on African countries, which are in favour of a supply-leading response.

Table 6.1 Studies in favour of a unidirectional causal flow from financial development to economic growth in African countries

Author(s)	Region/Country	Methodology	Direction of Causality
Ghali (1999)	Tunisia	• Annual time-series	Finance → Growth
Agbetsiafa (2004)	Eight SSA African countries	• Causality test based on error-correction model	Finance → Growth (Ghana, Nigeria, Senegal, South Africa, Togo, and Zambia.)
Ghimay (2004)	13 SSA countries	• VAR framework	Finance → Growth
Odhiambo (2007)	Three SSA countries — Kenya, South Africa and Tanzania	• ECM-based Granger causality model • Three proxies of finance	Finance → Growth (Tanzania)
Chukwu and Agu (2009)	Nigeria	• Multivariate VECM	Finance → Growth (when finance is measured by loan deposit ratio and bank deposit liabilities)
Odhiambo (2009)	Zambia	• ECM-based Granger causality model • A trivariate Granger-causality model	Finance → Growth
Akinlo and Egbetunde (2010)	Ten SSA countries	• ECM-based Granger causality model	Finance → Growth (Central African Republic, Congo Republic, Gabon, and Nigeria)
Ogwumike and Salisu (2012)	Nigeria	• VAR–Granger causality test	Finance → Growth
Odhiambo (2013)	Botswana	• ARDL-bounds testing approach	Finance → Growth (when finance is proxied by DCPS)
Menyah et al. (2014)	21 SSA countries	• Panel bootstrapped approach to Granger causality.	Finance → Growth (in three countries)
Phiri (2015)	South Africa	• Momentum threshold autoregressive (M-TAR) approach • Asymmetric cointegration and causality test	Finance → Growth (when finance is proxied by bank-based financial development)

(Continued)

Table 6.1 (Continued)

Author(s)	Region/Country	Methodology	Direction of Causality
Nyasha et al. (2017)	Ethiopia	• ARDL model • ECM-based multivariate Granger causality model	Finance → Growth (in the long run)
Olayungbo and Quadri (2019)	20 SSA countries	• Mean group and pooled mean group	Finance → Growth
Odhiambo and Nyasha (2020)	Uganda	• ARDL-bounds testing approach • ECM-based multivariate Granger causality model	Finance → Growth (when liquid liabilities and bank deposits are used as financial development proxies)
Olorugun et al. (2020)	Nigeria	• Toda–Yamamoto causality approach	Finance → Growth (when financial development from the banking sector is used as a proxy)
Yakubu et al. (2021)	Egypt	• ARDL • Error-correction model • Granger causality	Finance → Growth (in the short run)

6.3.2 The Demand-Following Response

Apart from the studies mentioned above, some other studies in Africa have found the finance-growth nexus to be demand-following rather than supply-leading. These studies include studies such as those by Agbetsiafa (2004), Boulila and Trabelsi (2004), Odhiambo (2008, 2009, 2013), Chukwu and Agu (2009), Akinlo and Egbetunde (2010), Kagochi et al. (2013), Menyah et al. (2014), Phiri (2015) and Fakudze et al. (2021), amongst others. Agbetsiafa (2004), while investigating the link between finance and growth in SSA countries, found a demand-following response to dominate in two countries, namely, Ivory Coast and Kenya. Boulila and Trabelsi (2004) also examined the causal link between finance and long-run growth in Tunisia during the period from 1962 to 1997. Using a bivariate model, the study found that causality runs from growth to finance during the sub-period of financial control from 1962 to 1987. In the main, the study found support for the finance-led growth hypothesis to be weak. In examining the dynamic linkage between financial depth, savings, and growth in Kenya, Odhiambo (2008) found a unidirectional causal flow from growth to finance during the study period. Likewise, Chukwu and Agu (2009) found a demand-following hypothesis to dominate in Nigeria when financial development is measured by real broad money supply and banking sector's private sector credit. In the same vein, Odhiambo (2009), while examining the finance-growth-poverty nexus in South Africa using a dynamic causality model, found a demand-following response to prevail. Akinlo and Egbetunde (2010), while analysing the linkage between finance and growth in ten SSA countries, found that the real sector growth Granger-causes financial sector development in Zambia. Kagochi et al. (2013) also found the same results in seven SSA countries when finance was proxied by banking indicators. Similar findings in favour of a demand-following response were found in Odhiambo (2013), for the case of Botswana when broad money supply and bank deposits were used as financial development proxies. Similar results were also found by Menyah et al. (2014) in one of the 21 studied African countries, and Phiri (2015) in the case of South Africa when stock market development is used as a proxy.

More recently, Fakudze et al. (2021) examined the link between finance and economic growth in Eswatini (formerly Swaziland). Using time-series data between 1996 and 2018, the study found that there is a unidirectional causal flow from the real sector growth to financial development, thereby validating the demand-following hypothesis in Eswatini. Table 6.2 gives a summary of some of the previous studies conducted in Africa, which are consistent with the demand-following hypothesis.

6.3.3 Bi-directional/Feedback Response

Although the finance–growth nexus debate has been largely dominated by the proponents of supply-leading versus demand-following response, some empirical studies have shown that there is a potential feedback relationship between financial sector development and economic growth. In other words, there is a bidirectional causal relationship between these two variables. Studies from African countries that are consistent with this view include studies such as those by Akinboade (1998), Ghirmay (2004), Abu-Bader and Abu-Qarn (2008), Acaravci et al. (2009), Wolde-Rufael (2009), Akinlo and Egbetunde (2010), Eita and Jordaan (2010), Fowowe (2011), Kagochi et al. (2013), Nyasha et al. (2017), Nyasha and Odhiambo (2018), Odhiambo and Nyasha (2020), and Ehigiamusoe (2021) amongst others. While examining the causal link between finance and economic growth in Botswana, Akinboade (1998) found that economic growth and the indicators used to measure financial sector development cause one another,

Table 6.2 Studies in favour of unidirectional causality from economic growth to financial development in African countries

Author(s)	Region/Country	Methodology	Direction of Causality
Agbetsiafa (2004)	Eight emerging SSA economies	• ECM-based causality test	Growth → Finance (Ivory Coast and Kenya)
Boulila and Trabelsi (2004)	Tunisia	• Bivariate Granger causality model	Growth → Finance (sub-sample period 1962–1987)
Odhiambo (2008)	Kenya	• Cointegration and error-correction techniques	Growth → Finance
Chukwu and Agu (2009)	Nigeria	• Multivariate VECM	Growth → Finance
Odhiambo (2009)	South Africa	• ARDL-bounds testing procedure	Growth → Finance
Akinlo and Egbetunde (2010)	Ten SSA countries	• ECM-based causality model	Growth → Finance (for Zambia)
Kagochi et al. (2013)	Seven SSA countries	• Panel Granger causality test	Growth → Finance (when finance is proxied by bank-based financial development)
Odhiambo (2013)	Botswana	• ARDL-bounds testing approach	Growth → Finance (when finance is proxied by M2/GDP and bank deposits)
Menyah et al. (2014)	21 African countries	• Panel bootstrapped approach to Granger causality	Growth → Finance (in one country)
Phiri (2015)	South Africa	• Momentum threshold autoregressive (M-TAR) approach • Asymmetric cointegration and causality test	Growth → Finance (when stock market development is used as a proxy)
Fakudze et al. (2021)	Eswatini	• ARDL model • Granger causality test	Growth → Financial development

which indicates that the causal link between financial development and growth in Botswana is bidirectional. Ghirmay (2004), while examining the link between finance and growth in 13 SSA countries, also found evidence of feedback causal relationships to prevail in six countries. Abu-Bader and Abu-Qarn (2008), in examining the causal relationship between financial development and economic growth in Egypt during the period between 1960 and 2001, found a strong support for a bidirectional causal relationship between financial development and economic growth in Egypt. Acaravci et al. (2009) also examined the causal link between finance and economic growth in SSA countries during the period from 1975 to 2005. Using the GMM approach, the study found bidirectional causality to prevail between economic growth and the domestic credit provided by the banking sector in the studied countries. Wolde-Rufael (2009), while re-examining the nexus between finance and growth in Kenya using Toda and Yamamoto (1995), found that neither the supply-leading nor the demand-following hypothesis is supported in Kenya. The study, therefore, concluded that finance and economic growth are either jointly determined, or that they complement each other. While examining the link between finance and growth in ten SSA countries, Akinlo and Egbetunde (2010) found bidirectional causality between finance and economic growth to prevail in Kenya, Chad, South Africa, Sierra Leone, and Swaziland. Eita and Jordaan (2010), while analysing the causality between finance and growth in Botswana during the period 1977–2006, found evidence of a feedback relationship between finance and growth, thereby suggesting that both the activity of financial markets and the real sector of the economy should be enhanced in Botswana. Fowowe (2011), while using panel cointegration and causality tests to examine the nexus between finance and growth in 17 SSA countries, found that there is homogenous bidirectional causal relationship between finance and growth in the studied countries. Kagochi et al. (2013), while investigating the relationship between finance and growth using data from seven SSA countries, also found a bidirectional causal relationship between finance and growth when stock market indicators were used as financial development proxies.

While examining the dynamic causal relationship between finance and growth in Ethiopia, Nyasha et al. (2017) found bidirectional causality between finance and growth to predominate in the short run. The same finding was revealed by Nyasha and Odhiambo (2018), for the case of Kenya in the short run between market-based financial development and economic growth. Odhiambo and Nyasha (2020), while using a wide arrange of proxies for financial development to examine the nexus between finance and growth in a multivariate setting in Uganda, found that strong bidirectional causality tends to predominate when financial development is measured by deposit money bank asset-to-bank asset ratio. More recently, Ehigiamusoe (2021) used Dumitrescu–Hurlin Granger non-causality approach to examine the nexus between tourism, financial development, and growth in 31 African countries. The study found *inter alia* that there is bidirectional causality between finance and growth. A summary of some of the studies in favour of bidirectional causality, which have been conducted in African countries, is provided in Table 6.3.

Table 6.3 Studies in favour of bidirectional causality between financial development and economic growth in African countries

Author(s)	Region/Country	Methodology	Direction of Causality
Akinboade (1998)	Botswana	• Granger causality model	Finance ↔ Growth
Ghirmay (2004)	13 SSA countries	• Vector autoregression (VAR) framework	Finance ↔ Growth (six countries)
Abu-Bader and Abu-Qarn (2008)	Egypt	• Vector error-correction model • A trivariate model	Finance ↔ Growth
Acaravci et al. (2009)	24 SSA	• GMM model	Finance ↔ Growth (when finance is proxied by domestic credit provided by the banking sector)
Wolde-Rufael (2009)	Kenya	• Toda and Yamamoto causality approach	Finance ↔ Growth (for three out of four measures of financial development)
Akinlo and Egbetunde (2010)	Ten SSA countries	• ECM model	Finance ↔ Growth (for Chad, Kenya, South Africa, Sierra Leone, and Swaziland)
Eita and Jordaan (2010)	Botswana	• Vector autoregression methods • Causality	Finance ↔ Growth
Fowowe (2011)	17 countries in SSA	• Panel causality test	Finance ↔ Growth
Kagochi et al. (2013)	Seven SSA countries	• Panel Granger causality test	Finance ↔ Growth (when finance is proxied by stock market development indicators)
Nyasha et al. (2017)	Ethiopia	• ARDL model • ECM-based Granger causality model	Finance ↔ Growth (in the short run)
Nyasha and Odhiambo (2018)	UK, Australia, Brazil, the USA, Kenya, and South Africa	• Granger causality	Finance ↔ Growth (in Kenya in the short run in the case of market-based financial development)
Odhiambo and Nyasha (2020)	Uganda	• ECM-based multivariate Granger causality model	Finance ↔ Growth (when deposit money bank assets to bank assets ratio is used as a proxy)
Ehigiamusoe (2021)	31 African countries	• Dumitrescu–Hurlin causality test	Finance ↔ Growth (individual causality)

6.4 Conclusion

This chapter reviewed the causal link between financial development and economic growth in African countries from both the theoretical and empirical fronts. While the theoretical literature is global in nature, the empirical literature focuses only on studies of African countries. The study was motivated by the debate on the causal link between financial development and economic growth, which has been ongoing for decades. Although some previous studies have attempted to conduct this review, the bulk of those studies have always lumped countries together, thereby proving little policy guidance for developing countries, such as African countries. Moreover, given the scanty scale of reliable empirical research on African countries, it is vital to take stock of the few studies that have been conducted in the region. Based on our analysis of the previous studies on this subject, we can safely conclude that, on the whole, the causal relationship between financial development and economic growth in SSA countries is largely dependent on a number of factors. These include (1) the level of financial development in the studied countries; (2) the financial system under consideration, i.e., whether bank-based or market-based; (3) the individual bank-based or market-based proxies used; (4) the nature of the data used, whether time-series or panel data; (5) the estimation techniques used; and (6) the causality model used, whether bivariate or multivariate. On the whole, the literature review shows that the bulk of the previous studies seems to support either a supply-following response or a feedback relationship, with studies in favour of the supply-leading response taking the lead, which may be consistent with the assertion of Schumpeter (1911).

Notes

1 See also Odhiambo (2014).
2 See also Nyasha and Odhiambo (2014).

References

Abu-Bader, S., and Abu-Qarn, A.S. (2008). Financial development and economic growth: The Egyptian experience. *Journal of Policy Modelling*, Volume 30, pp. 887–898.

Acaravci, S.K., Ozturk, I., and Acaravci, A. (2009). Financial development and economic growth: Literature survey and empirical evidence from sub-Saharan African countries. *South African Journal of Economic and Management Sciences*, Volume 12, issue 1, pp. 11–27.

Agbetsiafa, D. (2004). The finance growth Nexus: Evidence from sub-Saharan Africa. *Savings and Development*, Volume 28, issue 3, pp. 271–288.

Akinboade, O.A. (1998). Financial development and economic growth in Botswana, a test for causality. *Savings and Development*, Volume 22, issue 3, pp. 331–348.

Akinlo, A., and Egbetunde, T. (2010). Financial development and economic growth: The experience of 10 sub-Saharan African countries revisited. *The Review of Finance and Banking*, Volume 02, issue 1, pp. 017–028.

Arrieta, Gerardo M. (1988). Interest rates, savings and growth in LDCs: An assessment of recent empirical research. *World Development*, Volume 16, issue 5, pp. 589–605.

Boulila, G., and Trabelsi, M. (2004). Financial development and long-run growth: Evidence from Tunisia: 1962–1997. *Savings and Development*, Volume 28, issue 3, pp. 289–314.

Chukwu, J.O., and Agu, C.C. (2009). Multivariate causality between financial depth and economic growth in Nigeria. *African Review of Money Finance and Banking*, Supplementary Issue of *Savings and Development* (2009), pp. 7–21.

Clarke, R. (1996). Equilibrium interest rates and financial liberalisation in developing countries. *Journal of Development Studies*, Volume 32, issue 3, pp. 391–413.

Crichton, N., and De Silva, C. (1989). Financial development and economic growth: Trinidad and Tobago, 1973–1987. *Social and Economic Studies*, Volume 38, issue 4, pp. 133–162.

De Gregorio, J., and Guidotti, P. E. (1995). Financial development and economic growth. *World Development*, Volume 23, issue 3, pp. 433–448.

Ehigiamusoe, K.U. (2021). The nexus between tourism, financial development, and economic growth: Evidence from African countries. *African Development Review*, Volume 33, issue 2 pp. 382–396.

Eita, J.H. and Jordaan, A.C. (2010). A causality analysis between financial development and economic growth for Botswana. *African Finance Journal*, Volume 12, issue 1, pp. 72–89.

Fakudze, S-O., Tsegaye, A., and Sibanda, K. (2021). The relationship between financial development and economic growth in Eswatini (formerly Swaziland). *African Journal of Economic and Management Studies*, Vol. ahead-of-print No. ahead-of-print. https://doi.org/10.1108/AJEMS-06-2021-0291

Fowowe, B. (2011). The finance-growth nexus in sub-Saharan Africa: Panel cointegration and causality tests. *Journal of International Development*, Volume 23, issue 2, pp. 220–239.

Fry, M.J. (1978). Money and capital or financial deepening in economic development. *Journal of Money, Credit and Banking*, Volume 10, pp. 464–475.

Fry, M.J. (1982). Models of financial repressed developing economies. *World Development*, Volume 10, issue 9, pp. 731–750.

Fry, M.J. (1988), *Money, Interest and Banking in Economic Development*, Baltimore: John Hopkins University Press.

Ghali, K.H. (1999). Financial Development and Economic Growth: The Tunisian Experience. *Review of Development Economics*, Wiley Blackwell, Volume 3, issue 3, pp. 310–322, October.

Ghirmay, T. (2004). Financial development and economic growth in sub-Saharan African countries: Evidence from time series analysis. *African Development Review*, Volume 16, issue 3, pp. 415–432.

Gibson, H., and Tsakalotos, E. (1994). The scope and limits of financial liberalisation in developing countries: A critical survey. *The Journal of Development Studies*, Volume 30, issue 3, pp. 578–628.

Goldsmith, R. (1969). *Financial Structure and Development*, New Haven, CT: Yale University Press.

Gurley, J., and Shaw, E. (1955). Financial aspects of economic development. *American Economic Review*, Volume 44, issue 4, pp. 515–538.

Gurley, J. and Shaw, E. (1960). *Money in a Theory of Finance*, Washington DC: Brookings Institution.

Gurley, J., and Shaw, E. (1967). Financial structure and economic development. *Economic Development and Cultural Change*, Volume 15, issue 3.

Jung, W. (1986). Financial development and economic growth: International evidence. *Economic Development and Cultural Change*, Volume 34, issue January, pp. 333–346.

Kagochi, J.M., Al Nasser, O.M., and Kebede, E. (2013). Does financial development hold the key to economic growth? The case of sub-Saharan Africa. *The Journal of Developing Areas*, Volume 47, issue 2, pp. 61–79.

Khan, A., and Hasan, L. (1998). Financial liberalisation, savings and economic development in Pakistan. *Economic Development and Cultural Change*, Volume 46, issue 3, pp. 581–595.

King, R.G., and Levine, R. (1993). Finance and growth: Schumpeter might be right. Quarterly *Journal of Economics*, Volume 108, issue 3, pp. 713–737.

Lee, K. (2001). *"Note on Study of the Changes of Financial System."* Ref. 00.12-Department of Economics, University of Massachusetts.

Levine, R. (1997). Financial development and economic growth. *Journal of Economic Literature*, Volume 35, issue 2, pp. 688–727.

Levine, R., and Zervos, S. (1998). Stock markets, banks and economic growth. *American Economic Review*, Volume 98. issue June, pp. 537–558.

McKinnon, R.I. (1973). *Money and Capital in Economic Development,* Washington, DC: The Brookings Institution.

Menyah, K., Nazlioglu, S., and Wolde-Rufael, Y. (2014). Financial development, trade openness and economic growth in African countries: New insights from a panel causality approach. *Economic Modelling*, Volume 37, pp. 386–394.

Nyasha, S., and Odhiambo, N.M. (2014). Bank-based financial development and economic growth: A review of international literature. *Journal of Financial Economic Policy*, Volume 6, issue 2, pp. 112–132.

Nyasha, S. and Odhiambo, N.M. (2015). Banks, stock market development and economic growth in South Africa: a multivariate causal linkage. *Applied Economics Letters*. Volume 22, issue 18, pp. 1480–1485.

Odhiambo, N.M. (2004). Financial liberalisation and economic growth in sub-Saharan African countries: Dilemmas and prospects. Unpublished PhD (Economics) dissertation, University of Stellenbosch, South Africa.

Odhiambo, N.M. (2008). Financial Depth, Savings and Economic Growth in Kenya: A Dynamic Causal Linkage. *Economic Modelling*, Volume 25, issue 4, pp. 704–713.

Odhiambo, N.M., and Nyasha, S. (2020). Financial development and economic growth in Uganda: A multivariate causal linkage. *Journal of African Business*. https://doi.org/10.1080/15228916.2020.1Region/Country

Olayungbo, D.O. and Quadri, A. (2019). Remittances, financial development and economic growth in sub-Saharan African countries: evidence from a PMG-ARDL approach. *Financial Innovation*, Volume 5, Article Number 9, pp. 1–25.

Part II

Impact of Finance on Sustainable Economic Growth in Africa

7 Financial Development and Economic Growth in African Countries

Nicholas Mbaya Odhiambo and Talknice Saungweme

7.1 Introduction

Since the mid–18th century, when the industrial revolution began, economists and industrialists have tried to understand the factors that influence the level and rate of economic growth. They intended to figure out what was causing the disparities in economic growth rates between developed, emerging, and developing countries. Natural resource endowments, trade openness, human and physical capital development, macroeconomic stability, and legal and institutional systems were all recognised as proximate and linked fundamental determinants influencing growth rates among countries (Levine, 1997, 1999). However, financial depth was added to the list of growth determinants in the early 20th century. Since then, the discussion over the significance of financial structure and development in economic growth has intensified, with four distinct points of view emerging (see International Monetary Fund/IMF, 2000; Levine, 1997, 1999).

The first viewpoint contends that financial development not only precedes but also positively induces economic expansion – also called the supply-leading hypothesis (Nyasha and Odhiambo, 2019; Rehman and Hysa, 2021; Schumpeter, 1912). For example, without a properly structured and robust financial system, the industrialisation of the 18th century and technological innovation of today would not have been conceivable (Schumpeter, 1912). The absence of well-established financial systems in some global economies, according to Goldsmith (1970), is a barrier to capital development and foreign funding. In other words, financial intermediation is viewed as growth-enhancing because it performs the following critical functions: in trading, provision of investment information, determination of investment returns, catalysing savings and excess liquidity into more usage forms, economic and financial risk management, technological innovation, and poverty alleviation, among others (Levine, 1997, 2003; Patrick, 1966).

On the whole, a supply-leading financial system, in which financial development supports physical capital accumulation and increases total factor productivity, is an essential precondition for inducing real output growth. According to the Schumpeterian idea of financial innovation, industrialised

DOI: 10.4324/9781003215042-9

economies have more advanced and diverse financial institutions and markets, which foster entrepreneurial endeavours, than developing economies (Patrick, 1966).

On the contrary, the second perception asserts that economic progress precedes financial development – also called the demand-leading, or growth-led finance, hypothesis (see International Monetary Fund/IMF, 2012; Robinson, 1952). This viewpoint claims that a number of nonfinancial developments, such as governmental regulations and technological advancements, are assertive manifestations of the demand for these goods and services by economic agents in the real economy. These developments include the creation of contemporary financial institutions, the demand for financial instruments and related financial services by economic agents in the real economy, as well as a variety of other nonfinancial developments (Levine, 1997). The evolution of the financial system is thought to be a ubiquitous consequence of actual production development, according to Patrick (1966). This suggests that the demand-following method considers financial sector expansion to be largely passive, occurring more or less naturally as a result of the growth process. As the real economy expands, financial systems and markets develop, broaden, and become more efficient (Patrick, 1966). Thus, unlike Schumpeter (1912), Robinson (1952) believes in reverse causality from the real sector to financial sector.

According to the third perspective, financial advancement and economic progress are inextricably linked, and that the two cannot be separated easily. Economic growth is the outcome of a systematic interplay among savings, investment, consumption, and wealth accumulation that diversifies the flow of loanable funds and increases demand for diverse financial services and goods (Gurley and Shaw, 1955). Financial intermediaries, according to Gurley and Shaw (1955), are involved in the transmission and allocation of loanable funds between spending units, particularly to higher returning economic sectors. As a result, this theory indicates that economic growth and financial development are mutually reinforcing.

The fourth viewpoint claims that the finance-growth relationship has grown unduly stretched, concealing the role of other essential economic growth factors (Lucas, 1988). When compared to other factors such as labour productivity, public debt management, import substitution, and export promotion, financial depth may provide a minimal contribution to economic growth (Lucas, 1988). As a result, financial development and economic growth are considered unrelated, and causation linkages cannot be assumed explicitly (see Levine, 2003).

Another idea implies a nonlinear finance-growth relationship. That is, the real financial sector relationship is assumed to be convex and non-monotone (International Monetary Fund/IMF, 2012). As a result, despite years of empirical investigation on the financial depth-growth relationship, the conclusion is still equivocal. The nature of the link between these two variables, according to Nyasha and Odhiambo (2019), is complicated and sensitive to country-specific characteristics, applied econometric techniques, and financial development proxies utilised.

It is critical to recognise the existence of a growing corpus of research on the link between financial development and African economic progress. The research can be widely bundled into two bands, country (or sectorial)-specific studies (Ogbonna *et al.*, 2020; Okunlola *et al.*, 2020) and cross-country studies (Aluko and Ibrahim, 2020; An *et al.*, 2020; Ustarz and Fanta, 2021). While these prior empirical studies have made major contributions, the current study is significant on several fronts. Explicitly, the causation between financial development and economic growth in the African setting is empirically explored in this chapter using a panel Granger causality model for 24 African countries from 1980 to 2017. The analysis incorporates a number of proxies of financial development for a robustness check.

More so, the study employs a battery of cross-sectional dependence tests to address the cross-sectional dependency in the estimations, which has previously been overlooked. These tests include the (i) Breusch and Pagan (1980) LM, (ii) Pesaran (2004) scaled LM, (iii) Baltagi *et al.*, (2012) bias-corrected scaled LM, and (iv) Pesaran (2004) CD.

The chapter order is as follows: The second section contains a survey of relevant literature. This section is partitioned into two parts. The first part discusses financial sector development and economic growth dynamics in Africa, while the second part reviews the previous empirical literature on the subject. This is followed by the third section, which discusses the study's methodology, and the fourth section covers the empirical analysis. The last section presents the study summary and policy suggestions.

7.2 Literature Survey

7.2.1 *Financial Landscape and Economic Growth Dynamics in Africa*

The evolvement of global financial systems has been mostly shaped by repeated financial crises, increased globalisation, public policies, and the swift changes in economic actors' preferences. Furthermore, cross-country variation in financial landscape and economic growth patterns in Africa is influenced by (i) historical institutional factors, whose origin is mostly entrenched in colonial effects, and (ii) religion-based and ethnic divisions (see, for example, Emenalo *et al.*, 2018). These factors have influenced the rate and level of financial depth in African countries, as well as the degree of financial inclusion, efficiency, productivity, and economic well-being. The aspiration by member states to achieve Sustainable Development Goals by 2030, and to mobilise adequate local money for industrialisation and poverty reduction, has heightened the need to reconsider the possible links between financial systems and economic growth in Africa. With the severe impacts of the coronavirus pandemic, limited foreign direct investment and donor monies, and fast-changing climatic circumstances, understanding and developing domestic financial systems in Africa has become increasingly indispensable (see, for example, Tyson, 2021a).

Furthermore, inconsistencies between African and other world economies, notably in terms of key financial and economic players and economic structure, have had a substantial impact on the continent's economic convergence goal and other regional cooperation endeavours. Liquidity lenders, for example, have failed to provide appropriate credit to smallholder farmers and miners, women, and youths in Africa, preferring to support wealthier and politically linked households instead (Cramer *et al.*, 2020).

Financial development is broadly described as an amalgamation of (i) depth, which constitutes the size and liquidity of financial markets; (ii) accessibility, which measures the ability of players (households and firms) to obtain financial services; and (iii) efficiency, which focuses on liquidity providers' capacity to supply financial services at reasonable rates (Svirydzenka, 2016; Tyson and Beck, 2018). While financial access in Africa has improved moderately, there is still work to be done in terms of depth, efficiency, and capital market development (Tyson, 2021b).

Due to the increased use of digital banking and electronic transactions technologies, financial services accessibility in Africa has substantially improved (World Bank, 2020a). Domestic banks' use of digital infrastructures has not only allowed them to extend financial services to previously marginalised segments of the population, but it has also increased their profitability by lowering operational costs. In the SSA region, a number of telecommunication firms and microfinance institutions have established mobile payment services, as well as a host of other sophisticated financial services, including digital lending, deposits, bill payments, and insurance (OECD, 2020; World Bank, 2020a). With 21% of the adult population having a mobile money account, sub-Saharan Africa has established itself as a leader in the field (World Bank, 2020a).

Domestic bank credit to the private sector (as a share of GDP), broad money-to-GDP ratio, and the share of private sector credit to total credit are some of the proxies used to calculate quantitative financial sector growth. Typically, domestic bank credit to the private sector (as a share of GDP) is commonly used to determine financial depth. It assesses how well agents can save and invest using financial markets, and it is linked to long-term economic growth since it boosts the private sector's ability to participate in long-term and risky projects (Africa Development Bank, 2015). By recording claims on the private sector by deposit-taking financial entities relative to economic activity, it portrays the function of financial intermediaries in directing funds to productive sectors (King and Levine, 1993). Figure 7.1 displays the financial depth of the various African regions using this indicator.

Figure 7.1 shows that SSA has less financial depth than the global average, with period averages of 29.4% and 82.0%, respectively. According to the graph, West and Central Africa had the lowest percentages, averaging 11.6%

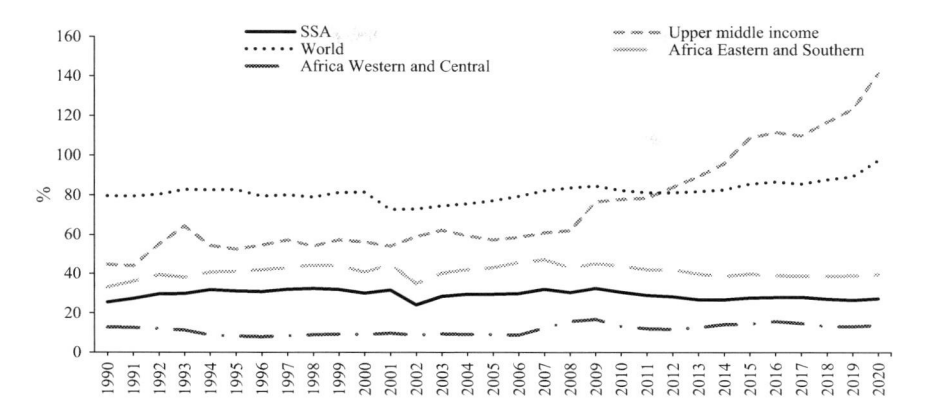

Figure 7.1 Domestic credit to private sector by banks (% of GDP) (1990–2020).
Source: Authors' computation from World Bank data.

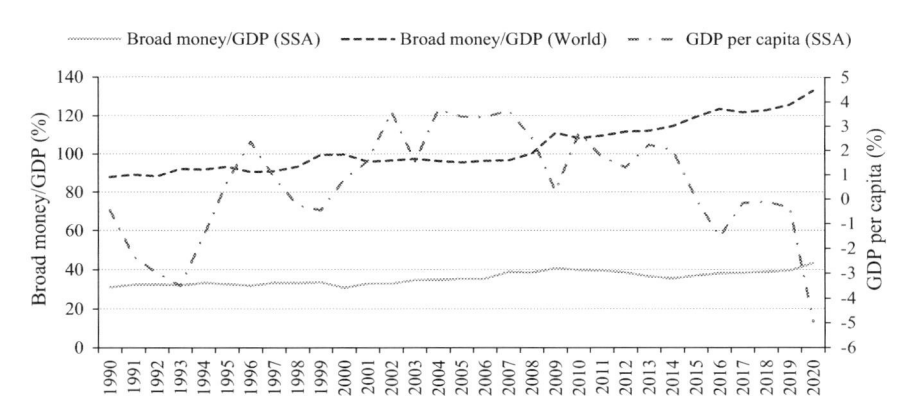

Figure 7.2 Money-to-GDP ratio and economic growth trends in SSA (1990–2020).
Source: Authors' computation from World Bank data.

between 1990 and 2020. Eastern and Southern Africa had a comparatively high ratio of 41.1%, owing primarily to Namibia and South Africa's strong financial depth (World Bank, 2020b). Furthermore, there is evidence of a rising gap in financial depth between SSA countries and the rest of the world between 2011 and 2020, with the globe's upward trend being led by upper-middle-income economies. Figure 7.2 shows the broad money-to-GDP ratio in SSA, in addition to the rate of economic growth patterns.

Figure 7.2 shows that the SSA region has a lower broad money-to-GDP ratio than the rest of the world, indicating less financial liquidity and depth. The figure also depicts a general positive finance-economic growth relationship in the sub-Saharan African region, except for the period after 2019, when a minor improvement in financial development was accompanied by a significant decline in GDP per capita. For example, the broad money/GDP ratio rose steadily between 1993 and 2008, when the region mostly recorded positive growth rates.

7.2.2 Empirical Literature Survey

Previous research on the causal flow linkage between financial depth and gross domestic product is divided into three categories in this study, in accordance with the theoretical literature discussed in Section 7.1. The first group comprises studies that suggest a one-way causal relationship between financial and economic progress. This group's theoretical foundations are the supply- and demand-leading theories. The second cluster emphasises the existence of a financial-economic growth feedback relationship. Aside from these two points of view, there is a third group of research that gives evidence for a causal relationship that is neutral.

There are two strands to previous empirical investigations that support a unidirectional connection between financial development and economic growth. The first strand of unidirectional causal flow is made up of research that buttresses the supply-leading theory, including Topcu and Coban (2017), Sehrawat and Giri (2016), Bojanic (2012), and Calderón and Liu (2003). Bist and Read (2018), Taivan and Nene (2016), and Bangake and Eggoh (2011) conducted studies that support the demand-leading hypothesis, which is the second premise of unidirectional causality. Furthermore, according to Odhiambo (2013), Guptha and Rao (2018), and Kar *et al.* (2018), the causal relationship between financial development and economic growth varies based on the financial development proxy used and, in certain situations, on the research country.

The conclusions reached by Aluko and Ibrahim (2020), Okunlola *et al.* (2020), Hsueh *et al.* (2013), and Fowowe (2011) produced outcomes that are consistent with two-way causality between financial deepening and economic growth. Finally, research by Menyah *et al.* (2014) and Bangake and Eggoh (2011), among others, found no direct causal association between financial advancement and economic growth. Table 7.1 summarises previous research on the finance-growth relationship from 2000 through 2021.

7.3 Methodology

7.3.1 Heterogeneous Granger Causality

In this chapter, we employed the recently developed heterogeneous panel Granger non-causality approach to examine the causal link among several proxies of financial development and economic growth in low-income and middle-income SSA countries. The approach, which was pioneered by Dumitrescu and Hurlin (2012), explains variation within cross-section units, and it outperforms earlier techniques by taking into account cross-sectional

Table 7.1 Previous research on the finance–growth causal link (2000–2021)

Author(s) & Year	Study Country/Region	Study Period	Methodology Applied	Finding
A: Studies consistent with unidirectional causality				
Bist and Read (2018)	16 countries (15 from Africa and one from South Asia)	1995–2014	FMOLS DOLS	Growth → Finance
Taivan and Nene (2016)	Ten SADC countries	1994–2013	VECM Panel Granger causality	Growth → Finance
Bangake and Eggoh (2011)	71 developed and developing countries	1960–2004	DOLS	Growth → Finance (for high-income countries)
Topcu and Çoban (2017)	Turkey (manufacturing sector)	1989–2010	Panel analysis Dumitrescu and Hurlin (2012) panel causality model	Growth ← Finance
Sehrawat and Giri (2016)	SAARC	1994–2013	FMOLS DOLS Panel Granger causality model	Growth ← Finance
Bojanic (2012)	Bolivia	1940–2010	ECM models Granger causality model	Growth → Finance
Calderón and Liu (2003)	109 developing and industrial countries	1960–1994	Panel analysis Geweke (1982) decomposition test	Growth → Finance
Guptha and Rao (2018)	BRICS countries	1996–2016	Toda-Yamamoto causality test	The direction of causality varies based on the financial growth indicator chosen and the study country.
Kar et al. (2018)	MENA countries	1980–2007	Granger causality test	The causality direction changes depending on the financial growth measure and the study country.

(*Continued*)

Table 7.1 (**Continued**)

Author(s) & Year	Study Country/Region	Study Period	Methodology Applied	Finding
Odhiambo (2013)	Botswana	–	ARDL Granger non-causality test	The direction of causation differs based on the financial development measure employed and the research country.
B: Studies consistent with bidirectional causality				
Aluko and Ibrahim (2020)	33 sub-Saharan African countries	1990–2015	Panel analysis Dumitrescu and Hurlin (2012) panel causality model	Growth ↔ Finance
Okunlola *et al.* (2020)	Nigeria	1985–2015	Time-series analysis TYDL approach	Growth ↔ Finance
Hsueh *et al.* (2013)	OECD countries	1980–2007	Panel Granger causality	Growth ↔ Finance
Fowowe (2011)	17 SSA countries	1975–2005	Panel Granger causality	Growth ↔ Finance
C: Studies consistent with no causality				
Menyah *et al.* (2014)	21 African countries	1965–2008	Panel bootstrapped approach to Granger causality	Growth [0] Finance
Bangake and Eggoh (2011)	71 developed and developing countries	1960–2004	DOLS	Growth [0] Finance

Note: Growth → Finance means economic growth causes financial development; Finance → Growth means financial development causes economic growth; Growth ↔ Finance means two-way causality; and Growth [0] Finance means no causality.

dependence between cross-sections. This technique can also account for the time span and the relative sizes of cross-section units. In panel causality testing, ignoring heterogeneity across cross-section units can lead to false causal relationships, such as assuming the presence of a causative link in all cross-section units when it is only present in a subset of them, or denying the presence of a causal relationship in all cross-section units when it exists in at least one subset (Dumitrescu and Hurlin, 2012). The following is the model representation:

$$y_{it} = \alpha_i + \sum_{k=1}^{K} \delta_i^k y_{i(t-k)} + \sum_{k=1}^{K} \beta_i^k x_{i(t-k)} + \varepsilon_{i,t} \tag{7.1}$$

where
y and x = variables, i.e., two stationary variables observed for N
     individuals on T periods.
T = time dimension, i.e., $t = 1...T$.
i = individuals, i.e., $i = 1...N$.

According to Dumitrescu and Hurlin (2012), the null hypothesis of homogeneous non-causality implies the absence of causality in any of the cross-section units, while the alternative hypothesis implies that there are two subgroups of cross-section units. The D-H test, which is based on the mean Wald statistic, can be computed as follows:

$$w_{N,T}^{HNC} = \frac{1}{N} \sum_{i=1}^{N} wi, T \tag{7.2}$$

where wi, T = the Wald statistic for each panel group.

Prior to conducting the heterogeneous Granger causality test, a battery of tests was conducted in line with previous studies. First, the current research applied four cross-sectional dependence tests to ascertain the existence of cross-sectional dependence among the study countries. These tests are the Breusch and Pagan (1980) LM, Pesaran (2004) scaled LM, Baltagi *et al.* (2012) bias-corrected scaled LM, and Pesaran (2004) CD. Second, panel unit root tests were performed to examine whether the variables used in this study are $I(0)$ or $I(1)$. These tests were the Levin *et al.* (LLC) (2002) test, a first-generation panel unit root test, which assumes that individual processes are cross-sectionally independent. The test incorporates separate deterministic trends in each series with varying lag spans of the dependent variable across the four models in the panel to remove autocorrelation. Because first-generation panel unit root tests cannot account for the impacts of international shocks, the study also applied the Pesaran – CIPS (a second-generation panel unit root test), which takes into account the cross-sectional dependency.

Last, panel cointegration tests were carried out to check whether the variables in each of the four models have a cointegration relationship. Traditional panel cointegration approaches, like Pedroni (1999) and Kao (1999), will not suffice if cross-sectional dependence is present. To obtain consistent results, the Westerlund (2007) cointegration test was employed to establish whether the variables were cointegrated. This method (1) incorporates unit-specific short-run dynamics, unit-specific trend and slope parameters, and cross-sectional dependence; (2) is valid when T is significantly greater than N; and (3) does not require any common-factor constraints because it relies on structural instead of residual dynamics (Persyn and Westerlund, 2008).

7.3.2 Data

The data for this study came from the World Development Indicators and the Global Financial Development Database, both of which are World Bank publications. The missing data points from these World Bank databases were filled using individual countries' national statistical databases/reports. Since the financial development in SSA countries is still developing, only bank-based financial development data were available for the study period covered. In total, the study used four proxies of financial development, i.e., bank deposits to GDP (BDGDP), deposit bank assets to GDP (DBAGDP), liquid liabilities to GDP (LLGDP), and private credit by deposit money banks to GDP (PCRDBGDP). GDP per capita (y), on the contrary, was used to measure economic growth, which is the second variable of interest in this study.

Although SSA has over 44 countries, only 24 countries have been included in this analysis as the data for the remaining countries during the period 1980–2017 were not sufficient. These 24 countries were further divided into 12 LICs and 12 MICs. The low-income countries include Burkina Faso, Burundi, Central African Republic, Chad, Gambia, Madagascar, Malawi, Mali, Niger, Rwanda, Sierra Leone, and Togo. The middle-income countries, on the contrary, include Benin, Cabo Verde, Cameroon, Côte d'Ivoire, Eswatini, Gabon, Ghana, Kenya, Lesotho, Nigeria, Senegal, and South Africa.

7.4 Empirical Analysis

7.4.1 Cross-Sectional Dependence Test

The results of the four cross-sectional dependence tests are reported in Table 7.2.

In Table 7.2, all tests reject the null hypothesis of no cross-sectional dependency across LICs and MICs, indicating that cross-sectional dependency does exist among the countries studied. The interdependence of countries means that a shock in one country may have ramifications in another – explained by neighbourhood effects (Pesaran, 2004). One reason for this result could be because countries and financial organisations in recent decades have become

Table 7.2 Results of cross-sectional dependence test

Series	Breusch-Pagan LM	Pesaran Scaled LM	Bias-Corrected Scaled LM	Pesaran CD
LICs				
BDGDP	1302.155★★★ (0.0000)	107.5935★★★ (0.0000)	107.4314★★★ (0.0000)	34.30081★★ (0.0000)
DBAGDP	960.7178★★★ (0.0000)	77.87519★★★ (0.0000)	77.71303★★★ (0.0000)	24.94262★★★ (0.0000)
LLGDP	831.1061★★★ (0.0000)	66.59394★★★ (0.0000)	66.43178★★★ (0.0000)	24.24062★★★ (0.0000)
PCRDBGDP	750.0838★★★ (0.0000)	59.54186★★★ (0.0000)	59.37969★★★ (0.0000)	20.23745★★★ (0.0000)
γ	785.6947★★★ (0.0000)	62.64138★★★ (0.0000)	62.47922★★★ (0.0000)	5.990862★★★ (0.0000)
MICs				
BDGDP	1108.369★★★ (0.0000)	90.72655★★★ (0.0000)	90.56439★★★ (0.0000)	26.94462★★★ (0.0000)
DBAGDP	921.5644★★★ (0.0000)	74.46732★★★ (0.0000)	74.30516★★★ (0.0000)	9.044640★★★ (0.0000)
LLGDP	983.1683★★★ (0.0000)	79.82926★★★ (0.0000)	79.66709★★★ (0.0000)	18.06165★★★ (0.0000)
PCRDBGDP	771.800★★★ (0.0000)	61.43204★★★ (0.0000)	61.26987★★★ (0.0000)	8.515796★★★ (0.0000)
Y	1245.473★★★ (0.0000)	102.6600★★★ (0.0000)	102.4978★★★ (0.0000)	16.26037★★★ (0.0000)

Note: ★★ and ★★★ denote significance at the 5% and 1% levels, respectively.

increasingly economically and financially intertwined, implying substantial cross-sectional interdependencies. The impact of these shocks on a single country is determined by factors such as trade openness and financial depth, among other factors (Karabiyik *et al.*, 2019).

7.4.2 First- and Second-Generation Panel Unit Root Tests

Table 7.3 displays the findings of the first- and second-generation panel unit root testing in both LICs and MICs.

Table 7.3 shows that all of the variables in this study are integrated of order one, i.e., [$I(1)$]. This finding is validated by the LLC t-statistics and the Pesaran (CIPS) statistics, which were found to be statistically significant at first difference.

7.4.3 Panel Cointegration Test

The findings of the Westerlund (2007) panel cointegration test are summarised in Table 7.4.

The *P*-value test for Model 1 reported in Table 7.4 indicates that Gt and Pa are statistically significant at 5% in LICs, whereas Pt and Pa are statistically

Table 7.3 First- and second-generation panel unit root test

	LICs				MICs			
	LLC t-Statistics		Pesaran − CIPS Panel Unit Root Test		LLC t-Statistics		Pesaran − CIPS Panel Unit Root Test	
	Level	First Difference	Level	First Difference	Level	First Difference	Level	First Difference
BDGDP	1.44280	−6.6990★★★	1.46433	−3.89769★★★	1.11361	−7.07472★★★	−1.30920	−4.29619★★★
DBAGDP	1.18391	−7.71165★★★	−1.53428	−3.88888★★★	0.76029	−7.30226★★★	−1.45610	−3.38162★★★
LLGDP	0.17514	−9.57403★★★	−1.33685	−3.58236★★★	1.51055	−7.33670★★★	−1.45421	−4.32294★★★
PCRDBGDP	−0.38777	−8.20307★★★	−1.37844	−4.34505★★★	−0.76374	−5.88556★★★	−0.89486	−3.60216★★★
γ	−0.74001	−7.21529★★★	−1.10291	−4.00670★★★	−0.56010	−5.47102★★★	−0.96401	−4.17544★★★

Note: ★★★ indicates rejection of the respective null hypothesis at the 1% significance level.

Table 7.4 Westerlund (2007) panel cointegration test results

Statistics	Value	Z-Value	P-Value	Robust P-Value	Value	Z-Value	P-Value	Robust P-Value
LICs					MICs			
Model 1								
Gt	−1.618	−2.138	0.016	0.000	−1.347	−1.234	0.108	0.000
Ga	−1.696	1.604	0.946	0.000	−4.133	−0.252	0.400	0.000
Pt	−3.244	−1.264	0.103	0.000	−5.038	−2.801	0.003	0.000
Pa	−2.548	−1.821	0.034	0.000	−3.787	−3.303	0.001	0.000
Model 2								
Gt	−1.372	−1.317	0.094	0.000	−2.119	−1.318	0.094	0.000
Ga	−1.852	1.485	0.931	0.000	−7.247	−0.067	0.473	0.000
Pt	−4.670	−2.486	0.007	0.000	−7.019	−2.016	0.022	0.000
Pa	−3.415	−2.858	0.002	0.000	−5.981	−1.366	0.086	0.000
Model 3								
Gt	−1.281	−1.015	0.155	0.000	−2.591	−0.957	0.169	0.000
Ga	−3.385	0.318	0.625	0.000	−12.283	−0.138	0.445	0.000
Pt	−3.751	−1.698	0.045	0.000	−9.458	−2.448	0.007	0.000
Pa	−2.105	−1.291	0.098	0.000	−11.818	−1.630	0.052	0.000
Model 4								
Gt	−1.426	−1.497	0.067	0.000	−2.404	−2.415	0.008	0.000
Ga	−3.953	−0.115	0.454	0.000	−9.055	−1.217	0.112	0.000
Pt	−4.250	−2.126	0.017	0.000	7.545	−2.545	0.006	0.000
Pa	−3.134	−2.522	0.006	0.000	−6.575	−1.829	0.034	0.000

significant at 1% in MICs. Overall, the *P*-value test statistic findings show that two Westerlund test statistics are statistically significant in Models 1, 2, and 4 for LICs, whereas two and three Westerlund test statistics are shown to be statistically significant in Models 1 and 4 for MICs, respectively. In all four models, the strong *P*-value test indicates the statistical significance of all the four Westerlund test statistics *Gt*, *Ga*, *Pt*, and *Pa* at 1%. These results generally suggest the presence of a cointegration relationship between the variables despite cross-sectional dependence.

7.4.4 *Heterogeneous Panel Causality Analysis*

Table 7.5 summarises the findings of heterogeneous panel Granger causality test.

Table 7.5 shows that there is a clear one-way causal flow from economic growth to financial development in the LICs examined. This conclusion is supported by the Zbar-statistics, which is statistically significant at 1% in the economic growth equation but not in the financial development equation in Models 1, 2, 3, and 4. The study's findings are consistent with those of Bist and Read (2018) for selected African and South Asian countries, as well as Taivan and Nene (2016) for selected SADC countries.

Whereas the major causal flow in MICs is from economic growth to financial development (Models 1, 3, and 4), the results of Model 2 suggest

Table 7.5 Dumitrescu and Hurlin Granger causality test

	Zbar-Stat.	Prob.	Causality	Zbar-Stat.	Prob.	Causality
	LICs			MICs		
Model 1						
Dy does not homogeneously cause DBDGDP	11.0859	0.0000	$y \to FD$	3.31248	0.0009	$y \to FD$
DBDGDP does not homogeneously cause Dy	0.84484	0.3982		−0.07963	0.9365	
Model 2						
Dy does not homogeneously cause DDBAGDP	4.5650	0.0000	$y \to FD$	0.16124	0.8719	$FD \perp y$
DDBAGDP does not homogeneously cause Dy	1.25840	0.2082		−1.65171	0.0986	
Model 3						
DY does not homogeneously cause DLLGDP	3.17666	0.0015	$y \to FD$	3.03030	0.0024	$y \to FD$
DLLGDP does not homogeneously cause Dy	−0.47186	0.6370		−0.96930	0.3324	
Model 4						
Dy does not homogeneously cause DPCRDBGDP	14.7639	0.0000	$y \to FD$	12.7098	0.0000	$y \to FD$
DPCRDBGDP does not homogeneously cause Dy	1.26078	0.2074		−0.59954	0.5488	

a neutral causal flow from financial development to economic growth based on the conventional 1% and 5% levels of significance. As a result, the relationship between economic growth and financial development in MICs varies depending on which financial development proxy is used. These findings are reinforced by Guptha and Rao (2018) for BRICS countries and Kar *et al.* (2018) for MENA countries.

7.5 Conclusion

This chapter revisits the causal relationship between financial development and sustainable economic growth in 24 SSA countries from 1980 to 2017. The goal of the study is to establish whether the relationship between financial development and economic growth in SSA follows a supply-leading or demand-following pattern. The chapter employs a battery of modern panel data estimation techniques. In the main, the study uses four estimation techniques, i.e., (i) four cross-sectional dependence tests; (ii) two panel unit root tests (Levin-Lin-Chu (LLC) and Pesaran – CIPS); (iii) two panel cointegration tests (Pedroni, 2004; Westerlund, 2007); and (iv) panel heterogeneous Granger non-causality test (Dumitrescu and Hurlin, 2012). The choice of Dumitrescu and Hurlin (2012) estimation technique instead of a multivariate ECM-based Granger causality is largely influenced by the presence of cross-sectional dependence, which was found to be prevalent in the data used in this study. For robustness check, the study used four proxies of financial development in a step-wise fashion, namely, bank deposits to GDP (BDGDP), deposit bank assets to GDP (DBAGDP), liquid liabilities to GDP (LLGDP), and private credit by deposit money banks to GDP (PCRDBGDP). The study also decomposes the selected SSA countries into two groups – low-income countries and middle-income countries. The findings of this study show that economic growth unambiguously Granger-causes financial development in both LICs and MICs in SSA. This finding applies, regardless of the financial development proxy used. The results, therefore, vehemently reject the supply-leading notion in favour of the demand-following view. The study recommends that SSA countries focus more on pro-growth policies to boost the development of their financial sectors.

References

African Development Bank (AfDB). (2015). The banking system in Africa: Main facts and challenges. *Africa Economic Brief*, 6(5), 1–16.

Aluko, O.A., and Ibrahim, M. (2020). Institutions and the financial development–economic growth nexus in sub-Saharan Africa. *Economic Notes*, 49(3), 1–16. https://doi.org/10.1111/ecno.12163

An, H., Zou, Q., and Kargbo, M. (2020). Impact of financial development on economic growth: Evidence from sub-Saharan Africa. *Australian Economic Papers*, 68(June), 1–35. https://doi.org/10.1111/1467-8454.12201

Baltagi, B. H., Feng, Q., and Kao, C. (2012). A Lagrange Multiplier test for cross-sectional dependence in a fixed effects panel data model. *Journal of Econometrics*, 170(1), 164–177. https://doi.org/10.1016/j.jeconom.2012.04.004

Bangake, C., and Eggoh, J.C. (2011). Further evidence on finance-growth causality: A panel data analysis. *Economic Systems*, 35(1), 176–188. https://doi. org/10.1016/j.ecosys.2010.07.001

Bist, J. P., and Read, R. (2018). Financial development and economic growth: Evidence from a panel of 16 African and non-African low-income countries. *Cogent Economics and Finance*, 6(1), 1–22. https://doi. org/10.1080/23322039.2018.1449780

Bojanic, A. N. (2012). The impact of financial development and trade on the economic growth of Bolivia. *Journal of Applied Economics*, 15(1), 51–70. https://doi.org/10.1016/S1514-0326(12)60003-8

Breusch, T. S. and Pagan, A. R. (1980). The Lagrange multiplier test and its applications to model specification in econometrics. *The Review of Economic Studies*, 47(1), 239–253. https://doi.org/10.2307/2297111

Calderón, C., and Liu, L. (2003). The direction of causality between financial development and economic growth. *Journal of Development Economics*, 72(1), 321–334. https://doi.org/10.1016/S0304-3878(03)00079-8

Cramer, C., Sender, J., and Oqubay, A. (2020). *African Economic Development: Evidence, Theory, Policy*. Oxford University Press. https://library.oapen.org/handle/20.500.12657/41802

Dumitrescu, E. I., and Hurlin, C. (2012). Testing for Granger non-causality in heterogeneous panels. *Economic Modelling*, 29(4), 1450–1460. https://doi.org/10.1016/j.econmod.2012.02.014

Emenalo, C. O., Gagliardi, F., and Hodgson, G. M. (2018). Historical institutional determinants of financial system development in Africa. *Journal of Institutional Economics*, 14(2), 345–372. https://doi.org/10.1017/S1744137417000042

Fowowe, B. (2011). The finance-growth nexus in sub- Saharan Africa: Panel cointegration and causality tests. *International Development*, 231, 220–239. https://doi.org/10.1002/jid.1660

Goldsmith, R.W. (1970). Financial structure and development. *The Economic Journal*, 80(318), 365–367.

Guptha, K. S. K., and Rao, R. P. (2018). The causal relationship between financial development and economic growth: An experience with BRICS economies. *Journal of Social and Economic Development*, 20(1), 308–326. https://doi.org/10.1007/s40847-018-0071-5

Gurley, J. G., and Shaw, E. S. (1955). Financial aspects of economic development. *The American Economic Review*, 45(4), 515–538.

Hsueh, S. J., Hu, Y. H., and Tu, C. H. (2013). Economic growth and financial development in Asian countries: A bootstrap panel Granger causality analysis. *Economic Modelling*, 32(1), 294–301. https://doi.org/ 10.1016/j.econmod.2013.02.027

International Monetary Fund (IMF). (2000). Financial development and economic growth: An overview. IMF Working Paper WP/OO/209.

International Monetary Fund (IMF). (2012). Too much finance. IMF Working Paper WP/12/161.

Kao, C. (1999). Spurious regression and residual-based tests for cointegration in panel data. *Journal of Econometrics*, 90(1), 1–44. https://doi.org/10.1016/S0304-4076(98)00023-2

Kar, M., Nazlıoğlu, S., and Ağır, H. (2018). Financial development and economic growth nexus in the MENA countries: Bootstrap panel granger causality analysis. *Economic Modelling*, 28(1), 685–693. https://doi.org/10.1016/j.econmod.2010.05.015

Karabiyik, H., Palm, F. C., and Urbain, J. P. (2019). Econometric analysis of panel data models with multifactor error structures. *Annual Review of Economics*, 11, 495–522. https://doi.org/10.1146/annurev-economics-063016-104338

King, R. G., and Levine, R. (1993). Finance, entrepreneurship and growth. *Journal of Monetary Economics*, 32(3), 513–542.

Levin, A., Chien-Fu, L., and Chia-Shang, J. C. (2002). Unit root tests in panel data: Asymptotic and finite-sample properties. *Journal of Econometrics*, 108(1), 1–24.

Levine, R. (1997). Financial development and economic growth: Views and agenda. *Journal of Economic Literature,* 35(2), 688–726.

Levine, R. (1999). Financial development and growth: Where do we stand. *Estudios de Economia*, 26(2): 113–136.

Levine, R. (2003). Finance and growth: Theory, evidence, and mechanisms. NBER Working Paper 10766. https://www.nber.org/papers/w10766

Lucas, R. E. (1988). On the mechanics of economic development. *Journal of Monetary Economics*, 22(1), 3–42.

Menyah, K., Nazlioglu S., and Wolde-Rufael, Y. (2014). Financial development, trade openness and economic growth in African countries: New insights from a panel causality approach. *Economic Modelling*, 37(2), 386–394.

Nyasha, S., and Odhiambo, N. M. (2019). Financial development and economic growth nexus: A rejoinder to Tsionas. *Economic Notes*, 48(2), 1–3.

Odhiambo, N. M. (2013). Financial development in Botswana: in search of a finance-led growth response. *International Journal of Sustainable Economy*, 5(4), 341–356.

Ogbonna, O. E., Mobosi, I. A., and Ugwuoke, O. W. (2020). Economic growth in an oil-dominant economy of Nigeria: The role of financial system development. *Cogent Economics and Finance*, 8(1), 1–16. https://doi.org/10.1080/23322039.2020.1810390

Okunlola, O. A., Masade, E. O., Lukman, A. F., and Abiodun, S. A. (2020). Investigating causal relationship between financial development indicators and economic growth: Toda and Yamamoto approach. *Iranian Economic Review*, 24(1), 225–246.

Organisation for Economic Co-operation and Development (OECD). (2020). Digital disruption in banking and its impact on competition. http://www.oecd.org/daf/competition/digital-disruption-in-financial-markets.htm

Patrick, H. T. (1966). Financial development and economic growth in underdeveloped countries. *Economic Development and Cultural Change*, 14(2), 174–189. https://doi.org/10.1086/450153

Pedroni, P. (1999). Critical values for cointegration tests in heterogeneous panels with multiple regressors. *Oxford Bulletin of Economics and Statistics*, 61(S1), 653–670.

Pedroni, P. (2004). Panel cointegration: Asymptotic and finite sample properties of pooled time series tests with an application to the PPP hypothesis. *Econometric Theory*, 20(3), 597–625.

Persyn, D., and Westerlund, J. (2008). Error-correction–based cointegration tests for panel data. *The Stata Journal*, 8(2), 232–241. https://journals.sagepub.com/doi/pdf/10.1177/1536867X0800800205

Pesaran, M. H. (2004). General diagnostic tests for cross section dependence in panels. Cambridge Working Papers in Economics 0435, Faculty of Economics, University of Cambridge.

Rehman, N. U., and Hysa, E. (2021). The effect of financial development and remittances on economic growth. *Cogent Economics and Finance*, 9(1). https://doi.org/10.1080/23322039.2021.1932060

Robinson, J. (1952). The generalisation of the general theory and other essays. 2nd edition. 67–142, London: Palgrave Macmillan.

Schumpeter, J. (1912). The theory of economic development. Leipzig: Dunker and Humblot, Translated by REDVERS OPIE. Cambridge, MA: Harvard University Press, 1934.

Sehrawat, M., and Giri, A. K. (2016). Financial development and poverty reduction in India: An empirical investigation. *International Journal of Social Economics*, 43(2), 106–122.

Svirydzenka, K. (2016). Introducing a new broad-based index of financial development. IMF Working Paper WP/16/5.

Taivan, A., and Nene, G. (2016). Financial development and economic growth. *The Journal of Developing Areas*, 50(4), 81–95.

Topcu, M., and Çoban, S. (2017). Financial development and firm growth in Turkish manufacturing industry: Evidence from heterogeneous panel based non-causality test. *Economic Research – Ekonomska Istrazivanja*, 30(1), 1758–1769. https://doi.org/10. 1080/1331677X.2017.1383179

Tyson, J. (2021a). Financial-sector development and inclusive and sustainable economic growth in sub-Saharan Africa: Progress and gaps. Joint FSD Africa and ODI Working Paper. London: Overseas Development Institute.

Tyson, J. (2021b). Differences in finance's role in economic development in sub-Saharan Africa. Joint FSD Africa and ODI Briefing Paper. London: Overseas Development Institute.

Tyson, J., and Beck, T. (2018). Capital flows and financial sector development in low-income countries. Growth Research Programme. Synthesis report. October 2018 Edition. degrp.odi.org

Ustarz, Y., and Fanta, A. B. (2021). Financial development and economic growth in sub-Saharan Africa: A sectoral perspective. *Cogent Economics and Finance*, 9(1), 1–21. https://doi.org/10.1080/23322039.2021.1934976

Westerlund, J. (2007). Testing for error correction in panel data. *Oxford Bulletin of Economics and Statistics*, 69(6), 709–748. https://doi.org/10.1111/j.1468-0084.2007.00477.x

World Bank. (2020a). Digital financial services. https://pubdocs.worldbank.org/en/230281588169110691/Digital-Financial-Services.pdf

World Bank. (2020b). Financial structure data base. https://www.worldbank.org/en/publication/gfdr/data/financial-structure-database

8 Bank-Based Financial Development and Economic Growth in African Countries

Nicholas Mbaya Odhiambo and Sheilla Nyasha

8.1 Introduction

The relationship between banking development and the growth of the economy has been at the hearts of both economists and policymakers for many decades. It has also enticed a superfluity of empirical studies from both developing and developed economies. While there has been an evolution of debate around whether financial development can be regarded as a growth instrument or as a mere greasing agent, it remains important to test whether its effect on economic progression is positive or negative. Furthermore, given the dire need for higher economic growth rates in Africa, any factor that can enhance the region's growth prospects significantly is worth receiving a detailed examination.

The core of this discussion has been centred on whether the effect of financial sector development on economic growth is significant or insignificant. Since time immemorial, the strongest view has been in support of the former, although empirical findings to the contrary have been increasing progressively – both in quantity and substance.

Despite a multitude of studies on the nexus between finance and growth, even in African countries, a significant number of these studies have weaknesses associated with the methodologies used. These paucities include the omission-of-variable bias (Odhiambo, 2008); the use of cross-sectional data even when it is now known that it does not address issues related to specific countries adequately (Quah, 1993); the failure to separate financial development into its major components, bank-based versus market-based financial development; and the assumption that the impact of each component of financial development on economic growth is uniform in an economy (Nyasha & Odhiambo, 2018).

To cover this void, this study is aimed at examining the impact of bank-based financial development on economic growth in 26 sub-Saharan African countries based on panel data for the period from 2013 to 2017. Unlike some of the earlier studies, the present study utilises four measures of bank development. These are bank deposits; private credit to deposit money banks and other financial institutions; liquid liabilities; and deposit money bank assets.

DOI: 10.4324/9781003215042-10

The selection of these measures was motivated by the financial development landscape in most African economies – characterised by the nascent developmental state and it being largely bank-based in nature.

Africa makes an interesting case in that, although it has received wide coverage of research work testing the effect of bank development on the growth of the economy, the results have been largely inconclusive. Furthermore, in the case of sub-Saharan Africa (SSA), where external demand is contracting and financing conditions are becoming considerably constricted, coupled with a less favourable regional growth outlook, ascertaining untapped and underutilised sources of growth has become even more urgent.

Financial systems in Africa are mostly bank-based, characterised by a handful of commercial banks in each country and numerous micro-finance institutions to bridge the financial access gap. The market-based financial systems in Africa are still shallow and growing, except for a few upper-middle-income countries such as South Africa, which possess a well-developed financial sector – in terms of both financial intermediation and stock market development – that compares well with those of the advanced economies (Nyasha & Odhiambo, 2015; Iheonu et al., 2020). Despite the overall underdevelopment of financial sectors in most African countries, there has been substantial progress in financial development in African countries, especially sub-Saharan African countries, compared with other regions (International Monetary Fund (IMF), 2016).

According to the IMF (2016), until recently, financial development standards in many sub-Saharan African countries had essentially relapsed compared to their level in the 1980s. The regional financial intermediary development is less than that in other emerging economies, except for the region's middle-income countries in SSA. However, in bridging the gap between the costly but good quality financial services and the high demand for basic and less costly financial services by most low-income customers, the region has been at the forefront of innovative financial services centred on the mobile telephone, raising the scoreboard for the continent's financial inclusion. The emergence of mobile banking has helped to advance the continent's financial inclusion agenda (African Development Bank, 2021), especially in East Africa. However, significant unexploited potential remains in this mobile banking space in other African regions, as it compensates for some of the traditional banking and non-banking infrastructure-related shortcomings that most countries face.

A new crop of banks has emerged in Africa, some in the form of designated banks, with the objective of driving home-grown financial development (IMF, 2016; African Development Bank, 2021). Although their rapid growth is believed to pose risks, such as inadequate supervisory oversight and relatively weak internal governance frameworks, which may jeopardise the continent's financial development efforts, these financial intermediary institutions have promoted greater economic integration, competition, and financial inclusion in Africa. They have also gradually closed the gap left by the European and American banks that had conventionally dominated the African financial landscape before the global financial crisis (African Development Bank, 2021).

In the main, empirical indications reveal that bank-based finance has buoyed growth and enhanced its stability in sub-Saharan Africa, and has helped to mobilise and allocate financial resources, as well as to facilitate other economic growth- and stabilisation-enhancing economic policies (Odhiambo, 2010; Aluko & Ibrahim, 2020). Although the recent literature on the non-linear relationship between bank development and economic growth has indicated the possibility of a threshold outside which the development of finance may be undesirable to economic growth (Sahay et al., 2015; Matei, 2020; Machado et al., 2021), all of the continent's countries in general, and the regional countries, in particular, are well below this threshold, and they still have the potential to benefit from financial development. However, looking ahead, there are fears that the prolonged forbearance of the COVID-19 pandemic would merely disguise the true state of the financial system and weaken its ability to support long-term growth (IMF, 2021).

The remainder of this chapter is structured as follows: Section 8.2 reviews the financial-growth literature, both theoretical and empirical, while Section 8.3 covers the methodology and the analysis of results, leaving Section 8.4 to conclude and offer recommendations.

8.2 Literature Review

The question of which financial system (bank-based or market-based) is better than the other at driving economic growth has been hotly debated over centuries, but one that is still largely inconclusive to this day. In this study, the focus is on the bank-based financial sector and its role in driving the growth of an economy, with a particular focus on sub-Saharan Africa. Whereas the preponderance of financial power in a market-based system is in the stock market, and the economic condition is tied to the performance of the stock market (Trehan, 2013), the power of the bank-based system and its development exists in the widening and deepening of the banks (Ahmed & Ansari, 1998). Ahmed and Ansari (1998) went on to define financial widening as the growth and expansion of financial institutions and the services they offer, whereas financial deepening is the rise in the per capita amount of financial services and institutions. According to Sanusi (2011), bank-based financial systems are key in the growth of economies through resource mobilisation and the provision of a channel for monetary policy discharge.

Bank development as a propeller of economic growth has been recognised extensively in the literature from the days of Schumpeter (Schumpeter, 1911; McKinnon, 1973; Shaw, 1973). Several growth models – Harrod-Domar, neoclassical, endogenous, and Schumpeterian growth models – have also demonstrated the finance-growth dynamics (Bencivenga & Smith, 1991; Levine, 1997, 2004; Bouton & Sumlinski, 1998).

Although the debate regarding the effect of bank development on the growth of an economy has been raging since the 19th century, the existing empirical evidence is still not conclusive. Three groups stand out, where the first group houses studies consistent with the positive effect of bank-based financial development on economic growth; the second group sheltering studies revealing the negative association between the two variables; while the third, a more unpopular group, pushed for the neutrality relationship. This points to the inconclusiveness of the results on this hot topic that has dragged on for years. Some empirical studies on the subject have utilised a time-series approach, while others have used panel estimation methods. However, there are some, though just a handful, that have also relied on cross-sectional methodologies, despite the known weaknesses of the methods.

Allen and Ndikumana (2000) studied the impact of bank development empirically in eight Southern African countries using cross-sectional data analysis and found a positive relationship. Studies by Agbetsiafa (2004) and by Kargbo and Adamu (2009) also led to the same conclusion, based on eight sub-Saharan African (SSA) countries and Sierra Leone, respectively. Sackey and Nkrumah (2012) used the Johansen cointegration analysis to assess the impact of financial sector development on the growth of the Ghanaian economy, and they concluded that the finance-growth nexus is positive. Ogunyiola (2013) explored the connection between bank development and growth in Cape Verde from 1980 to 2011, while Adu et al. (2013) examined the same nexus empirically in Ghana. The results for both studies were consistent with the first group of literature, confirming the positive effect of bank development on the real economy in the country under study. Samanhyia et al. (2014) also put the finance-growth nexus to the test, assessing the impact of bank development on the growth of the real sector in one country – Ghana. The results were mixed, some in support of positive impact and others in support of negative impact, depending on the measure of bank development used.

Other studies that attest to the positive finance-growth nexus include those conducted by Akinboade and Kinfack (2015) for South Africa, Puatwoe and Piabuo (2017) for Cameroon, Muazu and Alagidede (2018) in 29 SSA countries, Machado et al. (2021) in 36 SSA countries, Ncanywa and Mabusela (2019) in some of SSA, Haguiga and Amani (2019) for Algeria using panel data for 13 Algerian commercial banks, and An et al. (2020) in the upper middle-income sample and in the overall sample of 30 SSA countries, over the period from 1985 to 2015. Studies by Aluko and Ibrahim (2020) for SSA; Yusheng et al. (2020) in 32 SSA countries, and Ustarz and Fanta (2021) across sectors in SSA, were, in the main, consistent with the first group of empirical studies. However, the impact tended to vary depending on the financial institutions' level of development and the bank development measure used.

There are also studies on bank-based financial development and economic growth in Africa, which revealed that the impact of the former on the latter could be negative. Bolbol et al. (2005) confirmed this outcome in the case of Egypt using data from 1974 to 2002. Adu et al. (2013) found the same results in a study on Ghana, where bank-based financial development, when proxied by broad money stock-to-GDP ratio, exhibited negative growth effects on the real economy. Likewise, in the case of Ghana, Samanhyia et al. (2014) established that bank development has a negative impact on growth. Similar conclusions were reached by Puatwoe and Piabuo (2017) in the case of Cameroon, and by An et al. (2020) in 30 SSA countries, using dynamic and static panel data models and data from 1985 to 2015. On the contrary, the neutrality view within the context of Africa has found support from Ogunyiola (2013). The study examined the finance and growth link empirically, using data from 1980 to 2011 for Cape Verde, and found the link to be insignificant, however, in the short term.

Besides scholarly literature on the effects of intermediaries on the growth of the real sector specifically undertaken in African countries, there is also vast empirical evidence from other studies covering parts of the world other than Africa and, in some instances, inclusive of Africa or African countries. Although some of these studies are based on time-series data techniques, most of them are grounded on panel data methods. De Gregorio and Guidotti (1995), using panel data analysis for a big cross-country sample; Odedokun (1996), on the greater part of his 71 less-developed country sample; and Ahmed and Ansari (1998), in their sample of three countries in the southern part of Asia, found the development of the banking sector to be good for the growth of the economy. The same outcome was found by Christopoulos and Tsionas (2004), Nazmi (2005) in Latin America, Güryay et al. (2007) in Northern Cyprus, and Hassan et al. (2011). Yang (2019) tested how financial development impacts a nation's economic development positively among three income group economies. He concluded that the expansion of the banking sector contributes significantly to economic growth via the physical capital stock and total factor productivity channels. Meanwhile, Matei (2020) investigated both linear and non-linear relationships between finance and growth empirically in 11 emerging European countries using dynamic panel models during the period from 1995 to 2016. The findings validated the affirmative link between the two macroeconomic variables, although the outcome and its intensity tended to vary contingent on the measure of bank development employed.

Studies supporting the negative link that finance has with growth in other countries besides purely African countries include those by De Gregorio and Guidotti (1995) for Latin America, Odedokun (1996) in 15% of 71 less-developed economies, Petkovski and Kjosevski (2014) in 16 transition economies, and Nyasha and Odhiambo (2016) in the case of the UK. On the contrary, the neutrality view has also found empirical evidence in its support (Ram, 1999; Andersen & Tarp, 2003; Güryay et al., 2007).

Overall, the empirical literature reviewed has shown that Africa may not
be deficient in studies on the impact of bank development on growth, but
the available studies may be suffering from inconclusive outcomes, making
it difficult to use such studies for policy guidance purposes. The review of
empirical literature on this hotly debated topic has also revealed that whether
the studies are conducted on African or non-African countries, the results are
largely dependent on the proxy used for bank development, the developmental level of the economy under study, the analysis period, and the method of
analysis utilised.

Of all the measures and alternatives of bank development considered in
various studies, credit extension directed to the private sector has been found
consistently to have a desirable effect on the growth of the economy, except
in isolated cases. However, irrespective of the differences in methodological
approaches, the time frame of analysis, and the proxy of bank development
used, despite the availability of empirical evidence to lend support to the
three possible outcomes – positive, negative, and neutral – the conventional
wisdom, as revealed by these studies, emphasises that bank-based financial
development has a positive impact on economic growth.

8.3 Methodology

8.3.1 GMM Specification

Based on Asongu et al. (2019), Tchamyou et al. (2019a, 2019b), Asongu and
Odhiambo (2020), and Odhiambo (2020), the GMM model used in this
study can be presented as follows:

8.3.1.1 Variables in levels

$$y_{i,t} = \sigma_0 + \sigma_1 y_{i,t-\tau} + \sigma_2 FD_{i,t} + \sum_{h=1}^{4} \delta_h CV_{h,i,t-\tau} + \eta_i + \xi_t + \varepsilon_{i,t} \tag{8.1}$$

8.3.1.2 Variables in first difference

$$y_{i,t} - y_{i,t-\tau} = \sigma_1(y_{i,t-\tau} - y_{i,t-2\tau}) + \sigma_2(FD_{i,t} - FD_{i,t-\tau}) + \sum_{h=1}^{4} \delta_h(CV_{h,i,t-\tau}$$

$$-CV_{h,i,t-2\tau}) + \left(\xi_t - \xi_{t-\tau}\right) + \left(\varepsilon_{i,t} - \varepsilon_{i,t-\tau}\right) \tag{8.2}$$

where $y_{i,t}$ denotes economic growth of country i in period t; FD refers to the
four proxies of financial development, namely liquid liabilities (LL/GDP),
deposit money bank assets (DOMC/GDP), private credit to deposit money

banks and other financial institutions (PCD), and bank deposits (BD/GDP); CV refers to a vector of control variables, namely, interest rate, inflation, regulation, and trade; τ denotes the coefficient of auto-regression; $\hat{\imath}_t$ is the time-specific constant; η_i is the country-specific effect; $\acute{o}_0$ is a constant; and $\mathring{a}_{i,t}$ is the error term.

8.3.2 Identification and Exclusion Restrictions

Following Asongu and Odhiambo (2019), two procedures have been used to examine the impact of the various proxies of financial development on economic growth. While the GMM-style procedure has been used to estimate variables suspected to be endogenous, the 'ivstyle' − 'iv (years, eq (diff))' procedure has been used to address the time-invariant omitted variables. In addition, the endogeneity problem has been addressed by using the lagged regressors as instruments for forward-differenced variables. Consistent with previous studies, fixed effects, which may lead to biasness in the model, were removed using the Helmert transformation approach (see also Asongu and Nwachukwu, 2016; Asongu and De Moor, 2017). Likewise, the study also used the difference in the Hansen test (DHT) to test the validity of the exclusion restriction (see Asongu and Nwachukwu, 2016; Asongu and Odhiambo, 2019).

8.3.3 Data

The data for all the variables were obtained from the World Bank's World Development Indicators and the Financial Development and Structure Database. The definition of variables, data sources, and a priori expectations are presented in Table 8.1.

8.4 Empirical Analysis and Discussion

The results of the GMM model presented in Section 8.3 are reported in Table 8.2.

The empirical results reported in Table 8.2 show that the impact of banking sector development on economic growth in SSA is dependent on the variable used to measure banking sector development. While the impact of bank-based financial development on economic growth was found to be positive when bank-based financial development was measured by liquid liabilities, it was found to be statistically insignificant when proxied by the other three proxies, namely, deposit money bank assets, bank deposits, and private credit to deposit money banks and other financial institutions. Thus, an increase in liquid liabilities leads to an increase in economic growth. The positive impact of bank-based financial development (when measured by liquid liabilities) is supported by the coefficient of liquid liabilities in Model 1,

Table 8.1 Definitions of variables

Variables	Definitions of Variables (Measurements)	Expected Sign	Sources
Economic growth (y)	GDP per capita	N/A	World Development Indicators
Liquid liabilities (LL/GDP)	Liquid liabilities to GDP	(+)	Financial Development and Structure Data Base
Deposit money bank assets (DOMC/GDP)	Deposit money bank assets to GDP	(+)	Financial Development and Structure Data Base
Private credit to deposit money banks and other financial institutions PCD/GDP	Private credit to deposit money banks and other financial institutions (% of GDP)	(+)	Financial Development and Structure Data Base
Bank deposits (BD/GDP)	Bank deposits to GDP	(+)	Financial Development and Structure Data Base
Interest rate	Interest rate	(−)	World Development Indicators
Inflation	Inflation rate (CPI)	(−)	World Development Indicators
Regulation	Regulatory authority	(+) or (−)	World Governance Indicators
Trade	Exports + Imports (% of GDP)	(+)	World Governance Indicators

which has been found to be positive and statistically significant. Consistent with expectations, this outcome compares favourably with previous studies on the subject (see Hassan et al., 2011; Yang, 2019; Matei, 2020, among others).

Contrary to the liquid liabilities proxy, the empirical results show that private credit to deposit money banks and other financial institutions, deposit money bank assets, and bank deposits have no significant impact on economic growth in SSA. These findings, although contrary to our expectations, are consistent with some previous studies, such as those of Ram (1999) and Güryay et al. (2007).

The empirical results further show that interest rate has a positive impact on growth, while the impact of inflation on economic growth has been found to be negative and statistically significant. The results of these two variables

Table 8.2 Empirical results

	Dependent variable: Economic Growth[1]			
	Model 1 LL//GDP proxy	Model 2 DOMC/GDP proxy	Model 3 PCD/GDP proxy	Model 4 BD/GDP proxy
Constant	−80.5359★★★ (0.000)	−48.5029★★ (0.013)	−46.3136 (0.123)	−30.2158 (0.121)
LL/GDP	1.2309 ★★ (0.020)	– –	– –	– –
DOMC /GDP	–	0.6935 (0.202)	–	–
PCD/GDP	–	–	−1.2698 (0.435)	–
BD/GDP	–	–	–	−0.4392 (0.316)
Interest Rate	2.7986★★★ (0.001)	4.3038★★★ (0.000)	3.9545★★★ (0.000)	3.1155★★★ (0.000)
Inflation	−4.4308★★★ (0.000)	−5.5209★★★ (0.000)	−4.0834★★★ (0.000)	−3.8841★★★ (0.000)
Regulation	3.0190 (0.682)	35.3462★★★ (0.001)	78.5840★ (0.088)	58.6412★★★ (0.000)
Trade	0.2874 (0.121)	−0.0374 (0.881)	1.4991★★ (0.042)	0.7275★★★ (0.000)
Time Effects	Yes	Yes	Yes	Yes
AR (1)	0.347	0.363	0.353	0.353
AR (2)	0.627	0.681	0.602	0.629
Sargan OIR	0.000	0.017	0.002	0.000
Hansen OIR	0.440	0.764	0.488	0.810
DHT for instruments				
a) Instruments in levels				
H excluding group	0.212	0.320	0.189	0.229
Dif (null, H=exogenous)	0.592	0.883	0.648	0.952
b) IV (years, eq (diff))				
H excluding group	0.406	0.772	0.465	0.766
Dif (null, H=exogenous)	0.456	0.398	0.399	0.644
Fisher	35771.02★★★	81302.76★★★	46414.66★★★	168094.02★★★
Instruments	24	25	24	24
Countries	26	26	26	26
Observations	102	102	102	102

★, ★★, ★★★ denote statistical significance at 10%, 5% and 1%, respectively.
The lagged dependent variable was included in all models.

have been found to be consistent across all the four specifications irrespective of the proxy of bank-based financial development under consideration. However, regulation and trade had a mixed impact on economic growth, depending on the model under consideration.

While regulation was found to have a positive impact on economic growth in SSA, in Models 2–4, where bank-based financial development is measured by DOMC/GDP, PCD/GDP, and BD/GDP, its impact was insignificant in Model 1, where bank-banked financial development was proxied by LL/GDP. The coefficient of trade was also found to be positive and statistically significant in Models 3 and 4, but statistically insignificant in Models 1 and 2.

In order to examine the validity of the findings disclosed in Table 8.1, the study used four principal information criteria. These include AR(1), AR(2), Sargan OIR, and Hansen OIR. Based on these criteria, it can be concluded that the results reported in Table 8.2 are, on the whole, valid.

8.5 Conclusion

In this study, the relationship between banking sector development and economic growth is examined empirically in SSA using panel data from 26 countries during the period from 2013 to 2017. The study was motivated by the inconclusive findings on this subject, on the one hand, and the need for higher economic growth rates in Africa, prompting a detailed examination of any factors that could ameliorate growth prospects significantly for the continent or its regions, on the other hand. Unlike some previous studies for robustness, the current study uses four proxies of bank-based financial development, namely, private credit to deposit money banks and other financial institutions, deposit money bank assets, liquid liabilities, and bank deposits, thereby leading to four separate specifications for each growth model. In addition, four control variables, namely, interest rate, inflation, regulation, and trade, have been used. Using the GMM estimation techniques, the study found that the impact of bank-based financial development on economic growth is not unanimous across all the proxies used to measure the level of bank-based financial development. When liquid liabilities are used as a proxy for bank-based financial development, the results reveal that an increase in bank-based financial development leads to a rise in economic growth in SSA. However, when private credit to deposit money banks and other financial institutions, deposit money bank assets, and bank deposits are used as proxies, no significant impact of bank-based financial development on economic growth was found to exist. The insignificant impact of banking sector development on economic growth when measured by some proxies is not surprising, given the current quality of the financial sectors in some SSA countries. This finding is also consistent with previous studies, such as those by Ram (1999) and Güryay et al. (2007), who found and concluded that bank-based financial development does not affect economic growth significantly. Overall, the study found that only liquid liabilities promote economic growth in Africa. It is, therefore, recommended that African countries take cognisance of which bank-based financial development indicator to target as they draw up pro-growth policies.

References

Adu, G., Marbuah, G. and Mensah, JT. 2013. Financial development and economic growth in Ghana: Does the measure of financial development matter? *Review of Development Finance*, 3, 192–203. http://dx.doi.org/10.1016/j.rdf.2013.11.001

African Development Bank. 2021. African Economic Outlook. African Development Bank.

Agbetsiafa, D. 2004. The finance-growth nexus: Evidence from sub-Saharan Africa. *Savings and Development*, 28(3), 271–288.

Ahmed, SM. and Ansari, MI. 1998. Financial sector development and economic growth: The South-Asian experience. *Journal of Asian Economics*, 9(3), 503–517. http://dx.doi.org/10.1016/S1049-0078(99)80100-6

Akinboade, O. and Kinfack, EC. 2015. Financial development, economic growth and millennium development goals in South Africa: Is there a link? *International Journal of Social Economics*, 42, 459–479. http://dx.doi.org/10.1108/IJSE-01-2013-0006

Allen, DS. and Ndikumana, L. 2000. Financial intermediation and economic growth in Southern. *Journal of African Economics*, 9(2), 132–160. Africa. http://dx.doi.org/10.1093/jae/9.2.132

Aluko, OA. and Ibrahim, M. 2020. Institutions and the financial development–economic growth nexus in sub-Saharan Africa. *Economic Notes*, 49(3), e12163. https://doi.org/10.1111/ecno.12163

An, H., Zou, Q. and Kargbo, M. 2020. Impact of financial development on economic growth: Evidence from Sub-Saharan Africa. *Australian Economic Papers*, 60(2), 226–260, https://doi.org/10.1111/1467-8454.12201

Andersen, TB. and Tarp, F. 2003. Financial liberalization, financial development and economic growth. *Journal of International Development,* 15, 189–209.

Asongu, SA. and Nwachukwu, JC. 2016. The mobile phone in the diffusion of knowledge for institutional quality in sub-Saharan Africa. *World Development*, 86 (October), 133–147.

Asongu, SA. and De Moor, L. 2017. Financial globalisation dynamic thresholds for financial development: evidence from Africa. *European Journal of Development Research*, 29(1), 192–212.

Asongu, SA. and Odhiambo, NM. 2020. Economic development thresholds for a green economy in sub-Saharan Africa. *Energy Exploration and Exploitation*, 38(1), 3–17.

Asongu, S., Biekpe, N. and Tchamyou, V. (2019). Remittances, ICT and doing business in Sub-Saharan Africa. *Journal of Economic Studies*, Emerald Group Publishing Limited, 46(1), 35–54, January.

Bencivenga, VR. and Smith, BD. 1991. Financial Intermediation and endogenous growth. *Review of Economic Studies*, 58, 195–209. http://dx.doi.org/10.2307/2297964

Bolbol, A., Fatheldin, A. and Omran, M. 2005. Financial development, structure, and economic growth: The case of Egypt, 1974–2002. *Research in International Business and Finance*, 19(1), 171–194. https://doi.org/10.1016/j.ribaf.2004.10.008

Bouton, L. and Sumlinski, MA. 1998. Trends in private investment in developing countries. *International Finance Corporation, Discussion Paper Number 41*. The World Bank, Washington, DC. http://dx.doi.org/10.1596/0-8213-3874-9

Christopoulos, DK. and Tsionas, EG. 2004. Financial development and economic growth: Evidence from panel root and cointegration tests. *Journal of Development Economics*, 73, 55–74. http://dx.doi.org/10.1016/j.jdeveco.2003.03.002

De Gregorio, J. and Guidotti, PE. 1995. Financial development and economic growth. *World Development*, 23(3), 433–448. http://dx.doi.org/10.1016/0305-750X(94)00132-I

Güryay, E., Şafakli, OV. and Tüzel, B. 2007. Financial development and economic growth: Evidence from Northern Cyprus. *International Research Journal of Finance and Economics*, 8, 57–62.

Haguiga, M. and Amani, L. 2019. The impact of financial development on economic growth. *Journal of Applied Management and Investments*, 8(2), 107–116.

Hassan, KM., Sanchez, B. and Yu, J. 2011. Financial development and economic growth: New evidence from panel data. *The Quarterly Review of Economics and Finance*, 51, 88–104, http://dx.doi.org/10.1016/j.qref.2010.09.001

Iheonu, CO., Asongu, SA., Odo, KO. and Ojiem, PK. 2020. Financial sector development and Investment in selected countries of the Economic Community of West African States: empirical evidence using heterogeneous panel data method. *Financial Innovation*, 6(29), 1–15, https://doi.org/10.1186/s40854-020-00195-0

International Monetary Fund. 2016. *Financial Development in Sub-Saharan Africa*. International Monetary Fund, Washington, DC.

International Monetary Fund. 2021. *Regional Economic Outlook. Sub Saharan Africa*. International Monetary Fund, Washington, DC.

Kargbo, SM. and Adamu, PA. 2009. Financial development and economic growth in Sierra Leone. *West African Journal of Monetary and Economic Integration*, 9(2), 30–61.

Levine, R. 1997. Financial development and economic growth: Views and agenda. *Journal of Economic Literature*, 35, 688–726.

Levine, R. 2004. Finance and growth: Theory and evidence. *National Bureau of Economic Research*, Working Paper 10766. https://doi.org/10.3386/w10766

Machado, CMDC., Saraiva, AFMG. and Vieira, PDD. 2021. Finance-growth nexus in sub-Saharan Africa. *South African Journal of Economic and Management Sciences*, 24(1), a3435. https://doi.org/10.4102/sajems.v24i1.3435

Matei, I. 2020. Is financial development good for economic growth? Empirical insights from emerging European countries. *Quantitative Finance and Economics*, 4(4), 653–678. https://doi.org/10.3934/QFE.2020030

McKinnon, RI. 1973. *Money and Capital in Economic Development*. The Brookings Institution, Washington, DC.

Muazu, I. and Alagidede, I. 2018. Effect of financial development on economic growth in sub-Saharan Africa. *Journal of Policy Modeling*, 40(6), 1104–1125. http://dx.doi.org/10.1016/j.jpolmod.2018.08.001

Nazmi, N. 2005. Deregulation, financial deepening and economic growth: The case of Latin America. *The Quarterly Review of Economics and Finance*, 45(2–3), 447–459. https://doi.org/10.1016/j.qref.2004.12.014

Ncanywa, T. and Mabusela, K. 2019. Can financial development influence economic growth: The sub-Saharan analysis? *Journal of Economic and Financial Sciences*, 12(1), a194. https://doi.org/10.4102/jef.v12i1.194

Nyasha, S. and Odhiambo, NM. 2015. Financial development and economic growth in South Africa: An ARDL-Bounds testing approach to impact analysis. *Contemporary Economics*, 9(1), 93–108.

Nyasha, S. and Odhiambo, NM. 2016. The impact of bank-based and market-based financial development on economic growth: Time-series evidence from the United Kingdom. *Global Economy Journal*, 16(2), 389–410.

Nyasha, S. and Odhiambo, NM. 2018. Finance-growth nexus revisited: Empirical evidence from six countries. *Scientific Annals of Economics and Business*, 65(3), 247–268.

Odedokun, MO. 1996. Alternative econometric approaches for analysing the role of the financial sector in economic growth: Time-series evidence from LDCs. *Journal of Development Economics,* 50(1), 119–146. http://dx.doi.org/10.1016/0304-3878(96)00006-5

Odhiambo, NM. 2008. Financial depth, savings and economic growth in Kenya: A dynamic causal linkage. *Economic Modelling*, 25, 704–713. http://dx.doi.org/10.1016/j.econmod.2007.10.009

Odhiambo, NM. 2010. Finance-investment-growth nexus in South Africa: An ARDL-bounds testing procedure. *Economic Change and Restructuring,* 43(3), 205–219.

Odhiambo, NM. 2020. Financial Development, Income Inequality and Carbon Emissions in Sub-Saharan African Countries: A Panel Data Analysis. *Energy Exploration and Exploitation*, 38(5), 1914–1931. https://doi.org/10.1177/0144598720941999

Ogunyiola, A. 2013. Financial development and economic growth: The case of Cape Verde. MPRA Paper No. 49783.

Petkovski, M. and Kjosevski, J. 2014. Does banking sector development promote economic growth? An empirical analysis for selected countries in Central and South Eastern Europe. *Economic Research-Ekonomska Istraživanja*, 27(1), 55–66. http://dx.doi.org/10.1080/1331677X.2014.947107

Puatwoe, JT. and Piabuo, SM. 2017. Financial sector development and economic growth: evidence from Cameroon. *Financial Innovation*, 3(25), 2–18. http://dx.doi.org/10.1186/s40854-017-0073-x

Quah, D. 1993. Empirical cross-section dynamics in economic growth. *European Economic Review,* 37(2–3), 426–434.

Ram, R. 1999. Financial development and economic growth: Additional evidence. *Journal of Development Studies*, 35(4), 164–174. http://dx.doi.org/10.1080/00220389908422585

Sackey, FG. and Nkrumah, EM. 2012. Financial sector deepening and economic growth in Ghana. *Journal of Economics and Sustainable Development*, 3(8), 122–139.

Sahay, R., Cihak, M., N'Diaye, P. and Barajas, A. 2015. *Financial Inclusion: Can It Meet Multiple Macroeconomic Goals*? IMF Staff Discussion Note 15/17, International Monetary Fund, Washington, DC.

Samanhyia, S., Donbesuur, F. and Owusu-Ansah, I. 2014. financial development and economic growth in a post financial liberalization era in Ghana: Does the measure of financial development matter? *Journal of Economics and Sustainable Development*, 5(25), 51–59.

Sanusi, SL. 2011. Banks in Nigeria and national economic development – a critical review. *Bank for International Settlement*. [Online] Available from http://www.bis.org/review/r110323b.pdf [Accessed 08 January 2021].

Schumpeter, JA. 1911. The *Theory of Economic Development, An Inquiry into Profits, Capital, Credit, Interest, and the Business Cycle.* Harvard University Press Stern, Cambridge, 1989.

Shaw, ES. 1973. *Financial Deepening in Economic Development.* Oxford University Press, New York.

Tchamyou, VS., Erreygers, G. and Cassimon, D. 2019a. Inequality, ICT and financial access in Africa. *Technological Forecasting and Social Change* 139 (February), 169–184.

Tchamyou, VS., Asongu, SA. and Odhiambo, NM. 2019b. The role of ICT in modulating the effect of education and lifelong learning on income inequality and economic growth in Africa. *African Development Review* 31(3), 261–274.

Trehan, R. 2013. Market-based finance vs. bank-based finance. [Online] Available from http://www.prlog.org/10156113-market-based-finance-vs-bank-based-finance-robin-trehan.html [Accessed 02 May 2021].

Ustarz, U. and Fanta, AB. 2021. Financial development and economic growth in sub-Saharan Africa: A sectoral perspective. *Cogent Economics & Finance*, 9(1). http://dx.doi.org/10.1080/23322039.2021.1934976

Yang, F. 2019. The impact of financial development on economic growth in middle-income countries. *Journal of International Financial Markets, Institutions and Money*, 59, 74–89. https://doi.org/10.1016/j.intfin.2018.11.008

Yusheng, K., Bawuah, J., Nkwantabisa, AO., Atuahene, SOO. and Djan, GO. 2020. Financial development and economic growth: Empirical evidence from Sub-Saharan Africa. *International Journal of Finance & Economics*, 26(3), 3396–3416, https://doi.org/10.1002/ijfe.1967

Appendix

Appendix 8.1 Correlation Matrix

	Y	fin	domc	pcd	bd	lrate	inf	reg	trade
y	1.0000								
fin	0.4440	1.0000							
domc	0.4383	0.8270	1.0000						
pcd	0.2203	0.4848	0.8390	1.0000					
bd	0.4899	0.9108	0.9535	0.7200	1.0000				
lrate	−0.1437	−0.3551	−0.3287	−0.2560	−0.2765	1.0000			
inf	0.0722	−0.2669	−0.1301	−0.0973	−0.1319	0.5108	1.0000		
reg	0.1136	0.2204	0.4898	0.5161	0.4320	−0.1859	−0.0942	1.0000	
trade	0.3291	0.4005	0.2890	0.1477	0.4399	−0.0955	0.0110	0.1873	1.0000

9 Stock Market Development and Economic Growth in African Countries

Bosede Ngozi Adeleye, Nicholas Mbaya Odhiambo and Erasmus Larbi Owusu

9.1 Introduction

Continuous and sustained mobilization of resources is a prerequisite for economic growth and development. This process has long been the focus of many economists. To put it simply, for sustainable growth in any given economy, financial resources must be mobilized effectively and efficiently and allocated in a way to harness the synergies between human, material, and managerial resources for optimal economic output. The financial system of a country is, therefore, the framework within which capital formation takes place, and the stock market is one of the vehicles through which capital can be accumulated and channelled for effective economic growth across Africa. The stock markets do this by promoting efficient capital formation and allocation as a tool in the mobilization and allocation of savings among the competing choices, which are critical for economic growth; enabling governments and industry to raise long-term funds for new projects; and acting as an efficient capital allocator based on their rate of returns and level of risk (Owusu, 2016).

The role of the stock market in enhancing growth and development can be elucidated further through the argument that a well-functioning and efficient stock market system assists in lowering the costs of mobilizing investible financial resources and ensuring that they are allocated to high-yielding projects (Senbet, 2008). Studies have also shown that countries with more developed financial systems experience faster economic growth than countries with weak and shallow financial systems. This was evidenced by the East Asian countries in the 1970s and 1980s, where higher stock market capitalization was accompanied by higher economic growth (see Senbet, 2008).

Although a number of studies have been conducted on the impact of financial intermediaries on economic growth in a number of African countries, very few empirical studies exist on the role of stock market development on economic growth. This is mainly because many African stock markets are either underdeveloped or are still at a nascent stage. Some of the oldest stock exchanges in Africa include the Egyptian Exchange, which was established in 1883; Johannesburg Stock Exchange, which was established in 1887; Casablanca Stock Exchange (Morocco), which was established in

DOI: 10.4324/9781003215042-11

1929; Zimbabwe Stock Exchange, which was established in 1948; Nairobi Securities Exchange, which was founded in 1954, Nigerian Stock Exchange, which was established in 1960; Bourse de Tunis (Tunisia), which was established in 1969; and Stock Exchange of Mauritius, which was established in 1988, among others. In terms of the development of stock market size, South African Johannesburg remains the largest stock exchange in Africa. It is also one of the largest stock exchanges in the world in terms of stock market capitalization. With a total stock market capitalization of over USD1 trillion, South African stock market capitalization was ranked number 16 in the world in 2022. Other countries in the sub-Saharan region with notable stock markets in terms of total market capitalization include Nigeria, Kenya, Ghana, Ivory Coast, Tanzania, Mauritius, and Rwanda, among others.

In this chapter, the impact of stock market on economics in the selected sub-Saharan African countries is investigated during the period 2010–2017. Departing from some of the previous studies, the current study uses three proxies of stock market development, namely, (i) stock market capitalization as a percentage of GDP; (ii) the total value of stocks traded as a percentage of market capitalization; and (iii) the ratio of the value traded to market capitalization (turnover ratio). In addition, the studied countries were broadly divided into two groups, namely, (i) upper-middle-income countries (UMIC); and (ii) low-income and lower-middle-income countries combined (LI-LMIC). The merger of lower-middle-income and low-income countries was due to the lack of adequate data on stock market for many SSA countries. Indeed, out of 44 SSA countries, only 16 countries had a reasonable dataset on stock market that could be used in the current study. In order to address the weaknesses of some of the previous studies, the study used a wide range of estimation techniques to examine this linkage. Given the important role that governance plays in the finance-growth nexus, the study also examined the modulating impact of regulatory quality on the relationship between stock market and economic growth. For this purpose, the study computed interaction variables between stock market and regulation quality for each of the proxies of stock market development.

The rest of the chapter is structured as follows. Section 9.2 discusses the theoretical and empirical literature from across the African continent. Section 9.3 contains the methodology and analysis of the results. The last section contains the conclusions of the chapter.

9.2 Literature Review

The stock market brings up a multitude of markets and exchanges where regular interactions of buying, selling, and the discharge of shares take place. These activities are orchestrated in the form of institutionalized formal exchanges that can also be in the form of over-the-counter (OTC) marketplaces that function in terms of a well-defined set of rules. There are a variety of stock trading posts in a given country or region, where stock shares and other financial securities are sold and bought. More often than not, the terms 'stock market' and 'stock exchange' are used reciprocally. However, it must be understood that the former generally encompasses the latter (see Readthe-docs, n.d. and DalSpace, n.d.).

One may also consider the stock market as the sum of all the buyers and sellers of stocks, which designate ownership claims on businesses for which they have purchased the shares. These may include stocks that are traded pri-vately (such as shares of private companies) and the securities that are listed on a public stock exchange. Any investments in the stock market or exchange are principally conducted by way of stock brokerages and electronic trad-ing platforms. Stocks can be arranged by the country where the company is domiciled. Similarly, MTN Group Limited is domiciled in South Africa and traded on the Johannesburg Stock Exchange (JSE), so they may be considered to be part of the South African stock market, although the stocks are also traded on other exchanges such as the Ghana Stock Exchange (GSE).

Bekaert and Harvey (1995) are of the view that, firstly stock market devel-opment leads to an increase in international capital inflow, hence culmi-nating in a lower cost of capital. Secondly, it allows for risk diversification. In addition it stimulates investment in projects with higher returns, and it brings about the integration of the country's stock market into the world financial system with the ultimate benefits of economic growth. According to the endogenous growth literature, contemporary theoretical studies have engrossed on the links between the stock market development and endoge-nous growth models.

Other researchers like Bencivenga and Smith (1991) and Levine (1991) were among the pioneers who advanced the endogenous growth models to ascertain the channels through which stock markets may affect long-run eco-nomic growth. They highlighted that stock markets help to variegate the liquidity and investment risk of agents. Furthermore, they rationalized that it succours in pulling more savings into productive investment and prevents the early exodus of capital sunk in long-run projects. King and Levine (1993) also advocated another approach to identifying the channel of transference between financial markets and economic growth. Thus, financial markets assist in the function of efficient resource allocation. As a consequence, in an economy with efficient and well-functioning financial markets, there will be an elevated productivity growth rate (Owusu, 2016, 2018). In a 21st-century economy, banks and stock markets represent a major part of the financial system. Although they may accomplish different roles in the process of eco-nomic development and growth, their unrivalled characteristics can hardly be underestimated within the parameters of economic growth (Owusu, 2018).

Over the last few years, extensive empirical studies have been conducted on the dynamic relationship between stock market development and economic growth in many developing markets including African countries but with mixed results. For example, Quinn and Toyoda (2008) tested whether stock market development results in economic growth based on pooled time-series data from 93 developed and developing countries. The findings indicate that stock market developments have a positive connection or link with economic growth in both developed and emerging economies (Owusu, 2018).

Eita and Jordaan (2010) also dissected the causal relationship between financial development and economic growth in Botswana using yearly data from 1977 to 2006, applying Granger causality and co-integrated vector auto-regression methods and engaging these methods on two proxies for financial development. They discovered that there is a stable long-run relationship between stock market development and economic growth, heedless of which proxy for stock market development indicator is used. Furthermore, Owusu and Odhiambo (2014) utilized the ARDL-bounds testing approach and multidimensional stock market development proxies to investigate this linkage in Ghana. The findings of this investigation support the myriad of past studies, which have reported negative or inconclusive results in relation to the impact of stock market development on economic growth. They conclude, however, that it is rather the increase in credit to the private sector and not stock market development that spurs the real sector development in Ghana.

Moreover, Nyasha and Odhiambo (2015a and 2015b) scrutinized the dynamic causal relationship connecting bank-based financial development, stock market development, and economic growth in South Africa between 1980 and 2012, making use of a multivariate Granger causality model. Their results showed that there is a distinct unidirectional causal flow from stock market development to economic growth in the short run and in the long run in South Africa. The findings furthermore revealed that there is a unidirectional causality from bank-based financial development to stock market development in the short run. They surmised that there is a bond connecting stock market development and economic growth in South Africa.

Furthermore, Owusu (2016) studied the linkage between stock market advancement and sustainable economic growth in Nigeria, deploying the Auto-Regressive Distributed Lag (ARDL)-bounds testing approach and a constructed combined stock market indicator index to investigate the relationship. His research found that in the long run, stock market developments have no positive and, to a certain degree, inconclusive effect on economic growth in Nigeria.

Finally, Osakwe and Ananwude (2017) inquired about the short-run and long-run connectional linkage between stock market development and economic growth in Nigeria, as well as in South Africa from 1981 to 2015, using the ARDL co-integration methodology. They discovered that there is a long-run relationship allying stock market development and economic growth in the case of Nigeria, but that it was not the case in South Africa. They probed further using Granger causality and came to another conclusion that economic growth in South Africa is significantly affected by stock market capitalization, but that the same was not true in Nigeria. Their conclusion detected some support for the theory in Nigeria, but not in South Africa.

As can be seen from the available literature, the empirical results from many African countries may suggest that the linkage between stock market development and economic growth is at best inconclusive. This chapter uses the gross domestic product (GDP) as a proxy for economic growth and engages a multidimensional approach to interrogate the dynamics between stock market development and economic growth nexus in Africa, as elucidated in the following sections.

9.3 Variables, Methodology, and Empirical Analysis

9.3.1 *Variable Description and Expectations*

The chapter uses the gross domestic product (*GDP*) as the proxy for economic growth and engages a multidimensional approach to interrogate the market-growth nexus with the following indicators of capital market: (1) stock market capitalization as a % of GDP, which measures the size of the stock market, and its ability to mobilize funds and diversify risk; (2) total value of stocks traded as a % of market capitalization (*MKTVL*); and (3) the ratio of the value traded to market capitalization (turnover ratio), which captures trading relative to the stock market size (*MKTOVR*). Other control variables used are as follows: liquid liabilities (*LIQL*), which reflects financial liquidity required for stock trading; the inflation rate (*INFL*), which is included to capture macroeconomic fluctuations that may erode purchasing power causing a drag on the economy; and exchange rate (*EXR*), which is another macroeconomic variable that measures a country's competitiveness. It is measured by the exchange rate between the currency of a country and the US dollar. *Ceteris paribus* also determines the extent of capital inflows to the economy to boost development; and mobile subscription (*MOB*), which is the proxy for information technology to capture technology infusion in the economy. This chapter further probes the market-growth nexus to appraise if effective and strong regulatory institutions moderate the impact of the stock market on economic growth in Africa. We use regulatory quality *(RQ)* whose values range from −2.5 to 2.5 as the indicator of effective institutions. A value of −2.5 implies weak regulation, while 2.5 connotes strong regulation. In order words, we interact regulatory quality with each market proxy to weigh this nexus. The variables are sourced from World Development Indicators (WDI), World Bank Financial Structure Database (WBFSD), and World Governance Indicators (WGI).

On *a priori* expectations, an increase in stock market capitalization, the value of traded shares, and stock turnover will have a positive impact on the economy. Ditto, a regulated stock market, instils some level of confidence in market operations giving investors and shareholders the assurance to engage in stock trading activities with the attendant positive impact on economic growth. The expansion of liquid liabilities allows investors to engage in real and financial activities causing economic growth. Inflation may exert a negative impact on growth, while the exchange rate may boost or cause a lull in a trade depending on the structure of the economy. For instance, depreciation

Table 9.1 Variable description, expectations, and sources

Variables	Description	Expectations	Source
GDP	Gross domestic product	NA	WDI (2020)
MKTCAP	Market capitalization	+	WBFSD (2020)
MKTVL	The market value of shares	+	WBFSD (2020)
MKTOVR	Shares turnover	+	WBFSD (2020)
RQ	Regulatory quality	+	WGI (2020)
LIQL	Liquid liabilities (% of GDP)	+	WBFSD (2020)
INFL	Inflation rate	–	WDI (2020)
EXR	Official exchange rate	+/–	WDI (2020)
MOB	Mobile phone subscription	+	WDI (2020)

Source: Authors' compilations.

Note: WDI = World Development Indicators; WBFSD = World Bank Financial Structure Database; WGI = World Governance Indicators.

of the exchange rate (negative sign) can support economic growth (depending upon whether the country is a net exporter or importer). With mobile technology, economic activities which transcend the physical movement of goods and services are expected to increase since local and foreign transactions can be conducted within the comfort of homes and offices. In addition, up-to-date stock market information (such as share prices and volume traded) is delivered to investors and shareholders via mobile phones, which allows for informed decision making. Lastly, the interaction of stock market indicators with regulatory quality is expected to be favourable to enhance the *total* impact of stock market development on economic growth. Table 9.1 details the variables, description, expectations, and sources.

9.3.2 Methodology and Empirical Model

The methodology involves an unbalanced panel of 16 African countries whose inclusion is subject to having sufficient data on the variables of interest. The approach examines the market–growth nexus post-global financial crises; hence, the scope is from 2010 to 2017 with the following objectives: (1) to investigate the impact of each stock market indicator on economic growth; (2) to examine whether regulatory quality moderates the market–growth dynamics; and (3) to examine whether the respective impact under examination differs by income classification of countries. The recently published World Bank (2020),[1] World Bank Country and Lending Groups, classified countries into income groups based on gross national income (GNI) per capita. To facilitate income group analysis, we adopt this categorization such that our sample has lower middle income[2] (11) and upper middle income (5). Appendix Table 9.1A provides details of these countries and income groups. The income classification permits for examining whether the outcomes vary among income groups, leading to more specific policies and recommendations for each group.

To address the question of whether stock market development has a significant impact on economic growth and whether its impact is swayed by the quality of institutions, this paper adopts the empirical approach of Lakshmi, Saha, and Bhattarai (2021), Adusei and Adeleye (2020), and Adusei and Adeleye (2021) and specifies economic growth as a linear function of the stock market (*MKTCAP, MKTVL, MKTOVR*), regulatory quality, and other control variables. The market-institutions nexus is represented by the interaction of each stock market indicator and regulatory quality. The explicit form of the model is specified as:

$$\ln GDP_{it} = \xi_0 + \xi_1 \ln SM'_{it} + \xi_2 RQ_{it} \\ + \xi_3 \ln(SM \star RQ)_{it} + \xi_4 Z'_{it} + \lambda_t + e_{it} \tag{9.1}$$

where ln is natural logarithm; economic growth is proxied by gross domestic product (GDP); $\ln SM_{it}$ is each stock market indicator (*MKTCAP, MKTVL, MKTOVR*); RQ_{it} is regulatory quality; Z'_{it} is the vector of control variables (liquid liabilities, inflation rate, exchange rate, and mobile phone subscriptions); λ_t represents year dummies (which controls for variation of the dependent variable); and e_{it} is the general error term. Equation (9.1) is estimated for the full sample of 16 countries. However, in evaluating the RQ-SM-EG nexus, it becomes intrinsic to appraise this relationship alongside income classification – lower-middle- and upper-middle-income groups. Hence, the full sample is split into two sub-samples.

One of the contributions of this chapter hinges on the sign and statistical significance of ξ_3, which captures the moderation impact of regulatory quality on the stock market such that the impact of the stock market on economic growth will vary at different levels of regulatory quality. Hence, the *net* effect of stock market development on economic growth in the presence of effective regulation[3] is computed as:

$$\frac{\partial \ln GDP}{\partial \ln SM} = \xi_1 + \xi_3 RQ \tag{9.2}$$

Note, if the interaction term is positive, then equation (9.2) implies that a percentage change in stock market development yields a positive impact on economic growth as the degree of regulatory quality improves. In other words, extensive capital market activities boost economic growth as regulatory quality improves. But if the interaction term is negative, then the overall impact of stock market development on economic growth is contingent on the magnitude of weak regulations. In essence, if weakened regulatory quality prevails, then regulation distorts the impact of stock market development on economic growth. However, if no interaction effect exists, it is an indication that regulatory quality does not influence the market-growth nexus. Finally, to test the robustness of our results, financial system deposits (% of GDP) is used in place of liquid liabilities. To address the objectives of the chapter and estimate equation (9.1), the panel spatial correlation consistent (PSCC) technique for linear panel models is deployed. This technique eliminates the fixed effects and controls for other issues affecting panel data analysis, such as cross-sectional dependence, autocorrelation, and heteroscedasticity. In addition, it uses the Driscoll and Kraay (1998) robust standard error technique to compute correlation consistent standard errors that are robust to disturbances being heteroscedastic and auto-correlated and cross-sectionally dependent.

9.4 Results and Implications

9.4.1 Summary Statistics and Correlation Analysis

We begin by exploring the historical statistics of the essential variables. The upper panel of Table 9.2 details the summary statistics. It reveals that average growth is USD105 billion with the lowest value of USD6.9 billion (from Malawi in 2010) and the highest value of USD464 billion (from Nigeria in 2015). South Africa was shown to have the most developed capital market with the highest values across the three indicators (market capitalization, value, and turnover) recorded in the year 2018, 2017, and 2016, respectively, while the least developed markets are in Algeria (for market capitalization in 2010) and Uganda (for market value and turnover in the year 2010 and 2012). On the strength of institutions, the mean value of −0.248 is a reflection of weak institutions in Africa. From the sample, the country with the most effective regulatory control is Mauritius with 1.127 recorded in 2014, while Algeria has the most weakened institutions with −1.283 in 2014. It is interesting to see that the standard deviation of 0.534 indicates that the countries hover around the sample mean. In other words, most exhibit weak regulatory quality.

The lower panel of Table 9.2 displays the relative association between the variables. Concerning economic growth, the correlation shows that market value and turnover have a positive, strong, and statistically significant relationship at the 1% level, while the correlation with market capitalization is negative, weak, and statistically not significant. Regulatory quality shows a significant negative association at 1% suggesting an inverse relation with growth. Since correlation only quantifies the strength of the linear relationship between a pair of variables, it becomes imperative to investigate these relationships further with econometric analysis to evaluate the impact of a change in each explanatory variable on economic growth.

9.4.2 Main Results for Full Sample and Income Groups

Controlling for year dummies, liquid liabilities, inflation rate, exchange rate, mobile phone subscriptions, and the quality of institutions, the main results shown in Table 9.3 reveal that on aggregate (see columns 1, 4, and 7), the stock market exerts statistically insignificant impact on economic growth. This is contrary to expectations and a departure from previous

Table 9.2 Summary statistics and correlation analysis

Variables	GDP	MKTCAP	MKTVL	MKTOVR	LIQL	INFL	EXR	RQ	MOB
Observations	128	90	82	76	127	128	128	128	128
Mean	1.05E+11	44.958	9.473	10.871	45.968	7.382	375.365	−0.248	95.786
Std. deviation	1.34E+11	67.907	23.276	11.911	25.954	5.537	785.05	0.537	33.938
Minimum	6.96E+09	0.06	0.048	0.157	13.768	0.442	1.408	−1.283	21.44
Maximum	4.64E+11	328.361	123.245	50.346	110.812	29.507	3611.224	1.127	163.875
Variables	[1]	[2]	[3]	[4]	[5]	[6]	[7]	[8]	[9]
(1) lnGDP	1.000								
(2) lnMKTCAP	−0.098	1.000							
(3) lnMKTVL	0.557★★★	0.810★★★	1.000						
(4) lnMKTOVR	0.668★★★	0.419★★★	0.831★★★	1.000					
(5) lnLIQL	0.134	0.038	0.540★★★	0.400★★★	1.000				
(6) INFL	−0.007	−0.129	−0.229★★★	0.045	−0.373★★★	1.000			
(7) EXR	−0.133	−0.054	−0.508★★★	−0.617★★★	−0.538★★★	0.024	1.000		
(8) RQ	−0.34★★★	0.675★★★	0.305★★★	0.002	0.286★★★	−0.31★★★	−0.115	1.000	
(9) lnMOB	0.271★★★	0.176★	0.613★★★	0.482★★★	0.688★★★	−0.452★★★	−0.462★★★	0.442★★★	1.000

Source: Authors' computations.

Note: ★★★ $p < 0.01$, ★★ $p < 0.05$, and ★ $p < 0.1$; ln = natural logarithm; GDP = gross domestic product; MKTCAP = market capitalization; MKTVL = market value; MKTOVR = market turnover; LIQL = liquid liabilities; INFL = inflation rate; EXR = official exchange rate; RQ = regulatory quality; MOB = mobile phone subscribers; 1.05E+11 = 105,000,000,000.00.

studies (Ngare, Nyamongo, & Misati, 2014; Nyasha & Odhiambo, 2016; Owusu, 2016; Bundoo, 2017; Mensah & Alagidede, 2017; Mitra, 2017; Nyasha & Odhiambo, 2019). However, a disaggregation of the sample into lower-middle- and upper-middle-income countries reveals diverse and interesting results. For instance, a percentage increase in market capitalization in lower-middle-income countries results in a 0.98% increase in economic growth, while growth increases by 1.15% in upper-middle countries. Similarly, the impact on growth from an increase in market value is higher in lower-middle-income countries (0.73%) relative to upper-middle-income countries (0.68%). On market turnover, the impact on growth is not significantly different from zero in lower-middle-income countries, while growth is enhanced by 1.61% in upper-middle-income countries. Overall, given the clear disparities in these outcomes, we submit that income classification matters in appraising the market-growth nexus. This is because aggregation will lead to making wrong and erroneous inferences on the impact of stock market development on growth in Africa.

Next, we highlight the marginal effect of regulatory quality on growth. For the full sample, an improvement in regulatory quality shows to exert a positive and statistically significant impact at the 1% and 5% levels, respectively. It shows that Africa's economy grows by 0.0758, 0.110, and 0.212 percentage points when the quality of institutions improves. These outcomes align with *a priori* expectations and related studies (Gazdar & Cherif, 2014; Adeleye, Osabuohien, & Bowale, 2017; Lakshmi *et al.*, 2021). However, regulatory quality shows a disproportionate impact on growth relative to the market indicator and when countries are classified into income groups. For market capitalization, it reduces economic growth in lower-middle-income countries (−9.581) by a higher magnitude compared to upper-middle-income countries (−4.843). For market value, its impact is not significant in lower-middle-income countries but reduces growth by −1.106 in upper-middle-income countries. Lastly, while it boosts growth by 0.832 percentage points for market turnover in lower-middle-income countries, it reduces the same by −3.395 percentage points in upper-middle-income countries.

The overall impact of stock market development on economic growth is contingent on the level of regulatory quality. Bringing equation (9.2) into context, this is captured by the coefficients of the interaction term. We adopt the computations of Brambor, Clark, and Golder (2006) and Asongu and Nwachukwu (2018), but rather than evaluating the overall impact of the stock market at the mean values of regulatory quality, we expand the frontiers of knowledge to gauge the influence at the mean, minimum, and maximum values of regulatory quality. The results displayed in Table 9.4 reveal that the overall impact of market capitalization on growth is negative at the mean[4] and minimum values of regulatory quality, but it improves growth when regulation improves or is at its peak. The same pattern is observed in lower-middle-income countries, while regulation improves market impact in upper-middle-income countries.

Table 9.3 Full sample and income group results: main analysis

Variables	Market Capitalization			Market Value			Market Turnover		
	Full [1]	LMI [2]	UMI [3]	Full [4]	LMI [5]	UMI [6]	Full [7]	LMI [8]	UMI [9]
lnLIQL	−0.0861★★ (−2.874)	−0.579★★★ (−3.855)	−0.185 (−0.349)	−0.0621★★ (−2.174)	−1.689★★★ (−4.230)	2.066★★ (3.834)	−0.0658★ (−1.961)	−0.812★★ (−2.680)	3.953 (2.286)
INFL	0.000759 (0.441)	0.0731★★★ (3.707)	−0.144★★ (−3.135)	0.000446 (0.232)	0.0580★★ (2.897)	−0.0646 (−1.344)	0.000105 (0.0757)	0.0103 (0.512)	−0.304★★★ (−8.391)
EXR	8.18e−05 (0.849)	−0.000169★ (−2.197)	0.0161★★ (3.384)	9.48e−05 (0.923)	0.000354★★ (2.980)	−0.118★★★ (−6.598)	0.000141★ (1.843)	0.000314★ (1.861)	−0.0910★ (−2.383)
RQ	0.0758★★ (2.293)	−9.581★★★ (−14.09)	−4.843★★★ (−11.46)	0.110★★ (2.176)	−0.345 (−1.778)	−1.106★★ (−3.248)	0.212★★★ (5.027)	0.832★ (1.838)	−3.395★★ (−3.761)
lnMOB	0.0407★ (2.051)	2.467★★★ (5.775)	3.102★★ (3.982)	0.0486★★ (2.525)	2.055★★★ (5.225)	1.076 (1.944)	0.0338★★★ (3.122)	1.459★★★ (5.326)	7.819★★ (4.131)
lnMKTCAP	0.00347 (0.267)	0.976★★★ (10.91)	1.148★★★ (26.46)						
lnMKTCAP★RQ	0.0180★ (2.048)	3.062★★★ (16.39)	0.457★★★ (11.62)						
lnMKTVL				0.00569 (0.312)	0.733★★★ (5.597)	0.677★★★ (9.067)			
lnMKTVL★RQ				0.00259 (0.137)	0.0340 (0.220)	0.357 (1.535)			
lnMKTOVR							−0.00169 (−0.166)	0.380 (1.568)	1.605★★ (4.289)
lnMKTOVR★RQ							−0.0417★★ (−2.736)	−0.671 (−1.658)	0.446 (0.745)

Variables	Market Capitalization			Market Value			Market Turnover		
	Full [1]	LMI [2]	UMI [3]	Full [4]	LMI [5]	UMI [6]	Full [7]	LMI [8]	UMI [9]
Constant	24.88***	12.95***	7.814	24.69***	21.58***	12.14*	24.80***	20.58***	−26.98
	(135.9)	(9.717)	(1.379)	(139.2)	(13.52)	(2.861)	(188.6)	(13.08)	(−1.805)
Year dummies	Yes	Yes	Yes	Yes	Yes	Yes	Yes	Yes	Yes
Observations	90	55	35	82	58	24	76	52	24
R-squared		0.693	0.973		0.676	0.997		0.649	0.986
Countries	16	11	5	15	11	4	15	11	4
F-Statistics	5409	86460	5407	19897	17010	6.327e+06	1255	21784	1687

Source: Authors' computations.

Note: $*** \, p < 0.01$, $** \, p < 0.05$, and $* \, p < 0.1$; ln = natural logarithm; GDP = gross domestic product; MKTCAP = market capitalization; LIQL = liquid liabilities; INFL = inflation rate; EXR = official exchange rate; RQ = regulatory quality; MOB = mobile phone subscribers; LMI = lower middle income; UMI = upper middle income.

Table 9.4 Computation of the overall impact of stock market development on economic growth

Variables	Market Capitalization			Market Value			Market Turnover		
	Full [1]	LMI [2]	UMI [3]	Full [4]	LMI [5]	UMI [6]	Full [7]	LMI [8]	UMI [9]
Mean of RQ	−0.00446	−0.29687	1.203663	0	0.733	0.677	0.010342	0	1.605
Minimum of RQ	−0.02309	−1.85941	0.561669	0	0.733	0.677	0.053501	0	1.605
Maximum of RQ	0.020286	1.367936	1.663039	0	0.733	0.677	−0.047	0	1.605

Source: Authors' computations.

Note: RQ = regulatory quality.

For stock market value, the interaction with regulatory quality is statistically not significant across all models such that the market has no impact on economic growth for the full sample, while its impact across the income groups equates to its marginal impact on growth.[5] The overall impact of market values on growth is positive at the mean and minimum values of regulation but declines as regulatory quality are at its peak, while it has no impact in lower-middle-income and the impact in upper-middle-income countries equates to its marginal impact. Robustness checks using financial system deposits (see Appendix Table 9.1B) produced similar outcomes.

9.5 Conclusion

The motivation for the chapter hinges on the quest to test whether different indicators of the stock market have a similar or contradicting effect on economic growth given the presence of strong and effective institutions, which is a lacuna in the current literature. Using an unbalanced panel data of 16 African countries from 2010 to 2017, this chapter investigates the impact of stock market development on economic growth and probes further on whether regulatory quality improves the market-growth nexus. To harness the distinct heterogeneity in the data, the countries are grouped into two: lower-middle- and upper-middle-income countries. The chapter uses the gross domestic product as the proxy for economic growth; three indicators of the stock market, namely, (1) stock market capitalization as a % of GDP, (2) total value of stocks traded as a % of market capitalization, and (3) the ratio of the value traded to market capitalization (turnover ratio); and regulatory proxy to measure effective institutions.

From the full sample, the statistically insignificant results indicate that using an aggregated sample will not convey the true relationship between the stock market and growth in Africa. However, disaggregation into income groups visibly shows that for the most part, the stock market is a significant and positive predictor of economic growth. These outcomes lend credence to engaging an income group analysis. Also, the outcome of market-regulatory quality interaction depends on the market proxy used. Across the three models (full and sub-samples), the interaction is positive and significant with market capitalization, not different from zero using market value, and significantly negative using market turnover. Overall, we find that the market-growth nexus is contingent on the level of effective institutions. Subsequent research may further interrogate the institutions-market-growth dynamics using all the governance indicators to observe if the outcomes obtained in this chapter hold.

Notes

1 See https://datahelpdesk.worldbank.org/knowledgebase/articles/906519-world-bank-country-and-lending-groups
2 Given the small sample of low-income countries (Malawi, Tanzania, and Uganda), which made comparative analysis ineffective due to a significant loss

of observations, we reclassified the three countries as lower-middle-income countries.

3 For the full sample, net effect can be computed at the mean (−0.248), minimum (−1.283), or maximum values (1.127) of regulatory quality: lower middle income: −0.4157, −0.926, and 0.128; and for Upper middle income: 0.122, −1.283, and 1.127, respectively.

4 Overall impact = 0 + (0.018 × −0.248) = −0.00446. A coefficient that is statistically not significant is *not* significantly different from zero because its explanatory power is zero. Hence, the value 0 is assigned to such.

5 Since the interaction term is statistically not significant, the moderating impact of regulatory quality on the market-growth nexus is zero. Hence, the overall impact equates to the marginal impact.

References

Adeleye, N., Osabuohien, E., & Bowale, E. (2017). The Role of Institutions in the Finance-Inequality Nexus in Sub-Saharan Africa. *Journal of Contextual Economics - Schmollers Jahrbuch, 137*(1–2), 173–192.

Adusei, M., & Adeleye, N. (2020). Credit Information Sharing and Non-Performing Loans: The Moderating Role of Creditor Rights Protection. *International Journal of Finance and Economics*, 1–14. doi:10.1002/ijfe.2398

Adusei, M., & Adeleye, N. (2021). Corporate Disclosure and Credit Market Development. *Journal of Applied Economics, 24*(1), 205–230. doi:10.1080/15140326.2021.1901644

Asongu, S. A., & Nwachukwu, J. C. (2018). Openness, ICT and Entrepreneurship in Sub-Saharan Africa. *Information Technology & People, 31*(1), 278–303.

Bekaert, G., & Harvey, C. (1995). Market Integration and Investment Barriers in Emerging Equity Markets. *World Bank Economic Review, 9*(1), 75–107.

Bencivenga, V. R., & Smith, B.D. (1991). Financial Intermediation and Endogenous Growth. *Review of Economic Studies, 58*, 195–209.

Brambor, T., Clark, W. M., & Golder, M. (2006). Understanding Interaction Models: Improving Empirical Analyses. *Political Analysis, 14*(1), 63–82.

Bundoo, S. K. (2017). Stock Market Development and Integration in SADC (Southern African Development Community). *Review of Development Finance, 7*(1), 64–72. doi:10.1016/j.rdf.2017.01.005

DalSpace (n.d.). Available at DalSpace.library.dal.ca [Accessed 2 May 2022].

Driscoll, J. C., & Kraay, A. C. (1998). Consistent Covariance Matrix Estimation with Spatially Dependent Panel Data. *Review of Economics and Statistics, 80*, 549–560.

Eita, J. H., & Jordaan, A. C. (2010). A Causality Analysis between Financial Development and Economic Growth for Botswana. *The African Finance Journal, 12*(1), 72–89.

Gazdar, K., & Cherif, M. (2014). The Quality of Institutions and Financial Development in MENA Countries: An Empirical Investigation. *Risk Governance & Control: Financial Markets & Institutions, 4*(4), 1–16.

King, R. G., & Levine, R. (1993). Finance and Growth: Schumpeter Might Be Right. *Quantitative Journal of Economics., 108*, 717–737.

Lakshmi, G., Saha, S., & Bhattarai, K. (2021). Does Corruption Matter for Stock Markets? The Role of Heterogeneous Institutions. *Economic Modeling, 94*, 386–400. doi:10.1016/j.econmod.2020.10.011

Levine, R. (1991). Stock Markets. *Growth and Tax Policy Journal of Finance, 64*, 1445–1465.

Mensah, J. O., & Alagidede, P. (2017). How Are Africa's Emerging Stock Markets Related to Advanced Markets? Evidence from Copulas. *Economic Modelling, 60,* 1–10. doi:10.1016/j.econmod.2016.08.022

Mitra, R. (2017). Stock Market and Foreign Exchange Market Integration in South Africa. *World Development Perspectives, 6,* 32–34. doi:10.1016/j.wdp.2017.05.001

Ngare, E., Nyamongo, E. M., & Misati, R. N. (2014). Stock Market Development and Economic Growth in Africa. *Journal of Economics and Business, 74,* 24–39. doi:10.1016/j.jeconbus.2014.03.002

Nyasha, S., & Odhiambo, N. M. (2015a). The Impact of Banks and Stock Market Development on Economic Growth in South Africa: An ARDL-Bounds Testing Approach. *Contemporary Economics, 9*(1), 93–108.

Nyasha, S., & Odhiambo, N. M. (2015b). Banks, Stock Market Development and Economic Growth in South Africa: AMultivariate Causal Linkage. *Applied Economics Letters, 22*(18), 1480–1485. doi:10.1080/13504851.2015.1042132

Nyasha, S., & Odhiambo, N.M. (2016). Banks, Stock Market Development and Economic Growth in Kenya: An Empirical Investigation. *Journal of African Business, 18*(1), 1–23. doi:10.1080/15228916.2016.1216232

Nyasha, S., & Odhiambo, N. M. (2019). Do Financial Systems Spur Economic Growth in the USA? An Empirical Investigation. *Panoeconomicus, 66*(2), 165–185. doi:10.2298/pan160517012n

Osakwe, C. I. & Ananwude, A. C. (2017). Stock Market Development and Economic Growth: A Comparative Evidence from two Emerging Economies in Africa – Nigeria and South Africa. *Archives of Current Research International, 11*(1), 1–15.

Owusu, E. L. (2016). Stock Market and Sustainable Economic Growth in Nigeria. *Economies* MPDI, *4*(25). doi:10.3390/economies4040025

Owusu, E. L. (2018). Stock Market Development and Economic Growth: New Evidence from South Africa. *Open Journal of Economics and Commerce, 1*(2), 42–52.

Owusu, E. L & Odhiambo, N. M. (2014). Stock Market Developments and Economic Growth in Ghana: An ARDL-Bound Testing Approach. *Applied Economics Letter, 21*(4), 229–234. http://www.tandfonline.com/doi/abs/10.1080/13504851.2 013.844315#.UpoAr8xFDGg

Quinn, D. P. & Toyoda, A. M. (2008). Does Capital Account Liberalization Lead to Growth? *The Review of Financial Studies, 21*(3), 1403–1449.

Readthedocs (n.d.). Available at readthedocs.org. [Accessed 2 May 2022].

Appendixes

Appendix 9.1A List of Countries and Classifications

S/No.	Country	Region	Income Group
1	Algeria	North Africa	Upper middle income
2	Botswana	Southern Africa	Upper middle income
3	Cote d'Ivoire	West Africa	Lower middle income
4	Egypt, Arab Rep.	North Africa	Lower middle income
5	Ghana	West Africa	Lower middle income
6	Kenya	East Africa	Lower middle income
7	Malawi	East Africa	Lower middle income
8	Mauritius	East Africa	Upper middle income
9	Morocco	North Africa	Lower middle income
10	Namibia	Southern Africa	Upper middle income
11	Nigeria	West Africa	Lower middle income
12	South Africa	Southern Africa	Upper middle income
13	Tanzania	East Africa	Lower middle income
14	Tunisia	North Africa	Lower middle income
15	Uganda	East Africa	Lower middle income
16	Zambia	East Africa	Lower middle income

Source: Authors' compilation.

Appendix 9.1B Full Sample and Income Group Results: Robustness Analysis

Variables	Market Capitalization			Market Value			Market Turnover		
	Full	LMI	UMI	Full	LMI	UMI	Full	LMI	UMI
lnFSD	0.0263 (0.350)	−0.551★★ (−2.684)	0.804 (1.988)	0.0907 (1.633)	−0.994★★ (−2.842)	2.031★★★ (5.891)	0.0689 (0.968)	−0.559★ (−2.105)	3.773★★★ (10.71)
INFL	−0.000135 (−0.102)	0.0754★★★ (3.779)	−0.121★ (−2.513)	−0.000752 (−0.509)	0.0699★★★ (3.286)	−0.0485 (−1.378)	−0.00107 (−1.225)	0.0151 (0.655)	−0.178★★★ (−6.241)
EXR	0.000111 (1.339)	−0.000176★★ (−2.299)	0.0126★★★ (4.731)	0.000155★ (1.799)	0.000288★★ (2.482)	−0.102★★★ (−8.224)	0.000209★★★ (3.799)	0.000281 (1.567)	−0.0884★★★ (−15.99)
RQ	0.00251 (0.0741)	−9.889★★★ (−15.13)	−5.213★★★ (−23.52)	0.0904★★ (2.180)	−0.298 (−1.101)	−0.754★ (−3.051)	0.177★★★ (5.948)	0.978★ (2.046)	−1.182★ (−3.058)
lnMOB	0.0346 (1.658)	2.376★★★ (5.103)	4.015★★★ (7.177)	0.0441 (1.610)	1.679★★★ (5.285)	0.927★ (2.735)	0.0252★★ (2.227)	1.233★★★ (3.966)	5.544★★★ (6.550)
lnMKTCAP	0.0233 (1.639)	1.049★★★ (14.40)	1.133★★★ (33.18)						
lnMKTCAP★RQ	0.0354★★★ (3.254)	3.223★★★ (19.84)	0.416★★★ (8.332)						
lnMKTVL★RQ				0.00866 (0.537)	0.585★★★ (5.096)	0.584★★★ (15.41)			
lnMKTVL★RQ				0.0110 (0.775)	0.136 (0.736)	0.114 (1.031)			
lnMKTOVR							0.00320 (0.350)	0.303 (1.215)	1.242★★★ (14.87)
lnMKTOVR★RQ							−0.0328★★ (−2.625)	−0.725 (−1.639)	−0.353 (−1.858)

Variables	Market Capitalization			Market Value			Market Turnover		
	Full	*LMI*	*UMI*	*Full*	*LMI*	*UMI*	*Full*	*LMI*	*UMI*
Constant	24.41***	12.93***	−0.222	24.14***	20.41***	12.66**	24.32***	20.63***	−16.31**
	(74.10)	(8.900)	(−0.0563)	(119.1)	(13.55)	(4.936)	(93.65)	(12.16)	(−3.271)
Year Dummies	Yes	Yes	Yes	Yes	Yes	Yes	Yes	Yes	Yes
Observations	90	55	35	82	58	24	76	52	24
R-squared		0.692	0.974		0.617	0.998		0.628	0.994
Countries	16	11	5	15	11	4	15	11	4
F Statistic	50898	94780	5782	18953	7166	3.850e+08	6811	57007	277593

Source: Authors' computations.

Note: ★★★ $p < 0.01$, ★★ $p < 0.05$, and ★ $p < 0.1$; ln = natural logarithm; GDP = gross domestic product; MKTCAP = market capitalization; LIQL = liquid liabilities; INFL = inflation rate; EXR = official exchange rate; RQ = regulatory quality; MOB = mobile phone subscribers; LMI = lower middle income; UMI = upper middle income.

10 Financial Intermediaries, Stock Market Development and Economic Growth in African Countries

Nicholas Mbaya Odhiambo and Sheilla Nyasha

10.1 Introduction

It has been widely acknowledged that financial development is key in driving economic growth. However, it is still debatable whether financial intermediaries and stock markets complement or substitute each other in enhancing economic growth. The relationship between financial sector development and economic growth has been in the spotlight for decades, if not centuries, and has received extensive attention in both the developed and the developing economies. However, most previous studies on the subject have tended to concentrate mainly on the relationship between financial intermediaries and economic growth (see, Kargbo & Adamu, 2009; Hassan et al., 2011; Adu et al., 2013; Matei, 2020, among others).

Unlike studies on financial intermediaries and economic growth, pragmatic studies on stock market development and economic growth are scanty, and so are studies on financial intermediation and stock market development, and economic growth. Hence, only a few studies have empirically tested the three financial structure views – namely, the bank-based view, which suggests that financial intermediaries are better than stock markets in supporting economic growth; the market-based view, which assigns significant importance of stock market development in driving economic growth; and then the financial-services view, which downplays the power of financial intermediaries versus the stock market debate but instead emphasises the complementarity power of the two financial systems in providing sound financial products and services.

Consistent with the latter financial structure view, there is a new strand of literature, which has emerged in the recent past, questing the dynamic power of financial intermediaries and stock market in propelling economic growth. Although it is now well acknowledged that financial development in general is good for economic growth (Adu et al., 2013; Aluko & Ibrahim, 2020; Matei, 2020), the dynamics between the two key facets of financial development – financial intermediation and stock market development – in propelling economic growth is an underexplored area (Berlin, 2012; Nyasha & Odhiambo, 2017), in general, and has no known coverage on SSA,

DOI: 10.4324/9781003215042-12

in particular. It is not yet known whether the two components of financial development complement or substitute for each other in their role of growing the economy, yet this knowledge is critical to policymakers if appropriate growth-enhancing policies are to be crafted and implemented successfully.

It is against this background that the current study aims to examine the link between financial intermediaries and stock market development in propelling economic growth in SSA from 1993 to 2019 using dynamic panel data analysis. This study aims to examine whether financial intermediaries and stock markets complement each other or substitute for each other in the process of economic growth and development. The interaction of financial intermediaries and stock markets is captured by the interaction term – comprising an interaction between three proxies of stock market development and bank-based financial development. The three stock market proxies include stock market capitalisation, stock market traded value and turnover ratio, while the bank-based financial development is proxied by the domestic credit to the private sector by banks (% of GDP).

In order to address the omission-of-variable bias, two control variables have been included in the model, namely, inflation and trade. The study uses a wide range of modern econometric techniques in order to examine this linkage. These include (i) four cross-sectional dependence tests, (ii) first- and second-generation unit root tests, (iii) the Pedroni panel cointegration technique, and (iv) the dynamic ordinary least squares (DOLS) and the fully modified OLS (FMOLS) models.

Owing to the lack of adequate and reliable data on stock market development, only five countries that had sufficient data were included in this study, i.e., Cote d'Ivoire, Ghana, Kenya, Nigeria and South Africa. To our knowledge, this study may well be the first one of its kind to investigate the complementarity between market-based and bank-based financial development in driving economic growth in the studied countries using these techniques.

The study is organised as follows: Section 10.2 covers financial sector reforms and development in SSA, while Section 10.3 reviews the literature on financial intermediation, stock market and economic growth. Section 10.4 covers estimation techniques, empirical analysis and discussion of results. Section 10.5 concludes the study and proffers policy implications flowing from the study.

10.2 Financial Sector Reforms and Development in SSA

Although the financial systems in SSA are characterised by both banks and stock markets, just like any other financial system in the developed world, the former is more dominant than the latter. This can be confirmed by the lack of adequate data on stock market development in many SSA countries.

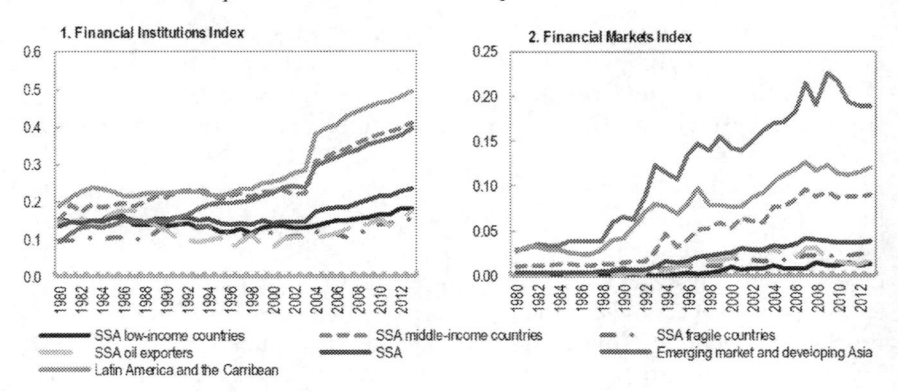

Figure 10.1 Sub-Saharan Africa: Dimensions of Financial Development (1 = highest development).

Source: Extracted from International Monetary Fund (IMF) (2016).

This could explain why coverage on SSA has been largely on either bank development or financial development, proxied by bank-based financial development indicators (see Aluko & Ibrahim, 2020; Matei, 2020; among others).

As revealed in Figure 10.1, in the main, financial intermediaries in SSA range from underdeveloped to moderately developed, scoring an index of about 0.2–0.5, where an index of 1 is the highest level of development (International Monetary Fund (IMF), 2016). On the contrary, stock markets are shown to be underdeveloped, with the highest index of 0.01 in 2012 (IMF, 2016). Although it is almost a decade later, the trend has not changed much. However, in comparison, the financial development index demonstrates that financial intermediaries in SSA are by far more developed than their stock market counterparts. This picture, however, may be different when individual countries are considered independently, where most are less developed than the trends revealed collectively, while a handful are more developed than portrayed by the average index. South Africa is one of the latter, as its financial systems, both bank- and market-based, are well developed and compare well with the financial systems of the developed economies.

Over the years, a number of financial sector reforms have been undertaken to tackle long-standing issues of competition, financial inclusion, financial stability and inclusive growth (IMF, 2016, 2021). The result was the rise of home-grown banks that gradually displaced foreign banks and branches of foreign banks in many parts of SSA. As the financial system opened up for non-bank financial institutions, competition improved, leading to reduced costs of financial products and services; so did financial inclusion. However, financial stability was compromised, leading to the call by the IMF (2016) and various financial regulators for customised regulation to restore and enhance financial stability in Africa.

In response to the financial sector reforms implemented, banking systems and financial markets in SSA have developed, though disproportionately – with financial intermediaries developing at a faster rate than the financial markets. There has also been an appetite for regional cooperation in financial-services offerings. According to the IMF (2016), despite fresh signs that efforts to fortify cross-border cooperation are increasing in the region, there is also still substantial scope to improve consolidated and cross-border supervisory and regulatory practices further.

Financial markets are still largely bourgeoning in many African countries. However, with isolated exceptions such as those of South Africa, Nigeria, Ghana and Kenya (Boamah, 2016), there have been some positive developments in SSA's financial markets that have not gone unnoticed. Despite the local debt market being dominated by government securities, there has been a steady increase in project bonds to finance investment in infrastructure (IMF, 2016). In addition, the IMF (2016) asserts that as compared to the non-marketable debt, the marketable instrument share is increasing, giving room for countries to establish more liquid benchmarks. The maturity of instruments has also, on average, increased substantially. Debt instruments with maturities longer than ten years in several low-income countries, such as Benin, Burkina Faso, Kenya, Mali, Tanzania and Zambia, have become a common phenomenon in recent times (IMF, 2016).

Despite substantial progress in financial development in Africa, in general, and in sub-Saharan Africa, in particular, over the past decade, challenges remain. From the financial intermediary side, these challenges include the lack of sufficient supervisory oversight and somewhat weak internal governance frameworks. According to IMF (2016), these vulnerabilities may cause systemic risks that could put financial development in danger if they are not addressed. From the financial markets side, the key challenges include market volatility, liquidity constraints as well as inclusion challenges since these markets are not readily accessible by many. The latter challenge is linked to information asymmetry, where some parts of the communities are not aware of such markets and how they operate, leading to automatic exclusion.

10.3 Financial Intermediation, Stock Market and Economic Growth: A Review of Literature

The link between financial market development and economic growth has been extensively explored empirically, particularly since the seminal works of Schumpeter (1911). Although various outcomes exist depending on a number of factors, such as the country under study, the methodology used, the proxies utilised, and the timeframe considered, it has become generally accepted that finance has a positive effect on growth. (Schumpeter, 1911; Levine, 1999, 2002; Nyasha & Odhiambo, 2019).

Despite this common understanding and acceptance that financial development is good for economic growth, economic theories differ radically on the role played by banks and markets in the real sector development. Ultimately, three competing views have been placed on the centre stage, namely the bank-based view, the market-based view and the financial-services view.

The bank-based view places more importance on the bank-based financial system than on the market-based system, arguing that economic growth is stimulated more by the bank-based financial system through long-term investment in the real sector. The advocates of the bank-based view claim that banks can cut the cost of acquiring information about firms through the assessment of potential borrowers, leading to increased savings and capital accumulation in the economy (Beck, 2010). Additionally, banks are believed to foster innovation and efficient resource allocation by identifying the most worthy projects. Banks can also reduce liquidity risk by pooling savings and investing in short-term securities and long-term investments (Beck, 2010). With banks, individual investors are able to share risk, permitting a move towards higher return and higher risk projects.

On the extreme end of the continuum is the market-based view, which assigns a high level of significance on market-based financial development in driving economic growth. This view also stresses the positive role that markets play in improving risk management, information dissemination, corporate control as well as capital allocation by facilitating takeovers and compensating managers according to performance (Beck, 2010). In elevating itself, the market-based view argues that banks can inhibit innovation by extracting informational rents and shielding established firms with close bank-firm connections from competition (Rajan, 1992).

Then, there is the third view, which is a compromise of the two extreme views, known as the financial-services view. This view diminishes the importance of the bank-based versus the market-based debate (Levine, 2002; Beck 2010). According to this view, the thrust of the matter is neither banks nor markets, but the existence of an enabling environment in which both banks and markets work together to foster both financial sector development and economic development. In light of this, the banking sector and stock market development are expected to complement each other in fostering economic growth.

It is, however, interesting to note that all these three divergent theoretical views have found empirical support. Although empirical literature is largely in support of the two financial systems being complements, some studies have found the two to be substitutes. To this day, the question of whether banks and markets are complements or substitutes remains largely unresolved, prompting further empirical scrutiny.

Levine (1999), after reviewing evidence on banks, markets and financial structures, concludes that both banks and markets offer complementary services with positive effects on economic performance. Levine (2002) empirically assessed contending extreme theoretical views placing one of the two financial systems – bank-based or market-based – at the helm of long-run economic growth promotion. Using data from 48 developed and developing countries, the results were, again, in support of the financial-services view. The study found no support for either the market-based or bank-based view, but rather, the two systems are found to be complementary.

Consistent with Levine's (1999, 2002) conclusion, Beck and Levine (2002) examined whether market-based or bank-based financial systems are better at financing industries that rely mainly on external finance. Using data from 36 industries across 42 countries, they found no evidence in support of either the bank-based or the market-based views, and their conclusion was a pro-financial-services view, giving credit to overall financial development. However, they further emphasised the importance of an efficient legal system in enhancing overall financial development that boosts industrial growth and efficient capital allocation.

Levine (2004) reviewed theoretical and empirical research on the relationship between the financial system and economic growth and found predominant evidence suggesting that both financial intermediaries and financial markets impact growth in their own ways, thus complementing each other. In the same mood, Yonezawa and Azeez (2010) investigated whether it is a bank-based or a market-based financial system that is superior at stimulating economic performance. Using a panel dataset on 40 countries for the period from 1990 to 2003, the results revealed that while a bank-based financial system is more effective in promoting productivity, a market-based financial system is more efficient at inducing capital accumulation. Based on these findings, the authors concluded that the two financial systems are complements in their efforts to drive economic growth.

Ujunwa et al. (2012) studied the channels used by banks and markets to stimulate economic growth in Nigeria and found evidence in support of banks and markets being complementary to each other. They, therefore, relegated the financial structure arguments while recommending a favourable macro-economic environment that fosters the overall development of the financial system. In the same year, Masoud and Hardaker (2012) reached matching conclusions after analysing the relationship between financial development and economic growth for 42 emerging markets, over 12 years, using an endogenous growth model. So did Berlin (2012), emphasising that while there is not much evidence that the relative scale of the financial activities performed via banks or via markets has a huge effect on a country's economic growth, there is, instead, overwhelming evidence that the combination of bank loans and bonds has real effects on the economy, even at the firm level.

Two years later, Odhiambo (2014) investigated the association between banks, stock markets and economic growth in South Africa, in an effort to find out whether financial intermediaries and stock markets are complements or substitutes in enhancing economic growth. The author found that complementarity between stock markets and banks is dependent on the proxy used to measure the level of stock market development. Complementarity existed when stock market development is proxied by stock market capitalisation. However, in the main, the complementarity between financial intermediaries and financial markets in the study country was found to be weak.

Nyasha and Odhiambo (2017) empirically tested whether banks and markets complement or substitute for one another in promoting economic growth in the USA, Brazil and Kenya using time series data for the period from 1980 to 2012. The ARDL-bounds testing approach was used, and the results varied depending on the study country. In the USA and Brazil, bank-based and market-based financial systems were found to complement each other in promoting economic growth. In the same year, Hassan and Kalim (2017) also put to empirical test the question of whether financial intermediaries and financial markets are complements or substitutes in driving economic growth. Using mean and common mean group estimators on a sample of low human development countries during the period from 1989 to 2013, the results of the study revealed that the two financial systems complement each other in their role to enhance economic growth in the study countries.

Although scant, the empirical literature has also found evidence in support of substitutability between financial intermediaries and financial markets in driving economic growth. Dey (2007) examined the determinants of stock market and bank liquidity using a panel dataset consisting of 32 exchanges from 27 countries over a period of 60–84 months between 1995 and 2001. Stock market turnover and available bank credit, respectively, proxied access to long-term and short-term capital. Although these two variables were found to be interdependent and the errors correlated, their coefficients were found to be inversely related, leading to the conclusion that banks and stock markets substitute for each other, rather than complement each other in their efforts to grow the economy. Nyasha and Odhiambo (2017), in their study on the USA, Brazil and Kenya, also found financial intermediaries and markets to substitute for each other in their efforts to enhance economic growth.

From the reviewed scant literature, it can be concluded that whether banks and stock markets are complements or substitutes is dependent on a number of factors, such as the specific proxies used to measure bank development and stock market development, country or countries studied, study period as well as the study methodology. However, despite these variation dynamics, in the main, the financial-services view has emerged as conventional wisdom – where financial intermediaries and financial markets are complements, rather than substitutes, in driving economic growth.

10.4 Estimation Techniques and Empirical Analysis

10.4.1 Empirical Model

The model used in this study to test whether banks and stock markets are complements or substitutes in the process of economic growth can be expressed as follows:

$$y = f\left(STK, Bank, Inf, Trade, STK \star Bank\right) \tag{10.1}$$

where
y = economic growth (proxied by GDP per capita)
STK = stock market development proxies
$Bank$ = bank-based financial development
Inf = inflation
$Trade$ = total trade
$STK \times Bank$ = Interaction term between market-based and bank-based financial development

Based on equation (10.1), the empirical models estimated in this study can be expressed as follows:

$$Model\ 1: y = f\left(Cap, Bank, Inf, Trade, Cap \star Bank\right) \tag{10.2}$$
$$Model\ 2: y = f\left(Strade, Bank, Inf, Trade, Strade \star Bank\right) \tag{10.3}$$
$$Model\ 3: y = f\left(Turnov, Bank, Inf, Trade, Turnov \star Bank\right) \tag{10.4}$$

where
Cap = stock market capitalisation
$Strade$ = stock market traded value
$Turnov$ = turnover ratio

The panel model employed to analyse the relationship between banks, stock market development and economic growth in the studied countries can be expressed as follows:

$$Y_{it} = \gamma_{it} + \delta_{it} + \beta_{1i}STK_{it} + \beta_{2i}Bank_{it} + \beta_{3i}Inf_{it} + \beta_{4i}Trade_{it}$$
$$+ \beta_{5i}STK \star Bank_{it} + \mu_{it} \tag{10.5}$$

where $i = 1,\ldots, N$ = cross-sectional observation
$t = 1,\ldots, T$ = time period
δ_{it} and β_{1i} = country-specific effects and deterministic trend effects, respectively.
μ_{it} = error term.

In this study, the DOLS and FMOLS, which have been found to be superior to the traditional OLS, are used to examine whether banks and stock markets are complementary or substitutes in the process of economic development. Unlike the OLS, the DOLS and FMOLS estimations are more robust as they can address the endogeneity and serial correlation issues, which have been found to be associated with panel regression analysis (Khan et al., 2019).

The study used annual data from 1993 to 2019 from selected SSA countries. The sample countries used in this study include South Africa, Ghana,

Table 10.1 Data source and definitions of variables

Variable		Definitions	Expected Sign	Source
Economic growth	*y*	GDP per capita	N/A	WDI
Stock market capitalisation	*Cap*	Stock market capitalisation/GDP	(+)	FDSB
Stock market total value traded	*Strade*	Stock market total value traded/GDP	(+)	FDSD
Stock market turnover	*Turnov*	Stock market turnover ratio	(+)	FDSD
Banking sector development	*Bank*	Domestic credit to the private sector by banks (as a % of GDP)	(+)	WDI/ FDSB
Inflation	*Inf*	Inflation	(−)	WDI
Trade	*Trade*	Exports + exports/GDP	(+)	WDI
Interaction between banks and stock market	*STK*Bank*	Interaction between banks and stock market	(+)/(−)	WDI/ FDSB
Stock market proxies	*STK*	Cap, Strade, Turnov	(+)	FDSD

WDI = World Bank Development Indicators of the World Bank. FDSD = Financial Development Structure Database.

Nigeria, Kenya and Botswana. The data were largely obtained from the World Development Indicators and World Bank Financial Development Structure Database. Table 10.1 gives a summary of the definitions of variables and specific data sources.

10.4.2 Empirical Analysis

10.4.2.1 Cross-Sectional Dependence Test

Since panel dataset may exhibit cross-sectional dependence owing to the presence of common shocks, it is vital first to conduct a cross-sectional dependence test before conducting the empirical analysis. The results of these tests are provided in Table 10.2.

The results reported in Table 10.2 show that the null hypothesis of no cross-sectional dependence in the data used in this study has been rejected by all cross-sectional dependience tests, with the exception of the Pesaran CD for the case of turnover ratio. This finding can be confirmed by the Breusch–Pagan LM, Pesaran scaled LM and bias–corrected scaled LM tests, which have been found to be statistically significant for all the variables used in this study. These findings have also been corroborated by the results of Pesaran CD, which have been found to be statistically significant for all the variables, with the exception of the turnover ratio. Hence, we can conclude that there is evidence of cross-sectional dependence in our dataset, which shows that there is strong evidence of interdependencies between cross-sectional units used in this study.

Table 10.2 Cross-sectional dependence test

Series	Cross-Sectional Dependency Results			
	Breusch-Pagan LM	Pesaran Scaled LM	Bias-Corrected Scaled LM	Pesaran CD
Cap	36.78916★★★	5.990238★★★	5.894085★★★	3.242278★★★
	(0.0001)	(0.0000)	(0.0000)	(0.0012)
Bank	56.67579★★★	10.43702★★★	10.34087★★★	4.795248★★★
	(0.0000)	(0.0000)	(0.0000)	(0.0000)
Strade	41.22372★★★	6.981837★★★	6.885683★★★	4.523335★★★
	(0.0000)	(0.0000)	(0.0000)	(0.0000)
Turnov	44.64871★★★	7.747688★★★	7.651534★★★	1.411530
	(0.0000)	(0.0000)	(0.0000)	0.1581
Y	147.3820★★★	30.71956★★★	30.62341★★★	10.99511★★★
	(0.0000)	(0.0000)	(0.0000)	(0.0000)
Inf	56.62337★★★	10.42530★★★	10.32915★★★	6.994176★★★
	(0.0000)	(0.0000)	(0.0000)	(0.0000)
Trade	32.33466★★★	4.994182★★★	4.898029★★★	2.642311★★★
	(0.0001)	(0.0000)	(0.0000)	(0.0082)

10.4.2.2 Unit Root Test

Given the presence of cross-sectional dependence detected in our dataset, it is important to apply the second-generation unit root test along with the first-generation test. Consequently, the study used both Pesaran – CIPS and LLC to test for the stationarity of the variables used in this study. The results of unit root tests are reported in Table 10.3.

Based on the results reported in Table 10.3, we can conclude that, on the whole, the variables used in this analysis are integrated order one. This has

Table 10.3 Unit root test results

Variables	LLC		Pesaran – CIPS	
	Level	First Difference	Level	First Difference
Cap	−0.99010	−5.38291★★★	−1.38108	−3.74296★★★
Bank	0.84937	−5.83669★★★	−1.31882	−6.17858★★★
Strade	−1.04318	−6.19427★★★	−1.55938	−5.11422★★★
Turnov	−0.35973	−8.62949★★★	−2.20713	−7.57186★★★
Y	1.19577	−4.21864★★★	−1.08647	−3.34701★★★
Cap★Bank	−0.43034	−9.91936★★★	−1.19740	−6.31059★★★
Strade★Bank	1.27607	−7.23862★★★	−0.84159	−5.07606★★★
Turnov★Bank	0.58964	−8.68609★★★	−1.16424	−8.10355★★★
Inf	−7.72239★★★	–	−2.43102	−6.79573★★★
Trade	−0.79642	−4.91046★★★	−2.62980	−4.92529★★★

Note: ★★★ indicates rejection of the respective null hypothesis at the 1% significance level.

been confirmed by the Pesaran – CIPS, which has been found to be statistically significant at 1% on the first difference.

10.4.2.3 Cointegration

In this section, the Pedroni (2004) residual-based cointegration approach is used to examine whether the variables used in this study are cointegrated. The Pedroni test has two dimensions, namely, (1) the 'between dimension', which is based on panel-specific AR parameters, and (2) the 'within dimension', which is based on the same AR parameters. The results of the cointegration test based on Pedroni (2004) are reported in Table 10.4.

The results reported in Table 10.4 show that there is evidence of cointegration among all the variables used in Models 1, 2 and 3. This finding has been confirmed by the Panel PP, Panel ADF, Group PP and Group ADF statistics, which have all been found to be statistically significant in all the three models.

10.4.2.4 DOLS and FMOLS Results

Since the cointegration results show that all the variables used in Models 1, 2 and 3 are cointegrated, we can now proceed to estimate the long-run relationships using the FMOLS and DOLS. The results of the FMOLS and DOLS are summarised in Table 10.5.

Table 10.4 Panel cointegration results

Pedroni Cointegration Test

	Model 1 Stock Capitalisation		Model 2 Stock Traded Value		Model 3 Stock Turnover Ratio	
	Statistic	*Probability*	*Statistic*	*Probability*	*Statistic*	*Probability*
Pedroni panel cointegration test – within dimension						
Panel v statistic	−1.346704	0.9110	0.706454	0.2400	0.321161	0.3740
Panel rho statistic	0.922746	0.8219	−0.205812	0.4185	−0.694412	0.2437
Panel PP statistic	−2.743444★★★	0.0030	−3.506747★★★	0.0002	−4.312466★★★	0.0000
Panel ADF statistic	−2.751124★★★	0.0030	−3.506037★★★	0.0002	−4.314061★★★	0.0000
Pedroni panel cointegration test – between dimension						
Group rho statistic	1.527604	0.9367	0.458585	0.6767	0.139564	0.5555
Group PP statistic	−3.009778★★★	0.0013	−4.031263★★★	0.0000	−4.125720★★★	0.0000
Group ADF statistic	−2.784072★★★	0.0027	−4.097946★★★	0.0000	−4.066220★★★	0.0000

Table 10.5 DOLS and FMOLS results

Explanatory Variable	Dependent Variable: Economic Growth (γ)					
	Model 1		Model 2		Model 3	
	FMOLS	DOLS	FMOLS	DOLS	FMOLS	DOLS
Cap	−1.056927 (−0.237565)	−1.545151 (−0.32294)	−	−	−	−
Strade	−		2.837530 (0.125868)	2.837530 (0.125868)	−	−
Turnov	−		−		−24.56745 (−1.645959)	78.27211★★ (2.151704)
Bank	25.35933★★ (2.361247)	23.24919★★ (2.07560)	23.43131★★ (2.011378)	23.43131★★★ (2.011378)	38.56852★★★ (4.447237)	28.84657★ (1.807522)
Cap★Bank	0.161717★★ (2.492840)	0.14088★★ (2.03381)	−	−	−	−
Strade★Bank	−		0.272346 (0.827380)	0.272346 (0.827380)	−	−
Turnov★Bank	−		−		2.069476★★★ (5.6415060)	1.1536★ (1.77226)
Inf	−11.71415★★★ (−3.123081)	−8.07565★★ (−2.1223)	−11.76087★★★ (−2.741826)	−11.76087★★★ (−2.741826)	−0.782379 (−0.121122)	13.08210 (0.95637)
Trade	−5.708696★ (−1.920451)	−3.48487 (−1.09465)	−6.177316★ (−1.846963)	−6.177316★ (−1.846963)	−11.78435★★★ (−3.105768)	3.6679 (0.78935)

Note: (1) The *t*-statistic is in parenthesis; (2) ★, ★★ and ★★★ denote statistical significance at the 10%, 5% and 1% levels, respectively.

The results reported in Table 10.5 show that the complementarity between banks and stock markets is dependent on the proxy used to quantify the level of stock market development.

When stock market capitalisation and turnover ratio are taken as proxies, the results show that there is complementarity between stock market development and banking sector development proxies by the domestic credit to the private sector. This finding is confirmed by the coefficients of the interaction terms *Cap*Bank* and *Turnov*Bank* in the growth model, which have been found to be positive and statistically significant. These results apply, regardless of whether the estimation is conducted using the FMOLS or the DOLS estimators. However, when the stock market is proxied for the traded value, no complementarity is found to exist, irrespective of the estimator used. This finding has been confirmed by the coefficient of the interaction term *Strade*Bank* in the growth model, which has been found to be statistically significant in both the FMOLS and DOLS models.

Although the complementarity between the stock market and the banking sector has been supported by two of the stock market proxies, the unconditional impact of stock market development on economic growth is, at best, very weak. This has been confirmed by the coefficients of all the stock market proxies in the growth equation, which have been found to be statistically significant in all the equations, with the exception of the turnover ratio in the DOLS model. This finding, although contrary to our expectations, is not surprising given the level of stock market development in many sub-Saharan African countries.

Contrary to the results of the stock market development, the results of bank-based financial development show that the banking sector has a positive and significant impact on economic growth in all specifications estimated in this analysis. This finding further confirms the narrative that the sub-Saharan African financial sector is largely bank-based. Other results show that both inflation and trade generally have a negative impact on economic development in the studied countries. This finding has been confirmed by the coefficients of inflation and trade in the growth equation, which have been found to be negative and statistically significant in four of the six specifications.

10.5 Conclusion

In this study, we examine the relationship between stock market development, bank-based financial development and economic growth using panel data from selected SSA countries during the period from 1993 to 2019. In the main, the study aims to examine whether stock markets and banks are complementary or substitutes in the process of economic growth and development. The interaction of financial intermediaries and stock markets is captured by the interaction term – comprising an interaction between three proxies of stock market development and a bank-based financial development proxy. The three stock market proxies used include stock market capitalisation, stock market traded value and turnover ratio, while the bank-based financial development is proxied by the domestic credit to the private sector by banks (% of GDP). Owing to the lack of adequate data on stock market development in many SSA countries, only five countries that have sufficient data on stock market during the study period were included in this study. These countries were Cote d'Ivoire, Ghana, Kenya, Nigeria and South Africa. In order to examine this linkage, the study used a wide range of panel data techniques, namely, (i) four cross-sectional dependence tests; (ii) first- and second-generation unit root tests based on LLC and Pesaran (CIPS), respectively; (iii) the Pedroni panel cointegration technique; and (iv) the dynamic ordinary least squares (DOLS) and the fully modified OLS (FMOLS) models. The results show that complementarity between banks and stock markets is sensitive to the proxy used to measure the level of stock market development. When stock market capitalisation and turnover ratio are used as proxies, complementarity was found to exist between stock market development and banking sector development. This finding applies, irrespective of whether the FMOLS or DOLS was used as the estimator. However, when the stock market is proxied by the stock market traded value, no complementarity is found to exist, irrespective of the estimator used. On the whole, we can conclude that the complementarity between stock market development and bank-based financial development exists in the selected countries since it has been supported by two out of three proxies and four out of six estimations. Although the findings show that there is support for complementarity between banks and stock markets in the process of economic growth, the study found that the impact of stock market development on economic growth is, at best, very weak as only the turnover ratio was found to have a positive and significant impact on economic growth when DOLS was used as the estimator. In contrast, the study found bank-based financial development to be positive and statistically significant in all of the specifications. This finding is not surprising given the nature of financial development in SSA countries, which is largely dominated by the banking sector. Based on the outcome of this study, policymakers in the study countries are recommended to consider which aspect of the financial sector to target should they wish to promote pro-growth policies.

References

Adu, G., Marbuah, G. and Mensah, J.T. 2013. Financial development and economic growth in Ghana: Does the measure of financial development matter? *Review of Development Finance*, 3, 192–203. http://dx.doi.org/10.1016/j.rdf.2013.11.001

Aluko, O.A. and Ibrahim, M. 2020. Institutions and the financial development–economic growth nexus in sub-Saharan Africa. *Economic Notes*, 49(3), e12–e163, https://doi.org/10.1111/ecno.12163

Baltagi, B.H., Feng, Q. and Kao, C. 2012. A Lagrange Multiplier test for cross-sectional dependence in a fixed effects panel data model. *Journal of Econometrics*, 170(1), 164–177.

Beck, T. 2010. Financial development and economic growth: Stock markets versus banks? In *Africa's financial markets. A Real Development Tool? Private Sector & Development,* 55, 23–25.

Beck, T. and Levine, R. 2002. Industry growth and capital allocation: Does having a market- or bank-based system matter? *Journal of Financial Economics, 64*(2), 147–180.

Berlin, M. 2012. Banks and markets: Substitutes, complements, or both? *Business Review,* Q2(1), 1–10.

Boamah, N.A. 2016. Regional and global market integration of African financial markets. African *Review of Economics and Finance, 8*(2), 234–268.

Breusch, T.S. and Pagan, A.R. 1980. The Lagrange Multiplier Test and its applications to model specification in econometrics. *The Review of Economic Studies, 47*(1), 239–253.

Dey, M.K. 2007. Are banks and stock markets complements or substitutes? NFI Working Papers –WP-04, Indiana State University, Scott College of Business, Networks Financial Institute.

Hassan, K.M., Sanchez, B. and Yu, J. 2011. Financial development and economic growth: New evidence from panel data. *The Quarterly Review of Economics and Finance, 51,* 88–104.

Hassan, M.S. and Kalim, R. 2017. Stock market and banking sector: Are they complementary for economic growth in low human developed economy? *Pakistan Economic and Social Review, 55*(1), 1–30.

International Monetary Fund. 2016. *Financial Development in Sub-Saharan Africa.* International Mononetary Fund, Washington, DC.

International Monetary Fund. 2021. *Regional Economic Outlook. Sub Saharan Africa.* International Monetary Fund, Washington, DC.

Kargbo, S.M. and Adamu, P.A. 2009. Financial development and economic growth in Sierra Leone. *West African Journal of Monetary and Economic Integration, 9*(2), 30–61.

Khan, S.A.R., Sharif, A., Golpîra, H. and Kumar, A. 2019. A green ideology in Asian emerging economies: From environmental policy and sustainable development. *Sustainable Development, 27*(6), 1063–1075.

Levine, R. 1999. Law, finance and economic growth. *Journal of Financial Intermediation, 8*(1/2), 36–67.

Levine, R. 2002. Bank-based or market-based financial systems: Which is better? *Journal of Financial Intermediation,* 11(4), 398–428.

Levine, R. 2004. Finance and growth: Theory and evidence. Working Paper 10766, National Bureau of Economic Research, Massachusetts, Cambridge, MA https://www.nber.org/system/files/working_papers/w10766/w10766.pdf

Masoud, N. and Hardaker, G. 2012. The impact of financial development on economic growth. *Studies in Economics and Finance, 29*(3), 148–173.

Matei, I. 2020. Is financial development good for economic growth? Empirical insights from emerging European countries. *Quantitative Finance and Economics, 4*(4), 653–678. http://dx.doi.org/10.3934/QFE.2020030

Nyasha, S. and Odhiambo, N.M. 2017. Are banks and stock markets complements or substitutes? Empirical evidence from three countries. *Managing Global Transitions, 15*(1), 81–101.

Nyasha, S. and Odhiambo, N.M. 2019. Do financial systems spur economic growth in the USA? An empirical investigation. *Panoeconomicus, 66*(2), 165–185. http://dx.doi.org/10.2298/PAN160517012N

Odhiambo, N.M. 2014. Financial systems and economic growth in South Africa: A dynamic complementarity test. *International Review of Applied Economics, 28*(1), 83–101.

Pedroni, P. 2004. Panel cointegration: Asymptotic and finite sample properties of pooled time series tests with an application to the PPP hypothesis. *Econometric Theory, 20*(03), 597–625. http://dx.doi.org/10.1017/S0266466604203073.

Pesaran, M.H. 2004. General diagnostic tests for cross section dependence in panels. Working Paper 0435, Faculty of Economics, University of Cambridge, Cambridge.

Rajan, R.G. 1992. Insiders and outsiders: The choice between informed and arm's length debt. *Journal of Finance, 47*(4), 1367–1400.

Schumpeter, J.A. 1911. *The Theory of Economic Development*. Harvard University Press, Cambridge, MA.

Ujunwa, A., Ekumankama, O., Umar, H.A., and Adamu, M.I. 2012. Finance and growth nexus in Nigeria: Do bank-based and market-based argument matter? *International Journal of Business and Management, 7*(23), 112–121.

Yonezawa, Y., and Azeez, A.A. 2010. Financial Systems and economic performance: A cross country analysis. *Global Economy and Finance Journal, 3*(2), 107–121.

11 Microfinance Performance and Economic Development in African Countries

Agyapomaa Gyeke-Dako, Elikplimi Komla Agbloyor and Joshua Yindenaba Abor

11.1 Introduction

Microfinance refers to the provision of financial services to the poor/under-privileged in society. These financial services include savings, loans, insurance and pensions, amongst others. Thus, microfinance goes beyond the provision of credit, though undeniably credit is a key feature of microfinance services. The credit provided by MFIs is typically small as they are typically directed to poor people. Indeed, MFIs who lend very large amounts are most likely not lending to the poor. This has been termed as 'mission drift' in the literature (see Mersland and Strøm, 2010; Armendáriz and Szafarz, 2011). The consequence of providing small loans and informal financial services such as microfinance is that it increases transaction costs (see CGAP, 2010). This is one of the main reasons why traditional financial institutions do not lend to this group of borrowers.

Further, the lending methodologies employed by MFIs differ to a certain extent from those employed by traditional providers of financial services such as banks. The unique methodologies that MFIs employ include group lending. With group lending, the MFI lends to a group of borrowers who may be jointly liable for servicing the loan. In other cases, group members do not receive loans until a member of the group who has taken a loan has fully paid off. Thus, there is some social pressure for members of the group to pay off their loans. MFIs use this approach as a substitute for taking collateral. This is so because the poor usually do not have collateral that they can use to borrow (Ghosh, Mookherjee, and Ray, 2000). MFIs also use the individual lending approach where they lend to individual borrowers. The extent of usage of the individual lending methodology varies across various regions in the world with larger MFIs employing individual lending more as opposed to group lending.

Modern microfinance was pioneered by Muhammad Yunus who showed that lending to the poor could be profitable. Yunus pioneered an experiment when he was at the University of Chittagong. He later went on to form the Grameen/Village Bank. For his contributions to the microfinance revolution, Yunus and the Grameen Bank received the Nobel Peace prize in

DOI: 10.4324/9781003215042-13

1996. The core idea behind microfinance is that financial services can be provided profitably to the poor. Indeed, there are two schools of thoughts about how microfinance should work. The welfarist approach believes that financial services such as loans should be provided to the poor at below market interest rates. This involves the provision of an inherent subsidy to the poor (see Chikalipah and Makina, 2019). The welfarist approach is also known as the poverty lending approach. On the contrary, the institutional approach believes that the poor can service loans at market interest rates. Consequently, there is no inherent subsidy. The proponents of the institutionalist approach believe that by charging market interest rates, MFIs do not need to rely on subsidies from donors, thus promoting their long-term sustainability and survival. The institutional approach is also known as the capitalist/financial systems approach. Indeed, it appears that proponents of the institutionalist approach have won this debate and microfinance services are now mostly provided on a commercial basis.

One of the key reasons why microfinance has been heralded as a panacea for poverty reduction and an improvement in household welfare is because access to finance and other financial services enable the poor to save, borrow (Kaboski and Townsend, 2012), invest in productive assets/accumulate assets (Stewart, Van Rooyen, Dickson, Majoro, and De Wet, 2010), insure against risks and smooth/increase consumption over time (see Attanasio, Augsburg, De Haas, Fitzsimons, and Harmgart, 2015). This helps to ultimately increase economic growth, human development and welfare and consequently leads to a reduction in poverty (see, for example, Morduch, 1999; Morduch and Armendariz, 2005; Banerjee and Duflo, 2011). In addition, the poor can take care of their health, education, housing and nutrition needs, thus improving their well-being.

Buera, Kaboski, and Shin (2021) find that in the short-run partial equilibrium state, microfinance increases output and capital but decreases total factor productivity. In the long-run after controlling for general equilibrium effects, they find that the impact of microfinance on per capita income is small because the increase in TFP is offset by a reduction in capital accumulation. They conclude, however, that microfinance has both direct and indirect beneficial effects for most of the population. Ahlin and Jiang (2008) propound that microfinance can promote development if borrowers are able to 'graduate' from self-employment to full-scale enterprises by being able to save because of their access to microcredit.

Banto and Monsia (2021) document that indicators of the social performance of MFIs such as the percentage of female borrowers, the average loan size per borrower, the number of active borrowers and the number of active clients, have a positive effect on GDP per capita growth in developing countries. Donou-Adonsou and Sylwester (2015) show that microfinance finance loans have a positive effect on economic growth and total factor productivity. Further, Donou-Adonsou and Sylwester (2017) find that whilst bank loans do not promote economic growth, microfinance loans do. Though Hermes

(2014) finds that microfinance can reduce income inequality, he concludes that the reduction in income inequality is modest given the nature of micro-finance. Some studies, however, dispute the ability of microfinance to reduce poverty at both the micro and macro levels. Banerjee, Duflo, Glennerster, and Kinnan (2013) using RCTs in India do not find any effects of microfi-nance on variables such as education, health and women empowerment. In Nigeria, Babajide (2012) finds no evidence that microfinance promotes the growth of small- and medium-sized enterprises (SMEs).

Indeed, most of the studies above focus on economic growth. However, in recent times the focus has shifted from economic growth to economic devel-opment. Economic development is broader than economic growth. Not all growth is pro-poor. Economic development which we proxy by the human development index in addition to income, captures education and health. Further, given the mixed evidence of the effect of microfinance on poverty reduction in the literature, it is important to examine the contribution of microfinance to economic development in the African context for several rea-sons. Firstly, Africa has a large informal sector compared to the formal sector. Given that microfinance institutions are engaged more in the informal sector, it is important to assess the impact of microfinance institutions on development. Secondly, many of the people who live in Africa live in rural areas, and indeed, informal financial markets thrive in these areas. Thirdly, because most of the population in Africa do not use formal financial services, microfinance is key to unlocking economic growth and development in Africa due to the compar-atively low levels of financial inclusion in the region (Demirguc-Kunt, Klap-per, Singer and Ansar, 2018). Fourthly, the low levels of institutional quality in Africa compared to other regions of the world (see Agbloyor, Gyeke-Dako, Kuipo and Abor, 2016) favour the provision of microfinance services which relies more on informal networks, and relationship-based lending as opposed to traditional financial services providers like banks who thrive better in rules-based exchanges that are more prevalent in countries with strong institutional arrangements. In addition, microfinance has a bigger chance of promoting the empowerment of women in the African setting as women are traditionally marginalized in the traditional African societal setting. Finally, most of the empirical literature, though scant, has focused on the relationship between microfinance and economic growth. There is urgent need to go beyond eco-nomic growth and examine the relationship between microfinance and eco-nomic development. Consequently, in this chapter we empirically examine whether various indicators of microfinance performance impact economic development. In particular, we examine whether various indicators of micro-finance sustainability, social performance and profitability improve economic development in Africa. The rest of the chapter is structured as follows: Section 11.2 provides stylized facts on microfinance performance and economic devel-opment in Africa. Section 11.3 details the methods that we employ. We discuss the results in Section 11.4 and provide our concluding comments and recom-mendations in Section 11.5.

11.2 Stylized Facts on MFI Performance and Economic Development in Africa

11.2.1 MFI Sustainability and Economic Development

Appendix 11.1A provides a list of the best-performing and worst-performing countries in terms of the Human Development Index (HDI) and microfinance sustainability (financial self-sufficiency (FSS) index, the subsidy dependence index (SDI) and the portfolio at risk (PaR)). We map countries based on their HDI index and how that compares to indicators of sustainability. Some countries score well on the HDI index and also score well on the sustainability indicators. Other countries do not score well on the HDI index and also score poorly on the sustainability indicators. Finally, some countries exhibit mixed performance on the HDI and the sustainability indicators.

MFIs in Guinea-Bissau are subsidy-independent (ranked 1), financially sustainable (ranked 1) and exhibited the highest quality loan book on the continent. Chad scores highly on the HDI index with MFIs in this country exhibiting subsidy independence. Nigeria was ranked Number 2 on the HDI, and its MFIs have a good quality loan book (ranked Number 3) and are fairly financially sustainable (ranked 10). However, MFIs in Nigeria are subsidy-dependent with yields on their loan book needing to increase by 23% for them to exit subsidy dependence. Liberia performs well on the HDI index, and MFIs in Liberia have a good quality loan book. However, MFIs in Liberia are not financially sustainable. Though Ghana scored well on the HDI index, MFIs in Ghana had the worst quality loan book on the continent.

Zimbabwe scores well on the HDI index; however, MFIs in Zimbabwe were the most subsidy-dependent. The Central African Republic (CAR) performs well on the HDI index, and MFIs in the CAR are subsidy-independent. However, MFIs in the CAR score poorly on financial sustainability and the quality of their loan book. Though Niger and Cameroon perform well on the HDI index, MFIs in these countries are highly subsidy-dependent with a poor quality loan book. Sierra Leonne on the contrary does well on the HDI index, but MFIs in Sierra Leone exhibit a poor quality loan book.

Senegal and Burundi did not perform well on the HDI index; however, MFIs in these countries exhibited financial sustainability. Similarly, Guinea doesn't perform well on the HDI index, but MFIs in Guinea had a good quality loan book. Benin also doesn't perform well on the HDI index; however, MFIs in Benin were subsidy-independent and exhibited good quality loan books. Further, Mali doesn't perform well on the HDI index and MFIs in Mali were subsidy-reliant. However, MFIs in Mali exhibit a high-quality loan portfolio. Togo equally does not perform well on the HDI index; however, Togo scored well on financial sustainability and its MFIs were not subsidy-dependent. Though South Africa has a high GDP per capita, it doesn't perform well on the HDI index. MFIs in South Africa exhibited subsidy independence. Burkina Faso and Mozambique do not perform well on the

HDI index. In addition, MFIs in these countries were not financially sustainable and exhibited poor quality loan books.

Overall, we notice a negative correlation between HDI and FSS, whilst HDI and SDI and HDI and PaR on the contrary were positively correlated. However, these correlations were not significant.

11.2.2 MFI Social Performance and Economic Development

Appendix 11.1B provides a list of the best-performing and worst-performing countries in terms of the Human Development Index (HDI) and microfinance social performance (the average loan size, the percentage of female borrowers and the percentage of rural borrowers). We map countries based on their HDI index and how that compares to indicators of MFI social performance.

Nigeria performs well in terms of the HDI index, and MFIs in Nigeria give comparatively large loans to microfinance borrowers. Whilst Chad scores highly on the HDI index, it falls in the bottom 10 on the continent with respect to the percentage of loans that its MFIs have granted to female borrowers. The Central African Republic falls in the top 10 in terms of HDI. MFIs in the Central African Republic give relatively small loans, so suffer less from 'mission drift'. However, MFIs in the Central African Republic perform poorly when it comes to lending to female borrowers. Cameroon performs well on the HDI index. In addition, MFIs in Cameroon perform well when it comes to lending to female borrowers. However, MFIs in Cameroon tend to give relatively large loans, suggesting that they may not be lending to the 'poorest of the poor'. Sierra Leone on the contrary performs well in terms of the HDI index. MFIs in Sierra Leonne also perform well in terms of extending their services to borrowers in rural areas. However, MFIs in Sierra Leone also tend to lend large loans, suggesting that they may not be lending to the 'poorest of the poor'.

Though Liberia scores highly on the HDI index, it performs poorly in terms of social performance. MFIs in Liberia give relatively large loans and lend less to borrowers in rural areas. Tanzania also scores well on the HDI index and performs poorly in terms of social performance. MFIs in Tanzania give relatively large loans. Further, they perform poorly in terms of lending to rural and female borrowers.

When it comes to countries with a low HDI, though Guinea performs poorly on the HDI index, it performs well in terms of social performance. MFIs in Guinea lend relatively small amounts, suggesting they are focusing on the poor. In addition, MFIs in Guinea perform well in terms of lending to female and rural borrowers. Similarly, Burkina Faso performs poorly in terms of the HDI. However, it performs well in terms of social performance. MFIs in Burkina Faso perform well in terms of lending to female borrowers. In addition, they tend to give small loan sizes suggesting a focus on the poor. Benin as well scores poorly on the HDI index, but performs well in terms of lending by MFIs in the country to female borrowers. Ethiopia and Senegal also score poorly on the HDI index, but MFIs in these countries perform well in terms of social performance. Specifically, they perform well in terms of lending to female borrowers.

Burundi, on the contrary, performs poorly in terms of the HDI index, and its performance on outreach is mixed. MFIs in Burundi score well in terms of lending to rural borrowers, but poorly in terms of lending to female borrowers. Similarly, South Africa scores poorly on the HDI index. However, it performs fairly well in terms of social performance. MFIs in South Africa lend relatively more to female and rural borrowers suggesting good outreach. However, the loan sizes by MFIs in South Africa are relatively large, suggesting that loans may not be reaching the very poor. Togo as well performs poorly on the HDI index. Its performance in terms of social performance is also mixed. It performs well in terms of lending to rural borrowers; however, loan sizes in Togo are relatively large compared to its counterparts in Africa. Finally, Mali performs poorly on the HDI index. In addition, MFIs in Mali perform poorly in terms of outreach. MFIs in Mali lend relatively large amounts and perform poorly in terms of lending to rural borrowers.

Indeed, our exploration of the data provides a lot of insight. Countries with high HDI generally do not perform well in terms of outreach, whilst countries with lower HDI tend to have higher MFI outreach. In particular, the HDI and the percentage of female borrowers and HDI and the percentage of rural borrowers have a negative and significant correlation. Though we are unable to conclude on causality, it appears that MFIs are very active in countries with low economic development (human development index). This may suggest an attempt by these institutions to tackle poverty in these countries and to lift the very poor and marginalized from poverty.

11.2.3 MFI Financial/Profitability Indicators and Economic Development

In this section, we explore how the HDI status of a country (high or low HDI) may map onto MFI profitability indicators (deposits, loans, yield on loan portfolio, return on equity, return on assets and efficiency). Appendices 11.2A and 11.2B present these indicators. In general, we do not observe any clear patterns. Most countries in the high HDI group (Nigeria, Tanzania, Ghana, Zimbabwe and Cameroon) had high deposits and high loans compared to countries in the low HDI group (Senegal and Togo) who had high deposits and loans. This suggests a positive correlation between HDI and deposits and loans respectively for countries in the high HDI and high MFI profitability sample. However, the correlation (for the entire sample) between HDI and deposits and loans respectively was negative, though insignificant.

In addition, several countries in the high HDI group (Chad, Central African Republic and Sierra Leonne) performed well in terms of returns on assets, returns on equity and efficiency compared to those in the low

HDI group. This suggests a positive correlation between HDI and return on assets and return on equity respectively. It also suggests a negative correlation between MFI cost and HDI. The correlation (for the entire sample) between return on assets and HDI was positive, whilst the correlations (for the entire sample) between return on equity and HDI were negative. These correlations, however, were not significant. On the contrary, the correlation between operating cost (efficiency) and HDI was negative as expected. However, this correlation as well was also not significant.

11.3 Methodology

This study employs panel data techniques to examine how microfinance sustainability, microfinance social performance and profitability variables affect economic welfare in high- and low-income countries using thirty (30) African economies between 2006 and 2016. The availability of the data allows us to employ a panel data strategy. Baltagi (2015, 2008) posits that the panel data technique presents more convincing and conclusive results than the traditional cross-sectional and time series techniques as the panel takes advantage of the strengths and corrects for the weaknesses of both time series and cross-sectional techniques. Similarly, the panel data presents that ability to control for omitted variables and allows for both long- and short-run effects, which controls for the weakness of cross-sectional and time series techniques (Imbens and Wooldridge, 2009). Data was obtained from the MFI MIX, World Development Indicators, World Governance Indicators and Global Finance Development. The panel data technique framework is expressed as

$$Y_{it} = \alpha_i + \gamma_t + \beta X_{it} + \varepsilon_{it} \tag{11.1}$$

$\varepsilon_{it} = \gamma_t + e_{it} : \alpha_i =$ country fixed effect; $\gamma_t =$ time fixed effect; $e_{it} = idiosyncratic\ term$, where subscript i denotes the cross-sectional dimension (country), $i = 1 \ldots N$, and t denotes the time series dimension (time), $t = 1 \ldots T$; Y_{it} is the dependent variable; α_i is scalar and constant term for all periods (t) and specific to a country fixed effect (i); γ_t is the time fixed effect t; β is a $k \times 1$ vector of parameters to be estimated on the independent variables for the explanatory variables; and X_{it} is a $1 \times k$ vector of observations on the independent variables comprising of independent variables in the model, which includes controlled variables, and ε_{it}, which is iid is the error term.

The study employs random-effect models to estimate the results following standard econometric procedures. Originally, Breusch and Pagan Lagrangian multiplier test is used to justify the selection between ordinary least square (OLS) and random-effect model. Given the Breusch and Pagan Lagrangian multiplier test results, there is evidence in favour of using the random-effect model, whilst between the random- and fixed-effect models, the Hausman test provides evidence in favour of using the random-effect model.

In modelling economic welfare, this study follows Agbloyor (2019) who investigated how economic welfare is influenced by political business cycles in Africa. Hence, this study adopts his model and modifies it by including microfinance sustainability, microfinance social performance and microfinance profitability as independent variables of interests. Hence, the modified model is expressed below. Equation (11.2) focuses on how microfinance sustainability and microfinance social performance affect economic welfare, whilst equation (11.3) focuses on how microfinance profitability affects economic welfare.

$$
\begin{aligned}
HDI_{it} = {} & \beta_0 + \beta_1 MFISUS_{it} + \beta_2 MFISocPerf_{it} + \beta_3 INCOME_{it} \\
& + \beta_4 TRADEOPEN_{it} + \beta_5 INFLATION_{it} \\
& + \beta_6 FDI_{it} + \beta_7 POPGROWTH_{it} + \beta_8 PERIMT_{it} \\
& + \beta_9 INSTITUTIONS_{it} \\
& + \beta_{10} PRIVATECREDITBUR_{it} + \varepsilon_{it}
\end{aligned}
\tag{11.2}
$$

$$
\begin{aligned}
HDI_{it} = {} & \beta_0 + \beta_1 MFIPROF_{it} + \beta_2 INCOME_{it} \\
& + \beta_3 TRADEOPEN_{it} + \beta_4 INFLATION_{it} \\
& + \beta_5 FDI_{it} + \beta_6 POPGROWTH_{it} + \beta_7 PERIMT_{it} \\
& + \beta_8 INSTITUTIONS_{it} + \beta_9 PRIVATECREDITBUR_{it} \\
& + \beta_9 ZSCORE_{it} + \varepsilon_{it}
\end{aligned}
\tag{11.3}
$$

MFISUS is a vector of MFI sustainability indicators, namely, financial self-sufficiency (FSS), subsidy dependence (SDI) and portfolio at risk (PaR).

MFISocPerf is a vector of MFI social performance indicators and includes the average loan size, the percentage of female borrowers and the percentage of rural borrowers.

MFIPROF is a vector of MFI financial/profitability indicators, namely, deposits, loans, yield on loan portfolio, return on equity, return on assets and efficiency

INCOME, TRADEOPEN, INFLATION, FDI, POPGROWTH, PERIMT, INSTITUTIONS and PRIVATECREDITBUR are control variables representing GDP per capita, trade openness, inflation, foreign direct investment, population growth, personal remittances, institutional quality, and private credit bureau coverage of the adult population and banking stability respectively.

11.4 Discussion of Findings

In this section, we present and discuss the results from the empirical estimations. We start with the presentation of the descriptive statistics in Table 11.1. This is then followed by a discussion of the regression results. The median HDI was 0.52, suggesting a low level of economic development in Africa. The HDI index ranges from 0 to 1, with higher values indicating higher human development. The median FSS ratio was 85%, indicating that on the average MFIs in Africa are not financially self-sufficient. The median SDI index was 0, indicating that MFIs in Africa are subsidy-independent. The median portfolio at risk for 90 days was 5%. This suggests that MFIs have a relatively performing loan portfolio. The descriptive statistics show that MFIs have a preference of lending to women. This is because there is evidence that women are more faithful borrowers. The percentage of female borrowers recorded a median of 57%. MFIs shun from lending to borrowers in rural areas. This is because the population in these areas is low increasing their transactional cost. The median percentage of loans granted to rural borrowers was 8%. The median yield on MFI loan books was 38%. This is indicative of the high rates that MFIs charge their borrowers.

The median ROA was almost 0%, whilst the median ROE was about 5%. On the average, operating expenses formed about 32% of MFI loan books in Africa. Trade openness had a median of 56%, suggesting that African countries are fairly open to international trade. Inflation recorded a median of 5.6%. The median level of FDI was 2.3% suggesting low levels of FDI inflows into Africa over the sample period. The median population growth rate was 2.7%. The median level of remittances was 1.1%. Institutions recorded a median of -0.641, suggesting that institutions in Africa are weak. The institutions index ranges from -2.5 to +2.5, with higher values indicating stronger institutions. Institutions is the average of the six governance indicators of Kaufmann, Kraay, and Mastruzzi (2010). The mean of the adult population covered by private credit bureaus was 11%. This is low, compared to other regions of the world. This compares to a ratio of 35% for North and South America (see Kusi, Agbloyor, Gyeke-Dako and Asongu, 2020).

11.4.1 Full Sample

Firstly, we examine the impact of microfinance sustainability and social performance on economic development using data at the country level. The results for these regression models are shown in Table 11.2. Generally, we do not detect any relationship between MFI sustainability, MFI social performance and economic development using the country-level data. The indicators of sustainability and social performance such as the financial self-sufficiency ratio, the subsidy dependence index, the portfolio at risk measure, the number of active borrowers, the average loan size, the percentage of female borrowers and the percentage of rural borrowers do not enter the regression models with significant coefficients.

In terms of the control variables, as expected, we observe a positive relationship between GDP per capita and human development or poverty reduction. Thus, an increase in GDP per capita leads to an increase in human development or a reduction in poverty. We also find a positive relationship between remittances and human development. This implies that an increase in remittances contributes to economic development or a reduction in poverty. It is well established that remittances are mostly sent by migrants to their families back home based on altruistic motives. Thus, part of the funds sent is used to take care of the educational and health needs of the family back

Table 11.1 Descriptive statistics

Variables	Obs	Mean	Std. Dev.	Min	Max	1%	25%	50%	75%	99%
Economic development	570	.555	.176	0	.866	0	.426	.52	.707	.866
Financial sustainability	653	.836	.34	0	2.343	0	.670	.846	.997	2.343
Subsidy dependence	586	.112	.397	−.464	2.025	−.464	−.085	−.003	.180	2.025
Portfolio at risk	617	.06	.049	0	.281	0	.029	.048	.079	.281
Number of active borrowers	661	11.109	2.094	5.069	14.731	5.069	9.799	11.453	12.689	14.731
Average loan size	612	1.512	1.882	.026	10.845	.026	.476	.980	1.601	10.845
Female borrowers	515	.572	.21	.093	1	.093	.443	.573	.709	1
Rural borrowers	668	.131	.182	0	.946	0	0	.075	.162	.946
Deposits	652	17.095	3.423	−.345	22.053	−.345	15.650	17.439	19.376	22.053
Loans	685	17.334	2.812	8.498	21.99	8.498	15.702	17.605	19.493	21.99
Yield on loan portfolio	593	.408	.191	.097	1.329	.097	.294	.377	.467	1.329
Return on assets	614	−.006	.096	−.408	.274	−.408	−.031	.008	.034	.274
Return on expenses	614	.029	.373	−1.436	1.32	−1.436	−.074	.046	.178	1.32
Operating expenses	609	.402	.336	.037	2.117	.037	.238	.323	.440	2.117
Income	559	6.707	.784	5.367	8.92	5.367	6.165	6.544	7.153	8.92
Trade openness	560	.579	.272	0	1.525	0	.408	.555	.704	1.525
Inflation	560	.073	.085	−.037	.448	−.037	.009	.056	.101	.448
FDI	560	.04	.067	−.037	.465	−.037	.008	.023	.045	.465
Population growth	560	.027	.007	.004	.044	.004	.024	.027	.029	.044
Remittances	560	.025	.032	0	.147	0	.002	.011	.032	.147
Institutions	560	−.63	.519	−1.619	.394	−1.619	−1.010	−.641	−.230	.394
Credit reference bureaus	533	.11	.229	0	1	0	0	0	.066	1
Bank stability	560	8.503	8.96	0	42.43	0	0	7.768	13.116	42.43

Table 11.2 Effect of microfinance sustainability and social performance on economic development

Variables	Model 1	Model 2	Model 3	Model 4	Model 5	Model 6	Model 7
MFI sustainability							
Financial sustainability	−0.00784 (0.0127)						
Subsidy dependence		−0.00634 (0.0206)					
Portfolio at risk			−0.0105 (0.118)				
MFI social performance							
Number of active borrowers				0.00719 (0.00464)			
Average loan size					−0.00114 (0.00577)		
Female borrowers						0.00641 (0.0283)	
Rural borrowers							−0.0181 (0.0393)
Controls							
Income	0.104★★ (0.0460)	0.115★★ (0.0457)	0.118★★ (0.0476)	0.116★★★ (0.0446)	0.118★★ (0.0498)	0.0984★★ (0.0438)	0.122★★★ (0.0468)
Trade openness	−0.0426 (0.0487)	−0.0416 (0.0684)	−0.0636 (0.0590)	−0.0776 (0.0472)	−0.0695 (0.0553)	−0.115★★ (0.0556)	−0.0678 (0.0536)
Inflation	0.0568 (0.0834)	0.0148 (0.0937)	0.0773 (0.0970)	0.0509 (0.0838)	0.0946 (0.0890)	0.0477 (0.106)	0.0555 (0.0842)
FDI	−0.162	−0.114	−0.142	−0.208★	−0.111	−0.103	−0.250★

Variables	Model 1	Model 2	Model 3	Model 4	Model 5	Model 6	Model 7
	(0.123)	(0.166)	(0.146)	(0.108)	(0.155)	(0.128)	(0.129)
Population growth	−2.083	−2.106	−1.614	−2.148	−2.072	−1.663	−1.611
	(2.057)	(2.166)	(2.307)	(1.970)	(2.406)	(2.423)	(2.091)
Remittances	0.811★	0.770	0.931★	0.934★	0.979★★	0.862	1.041★★
	(0.489)	(0.512)	(0.526)	(0.485)	(0.489)	(0.578)	(0.469)
Institutions	−0.0252	−0.0228	−0.0253	−0.0261	−0.0235	−0.0129	−0.0259
	(0.0263)	(0.0258)	(0.0257)	(0.0256)	(0.0255)	(0.0273)	(0.0252)
Credit reference bureaus	0.376★★★	0.379★★★	0.379★★★	0.388★★★	0.369★★★	0.393★★★	0.394★★★
	(0.0663)	(0.0708)	(0.0683)	(0.0660)	(0.0652)	(0.0660)	(0.0700)
Bank stability	0.00101★	0.000958★	0.000868	0.000932	0.000846	0.000416	0.000944★
	(0.000538)	(0.000581)	(0.000568)	(0.000577)	(0.000595)	(0.000589)	(0.000550)
Constant	−0.134	−0.213	−0.244	−0.291	−0.229	−0.0732	−0.266
	(0.293)	(0.302)	(0.313)	(0.312)	(0.326)	(0.296)	(0.307)
Observations	505	446	472	501	467	396	504
Number of countries	30	30	30	30	30	30	30

Robust standard errors in parentheses.

★★★ $p < 0.01$, ★★ $p < 0.05$ and ★ $p < 0.1$.

NB: Financial sustainability represents the financial self-sufficiency ratio. Subsidy dependence is the subsidy dependence index. Portfolio at risk is the portfolio at risk for 90 days. Number of active borrowers is the total number of active borrowers in a country. Average loan size is the average outstanding loan balance as a percentage of GNI. Female borrowers represent the percentage of female borrowers. Rural borrowers represent the percentage of rural borrowers. Income is GDP per capita in constant 2010 US dollars. Trade openness represents exports plus imports all divided by GDP. Inflation represents the changes in the consumer price index. FDI is net FDI inflows as a percentage of GDP. Population growth represents the growth in population. Remittances represents personal remittances as a percentage of GDP. Institutions is the average of the six indicators of governance from Kaufmann, Kraay, and Mastruzzi (2010). Credit reference bureaus is measured as the percentage of the adult population covered by private credit reference bureaus. Bank stability is measured as the Z score.

home. In addition, part of the money is used for investment purposes, which can contribute to income generation. These results are consistent with previous studies that show that remittances promote economic growth and development in Africa (see, for example, Fayissa and Nsiah, 2010; Nyamongo, Misati, Kipyegon, and Ndirangu, 2012). The results also provide support for a positive relationship between private credit bureau coverage and economic development. Thus, when more of the adult population is covered by private credit bureaus, information asymmetry between lenders and borrowers is reduced, leading to more supply of loans to borrowers and a reduction in the credit risk exposure of financial institutions (see, for example, Kusi, Agbloyor, Fiador, and Osei, 2016a,b). This contributes to economic activities and consequently an increase in human development or a reduction in poverty. Finally, the results indicated a positive and significant relationship between bank stability and economic development. This suggests that banking sector stability promotes economic development.

We observed a negative relationship between foreign direct investment and human development. This does not come as a surprise as the literature shows that the impact of FDI on economic growth/development depends on absorptive capacities such as financial development and institutions (see, for example, Agbloyor, Abor, Adjasi, and Yawson, 2014). We also find a negative relationship between trade openness and human development. This suggests that trade openness may not always be beneficial for poverty reduction.

We now examine the effect of MFI financial/profitability indicators on economic development at the country level. These results are presented in Table 11.3. Despite employing a large array of variables to explore the empirical relationships, only two of the variables enter the empirical regression models significantly. These are the deposits and loans of MFIs. Thus, by providing deposit taking and lending services, MFIs in Africa are able to improve the welfare of their clients leading to economic development. This occurs because the poor can accumulate assets and borrower to invest in productive activities. The other variables such as the yield on the loan portfolio of MFIs, the return on assets, the return on equity and the operational efficiency of MFIs do not exhibit any statistically significant relationship with economic development or poverty reduction. In terms of the control variables, the signs and significance of the variables employed are similar to the results presented earlier. Consequently, we do not discuss the control variables here.

11.4.2 *Sub-Sample (High and Low Income) Analysis*

Given the lack of significance of a number of the MFI indicators, we investigate further by splitting the sample into high-income groups as opposed to countries in low-income groups. We split the countries based on the sample median. Countries above the median are classified as high, whilst countries below the median are classified as low. We do this because the provision of microfinance and its impact are likely to be felt more in low-income countries

Table 11.3 Effect of microfinance financial/profitability indicators on economic development

Variables	Model 8	Model 9	Model 10	Model 11	Model 12	Model 13
MFI financial/profitability indicators						
Deposits	0.00751** (0.00295)					
Loans		0.00755** (0.00296)				
Yield on loan portfolio			0.0176 (0.0288)			
Return on assets				−0.0266 (0.0946)		
Return on equity					−0.0151 (0.0124)	
Operating expenses						0.00735 (0.0235)
Controls						
Income	0.0967** (0.0434)	0.0958** (0.0426)	0.118** (0.0486)	0.113** (0.0478)	0.113** (0.0476)	0.109** (0.0468)
Trade openness	−0.0451 (0.0492)	−0.0456 (0.0432)	−0.0499 (0.0653)	−0.0468 (0.0614)	−0.0493 (0.0611)	−0.0529 (0.0591)
Inflation	0.0618 (0.0823)	0.0622 (0.0789)	0.0232 (0.0938)	0.0332 (0.0931)	0.0307 (0.0914)	0.0417 (0.0927)
FDI	−0.168 (0.117)	−0.175 (0.112)	−0.102 (0.171)	−0.139 (0.149)	−0.139 (0.150)	−0.128 (0.155)
Population growth	−2.407 (1.932)	−2.331 (1.932)	−2.197 (2.147)	−2.124 (2.127)	−1.984 (2.105)	−2.135 (2.156)
Remittances	0.770*	0.721	0.800	0.807	0.786	0.825

(Continued)

Table 11.3 (Continued)

Variables	Model 8	Model 9	Model 10	Model 11	Model 12	Model 13
	(0.468)	(0.458)	(0.533)	(0.539)	(0.532)	(0.533)
Institutions	−0.0221	−0.0244	−0.0168	−0.0156	−0.0160	−0.0157
	(0.0278)	(0.0268)	(0.0269)	(0.0272)	(0.0274)	(0.0272)
Credit reference bureaus	0.371★★★	0.372★★★	0.380★★★	0.383★★★	0.384★★★	0.381★★★
	(0.0655)	(0.0629)	(0.0719)	(0.0692)	(0.0697)	(0.0700)
Bank stability	0.000688	0.000928★	0.000616	0.000563	0.000542	0.000568
	(0.000637)	(0.000550)	(0.000602)	(0.000601)	(0.000619)	(0.000611)
Constant	−0.207	−0.206	−0.232	−0.188	−0.191	−0.165
	(0.298)	(0.301)	(0.316)	(0.310)	(0.308)	(0.303)
Observations	503	519	457	472	470	470
Number of countries	30	30	30	30	30	30

Robust standard errors in parentheses.

★★★ $p < 0.01$, ★★ $p < 0.05$ and ★ $p < 0.1$.

NB: Deposits is the sum of deposits of MFIs in a country. Loans is the sum of loans of MFIs in a country. Yield is the average yield on an MFI loan portfolio. Return on assets is the average return on MFI assets in a country. Return on equity is the average return on MFI equity in a country. Operating expenses is the MFI operating expenses as a percentage of its loan book.

as opposed to high-income countries. As indicated earlier, informal finance thrives in countries where institutions are weak.

11.4.2.1 *Microfinance Sustainability, Social Performance and Economic Development*

We find interesting results when we split the sample based on income. The results for MFI sustainability, social performance and economic development are presented in Appendix 11.3. In terms of the social performance measures, for the high-income sample, we find that the number of active borrowers has a positive effect on economic development; however, the average loan size has a negative effect on economic development. When we interpret these results together, it suggests that in relatively high-income countries, what matters is giving more loans to borrowers and not the size of the loan. Further, lending to female borrowers was found to promote economic development. On the contrary, results in the low-income countries were similar to those of the full sample; most of the indicators were not significant. The only difference was that subsidies enter the regression models being marginally significant at the 10% level. This suggests that in low-income economies, the provision of subsidies helps to improve economic development. The results were overall surprising, because we expected microfinance to have a bigger impact in lower income countries because of the prevalence of weak institutions and informal financial markets.

In terms of the control variables, we noticed some differences in the two samples. We find that population growth has no effect in high-income countries, whilst it has a negative effect in low-income countries. This is not surprising as a high level of population growth can put pressure on educational and health facilities. In addition, if jobs are not created fast enough, it could lead to high unemployment and the prevalence of crime resulting from a demographic 'curse'. In addition, whilst remittances have a positive effect on economic development in high-income countries, it has a negative effect on economic development in low-income countries. On the contrary, institutions have a negative effect in high-income countries but a positive effect in low-income countries. Finally, whilst financial stability has no effect on economic development in high-income countries, it has a positive effect on economic development in low-income countries. Interestingly, the coverage of credit reference bureaus in both low- and high-income countries has a consistently positive impact on economic development.

11.4.2.2 *Microfinance Financial/Profitability Indicators and Economic Development*

We now examine how microfinance profitability indicators are related to economic development when we split the sample into high- and low-income economies. The results are presented in Appendix 11.4. Whilst loans and deposits were significant in the full sample, they were not significant in either high- or low-income samples. In terms of the control variables, the results are similar to the earlier results discussed.

11.5 Conclusion

In this chapter, we examine the relation between microfinance sustainability, microfinance social performance and economic development in Africa. The findings in the full sample did not reveal any significant relationship between MFI sustainability and social performance indicators and economic development. In the high-income sample, however, as more people access deposit and lending services from MFIs, it leads to an improvement in economic development. We also found that when MFIs focus on their core mission of lending to the poor, this promotes economic development. Finally, the findings also suggested that lending to females leads to economic development. In low-income countries, the provision of subsidies was found to be important in explaining economic development. In particular, the findings revealed a marginally significantly positive relationship between subsidy dependence and economic development. In terms of profitability, we found in the full sample that the provision of deposit and lending services by MFIs promotes economic development. Overall, the findings provide support for microfinance as one way to reduce poverty or promote economic development in Africa. In particular, promoting the deposit and lending services of MFIs to those at the bottom of the economic ladder can make a dent in poverty reduction. We also find support that MFI social performance (number of active borrowers, number of female borrowers and small loan sizes) impacts positively on economic development, at least in high-income African countries. Low-income countries should seek to learn from the experiences of higher income countries in the continent, so they can also realize the benefits of the microfinance 'promise'.

In the full sample, we found that income, remittances, credit reference bureaus and banking stability were positively related to economic development. On the contrary, FDI and trade openness were found to be negatively related to economic development. In terms of the control variables for the sub-samples, we noticed some differences in the two samples. We find that population growth has no effect in high-income countries, whilst it has a negative effect in low-income countries. In addition, whilst remittances have a positive effect on economic development in high-income countries, it has a negative effect on economic development in low-income countries. On the contrary, institutions have a negative effect in high-income countries but a positive effect in low-income countries. Finally, whilst financial stability has no effect on economic development in high-income countries, it has a positive effect on economic development in low-income countries. Interestingly, the coverage of credit reference bureaus in both low- and high-income countries has a consistently positive impact on economic development.

References

Agbloyor, E. K. (2019). Foreign direct investment: Political business cycles and welfare in Africa. *Journal of International Development, 31*(5), 345–373.

Agbloyor, E. K., Abor, J. Y., Adjasi, C. K. D., & Yawson, A. (2014). Private capital flows and economic growth in Africa: The role of domestic financial markets. *Journal of International Financial Markets, Institutions and Money, 30*, 137–152.

Agbloyor, E. K., Gyeke-Dako, A., Kuipo, R., & Abor, J. Y. (2016). Foreign direct investment and economic growth in SSA: The role of institutions. *Thunderbird International Business Review, 58*(5), 479–497.

Ahlin, C., & Jiang, N. (2008). Can micro-credit bring development? *Journal of Development Economics, 86*(1), 1–21.

Armendáriz, B., & Szafarz, A. (2011). On mission drift in microfinance institutions. In S. D'Agnes & S. G. Prabhakar (Eds.), *The Handbook of Microfinance* (Volume 2, pp. 341–366). Singapore: World Scientific Publishing.

Attanasio, O., Augsburg, B., De Haas, R., Fitzsimons, E., & Harmgart, H. (2015). The impacts of microfinance: Evidence from joint-liability lending in Mongolia. *American Economic Journal: Applied Economics, 7*(1), 90–122.

Babajide, A. (2012). Effects of microfinance on micro and small enterprises (MSEs) growth in Nigeria. *Asian Economic and Financial Review, 2*(3), 463–477.

Baltagi, B. H. (2008). *Econometric analysis of panel data.* Chichester: John Wiley & Sons.

Baltagi, B. H. (Ed.). (2015). *The Oxford handbook of panel data.* Oxford Handbooks. Oxford: Oxford University Press.

Banerjee, A. V., Banerjee, A., & Duflo, E. (2011). *Poor economics: A radical rethinking of the way to fight global poverty.* New York, NY: Public Affairs.

Banerjee, A., Duflo, E., Glennerster, R., & Kinnan, C. (2015). The miracle of microfinance? Evidence from a randomized evaluation. *American Economic Journal: Applied Economics, 7*(1), 22–53.

Banto, J. M., & Monsia, A. F. (2021). Microfinance institutions, banking, growth and transmission channel: A GMM panel data analysis from developing countries. *The Quarterly Review of Economics and Finance, 79*, 126–150.

Buera, F. J., Kaboski, J. P., & Shin, Y. (2021). The macroeconomics of microfinance. *The Review of Economic Studies, 88*(1), 126–161.

Demirguc-Kunt, A., Klapper, L., Singer, D., & Ansar, S. (2018). *The Global Findex Database 2017: Measuring financial inclusion and the fintech revolution.* Washington, DC: World Bank Publications.

Donou-Adonsou, C. F., & Sylwester, K. (2015). Macroeconomic effects of microfinance: Evidence from developing countries. *Journal Economics, 41*(1), 21–35.

Donou-Adonsou, C. F., & Sylwester, K. (2017). Growth effect of banks and microfinance: Evidence from developing countries. *The Quarterly Review of Economics and Finance, 64*, 44–56.

Fayissa, B., & Nsiah, C. (2010). The impact of remittances on economic growth and development in Africa. *The American Economist, 55*(2), 92–103.

Ghosh, P., Mookherjee, D., & Ray, D. (2000). Credit rationing in developing countries: An overview of the theory. In J. Behrman & T. N. Srinivasan (Eds.), *Readings in the Theory of Economic Development* (pp. 383–401). Oxford, UK: Blackwell Publishers.

Hermes, N. (2014). Does microfinance affect income inequality? *Applied Economics, 46*(9), 1021–1034.

Imbens, G. W., & Wooldridge, J. M. (2009). Recent developments in the econometrics of program evaluation. *Journal of Economic Literature, 47*(1), 5–86.

Kaboski, J. P., & Townsend, R. M. (2012). The impact of credit on village economies. *American Economic Journal: Applied Economics, 4*(2), 98–133.

Kaufmann, D., Kraay, A., & Mastruzzi, M. (2010). The worldwide governance indicators: Methodological and analytical issues. *World Bank Policy Research Paper* No. 5430.

Kusi, B. A., Agbloyor, E. K., Fiador, V. O., & Osei, K. A. (2016a). Does information sharing promote or detract from bank returns: Evidence from Ghana. *African Development Review, 28*(3), 332–343.

Kusi, B. A., Agbloyor, E. K., Fiador, V. O., & Osei, K. A. (2016b). Credit referencing bureaus and bank credit risk: Evidence from Ghana. *African Finance Journal, 18*(2), 69–92.

Kusi, B. A., Agbloyor, E. K., Gyeke-Dako, A., & Asongu, S. A. (2020). Financial Sector transparency and net interest margins: Should the private or public Sector lead financial Sector transparency? *Research in International Business and Finance, 54*, 101–260.

Mersland, R., & Strøm, R. Ø. (2010). Microfinance mission drift?. *World Development, 38*(1), 28–36.

Morduch, J. (1999). The microfinance promise. *Journal of Economic Literature, 37*(4), 1569–1614.

Morduch, J., & Armendariz, B. (2005). *The economics of microfinance.* Cambridge: MIT Press.

Nyamongo, E. M., Misati, R. N., Kipyegon, L., & Ndirangu, L. (2012). Remittances, financial development and economic growth in Africa. *Journal of Economics and Business, 64*(3), 240–260.

Stewart, R., Van Rooyen, C., Dickson, K., Majoro, M., & De Wet, T. (2010). What is the impact of microfinance on poor people?: A systematic review of evidence from sub-Saharan Africa. *African Journal of Economic and Management Studies, 1*(1), 18–31.

Appendices

Appendix 11.1A MFI Sustainability and Economic Development

Best-Performing Countries

Rank	Country	HDI	Country	FSS	Country	SDI	Country	Portfolio at Risk
1	Chad	0.739	Guinea-Bissau	1.39	Guinea-Bissau	−0.37	Guinea-Bissau	0.0299
2	Nigeria	0.739	Uganda	1.27	Zambia	−0.12	Malawi	0.0336
3	Liberia	0.708	Senegal	1.07	Central African Republic	−0.10	Nigeria	0.0346
4	Tanzania	0.689	Burundi	1.04	Togo	−0.06	Zambia	0.0350
5	Ghana	0.687	Kenya	1.02	Rwanda	−0.05	Guinea	0.0390
6	Zimbabwe	0.687	Congo Republic	1.00	Chad	−0.04	Sudan	0.0390
7	Central African Republic	0.682	Cote d'Ivoire	0.99	Benin	−0.03	Namibia	0.0414
8	Niger	0.675	Madagascar	0.96	South Africa	−0.02	Benin	0.0420
9	Cameroon	0.652	Togo	0.95	Congo Republic	−0.01	Liberia	0.0438
10	Sierra Leone	0.651	Nigeria	0.93	South Sudan	−0.01	Mali	0.0445

Worst-Performing Countries

Rank	Country	HDI	Country	FSS	Country	SDI	Country	Portfolio at Risk
10	Guinea	0.123	Swaziland	−0.15	Zimbabwe	1.51	Ghana	0.5279
9	Burkina Faso	0.367	South Sudan	0.48	Kenya	1.35	Angola	0.1193
8	Benin	0.394	Angola	0.63	Niger	0.54	Niger	0.1185

(Continued)

Appendix 11.1A (Continued)

Worst-Performing Countries

Rank	Country	HDI	Country	FSS	Country	SDI	Country	Portfolio at Risk
7	Mali	0.394	Central African Republic	0.65	Comoros	0.40	Mozambique	0.1120
6	Ethiopia	0.403	Liberia	0.65	Swaziland	0.34	Sierra Leone	0.1120
5	Senegal	0.411	Sudan	0.65	Sudan	0.31	Burkina Faso	0.0937
4	Burundi	0.433	Burkina Faso	0.68	Mali	0.23	Central African Republic	0.0886
3	South Africa	0.456	Comoros	0.69	Uganda	0.23	Kenya	0.0714
2	Togo	0.470	Mozambique	0.73	Nigeria	0.23	Comoros	0.0712
1	Mozambique	0.487	Zambia	0.73	Cameroon	0.22	Cameroon	0.0711

Appendix 11.1B MFI Social Performance and Economic Development

Best-Performing Countries

Rank	Country	HDI		Loan Size		Female Borrowers		Rural Borrowers
1	Chad	0.739	Swaziland	−0.012	South Sudan	0.885	Swaziland	0.932
2	Nigeria	0.739	Central African Republic	0.072	Guinea	0.841	Benin	0.366
3	Liberia	0.708	Comoros	0.290	Zambia	0.720	South Africa	0.299
4	Tanzania	0.689	Gambia, The	0.320	Uganda	0.702	Angola	0.268
5	Ghana	0.687	Guinea	0.432	Cameroon	0.697	Congo Republic	0.234
6	Zimbabwe	0.687	Angola	0.494	Burkina Faso	0.671	Burundi	0.221
7	Central African Republic	0.682	Burkina Faso	0.664	South Africa	0.657	Guinea	0.209
8	Niger	0.675	Kenya	0.735	Ethiopia	0.642	Togo	0.197

| 9 | Cameroon | 0.652 | South Sudan | 0.738 | Senegal | 0.642 | Sierra Leone | 0.178 |
| 10 | Sierra Leone | 0.651 | Zambia | 0.771 | Congo Republic | 0.635 | The Gambia | 0.167 |

Worst-Performing Countries

Rank	Country	HDI		Loan Size		Female Borrowers		Rural Borrowers
10	Guinea	0.123	Liberia	6.207	Central African Republic	0.144	Liberia	0.027
9	Burkina Faso	0.367	Sierra Leone	6.205	Angola	0.269	Cote d'Ivoire (Ivory Coast)	0.040
8	Benin	0.394	Nigeria	3.411	Chad	0.312	Tanzania	0.054
7	Mali	0.394	South Africa	2.196	Namibia	0.384	Namibia	0.057
6	Ethiopia	0.403	Togo	2.105	The Gambia	0.464	Congo, Democratic Republic	0.062
5	Senegal	0.411	Congo, Democratic Republic	1.999	Comoros	0.475	Rwanda	0.065
4	Burundi	0.433	Cameroon	1.995	Tanzania	0.481	Malawi	0.068
3	South Africa	0.456	Tanzania	1.814	Burundi	0.484	Uganda	0.071
2	Togo	0.470	Mali	1.718	Rwanda	0.503	Kenya	0.071
1	Mozambique	0.487	Malawi	1.702	Guinea-Bissau	0.505	Mali	0.071

Appendix 11.2 MFI Profitability and Economic Development
Appendix 11.2A High HDI Sample

HIGH HDI

Variables	Top 10	Top 10	Top 10	Top 10	Top 10	Top 10	Top 10	Top 10	Top 10	Top 10
MFI deposits		Nigeria		Tanzania	Ghana	Zimbabwe			Cameroon	
MFI loans		Nigeria		Tanzania	Ghana	Zimbabwe			Cameroon	
Yield on MFI loan portfolio			Liberia				CAR			
Return on assets	Chad						CAR			Sierra Leone
Return on equity	Chad					Zimbabwe	CAR	Niger		Sierra Leone
Operating expense to loans	Chad						CAR			Sierra Leone

Variables	Bottom 10	Bottom 10	Bottom 10	Bottom 10	Bottom 10	Bottom 10	Bottom 10	Bottom 10	Bottom 10	Bottom 10
MFI deposits			Liberia				CAR			Sierra Leone
MFI loans	Chad						CAR			
Yield on MFI loan portfolio				Tanzania						Sierra Leone
Return on assets			Liberia	Tanzania				Niger	Cameroon	
Return on equity			Liberia	Tanzania	Ghana					
Operating expense to loans			Liberia			Zimbabwe				

LOW HDI

Variables	Top 10	Top 10	Top 10	Top 10	Top 10	Top 10	Top 10	Top 10	Top 10	Top 10
MFI deposits						Senegal			Togo	
MFI loans						Senegal		SA	Togo	
Yield on MFI loan portfolio					Ethiopia					Mozambique
Return on assets			Benin						Togo	
Return on equity								SA		
Operating expense to loans								SA		Mozambique

Variables	Bottom 10	Bottom 10	Bottom 10	Bottom 10	Bottom 10	Bottom 10	Bottom 10	Bottom 10	Bottom 10	Bottom 10
MFI deposits										Mozambique
MFI loans	Guinea									
Yield on MFI loan portfolio		Burkina Faso					Burundi			
Return on assets	Guinea									Mozambique
Return on equity		Burkina Faso								Mozambique
Operating expense to loans					Ethiopia					

Appendix 11.3A Microfinance Sustainability, Social Performance and Economic Development in High-Income Economies

Variables	Model 14	Model 15	Model 16	Model 17	Model 18	Model 19	Model 20
MFI sustainability							
Financial sustainability	−0.00603						
	(0.00955)						
Subsidy dependence		−0.0225					
		(0.0197)					
Portfolio at risk			0.0706				
			(0.166)				
MFI sustainability							
Number of active borrowers				0.0112★★			
				(0.00546)			
Average loan size					−0.0142★★★		
					(0.00507)		
Female borrowers						0.0644★★	
						(0.0310)	
Rural borrowers							−0.0461
							(0.0316)
Income	0.0342	0.0433	0.0462	0.0588	0.0225	0.0578	0.0528
	(0.0687)	(0.0726)	(0.0627)	(0.0669)	(0.0548)	(0.0633)	(0.0601)
Trade openness	−0.0854	−0.0987	−0.116	−0.145★★	−0.114	−0.230★★★	−0.132★
	(0.0751)	(0.109)	(0.0814)	(0.0669)	(0.0741)	(0.0861)	(0.0728)
Inflation	0.0483	0.0411	0.0732	0.0175	0.0291	−0.00312	0.0391
	(0.155)	(0.195)	(0.176)	(0.154)	(0.156)	(0.195)	(0.145)
FDI	0.439	0.469	0.528★	0.165	0.460★	0.198	0.279
	(0.336)	(0.373)	(0.289)	(0.228)	(0.273)	(0.423)	(0.270)
Population	2.592	0.694	2.804	2.871	2.280	3.788★	2.738
	(2.275)	(3.648)	(2.543)	(2.578)	(2.031)	(2.266)	(2.558)
Remittances	1.486★★★	1.572★★★	1.625★★★	1.511★★★	1.551★★★	1.323★★★	1.516★★★
	(0.291)	(0.299)	(0.268)	(0.286)	(0.240)	(0.437)	(0.283)

Institutions	−0.0523	−0.0413	−0.0398	−0.0418	−0.0480	−0.0577	−0.0476
	(0.0325)	(0.0332)	(0.0286)	(0.0301)	(0.0315)	(0.0392)	(0.0340)
Credit reference bureaus	0.412★★★	0.430★★★	0.384★★★	0.402★★★	0.386★★★	0.375★★★	0.411★★★
	(0.0999)	(0.108)	(0.105)	(0.106)	(0.0938)	(0.107)	(0.0987)
Bank stability	−2.26e−05	−0.000588	−0.000206	0.000196	−0.000183	−0.000175	8.86e−05
	(0.000760)	(0.00100)	(0.000749)	(0.000699)	(0.000727)	(0.000818)	(0.000710)
Constant	0.232	0.228	0.151	−0.0354	0.359	0.0898	0.127
	(0.516)	(0.594)	(0.488)	(0.535)	(0.409)	(0.498)	(0.457)
Observations	250	211	236	249	237	193	253
Number of country code	17	17	17	17	17	17	17

Robust standard errors in parentheses.
★★★ $p < 0.01$, ★★ $p < 0.05$ and ★ $p < 0.1$.

Appendix 11.3B Microfinance Sustainability, Social Performance and Economic Development in Low-Income Economies

Variables	Model 21	Model 22	Model 23	Model 24	Model 25	Model 26	Model 27
MFI sustainability							
Financial sustainability	−0.0142						
	(0.0227)						
Subsidy dependence		0.0264★					
		(0.0151)					
Portfolio at risk			0.00845				
			(0.0967)				
MFI sustainability							
Number of active borrowers				0.000780			
				(0.00594)			
Average loan size					0.00548		
					(0.00353)		
Female borrowers						−0.0110	
						(0.0319)	
Rural borrowers							0.0309
							(0.0737)
Income	0.0790	0.0869	0.0723	0.0571	0.0658	0.0264	0.0649
	(0.0656)	(0.0639)	(0.0616)	(0.0608)	(0.0703)	(0.0646)	(0.0636)
Trade openness	0.0211	0.0418	0.0346	0.0182	0.0365	0.0122	−5.63e−05
	(0.0423)	(0.0568)	(0.0457)	(0.0399)	(0.0493)	(0.0358)	(0.0396)
Inflation	−0.00868	−0.0237	−0.0227	−0.00434	−0.0360	0.0294	−0.00355
	(0.0553)	(0.0593)	(0.0531)	(0.0553)	(0.0485)	(0.0715)	(0.0558)
FDI	0.0261	0.0362	0.0256	0.0266	0.0327	−0.000608	0.0605
	(0.0702)	(0.0689)	(0.0661)	(0.0653)	(0.0543)	(0.0731)	(0.0910)
Population	−4.591★★★	−4.143★★★	−4.689★★★	−4.299★★★	−4.830★★★	−3.914★	−4.761★★★
	(1.206)	(1.210)	(0.987)	(1.090)	(1.037)	(2.032)	(0.877)

Remittances	−0.829★	−1.026★★	−0.967★★	−0.744	−0.852★	−0.928★	−0.912★
	(0.477)	(0.520)	(0.489)	(0.497)	(0.438)	(0.540)	(0.538)
Institutions	0.0333★	0.0271	0.0302	0.0315★	0.0274	0.0313	0.0277
	(0.0193)	(0.0171)	(0.0193)	(0.0189)	(0.0216)	(0.0221)	(0.0185)
Credit reference bureaus	0.333★★★	0.331★★★	0.343★★★	0.330★★★	0.319★★★	0.359★★★	0.323★★★
	(0.0665)	(0.0706)	(0.0652)	(0.0661)	(0.0617)	(0.0605)	(0.0657)
Bank stability	0.00122★	0.00184★★★	0.00106	0.00104	0.00103	0.000321	0.00102
	(0.000682)	(0.000624)	(0.000705)	(0.000770)	(0.000750)	(0.000815)	(0.000784)
Constant	0.146	0.0500	0.163	0.241	0.194	0.443	0.223
	(0.376)	(0.371)	(0.360)	(0.375)	(0.421)	(0.355)	(0.379)
Observations	255	235	236	252	230	203	251
Number of country code	18	18	18	18	18	18	18

Robust standard errors in parentheses.
★★★ $p < 0.01$, ★★ $p < 0.05$ and ★ $p < 0.1$.

Appendix 11.4A Microfinance Profitability and Economic Development in High-Income Economies

Variables	Model 28	Model 29	Model 30	Model 31	Model 32	Model 33
Deposits	0.00560 (0.00358)					
Loans		0.00559 (0.00348)				
Yield on loan portfolio			0.0165 (0.0301)			
Return on assets				0.0618 (0.0487)		
Return on equity					−0.00808 (0.00725)	
Operating expenses						−0.0132 (0.0142)
Income	0.0267 (0.0659)	0.0352 (0.0674)	0.0354 (0.0744)	0.0404 (0.0699)	0.0393 (0.0725)	0.0407 (0.0714)
Trade openness	−0.0783 (0.0690)	−0.0881 (0.0653)	−0.0985 (0.0914)	−0.0834 (0.0988)	−0.0868 (0.101)	−0.0920 (0.0883)
Inflation	0.0352 (0.171)	0.0315 (0.157)	0.0470 (0.190)	0.0482 (0.194)	0.0382 (0.199)	0.0623 (0.188)
FDI	0.310 (0.231)	0.324 (0.245)	0.472 (0.337)	0.442 (0.351)	0.462 (0.368)	0.462 (0.332)
Population growth	0.205 (2.775)	1.821 (2.634)	2.065 (3.200)	2.354 (2.855)	3.125 (2.931)	2.852 (2.811)
Remittances	1.463★★★ (0.371)	1.358★★★ (0.332)	1.604★★★ (0.298)	1.586★★★ (0.296)	1.549★★★ (0.296)	1.556★★★ (0.295)

Institutions	-0.0497	-0.0493	-0.0435	-0.0402	-0.0443	-0.0416
	(0.0329)	(0.0326)	(0.0348)	(0.0339)	(0.0348)	(0.0335)
Credit reference bureaus	0.420***	0.409***	0.420***	0.428***	0.426***	0.427***
	(0.109)	(0.102)	(0.105)	(0.105)	(0.106)	(0.107)
Bank stability	-9.39e-05	9.38e-05	-0.000369	-0.000241	-0.000209	-0.000241
	(0.000826)	(0.000753)	(0.000899)	(0.000830)	(0.000864)	(0.000894)
Constant	0.246	0.152	0.235	0.192	0.182	0.185
	(0.502)	(0.519)	(0.578)	(0.545)	(0.559)	(0.548)
Observations	248	260	220	228	227	227
Number of country code	17	17	17	17	17	17

Robust standard errors in parentheses.
*** $p < 0.01$, ** $p < 0.05$ and * $p < 0.1$.

Appendix 11.4B Microfinance Profitability and Economic Development in Low-Income Economies

Variables	Model 34	Model 35	Model 36	Model 37	Model 38	Model 39
Deposits	0.00625					
	(0.00441)					
Loans		0.00582				
		(0.00530)				
Yield on loan portfolio			0.0423			
			(0.0446)			
Return on assets				−0.217★		
				(0.130)		
Return on equity					−0.0337	
					(0.0274)	
Operating expenses						0.0484
						(0.0333)
Income	0.0581	0.0559	0.0778	0.0678	0.0614	0.0693
	(0.0629)	(0.0623)	(0.0617)	(0.0583)	(0.0610)	(0.0578)
Trade openness	0.0342	0.0315	0.0432	0.0429	0.0360	0.0287
	(0.0458)	(0.0441)	(0.0542)	(0.0481)	(0.0480)	(0.0464)
Inflation	0.00460	−0.00260	−0.0405	−0.00754	−0.0108	−0.0140
	(0.0601)	(0.0553)	(0.0549)	(0.0572)	(0.0575)	(0.0644)
FDI	0.00875	0.00423	0.0682	0.0420	0.0324	0.0752
	(0.0532)	(0.0553)	(0.0735)	(0.0596)	(0.0672)	(0.0518)
Population growth	−4.723★★★	−4.694★★★	−4.150★★★	−4.317★★★	−4.102★★★	−4.046★★★
	(1.098)	(1.034)	(1.182)	(1.277)	(1.166)	(1.332)

Remittances	−0.835★	−0.833★	−1.026★★	−1.100★★	−1.029★★	−0.974★
	(0.474)	(0.471)	(0.522)	(0.480)	(0.494)	(0.519)
Institutions	0.0398★	0.0347★	0.0369	0.0340	0.0375	0.0365
	(0.0238)	(0.0199)	(0.0227)	(0.0255)	(0.0245)	(0.0242)
Credit reference bureaus	0.328★★★	0.330★★★	0.334★★★	0.338★★★	0.333★★★	0.334★★★
	(0.0664)	(0.0647)	(0.0724)	(0.0664)	(0.0672)	(0.0664)
Bank stability	0.000572	0.00102	0.000974	0.00104	0.000834	0.00102
	(0.000835)	(0.000705)	(0.000672)	(0.000710)	(0.000782)	(0.000690)
Constant	0.158	0.174	0.102	0.185	0.225	0.155
	(0.383)	(0.376)	(0.357)	(0.338)	(0.353)	(0.332)
Observations	255	259	237	244	243	243
Number of country code	18	18	18	18	18	18

Robust standard errors in parentheses.
★★★ $p < 0.01$, ★★ $p < 0.05$ and ★ $p < 0.1$.

Part III

Impact of Finance on Poverty Alleviation in Africa

12 Information and Communications Technology (ICT) Diffusion and Financial Development Nexus in African Countries

Charles Shaaba Saba, Nicholas Ngepah and Nicholas Mbaya Odhiambo

12.1 Introduction

Poverty and inequality, income, inflation, FDI, etc., are some of the prominent factors identified in the empirical literature that could drive the levels of financial development across countries (inter alia: Beck, 2002; Beck et al., 2007; Alfaro et al., 2009; Bittencourt, 2011). While other factors are considered in the literature, ICT being a possible factor that could drive financial development has not attracted much attention for the case of Africa. Focusing on Africa is very important given that it is a developing region, and there is a need to harness ICT/telecommunication services for financial development.

Most financial development studies in literature, whether they focus on the effect of ICT diffusion or other macroeconomic variables, hardly explore the outcome of ICT diffusion on the complex multidimensional nature of financial development. To consider the effect of the ICT diffusion on the complex multidimensional nature of financial development has become essential for the case of Africa. This is because the financial sector across the globe has offered support to the ICT/telecommunication sector in the form of loans, technical assistance, etc. (World Bank, 2017). As Africa's economy is becoming more connected with the global economy, its enterprises/businesses and citizens in the countries increasingly need access to financial services tools in order to be able to compete favourably. And because ICT and financial services could complement each other, ICT is one way to increase financial access. Financial inclusion could be facilitated by ICTs, and the financial services sector is also among the main drivers of communications and network technology (World Bank, 2012). Many financial companies have combined ICT/telecommunication services with internal process modernization to deliver enhanced services such as cash transfers via mobile phones, remittances, bill payments (Cheng et al., 2021).

Most empirical research use one of two financial depth measures – the ratio of private credit to GDP or the ratio of stock market capitalization to GDP – to estimate financial development. However, these indicators do not take into consideration the multidimensional dynamics and character of financial development. The complex multidimensional nature of the financial development is captured or summarized as how developed financial

DOI: 10.4324/9781003215042-15

institutions and the financial market are in terms of their (i) depth (size and liquidity); (ii) access (the ability of individuals and companies to access financial services); (iii) and efficiency (the ability of institutions to provide financial services at low cost and with sustainable revenues and the level of activity of capital markets) (Svirydzenka, 2016). The advantage of using the multidimensional nature of the financial development provided by the International Monetary Fund (IMF) is that it covers (i) the financial markets (for example, stock and bond markets) and (ii) the banking sector (for example, the bank financial institutions (such as pension funds, insurance companies, mutual funds) and non-bank financial institutions). This measure will give a holistic dynamic insight into the ICT diffusion-financial development nexus by using a different methodological approach.

Yartey (2008), Pradhan et al. (2016), Nguyen et al. (2020), Mignamissi (2021) among others, have done research that is similar to this current study. However, our research differs from past studies in several areas. Firstly, Pradhan et al. (2016) used the traditional panel VAR to investigate the nexus of the theme at hand with other macroeconomic variables, while this current paper uses the newly developed panel VAR (PVAR) in GMM framework, which takes into account endogeneity problems to examine the causal-effect linkage between ICT diffusion and the overall financial development, and its multidimensional indices. This is a key methodological contribution of the study. Secondly, we take into account the three main dimensions of financial development (which include depth, accessibility, and efficiency) within the PVAR in GMM framework approach. Thirdly, our study focuses on Africa and covers more sample size in terms of the number of countries used and time dimension. Despite the level of financial development in Africa, has ICT diffusion contributed to financial depth, access, and efficiency in Africa? This is a crucial question that this research aims to answer. Seeking to answer this question will guide policy direction for African countries, hence the rationale to contribute to the empirical literature. Based on the above discussion, the contribution of this paper is to explore the nexus between ICT diffusion and the complex multidimensional nature of financial development in Africa. In this chapter, a panel of 45 African countries is used, and the period covers between 2000 and 2018.

The remaining sections of this article are organized as follows: Section 12.2 reviews related literature; Section 12.4 focuses on the methodology; Section 12.5 presents the empirical results and discussion; and Section 12.6 presents the conclusion and policy recommendations.

12.2 Literature Review

Given that the effect of ICT on economic and financial growth on long-term development has become clear (Grace et al., 2003), and because of its economic, financial, and social repercussions on several other sectors, ICT is one of the most significant industries for governments. As the world economies are becoming more digitalized, it is important to investigate the role that ICT plays in the complex multidimensional nature of the financial development for a continent like Africa for the purpose of policy direction, since ICT enables easy access to information, improved bank credit, transfer of funds/remittances, etc. (Asongu, 2013). Prior to this particular study, when ICT is measured by mobile phone penetration, Donner and Tellez (2008) point to the fact that (i) when users have a bank account, they are usually able to store value (currency), which is accessible through a handset; (ii) they are able to convert their cash both into and out of the store value account; and (iii) they are able to transfer stored value between different banks and accounts. For a sample of 52 African countries, Asongu (2013) investigates the relationship between mobile phone penetration and financial development. The study shows that informal finance is becoming more important and that traditional financial development indicators may not be able to accurately estimate mobile phone usage at a macroeconomic level. Asongu and Acha-Anyi (2017) investigate the role of ICT in conflicts of financial intermediation for financial access for 53 African countries spanning from 2004 to 2011 using a quantile regression approach. The results of the study show that ICT has a positive threshold impact on the banking system while a negative threshold impact on the financial system.

Studies that focus on the nexus between ICT and financial development include Lashitew et al. (2019), Karakara and Osabuohien (2019), Chatterjee and Das (2021), among others. Although these studies focused on different countries/regions, they were able to establish the fact that ICT penetration in one way or the other boosts up financial inclusion/financial development. For example, Yartey (2008) examines the nexus between ICT, financial structure, and financial development for 76 emerging and advanced countries for the period 1990–2003. The dynamic GMM estimator was used by the study to achieve its objective. The study finds that the measures of financial development (that is, credit and stock market development) promote ICT diffusion and vice versa for the case of financial structure. Marszk and Lechman (2021) explore the role of ICT in the diffusion of financial innovations with the aim of reshaping the financial system among the European countries between 2004 and 2019. The study uses panel and country–specific regression models to achieve its objective. The findings reveal that innovative financial product development was made possible as a result of ICT penetration across all the countries used for the study. ICT also plays a significant role in the diffusion of exchange-traded funds even though exchange-traded fund market development has not gained ground between the countries. Alshubiri's (2020) study investigates the impact of ICT price basket on financial development indicators for Gulf Cooperation Council (GCC) countries over the period 2008–2016. The study applied a number of econometric techniques such as GMM, fixed effect, etc. The study measured financial development by using domestic credit and market capitalization. The results reveal high (for Saudi Arabia and Oman) and low (for Kuwait) ICT price baskets. The findings further reveal a positive relationship between financial development and ICT basket price when financial development is proxied by stock market. While Nguyen et al.'s (2020) study explore the impact of internet and mobile usage on financial development indicators, as well as the overall financial development for 109 economies over the period of 1998–2017. The countries were further sub-divided into 62 low- and middle-income economies and 47 high-income economies. They used a two-step system GMM estimation technique, as well as Granger causality, cointegration tests, PMG, ARDL, and PDOLS. The findings show a long-run bidirectional causality between internet/mobile usage and financial progress. According to the findings, internet use has a large detrimental influence on financial institutions and overall financial development, while having a significant favourable impact on financial markets. In addition, internet and mobile usage have a strong significant positive impact on all nine financial development indices. This current study is different from previous studies in that it amalgamates ICT/telecommunication indicators (by constructing a composite index of ICT) and also uses the complex multidimensional nature of the financial development in a newly proposed GMM panel VAR setting for the case of the Africa continent.

12.3 Methodology and Data

12.3.1 Empirical Specification

This study explores the nexus between ICT diffusion and financial development by employing panel VAR (PVAR) in the GMM estimation framework, which is an extension of the traditional panel vector autoregression (PVAR) model introduced by Sims (1980) to explore the ICT-financial development nexus. The newly developed PVAR in GMM approach is more preferable and differs from the traditional PVAR in the following ways: (i) concerns about the direction of causality are of no importance because all the variables in the model are treated as independent and endogenous; (ii) it has more than one equation compared to other models; (iii) variables in the model are explained by their own lags and by the other variables' lagged values; (iv) unobserved individual heterogeneity in the panel data are taken into account; and (v) the choice and appropriateness of instruments along with improved asymptotic results are attributed to this estimation technique. Canova and Ciccarelli (2004) simplified the general way of presenting the PVAR model, and it is given below as

$$Q_{i,t} = M_\theta \breve{A}_{i,t} + H_1 y_{i,t-1} + \ldots + H_\beta y_{i,t-\beta} + P_t \tag{12.1}$$

where $Q_{i,t}$ is a $K \times 1$ vector of a K panel data variables, $i = 1,\ldots,I$, $\breve{A}_{i,t}$ is a vector of deterministic terms, M_θ is the associated parameter matrix, and the Hs are a $K \times K$ parameter matrices attached to the lagged variables $Q_{i,t-\beta}$. The lag order (VAR order) is denoted by β, while the error term is p_t. We included nine variables in our empirical model, and they can be found in Table 12.1. This approach follows Abrigo and Love's (2016) estimation

Table 12.1 Summary of dataset

Variables	Indicators	Variable Description	Source of Data
FDE	Financial development	Financial development index proxy for financial development	International Monetary Fund (IMF) financial development database.
FIS	Financial institutions' development	Financial institution index proxy financial institution development	
FISD	Financial institutions depth	Financial institutions depth index proxy for financial institutions depth	
FISA	Financial institutions access	Financial institutions access index proxy for financial institutions access	
FISE	Financial institutions efficiency	Financial institutions efficiency index proxy for financial institutions efficiency	
FM	Financial markets' development	Financial markets index proxy for financial markets' development	
FMD	Financial markets depth	Financial markets depth index proxy for financial markets depth	
FMA	Financial markets access	Financial markets access index proxy for financial markets access	
ICT	Information and communications Technology	ICT diffusion is captured by a composite index of ICT indicators (which comprises of three indicators) by applying principal component method/ analysis (PCA). These indicators include (i) mobile-cellular telephone subscriptions per 100 inhabitants (penetration of connected mobile lines); (ii) fixed-telephone subscriptions per 100 inhabitants (penetration of connected fixed lines); and (iii) percentage of Individuals using the internet (percentage of population with access to the internet).	International Telecommunication Union database.

Note: To compose the composite index ICT, we follow the study conducted by Saba and David (2020), Saba and Ngepah (2022), among others. Similarly, to compose the composite index of financial development,[2] we follow the recent study of Sassi and Goaied (2013) and Cheng et al. (2021). International Monetary Fund (IMF) financial development database, 2021; see https://data.imf.org/?sk=F8032E80-B36C-43B1-AC26-493C5B1CD33B. There were few missing data, and this was taken care of through extrapolation and interpolation procedure of filling missing data. Studies that have used these methods include David (2019), Saba and Ngepah (2019, 2020a, 2020b), and Saba (2020, 2021).

technique which had its foundation on Hamilton's (1994) and Lutkepohl's (2005) Arellano and Bond (1991), Arellano and Bover (1995), and Blundell and Bond (1998) approaches.[1]

12.3.2 Data

This study used annual panel data spanning 2000–2018 for 45 African countries. The summary of the dataset is shown in Table 12.1, while Table 12.2 consists of the list of selected countries used for this study.

12.4 Empirical Results and Discussion

12.4.1 *Principal Component Analysis, Descriptive Statistics, and Correlation Matrix Results*

Before going into the analysis of the study, we first estimate the ICT diffusion variable via the principal component analysis/method (PCA/M). Given that there is a significant correlation at least at the 1% significance level between the ICT indicators (that is, internet access, mobile-telephone, and fixed-telephone), we, therefore, proceed to apply the PCA to the indicators. Table 12.3 presents the PCA results, and as a rule of thumb, we retained component 1 that has eigenvector >1, because it has a loading value that exceeded 0.40 in absolute value (Chen, 2014). We ignore the remaining components because they did not meet the above condition.

12.4.2 *Panel Causality Result Analysis*

This study utilized the panel VAR–Granger causality test to examine the causal relationship between ICT diffusion, FDE, FIS, FM, FISD, FISA, FISE, FMD, and FMA. We focused our attention more on the causality between ICT diffusion and the rest of the variables in the model, given the focus of this study. In Table 12.4, the results suggest strong evidence of bidirectional causality between (i) ICT diffusion and financial development (FDE); (ii) ICT diffusion and financial market development (FM); (iii) ICT diffusion and financial institutions depth (FISD); (iv) ICT diffusion and financial institutions efficiency (FISE); (v) ICT diffusion and financial markets depth (FMD); and (vi) ICT diffusion and financial markets access (FMA), while the results further suggest that unidirectional causality runs from (i) financial institution development (FIS) to ICT diffusion; and (ii) financial institution access (FISA) to ICT diffusion. This implies interdependence and mutual reinforcement between the ICT sector and the financial sector of the economy across African countries. This shows that at the Africa level, governments should not pursue ICT policy aims and objectives independently to achieve growth and development, but also consider all the complex multidimensional nature of financial development given that the two sectors are mutually reinforcing. This is

Table 12.2 List of 45 African countries

Angola	Cabo Verde	Côte d'Ivoire	Ethiopia	Guinea-Bissau	Malawi	Namibia	Senegal	Tanzania
Benin	Cameroon	Dem. Rep. of the Congo	Gabon	Kenya	Mali	Niger	Seychelles	Togo
Botswana	Central African Rep.	Equatorial Guinea	Gambia	Lesotho	Mauritania	Nigeria	Sierra Leone	Uganda
Burkina Faso	Chad	Eritrea	Ghana	Liberia	Mauritius	Rwanda	South Africa	Zambia
Burundi	Congo (Rep. of the)	Eswatini	Guinea	Madagascar	Mozambique	Sao Tome & Principe	Sudan	Zimbabwe

Table 12.3 Principal component and correlation matrix results

Panel (A): Principal Component Results for ICT Variable

Component	Eigenvalue	Difference	Proportion	Cumulative
Component 1	2.148	1.407	0.716	0.716
Component 2	0.740	0.628	0.247	0.963
Component 3	0.112	–	0.037	1.000

Principal component (eigenvector) results

Variable	Component 1	Component 2	Component 3	Unexplained
Fixed-telephone	0.437	0.891	0.124	0
Mobile-telephone	0.622	-0.399	0.674	0
Internet access	0.649	-0.218	-0.729	0

Retained eigenvector results

Variable	Component 1	Unexplained
Fixed-telephone	0.437	0.589
Mobile-telephone	0.622	0.169
Internet access	0.649	0.095

Correlation matrix results

Variables	Fixed-telephone	Mobile-telephone	Internet access
Fixed-telephone	1.000		
Mobile-telephone	0.331***	1.000	
	(0.000)		
Internet access	0.456***	0.877***	1.000
	(0.000)	(0.000)	

Source: Author's computations.
Note: *** $p < 0.01$, ** $p < 0.05$, and * $p < 0.1$ are significance levels, respectively.

pertinent given the possible degree of backward and forward linkages that ICT and financial development could have on the economy of African countries. This is pertinent given the possible degree of backward and forward linkages that ICT and financial development could have on the economy of African countries. Based on the feedback causality between the variables suggested a possible endogeneity problem that needs to be accounted for in the next phase of our analysis. The bidirectional causality result between ICT diffusion and FDE is in line with Pradhan et al. (2016) and Nguyen et al. (2020) findings. This justified the use of a panel causality test based on the GMM estimator, which takes care of endogeneity problems in the panel VAR model through instrumentation (Abrigo & Love, 2016).

12.4.3 Panel VAR in GMM Result Analysis

Table 12.5 presents the panel VAR in GMM results. Firstly, the financial institutions depth (FISD), financial institutions efficiency (FISE), financial market development (FM), and financial markets access (FMA) equations revealed

Table 12.4 Panel VAR–Granger causality Wald test, Chi-squared value results

Model	Null hypothesis	chi2	p-value	Direction of relationship observed	Conclusion
1	ICT ↛ FDE	149.555★★★	0.000	ICT↔FDE	Bidirectional
	FDE ↛ ICT	44.217★★★	0.000		causality
2	ICT ↛ FIS	0.500	0.480	FIS→ICT	Unidirectional
	FIS ↛ ICT	49.045★★★	0.000		causality
3	ICT ↛ FM	418.128★★★	0.000	ICT↔FM	Bidirectional
	FM ↛ ICT	161.472★★★	0.000		causality
4	ICT ↛ FISD	288.504★★★	0.000	ICT↔FISD	Bidirectional
	FISD ↛ ICT	242.636★★★	0.000		causality
5	ICT ↛ FISA	0.000	0.995	FISA→ICT	Unidirectional
	FISA ↛ ICT	757.898★★★	0.000		causality
6	ICT ↛ FISE	230.103★★★	0.000	ICT↔FISE	Bidirectional
	FISE ↛ ICT	6.942★★★	0.008		causality
7	ICT ↛ FMD	382.547★★★	0.000	ICT↔FMD	Bidirectional
	FMD ↛ ICT	153.817★★★	0.000		causality
8	ICT ↛ FMA	8.544★★★	0.003	ICT↔FMA	Bidirectional
	FMA ↛ ICT	186.012★★★	0.000		causality

Source: Author's computations.
Note: ↔ and → denote bidirectional and unidirectional causality respectively. ↛ denotes **H₀**: excluded variable does not Granger-cause equation variable. Here, the **H₁** is excluded variable that does Granger-cause equation variable. ★★★ $p < 0.01$, ★★ $p < 0.05$, and ★ $p < 0.1$.

that at 1% significance level, ICT diffusion is positive to FISD, FISE, FM, and FMA. However, ICT diffusion is significant and negative to financial development (FDE) and financial markets depth (FMD). This suggests that if ICT diffusion increases by 1%, the FISD, FISE, FM, and FMA will increase by 0.20, 0.77, 0.17, and 0.05%, respectively. But an increase in ICT diffusion by 1% decreases the level of financial development (FDE) and financial markets depth (FMD) by −0.82 and −0.16%, respectively. ICT diffusion has an insignificant impact on financial institution development (FIS) and financial institutions access (FISA). The policy implications of these results are to promote financial institutions depth (FISD), financial institutions efficiency (FISE), financial market development (FM), and financial markets access (FMA) by 0.20, 0.77, 0.17, and 0.05%, respectively; then, there is a need to increase ICT diffusion by 1% in African countries. The result suggests that there is a need to enact policies that will speed up the rate of ICT diffusion meant to promote the level of financial development (FDE), financial markets depth (FMD), financial institution development (FIS), and financial institutions access (FISA) in Africa.

Secondly, ICT diffusion equation revealed that at 1% significance level, the financial development (FDE), financial institution development (FIS), financial institutions depth (FISD), and financial institutions access (FISA) have a positive impact on ICT diffusion, while financial institutions efficiency

(FISE), financial market development (FM), financial markets depth (FMD), and financial markets access (FMA) have a negative impact on ICT diffusion. This suggests that if the levels of FDE, FIS, FISD, and FISA rise by 1%, each of them will contribute to the increase in ICT diffusion in Africa by 0.02, 0.03, 0.05, and 0.21%, respectively. However, if the levels of FISE, FM, FMD, and FMA rise by 1%, each of them will contribute −0.01, −1.04, −1.00, and −0.04% decrease to ICT diffusion in Africa, respectively. The policy implications of these results are that for the levels of financial development (FDE), financial institution development (FIS), financial institutions depth (FISD), and financial institutions access (FISA) to contribute 0.02, 0.03, 0.05, and 0.21% to the improvement of ICT diffusion, respectively, there is a need to improve the levels of these variables. The result further suggests that there is a need to enact policies that will deepen financial institutions efficiency (FISE), financial market development (FM), financial markets depth (FMD), and financial markets access (FMA) in order to accelerate ICT diffusion, given that they contributed negatively to the ICT diffusion.

Thirdly, the financial development (FDE) equation revealed that at 1% significance level, financial institution development (FIS), financial institutions efficiency (FISE), and financial markets access (FMA) are positive to financial development (FDE) in Africa. This implies that these variables have contributed more to the level of financial development (FDE) in Africa, while other variables such as financial institutions depth (FISD), financial institutions access (FISA), financial market development (FM), and financial markets depth (FMD) have contributed negatively to financial development (FDE) in Africa. The financial institution development (FIS) equation revealed that at 1% significance level, FISD, FISA, FM, and FMD are positive to financial institution development (FIS). This implies that these variables have contributed more to the level of financial institution development (FIS) in Africa, while variables such as FISE and FMA have contributed negatively to financial institution development (FIS) in Africa. A similar interpretation holds for the other equations.

In order not to embark on a meaningless analysis, we test the validity of our PVAR models by performing the stability condition test. Table 12.6 shows that our models were correctly specified, given that the eigenvalues and modulus values are less than 1. This implies that all the nine estimated panel models have stationary roots (Hamilton, 1994; Lutkepohl, 2005; Abrigo & Love, 2016). Hence, the condition of the eigenvalue stability test is therefore satisfied.

12.4.4 *Variance Decomposition and Impulse Response Analysis*

In addition to the panel VAR tests, this study also utilizes forecast error variance decompositions (FEVDs) and impulse response function (IRF) analysis

Table 12.5 Panel VAR-GMM results

	ICT $(t-1)$	FDE $(t-1)$	FIS $(t-1)$	FISD $(t-1)$	FISA $(t-1)$	FISE $(t-1)$	FM $(t-1)$	FMD $(t-1)$	FMA $(t-1)$
ICT (t)	0.911★★★ (0.000)	−0.823★★★ (0.000)	0.068 (0.480)	0.204★★★ (0.000)	0.000 (0.995)	0.767★★★ (0.000)	0.174★★★ (0.000)	−0.157★★★ (0.000)	0.054★★★ (0.003)
FDE (t)	0.024★★★ (0.000)	2.431★★★ (0.000)	−2.031★★★ (0.000)	0.100★★★ (0.000)	0.033★★★ (0.000)	0.357★★★ (0.000)	−0.057★★★ (0.000)	0.062★★★ (0.000)	−0.210★★★ (0.000)
FIS (t)	0.025★★★ (0.000)	1.897★★★ (0.000)	−1.563★★★ (0.000)	0.119★★★ (0.000)	0.026★★★ (0.000)	0.463★★★ (0.000)	−0.047★★★ (0.000)	0.054★★★ (0.000)	−0.181★★★ (0.000)
FISD (t)	0.054★★★ (0.000)	−1.045★★★ (0.000)	0.566★★★ (0.000)	0.917★★★ (0.000)	−0.029★★★ (0.000)	0.614★★★ (0.000)	−0.196★★★ (0.000)	0.199★★★ (0.000)	−0.095★★★ (0.000)
FISA (t)	0.206★★★ (0.000)	−3.949★★★ (0.000)	3.621★★★ (0.000)	0.415★★★ (0.000)	0.441★★★ (0.000)	0.543★★★ (0.000)	−0.133★★★ (0.000)	0.157★★★ (0.000)	0.292★★★ (0.000)
FISE (t)	−0.013★★★ (0.008)	3.445★★★ (0.000)	−4.082★★★ (0.000)	0.140★★★ (0.000)	0.089★★★ (0.000)	1.519★★★ (0.000)	0.032★★ (0.003)	−0.024★★ (0.023)	−0.231★★★ (0.000)
FM (t)	−1.036★★★ (0.000)	−20.497★★★ (0.000)	26.319★★★ (0.000)	1.917★★★ (0.000)	−1.153★★★ (0.000)	−5.217★★★ (0.000)	−0.802★★★ (0.000)	1.035★★★ (0.000)	8.536★★★ (0.000)
FMD (t)	−1.004★★★ (0.000)	−20.669★★★ (0.000)	26.548★★★ (0.000)	1.809★★★ (0.000)	−1.156★★★ (0.000)	−5.286★★★ (0.000)	−1.565★★★ (0.000)	1.800★★★ (0.000)	8.468★★★ (0.000)
FMA (t)	−0.038★★★ (0.000)	0.156★★★ (0.000)	−0.067 (0.118)	0.043★★★ (0.000)	0.011★★★ (0.000)	0.112★★★ (0.000)	−0.074★★★ (0.000)	0.076★★★ (0.000)	1.048★★★ (0.000)

Source: Author's computations.
Note: ★★★ $p < 0.01$, ★★ $p < 0.05$, and ★ $p < 0.1$. p-values in parenthesis; the error terms include country-specific effect.

Table 12.6 Eigenvalue stability condition test results

	Eigenvalue		
	Real	*Imaginary*	*Modulus*
1	0.8196	−0.5170	0.9691
2	0.8196	0.5170	0.9691
3	0.8635	0.0000	0.8635
4	0.8383	0.0073	0.8383
5	0.8383	−0.0073	0.8383
6	0.8089	−0.1678	0.8261
7	0.8089	0.1678	0.8261
8	0.4671	0.0000	0.4671
9	0.3416	0.0000	0.3416

Source: Author's computations.
Note: All the eigenvalues values are less than 1. This implies the panel VAR satisfies stability condition.

of unrestricted VAR estimation process using the orthogonalized Cholesky ordering technique. These two methods were used in order to further explain the magnitude of the causation among the variables. The variance decomposition results revealed that (i) ICT diffusion, financial institution development (FIS), financial institutions access (FISA), financial institutions depth (FISD), and financial market access (FMA) are more sensitive to shocks in the levels of financial development (FDE) in the short run and long run when compared to other variables; (ii) financial development (FDE) is more sensitive to shocks in financial institution development (FIS) (short run) and financial markets access (FMA) (long run); (iii) financial market development (FM) is more sensitive to shocks in financial markets access (FMA) (short run) and financial development (FDE) (long run); (iv) financial institutions efficiency (FISE) is more sensitive to shocks in FDE (short run) and FMA (long run); and (v) financial market efficiency (FMD) is more sensitive to shocks in FM (short run) and FDE (long run). Table 12.7 shows the results of the variance decomposition.

We estimated the IRFs for the African countries to further explain the magnitude of the causation between the variables. Figure 12.1 presents the summary of the IRF outcome for the variables. The IRF plots show that a positive shock in ICT diffusion leads to a steady fall in FMA, FMD, FM, FISA, and FISD, but a steady rise in FISE, FIS, and FDE. It is also noteworthy that a shock in financial development (FDE) leads to a rise in FMA, FMD, FM, FISA, and ICT, but a steady fall in FISE, FISD, and FIS. However, these shocks are short-lived, but they can be observed for Africa. Most shocks have a noticeable influence on one another/the economy only in the first five years, and they are fully absorbed within ten years.

Table 12.7 Forecast error variance decomposition

Response Variable and Forecast Horizon	Impulse Variable								
Panel A	ICT	FDE	FIS	FM	FISD	FISA	FISE	FMD	FMA
ICT									
0	0.000	0.000	0.000	0.000	0.000	0.000	0.000	0.000	0.000
1	1.000	0.000	0.000	0.000	0.000	0.000	0.000	0.000	0.000
2	0.860	0.030	0.028	0.034	0.014	0.009	0.020	0.005	0.000
3	0.632	0.130	0.037	0.057	0.047	0.023	0.057	0.011	0.005
4	0.418	0.266	0.024	0.062	0.082	0.032	0.095	0.012	0.008
5	0.264	0.384	0.014	0.055	0.110	0.035	0.121	0.010	0.008
6	0.167	0.463	0.020	0.043	0.127	0.034	0.135	0.007	0.005
7	0.108	0.504	0.038	0.032	0.137	0.031	0.142	0.005	0.004
8	0.074	0.517	0.063	0.023	0.142	0.028	0.143	0.003	0.008
9	0.052	0.509	0.088	0.016	0.144	0.025	0.142	0.002	0.021
10	0.039	0.488	0.110	0.012	0.144	0.023	0.140	0.002	0.043
Panel B									
FDE									
0	0.000	0.000	0.000	0.000	0.000	0.000	0.000	0.000	0.000
1	0.012	0.988	0.000	0.000	0.000	0.000	0.000	0.000	0.000
2	0.008	0.885	0.076	0.001	0.009	0.001	0.004	0.002	0.014
3	0.005	0.756	0.154	0.001	0.024	0.001	0.007	0.006	0.045
4	0.004	0.639	0.200	0.004	0.035	0.001	0.008	0.008	0.099
5	0.005	0.539	0.213	0.011	0.040	0.001	0.009	0.009	0.173
6	0.007	0.457	0.201	0.018	0.041	0.002	0.009	0.008	0.257
7	0.010	0.393	0.178	0.026	0.038	0.002	0.008	0.007	0.338
8	0.014	0.346	0.154	0.031	0.033	0.003	0.007	0.007	0.404
9	0.018	0.314	0.135	0.034	0.029	0.005	0.006	0.010	0.448
10	0.021	0.292	0.124	0.036	0.026	0.006	0.006	0.016	0.473
Panel C									
FIS									
0	0.000	0.000	0.000	0.000	0.000	0.000	0.000	0.000	0.000
1	0.006	0.934	0.060	0.000	0.000	0.000	0.000	0.000	0.000
2	0.004	0.906	0.055	0.005	0.010	0.003	0.007	0.002	0.009
3	0.003	0.810	0.105	0.003	0.027	0.004	0.014	0.004	0.030
4	0.002	0.702	0.152	0.004	0.043	0.005	0.019	0.006	0.068
5	0.002	0.602	0.179	0.007	0.052	0.005	0.022	0.007	0.124
6	0.003	0.514	0.184	0.012	0.055	0.005	0.023	0.006	0.197
7	0.005	0.438	0.173	0.019	0.054	0.006	0.023	0.005	0.276
8	0.008	0.377	0.154	0.025	0.051	0.007	0.023	0.005	0.351
9	0.011	0.329	0.134	0.030	0.046	0.008	0.021	0.007	0.414
10	0.014	0.293	0.118	0.033	0.041	0.009	0.020	0.011	0.461
Panel D									
FM									
0	0.000	0.000	0.000	0.000	0.000	0.000	0.000	0.000	0.000
1	0.030	0.116	0.001	0.853	0.000	0.000	0.000	0.000	0.000
2	0.025	0.091	0.041	0.729	0.026	0.000	0.002	0.000	0.086
3	0.020	0.082	0.067	0.603	0.042	0.000	0.002	0.002	0.181

(Continued)

Table 12.7 (Continued)

Response Variable and Forecast Horizon	Impulse Variable								
4	0.017	0.107	0.064	0.504	0.049	0.000	0.002	0.007	0.251
5	0.016	0.155	0.052	0.422	0.052	0.000	0.003	0.014	0.286
6	0.016	0.210	0.049	0.354	0.053	0.000	0.007	0.022	0.289
7	0.016	0.258	0.061	0.299	0.054	0.000	0.010	0.031	0.270
8	0.017	0.292	0.084	0.257	0.054	0.000	0.014	0.040	0.242
9	0.017	0.311	0.113	0.226	0.055	0.000	0.016	0.048	0.215
10	0.016	0.318	0.140	0.204	0.055	0.000	0.018	0.055	0.194

Panel E

FISD

0	0.000	0.000	0.000	0.000	0.000	0.000	0.000	0.000	0.000
1	0.083	0.024	0.001	0.035	0.856	0.000	0.000	0.000	0.000
2	0.078	0.079	0.029	0.028	0.774	0.004	0.003	0.004	0.001
3	0.066	0.164	0.035	0.024	0.672	0.012	0.015	0.009	0.003
4	0.053	0.259	0.026	0.020	0.569	0.020	0.035	0.010	0.007
5	0.041	0.339	0.023	0.016	0.475	0.025	0.056	0.010	0.015
6	0.031	0.386	0.035	0.012	0.396	0.027	0.074	0.009	0.030
7	0.024	0.401	0.057	0.009	0.334	0.027	0.087	0.007	0.053
8	0.019	0.391	0.082	0.008	0.287	0.026	0.095	0.006	0.087
9	0.015	0.365	0.101	0.009	0.251	0.025	0.098	0.005	0.132
10	0.013	0.329	0.113	0.012	0.221	0.024	0.098	0.004	0.187

Panel F

FISA

0	0.000	0.000	0.000	0.000	0.000	0.000	0.000	0.000	0.000
1	0.238	0.045	0.003	0.148	0.115	0.453	0.000	0.000	0.000
2	0.233	0.035	0.164	0.163	0.153	0.241	0.003	0.001	0.006
3	0.180	0.131	0.202	0.149	0.167	0.132	0.020	0.002	0.018
4	0.123	0.283	0.144	0.122	0.169	0.084	0.047	0.002	0.026
5	0.080	0.417	0.086	0.092	0.164	0.061	0.073	0.002	0.024
6	0.052	0.500	0.067	0.066	0.158	0.047	0.092	0.002	0.017
7	0.035	0.535	0.078	0.047	0.151	0.037	0.103	0.003	0.011
8	0.024	0.536	0.102	0.033	0.146	0.031	0.109	0.003	0.014
9	0.018	0.516	0.129	0.025	0.142	0.026	0.112	0.004	0.029
10	0.014	0.483	0.151	0.020	0.137	0.023	0.112	0.003	0.057

Panel G

FISE

0	0.000	0.000	0.000	0.000	0.000	0.000	0.000	0.000	0.000
1	0.016	0.846	0.061	0.003	0.013	0.021	0.040	0.000	0.000
2	0.014	0.814	0.072	0.003	0.007	0.022	0.062	0.000	0.006
3	0.012	0.713	0.150	0.002	0.011	0.018	0.071	0.000	0.022
4	0.010	0.610	0.217	0.003	0.019	0.015	0.071	0.000	0.055
5	0.008	0.518	0.253	0.008	0.026	0.012	0.068	0.000	0.106
6	0.007	0.440	0.261	0.015	0.029	0.011	0.063	0.000	0.175
7	0.006	0.375	0.246	0.023	0.029	0.010	0.057	0.000	0.254
8	0.007	0.326	0.219	0.030	0.027	0.009	0.050	0.001	0.330
9	0.008	0.292	0.191	0.036	0.024	0.009	0.044	0.004	0.392
10	0.010	0.271	0.167	0.039	0.021	0.009	0.039	0.009	0.435

Response Variable and Forecast Horizon	Impulse Variable								
Panel H									
FMD									
0	0.000	0.000	0.000	0.000	0.000	0.000	0.000	0.000	0.000
1	0.029	0.121	0.001	0.847	0.000	0.000	0.000	0.002	0.000
2	0.025	0.096	0.042	0.723	0.024	0.000	0.002	0.003	0.085
3	0.020	0.085	0.068	0.600	0.037	0.000	0.002	0.006	0.181
4	0.017	0.105	0.066	0.503	0.043	0.000	0.002	0.012	0.252
5	0.016	0.149	0.054	0.423	0.045	0.000	0.003	0.020	0.290
6	0.016	0.201	0.051	0.357	0.045	0.000	0.006	0.029	0.296
7	0.016	0.246	0.062	0.303	0.046	0.000	0.009	0.038	0.280
8	0.017	0.279	0.084	0.262	0.047	0.000	0.012	0.046	0.253
9	0.017	0.298	0.111	0.231	0.047	0.000	0.014	0.054	0.226
10	0.017	0.305	0.138	0.210	0.047	0.000	0.016	0.061	0.205
Panel I									
FMA									
0	0.000	0.000	0.000	0.000	0.000	0.000	0.000	0.000	0.000
1	0.013	0.002	0.001	0.075	0.000	0.003	0.016	0.009	0.882
2	0.008	0.049	0.000	0.086	0.004	0.002	0.019	0.004	0.828
3	0.004	0.129	0.002	0.089	0.011	0.002	0.023	0.003	0.738
4	0.003	0.217	0.009	0.083	0.021	0.001	0.029	0.006	0.630
5	0.003	0.296	0.027	0.074	0.032	0.001	0.034	0.011	0.522
6	0.003	0.357	0.053	0.062	0.043	0.001	0.040	0.018	0.424
7	0.003	0.400	0.084	0.052	0.052	0.000	0.045	0.024	0.340
8	0.003	0.424	0.117	0.043	0.059	0.000	0.049	0.030	0.275
9	0.003	0.433	0.147	0.036	0.065	0.000	0.052	0.034	0.230
10	0.003	0.429	0.173	0.031	0.069	0.001	0.054	0.036	0.205

Source: Author's computations.
Note: Orthogonalized Cholesky ordering used.

12.6 Conclusion and Policy Recommendations

We analyse the ICT diffusion–financial development nexus for 45 African countries over the period 2000–2018. We provide a precise quantitative analysis by applying the recently developed novel panel VAR models in a generalized method of moments (GMM) estimation framework, which takes into account the endogeneity problem. This study differs from the previous studies because ICT diffusion is measured by a composite index of ICT/telecommunications indicators, which comprises of mobile line, fixed line, and internet access penetration, using the principal component method. It also used all the complex multidimensional nature of the financial development (FDE).

The main result from the panel VAR in GMM analysis revealed that ICT diffusion has a positive impact on financial institutions depth (FISD), financial institutions efficiency (FISE), financial markets' development (FM),

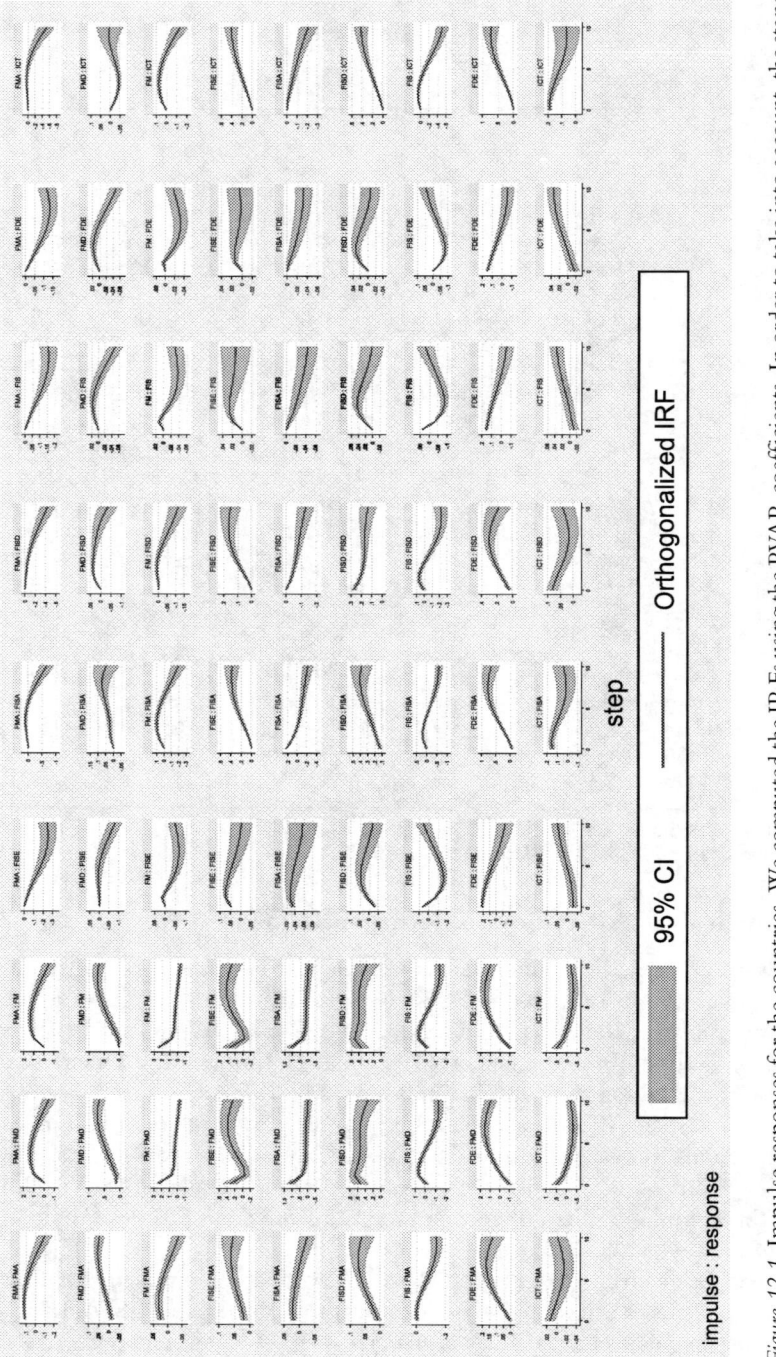

Figure 12.1 Impulse responses for the countries. We computed the IRFs using the PVAR coefficients. In order to take into account, the standard errors of these coefficients we used the Monte Carlo simulation, in which the parameters of the model are re-calculated 200 times using the estimated coefficients and their variance-covariance matrices as underlying distribution. The 5th and 95th percentiles from the resulting distribution were then used to generate the lower and upper bounds of the impulse response functions.

and financial markets access (FMA), but a negative impact on financial development (FDE) and financial markets depth (FMD). Secondly, the financial development (FDE), financial institution development (FIS), financial institutions depth (FISD), and financial institutions access (FISA) have a positive and significant impact on ICT diffusion, while financial institutions efficiency (FISE), financial market development (FM), financial markets depth (FMD), and financial markets access (FMA) have a negative and significant impact on ICT diffusion. Finally, for policy direction, firstly, this study recommends that the governments should make a concerted effort to revamp the ICT and financial sector concomitantly since mutual causality exists between them. This is because with improved ICT infrastructures, digital devices meant to promote financial activities are attainable in Africa. Although policies that emphasize financial development are important, they should not be treated as stand-alone policies. Instead, governments should adopt holistic policy reforms that take the multidimensional nature of financial development into account, along with other ICT indicators. ICT policies should be formulated, implemented, coordinated, and periodically reviewed with the aim of enhancing customer's easy access to financial services both at the financial institution and at the financial market levels. As the financial sector uses ICT services for the purpose of easy transactions, there is a need to coordinate and promote policies in the ICT/telecommunication sector, which will enhance affordability, improvement and easy accessibility to mobile-cellular telephone penetration, fixed line penetration, and internet access penetration for financial personnel. There should be holistic policies in terms of technology transfer. In addition, training and investment should be supported by the financial sector to boost the domestic production of smart phones in African countries since there is rapid migration from feature phones. These will especially create more economic benefits for African countries. Given that the efficiency of the financial system depends on the depth and accessibility, it is important to put policies in place that will encourage control over the return on assets, equity, interest margin, non-interest income, lending-deposits spread, etc. Since the financial system's functionality, production, and profitability are all tied to efficiency (Mignamissi, 2021), stakeholders in the financial sector should enact policies that will enable the ICT to strengthen its depth, accessibility, and efficiency. In conclusion, effective knowledge-sharing policies between the ICT and financial sectors are substantially required for a financially digitalized economy in African countries.

Notes

1 Interested readers are referred to Abrigo and Love (2016) for more details. We refer readers to this paper to save space.
2 The reader(s) should note that we did not use financial markets efficiency data because most of the countries have missing data for it. Therefore, we had to exclude it from our analysis.

References

Abrigo, M. R., & Love, I. (2016). Estimation of panel vector autoregression in Stata. *The Stata Journal, 16*(3), 778–804.

Alfaro, L., Kalemli-Ozcan, S., & Sayek, S. (2009). FDI, productivity and financial development. *World Economy, 32*(1), 111–135.

Alshubiri, F. (2020). Analysis of the financial model of the ICT Price Basket on financial development indicators of GCC countries. *The Review of Socionetwork Strategies, 14*(1), 147–170.

Arellano, M., & Bond, S. (1991). Some tests of specification for panel data: Monte Carlo evidence and an application to employment equations. *The Review of Economic Studies, 58*(2), 277–297.

Arellano, M., & Bover, O. (1995). Another look at the instrumental variable estimation of error-components models. *Journal of Econometrics, 68*(1), 29–51.

Asongu, S. A. (2013). How has mobile phone penetration stimulated financial development in Africa? *Journal of African Business, 14*(1), 7–18.

Asongu, S. A., & Acha-Anyi, P. N. (2017). ICT, conflicts in financial intermediation and financial access: Evidence of synergy and threshold effects. *NETNOMICS: Economic Research and Electronic Networking, 18*(2), 131–168.

Beck, T. (2002). Financial development and international trade: Is there a link? *Journal of International Economics, 57*(1), 107–131.

Beck, T., Demirgüç-Kunt, A., & Levine, R. (2007). Finance, inequality and the poor. *Journal of Economic Growth, 12*(1), 27–49.

Bittencourt, M. (2011). Inflation and financial development: Evidence from Brazil. *Economic Modelling, 28*(1–2), 91–99.

Blundell, R., & Bond, S. (1998). Initial conditions and moment restrictions in dynamic panel data models. *Journal of Econometrics, 87*(1), 115–143.

Canova, F., & Ciccarelli, M. (2004). Forecasting and turning point predictions in a Bayesian panel VAR model. *Journal of Econometrics, 120*(2), 327–359.

Chatterjee, A., & Das, S. (2021). Information communication technology diffusion and financial inclusion: An inter-state analysis for India. *Innovation and Development, 11*(1), 1–23.

Chen, I. J. (2014). Financial crisis and the dynamics of corporate governance: Evidence from Taiwan's listed firms. *International Review of Economics & Finance, 32*, 3–28.

Cheng, C. Y., Chien, M. S., & Lee, C. C. (2021). ICT diffusion, financial development, and economic growth: An international cross-country analysis. *Economic Modelling, 94*, 662–671.

David, O. O. (2019). Nexus between telecommunication infrastructures, economic growth and development in Africa: Panel vector autoregression (P-VAR) analysis. *Telecommunications Policy, 43*(8), 101816.

Donner, J., & Tellez, C. A. (2008). Mobile banking and economic development: Linking adoption, impact, and use. *Asian Journal of communication, 18*(4), 318–332.

Grace, J., Charles K., & Christine Z. (2003). Information and communication technologies and broad-based development: A partial review of the evidence, World Bank working paper, technical report 12 (Washington, World Bank).

Hamilton, J. (1994). *Time series econometrics.* Cambridge: Cambridge University Press.

Karakara, A. A., & Osabuohien, E. S. (2019). Households' ICT access and bank patronage in West Africa: Empirical insights from Burkina Faso and Ghana. *Technology in Society*, *56*, 116–125. https://doi.org/10.1016/j.techsoc.2018.09.010

Lashitew, A. A., van Tulder, R., & Liasse, Y. (2019). Mobile phones for financial inclusion: What explains the diffusion of mobile money innovations? *Research Policy*, *48*(5), 1201–1215.

Lutkepohl, H. (2005). *New Introduction to Multiple Time Series Analysis*. New York: Springer.

Marszk, A., & Lechman, E. (2021). Reshaping financial systems: The role of ICT in the diffusion of financial innovations–Recent evidence from European countries. *Technological Forecasting and Social Change*, *167*, 120683. https://doi.org/10.1016/j.techfore.2021.120683

Mignamissi, D. (2021). Digital divide and financial development in Africa. *Telecommunications Policy*, *45*(9), 102199.

Nguyen, C. P., Su, T. D., & Doytch, N. (2020). The drivers of financial development: Global evidence from internet and mobile usage. *Information Economics and Policy*, *53*, 100892. https://doi.org/10.1016/j.infoecopol.2020.100892

Pradhan, R. P., Arvin, M. B., & Hall, J. H. (2016). Economic growth, development of telecommunications infrastructure, and financial development in Asia, 1991–2012. *The Quarterly Review of Economics and Finance*, *59*, 25–38. https://doi.org/10.1016/j.qref.2015.06.008

Saba, C. S. (2020). Security as an outcome for promoting economic prosperity in the regional economic communities of Africa: Evidence from a panel data analysis. *African Security Review*, *29*(4), 376–400.

Saba, C. S. (2021). Convergence or divergence patterns in global defence spending: Further evidence from a nonlinear single factor model. *Peace Economics, Peace Science and Public Policy*, *27*(1), 51–90.

Saba, C. S., & David, O. O. (2020). Convergence patterns in global ICT: Fresh insights from a club clustering algorithm. *Telecommunications Policy*, *44*(10), 102010.

Saba, C. S., & Ngepah, N. (2019). A cross-regional analysis of military expenditure, state fragility and economic growth in Africa. *Quality & Quantity*, *53*(6), 2885–2915.

Saba, C. S., & Ngepah, N. (2020a). Military expenditure and security outcome convergence in African regional economic communities: evidence from the convergence club algorithm. *Peace Economics, Peace Science and Public Policy*, *26*(1), 1–28.

Saba, C. S., & Ngepah, N. (2020b). Empirical analysis of military expenditure and industrialisation nexus: A regional approach for Africa. *International Economic Journal*, *34*(1), 58–84.

Saba, C. S., & Ngepah, N. (2022). ICT diffusion, industrialisation and economic growth Nexus: An international cross-country analysis. *Journal of the Knowledge Economy*, *13*(3), 1–40.

Sassi, S., & Goaied, M. (2013). Financial development, ICT diffusion and economic growth: Lessons from MENA region. *Telecommunications Policy*, *37*(4–5), 252–261.

Sims, C. A. (1980). Macroeconomics and reality. *Econometrica: Journal of the Econometric Society*, *48*(1), 1–48.

Svirydzenka, K. (2016). *Introducing a new broad-based index of financial development*. International Monetary Fund (IMF) Working Paper No. WP/16/5. https://www.imf.org/external/pubs/ft/wp/2016/wp1605.pdf

World Bank (2012). ICTs for financial services in Africa. https://openknowledge.worldbank.org/bitstream/handle/10986/19019/882280WP0Box380cialServices-0summary.pdf?sequence=1&isAllowed=y

World Bank (2017). World Bank annual report. https://thedocs.worldbank.org/en/doc/908481507403754670-0330212017/original/AnnualReport2017WBG.pdf

Yartey, C. A. (2008). Financial development, the structure of capital markets, and the global digital divide. *Information Economics and Policy, 20*(2), 208–227.

13 Financial Development and Remittance in African Countries

Nicholas Mbaya Odhiambo and Mercy T. Musakwa

13.1 Introduction

Despite the COVID-19 pandemic and economic slowdown, remittance inflows remained strong in 2020 for low- and middle-income countries. Low- and middle-income countries received $540 billion in 2020, a decline of $8 billion from 2019 receipts (World Bank, 2021a). This decline is small when compared to the decline of 4.8% that was reported during the 2009 global financial crisis, and far below the fall of over 30% in foreign direct investment (FDI) in low- and middle-income countries in 2020 (World Bank, 2021a). Remittance inflows to low- and middle-income countries exceeded the sum of $179 billion overseas development assistance and FDI of $259 billion and in 2020 (World Bank, 2021a). Egypt was among the top recipients of remittances in 2020, while the United Arab Emirates, United States, Arabia and Russian Federation were the largest sources of remittances in the same year (World Bank, 2021a) The true size of remittances, which include informal and formal flows, is larger than the official reported data (World Bank, 2021a). According to the World Bank (2021a), remittance inflows globally are expected to increase to $553 as the global growth rebounds further in 2021 and are expected to increase to $565 billion in 2022. The Middle East and North Africa recorded an increase of 2.3% in remittance inflows (World Bank, 2021a). In 2021, remittance inflows are expected to rise by 2.6% in the same region (World Bank, 2021a). This also holds for sub-Saharan Africa (excluding Nigeria), where remittance inflows increased by 2.3% in 2020 (World Bank, 2021a). This was linked to strong remittance growth reported for Zambia (37%), Mozambique (16%), Kenya (8%) and Ghana (5%) during the period (Ratha *et al.*, 2020). It is evident that remittance inflows have remained strong in low- and middle-income countries. The question is: Can African countries harness remittance inflows to accelerate financial development?

The surge in remittance inflows has sparked interest among researchers and policymakers who seek to establish how economies can benefit from the surge. Unlike other sources of funding, remittances are not associated with any conditionalities or interest payments. This makes this source of

DOI: 10.4324/9781003215042-16

external funding very attractive. The United Nations has also highlighted the importance of remittances as a source of funding needed to achieve the 17 Sustainable Development Goals (SDGs). Some of the clauses that support remittances include Section 10.c.1, which emphasises the reduction in remittance cost to 3%; Section 10.7.1, which captures the reduction in recruitment cost for migrant workers; and Section 17.3.2, which emphasises an increase in the volume of remittances as a percentage of GDP (World Bank, 2019).

On the financial development front, Africa has gone through transformation for decades, with the main objective of increasing and simplifying the mobilisation of savings and channelling the resources to productive investment. The transformation includes the development of a wide range of products that are accessible to both borrowers and savers, financial inclusion, an overhaul of the legislation and central bank supervisory reforms. The formation of monetary unions like the East Africa Monetary Union (EAMU) by 2024, West African Economic and Monetary Union (UEMOA) and the proposed monetary union in the Economic Community of West African States (ECOWAS) to be launched in 2027, has put pressure on member countries to rationalise their financial processes in preparation for the monetary unions. The same financial sector rationalisation is anticipated with the introduction of one currency in the African Union member countries. In sub-Saharan Africa, for instance, private sector credit to GDP has doubled from the 1995 level (IMF, 2016). Another interesting occurrence in the financial development landscape in Africa is the widespread financial liberation and overhaul of financial policies to embrace a more accessible financial system in line with best standards of financial development. There has been an ongoing transformation, although the financial systems of most African countries are still in the nascent stage, except for a few countries that have advanced financial systems, such as South Africa, Nigeria and Ghana (IMF, 2016).

Despite the nascent financial development, there has been a gradual introduction of marketable debt that has improved liquidity in the market (IMF, 2016). For example, Africa leads in innovation in the field of mobile telephone financial services (IMF, 2016). There has been a fast spread of telephonic financial service access in the form of M-Shwari, M-Pesa, M-Kopa in Kenya and EcoCash in Zimbabwe (IMF, 2016). The telephone-backed financial access has assisted in facilitating transactions even in the absence of traditional financial infrastructure (IMF, 2016). Figure 13.2 shows a general increase in domestic credit to the private sector by banks, broad money and domestic credit to the private sector from 1990 to 2017 (World Bank, 2021b). According to Figure 13.2, domestic credit to the private sector, among other selected bank-based financial development proxies, has experienced outstanding growth in Middle and North and Western and Central African countries, while East and Southern African countries had a modest growth (World Bank, 2021b).

Although the relationship between remittances and economic growth is comprehensively covered in the literature, the relationship between remittances and financial development has not been fully explored. The studies that investigated the relationship between remittances and financial development are more inclined to the impact of financial development on remittances, or the impact of remittances on financial development (see Olayungbo & Quadri, 2019; Masuduzzaman, 2014; Aggarwal, Demirguc-Kunt & Martinez Peria, 2011; Giuliano & Ruiz-Arranz, 2009). Although the findings of these studies are tilted in favour of a positive impact of remittances on financial development, another strand of literature also supports financial development having a positive impact on remittances. The variance in the findings of these studies is also confirmed by causality studies that found inconclusive causal relationship. Some studies found bidirectional causality between financial development and remittances (Karikari, Mensah & Harvey, 2016; Masuduzzaman, 2014) and a unidirectional causal relationship running from financial development to remittances (see Karikari *et al.*, 2016). In other studies, no causal relationship was found between the two (Olayungbo & Quadri, 2019). This necessitates a relook into the impact of remittances on financial development in sub-Saharan Africa using current data and statistical methods.

Financial development proxies that have been used in previous studies to examine the link between remittances and financial development are bank deposits, bank credit and money supply to financial liabilities, among others. Given the complexity of measuring financial development, a combination of bank-based financial development and market-based financial development measures is preferred (see Demirguc-Kunt & Levine, 2001).

The current study, therefore, employs six proxies of financial development to examine the dynamic relationship between remittances and financial development in five selected middle-income sub-Saharan African countries. The bank-based financial development proxies used in the study include the variables of bank deposits, liquid liabilities and bank deposit assets, while the market-based proxies include stock-market turnover ratio, stock-market capitalisation and stock-market traded value. The countries included in the empirical analysis were South Africa, Nigeria, Cote d'Ivoire, Kenya and Ghana. The motivations for the selection of these countries were the countries' level of financial development and the availability of long-term annual data on remittance inflows and stock-market development. Owing to the inadequate availability of longer term annual data, the variables used in this study were restricted to the period from 2000 to 2017. The study employed a wide range of estimation techniques, such as the cross-sectional dependence test, first- and second-generation unit root tests, first- and second-generation cointegration tests, and the DOLS and FMOLS dynamic models. In order to account for the omission-of-variable bias, the study included three control variables, namely, economic growth, trade and external debt.

The remainder of the chapter is organised as follows: Section 13.2 provides an overview of some of the previous studies that have been conducted on the relationship between remittances and financial development. Section 13.3 deals with the empirical analysis and the discussion of the results, while Section 13.4 concludes the study and offers policy recommendations.

13.2 Remittance in Flows and Financial Development: A Review of the Literature

Lucas and Stark (1985) highlighted altruism, coinsurance and savings as some important motives for emigrants to remit back home. The coinsurance motive rests on the need to save resources back home as a fallback when anything happens in the foreign country that leads to a loss of income. Emigrants remit to invest in projects that would enable them to generate income when they come back home. Unlike the coinsurance motive, the altruism motive is centred on alleviating struggling families back home: financially. This motive is rooted in the empathy of the emigrants, knowing the difficulties of the family members they left behind. Yang (2011) and Stark (1995) also confirm the altruistic and insurance motives for remittances. Among the three motives, this motive is also the main reason for emigrants to take the initiative to seek greener pastures. The savings motive is closely related to coinsurance and is anchored on the need for the emigrants to build savings back home to cater for a fall in income of loss of employment. According to Adam Jr and Page (2005), remittances are associated with investment in human capital and cash assets. Ratha (2007) also added real estate and support to small businesses. Most importantly, remittance inflows provide a stable and counter-cyclical income, especially during social shocks like pandemics, drought and wars. Ratha (2007) and Kapur (2004) further suggest an indirect positive impact of remittances on poverty reduction realised through the multiplier effect. This is felt at a national level through consumption and investment stimulation because of additional funds received from emigrants. The multiplier effect results in high national income that is associated with improved living standards, assuming equitable distribution of income. Remittance inflows have been identified as a potential source of development finance by the United Nations; this is encapsulated in by SDG 10.7 – reducing inequality within and among countries (United Nations, 2017).

Historically, financial development has been used as a conduit to mobilise savings from surplus units to deficit units (Levine, 1997). According to the IMF (2016), the financial sector helps in mobilising savings and directs them into productive uses such as start-up capital for innovative enterprises. Further, according to IMF (2016), financial institutions help in the management of risk, make payments easier, assist lenders in monitoring their clients, provide coinsurance and make stable investment and consumption possible. The benefits of a well-developed financial system can never be underestimated in economic development. Financial systems can be divided into market-based systems and bank-based, depending on the role that financial markets and financial intermediaries play in the economy. In economies where the financial intermediaries play an important role, the financial system is bank-based, while if the financial markets play a key role, the financial system is market-based (Nyasha & Odhiambo, 2014, 2015; Demirguc-Kunt & Levine, 2001). Under a bank-based, financial system financial widening and financial deepening are important growth metrics. Financial widening happens when there is growth of financial institutions and an expansion of financial services, while financial deepening occurs when there is an increase in the per capita number of financial services or in the ratio of financial assets to income (Demirguc-Kunt & Levine, 2001).

The theoretical link between financial development and remittances is based on the financial intermediation role financial institutions play during the remitting stage and receipting of the remitted funds. It is not clear which of the two Granger-causes the other. An advanced financial market provides affordable charges for emigrants, thereby encouraging them to use formal channels. The remittances in Africa have shown a consistent increase although Ratha *et al.* (2020) have indicated that the figures could be higher as statistics on informal channels are not available. The use of informal channels could be because of high charges, as supported by the SDG remittance charge reduction target of 3%, lack of financial inclusion of the recipients and lack of knowledge of the benefits of using the formal channels.

There is growing literature on the impact of remittances on financial development and the impact of financial development on remittances (see, for example, Olayungbo & Quadri, 2019; Masuduzzaman, 2014; Giuliano & Ruiz-Arranz, 2009). The findings from these studies suggest that remittances have a positive impact on financial development, while other studies confirm a positive impact of financial development on remittances (see Karikari *et al.*, 2016; Giuliano & Ruiz-Arranz, 2009). Some studies, however, found a negative impact of remittances on financial development (Karikari *et al.*, 2016), while others found the impact to be insignificant (Coulibaly, 2015). These inconsistent results on the impact studies are also reflected in the inconclusive causal relationship between the two (see Olayungbo & Quadri, 2019; Karikari *et al.,* 2016; Masuduzzaman, 2014). This section outlines studies on the impact of remittances on financial development and those studies that analysed the causality between the two.

Adekunle, Tella and Subair (2020) examined the relationship between remittances and financial development in 53 African countries using pooled mean group estimation and data spanning from 1986 to 2017. The study found a positive long-run relationship between remittances and financial development. In the same vein, Misati, Kamau and Nassir (2019) examined the relationship between remittances and financial development in Kenya using data from 2006 to 2016. Employing the autoregressive distributed lag (ARDL)–bounds approach, the study found remittances to have a positive impact on financial development.

Karikari *et al.* (2016) investigated the causal relationship between remittances and financial development in 50 African countries using data from

1990 to 2011. In the study, credit to the private sector and money supply were used as financial development proxies. Using random-effects and fixed-effects estimation, the study found that remittances promote financial development in the short run. However, remittances were found to have a negative impact on financial development in the long run. Williams (2016) also investigated the relationship between remittances and financial development in sub-Saharan African countries using panel data from 1970 to 2013. The study found remittances to have a positive impact on financial development. A 10% increase in remittances was found to increase domestic private credit by 0.43%, with a cumulative effect of 1.84%.

Similarly, Coulibaly (2015) investigated the relationship between financial development and remittances in 19 sub-Saharan African countries using panel-Granger causality testing on data from 1980 to 2010. The study found remittances to have a positive influence on financial development in Niger, Sierra Leone, Senegal and Sudan, and financial development was found to have a positive influence on remittances in Gambia when liabilities were used as a proxy for financial development. In the same study, when credit was used to measure financial development, remittances influenced financial development in Sudan, while no significant relationship was established regarding the influence of financial development on remittances in the other countries studied. The inconclusive results from studies such as those by Karikari *et al.* (2016) and Coulibaly (2015) suggest that more work still needs to be done on the relationship between the two variables to make informed policies.

Masuduzzaman (2014) examined the interaction of remittances and financial development in Bangladesh using annual data from 1981 to 2013. The study found remittances to have a positive impact on financial development in Bangladesh. These findings are in line with the study by Karikari *et al.* (2016) in Africa. They suggest that remittances contribute positively to financial development, irrespective of where the studies were done. In the same study by Masuduzzaman (2014), a bidirectional causal relationship was confirmed between remittances and financial development. This contrasts with the findings by Karikari *et al.* (2016), who found a unidirectional causal flow.

Aggarwal *et al.* (2011) analysed the impact of financial development on remittance inflows in 109 developing countries using data from 1975 to 2007. The study found a positive association between remittances and financial development. The same authors (Aggarwal, Demirguc-Kunt & Martinez Peria, 2006) investigated the impact of remittances on financial development in 99 developing countries employing data from 1975 to 2003. This study also found a positive association between remittances and financial development.

Aslam and Sivarajasigham (2020) examined the relationship between remittances and financial development in Sri Lanka employing data from 1975 to 2017. Using the Granger causality test and impulse response function analysis, the study found a bidirectional causal relationship between financial development and remittances. The impulse response indicated a positive shock on remittances to have an immediate significant positive impact on financial development. Olayungbo and Quadri (2019) investigated the relationship between financial development and economic growth in a panel of 20 sub-Saharan African countries using data from 2000 to 2015. No causality was confirmed between remittances and financial development in the study.

Overall, the literature reviewed provides prodigious evidence of a positive impact of remittances on financial development. However, the presence of some studies that found a negative or insignificant relationship between the two, and inconclusive causal relationship findings, warrants a relook on the relationship using current data and methodology. This points to a need for another study that investigates the obtaining relationship in the face of consistently increasing remittances. This will inform policy on how sub-Saharan African economies can harness remittances to facilitate financial development and ultimately economic development. This is increasingly becoming important, as most sub-Saharan African (SSAn) countries are faced with declining savings that cannot support investment demands.

13.3 Estimation Techniques and Empirical Analysis

13.3.1 Empirical Model

The following general model was used to examine the impact of remittances on financial development in the selected SSAn countries.

$$Fin_{it} = \gamma_{it} + \delta_{it} + \beta_{1i}Remit_{itj} + \beta_{2i}\gamma_{it} + \beta_{3i}Extdebt_{it} + \beta_{4i}Trade_{it} + \mu_{it} \qquad (13.1)$$

where i = Cross-sectional observation
t = Time period
Fin = Financial development – proxied by market-based financial development indicators (CAP = Stock-market capitalisation, STRADE = Stock-market traded value, and TURNOV = Stock-market turnover ratio) and bank-based financial development indicators (BD = Bank deposits, LL = Liquid liabilities, and DMBA = Bank deposit assets).
$Remit$ = Remittance
γ = Economic growth proxied by GDP per capita
$Extdebt$ = External debt
$Trade$ = Trade volume
δ_{it} and β_{1i} = Country-specific effects and deterministic trend effects, respectively.
μ_{it} = Error term expected to be normally and identically distributed with zero mean and constant variance.
Based on equation (13.1), the empirical models estimated in this study can be expressed as follows:

Model 1
Model 1A: [CAP = f (*Remit, Trade, Exdebt, y*)]
Model 1B: [STRADE = f (*Remit, Trade, Exdebt, y*)]

Model 1C: [TURNOV = f(Remit, Trade, Exdebt, y)]
Model 2
Model 2A: [BD = f(Remit, Trade, Exdebt, y)]
Model 2B: [LL = f(Remit, Trade, Exdebt, y)]
Model 2C: [DMBA = f(Remit, Trade, Exdebt, y)]

Although there are various ways by which equation (13.1) can be estimated, in this study the DOLS (dynamic ordinary least squares) and FMOLS (fully modified ordinary least squares) were used to examine the impact of remittances on the various proxies of financial development. Previous studies have demonstrated that using the normal OLS techniques on non-stationary panel data may lead to false inferences. In addition, OLS estimates have been found to be asymptotically biased (Jebli, Youssef & Apergis, 2019). The data used in this study were obtained from the World Bank Financial Development and Structure Database and the World Development Indicators. The missing data points were sourced from individual countries' statistical reports. Table 13.1 gives a summary of the definitions of variables, as well as specific data sources.

13.3.2 Cross-Sectional Dependence Test

Before conducting a stationarity test, it is important to carry out a cross-sectional dependence test to establish whether there is cross-sectional dependence in the data used in this study. For this purpose, four cross-sectional dependence tests were used, namely, the bias-corrected scaled LM, Pesaran CD, Breusch-Pagan LM and Pesaran scaled LM tests. The results of these tests are reported in Table 13.2.

Table 13.1 Data sources and definitions of variables

Variable		Definitions of Variable (Measurement)	Source
Remittance	*Remit*	Remittance inflows	FDSD/WDI
Trade	*Trade*	Exports + Exports/GDP	WDI
Economic growth	y	Real GDP per capita	WDI
External debt	*Extdebt*	Total external debt	WDI
Stock-market capitalisation	CAP	Stock-market capitalisation/GDP	FDSD
Stock-market total value traded	STRADE	Stock-market total value traded/GDP	FDSD
Stock-market turnover	TURNOV	Stock market turnover ratio (%)	FDSD
Bank deposits	BD	Bank deposits/GDP	FDSD
Liquid liabilities	LL	Liquid liabilities/GDP	FDSD
Deposit money bank assets	DMBA	Deposit money bank assets/GDP	FDSD

WDI = World Bank Development Indicators; FDSD = Financial Development Structure Database.

Table 13.2 Cross-sectional dependence tests

Series	Cross-Section Dependence Results			
	Breusch-Pagan LM	Pesaran Scaled LM	Bias-Corrected scaled LM	Pesaran CD
CAP	49.29485★★★ (0.0000)	8.786597★★★ (0.0000)	8.639538★★★ (0.0000)	6.336890★★★ (0.0000)
STRADE	23.17103★★ (0.0101)	2.945132★★★ (0.0032)	2.798073★★★ (0.0051)	3.346364★★★ (0.0008)
TURNOV	26.94515★★★ (0.0027)	3.789051★★★ (0.0002)	3.641993★★★ (0.0003)	1.493048 (0.1354)
BDGDP	136.3984★★★ (0.0000)	28.26353★★★ (0.0000)	28.11647★★★ (0.0000)	11.64959★★★ (0.0000)
LLGDP	89.46028★★★ (0.0000)	17.76786★★★ (0.0000)	17.62080★★★ (0.0000)	5.924490★★★ (0.0000)
DMBAGDP	97.58629★★★ (0.0000)	19.58489★★★ (0.0000)	19.43783★★★ (0.0000)	9.582197★★★ (0.0000)
REMIT	17.64655★ (0.0612)	1.709821★ (0.0873)	1.562762 (0.1181)	3.388508★★★ (0.0007)
TRADE	44.57000★★★ (0.0000)	7.730087★★★ (0.0000)	7.583028★★★ (0.0000)	2.723850★★★ (0.0065)
EXDEBT	101.4511★★★ (0.0000)	20.44910★★★ (0.0000)	20.30204★★★ (0.0000)	4.360298★★★ (0.0000)
y	104.3124★★★ (0.0000)	21.08889★★★ (0.0000)	20.94183★★★ (0.0000)	9.544681★★★ (0.0000)

Note: ★, ★★ and ★★★ denote significance at the 10%, 5% and 1% levels, respectively.

The results of the cross-sectional dependence tests reported in Table 13.2 show that there is sufficient evidence that cross-sectional dependence exists among the countries used in this study. The null hypothesis of no cross-sectional dependence was rejected by all four tests for all the variables, with the exception of remittance in the case of the Bias-corrected scaled LM test and turnover ratio in the case of the Pesaran CD test. Based on these results, we can conclude that there is cross-sectional dependence among the cross-sections. This implies that it is important to use the second-generation unit root test alongside the first-generation unit root tests.

13.3.3 Stationarity Test

Considering the presence of cross-sectional dependence in the data, both first- and second-generation unit root tests were used to examine the order of integration. The advantage of the second-generation unit root test is that, unlike the first-generation test, it accounts for the cross-sectional dependence in the series. Consequently, Pesaran's (2007) Cross-sectionally Augmented IPS (CIPS) panel unit root test was used as the second-generation unit root

Table 13.3 LLC and Pesaran – CIPS unit root tests

Variables	LLC		Pesaran – CIPS	
	Level	First Difference	Level	First Difference
CAP	0.5590	−8.0539★★★	−0.81797	−3.06346★★★
STRADE	−0.6734	−7.7864★★★	−1.06893	−4.0809★★★
TURNOV	−0.9256	−7.9395★★★	−1.29745	−4.6256★★★
BDGDP	1.6697	−4.8101★★★	−0.82332	−3.70841★★★
LLGDP	1.10496	−6.2123★★★	−1.59784	−3.4334★★★
DMBAGDP	1.35900	−5.0941★★★	−1.11901	−2.74060★★★
REMIT	−0.5080	−6.5372★★★	−1.34135	−3.88014★★★
TRADE	−0.68264	−4.1591★★★	−1.65294	−3.81518★★★
EXTDEBT	1.0548	−4.0234★★★	−0.98819	−5.64650★★★
y	−0.8899	−3.4983★★★	−1.37446	−3.23591★★★

Note: ★★★ indicates rejection of the respective null hypotheses at the 1% significance level.

test and the Levin-Lin-Chu test (LLC) as the first-generation unit root test. Table 13.3 gives a summary of the results of these tests.

From the results reported in Table 13.3, it is clear that both the LLC and Pesaran (CIPS) test results reject the stationarity of all the variables in levels but accept the stationarity in first difference. This has been confirmed by the LCC and Pesaran (CIPS) statistics, which were found to be insignificant in levels, but statistically significant after the first difference. Consequently, we can conclude that all the variables included in all the six equations are integrated of order one, i.e., $I(1)$.

13.3.4 Cointegration

As in the case of the unit root test, the second-generation cointegration test was used to test whether there is a cointegration relationship between the variables included in the six models, i.e., Models 1A, 1B, 1C, 2A, 2B and 2C. Specifically, the Westerlund (2007) cointegration test was used, which has been found to be robust when there is cross-sectional dependence in data. The advantage of Westerlund (2007) is that, unlike some of the first-generation cointegration tests, it is based on structural rather than residual dynamics (see Persyn & Westerlund, 2008). Table 13.4 gives a summary of the Westerlund (2007) cointegration test.

The results reported in Table 13.5 show that, overall, there was cointegration among the variables included in Models 1A, 1B, 1C, 2A, 2B and 2C. This finding was supported by the *Gt, Ga, Pt* and *Pa*, which were found to be statistically significant in most of the specifications.

This was also supported by the robust *P*-values of *Gt, Ga, Pt* and *Pa*, which were found to be statistically significant at the 1% level of significance in most

Table 13.4 Westerlund ECM panel cointegration test

Statistic	Value	Z-Value	P-Value	Robust P-Value	Value	Z-Value	P-Value	Robust P-Value
Stock-market development					Bank-based financial development			
Model 1A					Model 2A			
Gt	−3.200	−2.655	0.004	0.000	−3.141	−2.527	0.006	0.000
Ga	−6.790	0.971	0.834	0.000	−6.709	0.997	0.841	0.000
Pt	−7.169	−2.805	0.003	0.000	−5.682	−1.631	0.051	0.000
Pa	−5.505	0.186	0.574	0.200	−4.877	0.378	0.647	0.000
Model 1B					Model 2B			
Gt	−3.170	−2.590	0.005	0.200	−3.396	−3.080	0.001	0.200
Ga	−8.092	0.562	0.713	0.000	−7.066	0.885	0.812	0.000
Pt	−6.276	−2.101	0.018	0.200	−5.668	−1.620	0.053	0.000
Pa	−6.969	−0.261	0.397	0.000	−5.857	0.079	0.531	0.400
Model 1C					Model 2C			
Gt	−3.232	−2.724	0.003	0.000	−3.967	−4.322	0.000	0.000
Ga	7.914	0.618	0.732	0.000	−6.013	1.216	0.888	0.000
Pt	−6.413	−2.208	0.014	0.000	−7.340	−2.940	0.002	0.000
Pa	−6.100	0.004	0.502	0.200	−4.825	0.394	0.653	0.000

of the specifications. Based on the results, we can therefore conclude that there was a cointegration relationship among the variables used in this study, even in the presence of cross-sectional dependence.

13.3.5 Dynamic OLS (DOLS) and Fully Modified OLS (FMOLS)

Following the results of the cointegration test, DOLS and FMOLS were used to investigate the impact of remittances on the various proxies of financial development. Previous studies have shown that both the DOLS and FMOLS estimators provide robust estimations by addressing the endogeneity and serial correlation issues in a panel regression analysis (Khan *et al.*, 2019). Although the results from both DOLS and FMOLS are usually more reliable than those from OLS, the results yielded by DOLS are more popular because DOLS uses a parametric approach to resolve endogeneity and autocorrelation problems. Consequently, the DOLS estimates are preferred over the FMOLS. A summary of the DOLS and FMOLS results is given in Table 13.5.

The empirical results presented in Table 13.5 show that the impact of remittances on financial development depends largely on the type of financial development in question. While the coefficient of remittances is found to be positive and statistically significant in all bank-based financial development specifications, in stock-market development it is only significant in one of the three specifications, namely, turnover ratio (TURNOV) in the

Table 13.5 DOLS and FMOLS results

| | FMOLS | | | | | | DOLS | | | | | |
| | Stock-Market Development | | | Bank-Based Financial Development | | | Stock-Market Development | | | Bank-Based Financial Development | | |
	Model 1A (CAP)	Model 1B (STRADE)	Model 1C (TURNOV)	Model 2A (BD)	Model 2B (LL)	Model 2C DMBA	Model 1A (CAP)	Model 1B (STRADE)	Model 1C (TURNOV)	Model 2A (BD)	Model 2B (LL)	Model 2C (DMBA)
REMIT	−2.618683 (−1.4783)	−1.1911 (−1.5721)	0.8842*** (3.0230)	24.820*** (8.297)	0.4205*** (2.856)	39.879*** (7.051)	−1.6377 (−1.5898)	0.7464*** (3.7008)	−0.4039 (−1.2509)	0.3908*** (2.049)	1.0985*** (3.8353)	0.4372* (1.888)
TRADE	0.54678** (1.9937)	0.1717 (1.4640)	0.0737* (1.8737)	0.1058*** (4.828)	−0.0194 (−0.849)	0.066** (2.236)	0.3516** (1.9913)	0.0195 (0.6383)	0.0182 (1.044)	0.0430 (1.336)	−0.0058 (−0.1164)	−0.0606 (−1.295)
EXDEBT	0.0190 (0.1392)	0.0981* (1.6793)	−0.1086*** (−4.4625)	−0.0295 (−1.118)	−0.1027*** (−9.047)	0.0365 (1.403)	−0.0837 (−1.2119)	−0.0470*** (−3.331)	−0.0423** (−2.4788)	−0.0791*** (−5.2327)	−0.0812*** (−3.562)	−0.034* (−1.772)
y	0.0553*** (6.2222)	0.0261*** (6.858)	0.0066*** (2.4598)	−0.0039 (−1.337)	0.0035*** (4.802)	0.0194*** (9.858)	0.0271** (2.494)	0.0017 (0.3069)	0.0042*** (15.352)	0.0072*** (10.579)	−0.00046 (−0.3614)	0.0062*** (3.0984)

Note: (1) The *t*-statistic is in parentheses; (2) *, ** and *** denote statistical significance at the 10%, 5% and 1% levels, respectively.

case of the FMOLS estimator and the stock–market traded value (STRADE) in the case of the DOLS estimator. This implies that although remittance inflows have a positive impact on financial development in the studied SSAn countries, their impact largely affects the bank–based financial sector, rather than the stock–market sector. This finding is, however, not surprising, given the nature of financial systems in many SSAn countries. Indeed, the financial systems in many SSAn countries are largely dominated by bank-based rather than market-based financial systems.

Other results show that in Model 1A, both trade and economic growth had a positive impact on stock–market development, but only when the stock market is proxied by stock–market capitalisation. This applies irrespective of whether the estimation is done using DOLS or FMOLS. In Model 1B, the results show that while both economic growth and external debt had a positive impact on stock–market traded value when the FMOLS estimator was used, when the DOLS estimator was used, external debt seemed to negatively affect stock–market traded value. In Model 1C, external debt and economic growth, respectively, had a negative and positive impact on the stock–market turnover ratio with both the FMOLS and DOLS estimators, while trade had a positive impact on the turnover ratio only with the FMOLS estimator. In Model 2A, trade was found to have a positive impact on bank deposits when FMOLS was used as the estimator, while economic growth and external debt had positive and negative impacts on bank deposits, respectively, when DOLS was used as the estimator. In Model 2B, external debt was found to have a negative impact on liquid liabilities in both FMOLS and DOLS specifications, while economic growth had a positive impact on liquid liabilities only when FMOLS was used as the estimator. Finally, the results of Model 2C showed that although economic growth had a positive impact on deposit money bank assets with both FMOLS and DOLS, trade had a positive effect on deposit money bank assets in the FMOLS specification, while external debt had a negative effect in the DOLS specification.

13.4 Conclusion

In this chapter, we examined the impact of remittances on financial development in selected SSAn countries during the period from 2000 to 2017. Although recent data show that the amount remitted by migrants from sub–Saharan Africa (SSA) has grown from $4.8 billion in 2000 to $48 billion in 2018, the link between this important income stream and financial development has not been fully explored in African countries, especially in the sub–Saharan African region. Contrary to some of the previous studies, the current study used a wide range of financial development proxies in a stepwise fashion to examine the link between remittance inflows and financial development in the studied countries. In total, six proxies were used – three proxies for bank-based financial development and another three proxies for stock–market development. The bank-based financial development proxies used included bank deposits, liquid liabilities and deposit money bank assets, while the market-based proxies included stock-market turnover ratio, stock-market capitalisation and stock-market traded value. Owing to the inadequate availability of long-term annual data for stock-market development in many SSAn countries, only five countries were included in this study, namely, Kenya, South Africa, Cote d'Ivoire, Ghana and Nigeria. To address the weaknesses of some of the previous studies, the study employed a wide number of modern econometric techniques to examine this linkage. These techniques included the cross-sectional dependence test, first- and second-generation unit root tests, first- and second-generation cointegration tests, and the DOLS and FMOLS dynamic models. To account for the omission-of-variable bias, the study included three control variables, namely, economic growth, trade and external debt. The results of the study confirm that the impact of remittance inflows on financial development in SSA depends on whether the financial sector is market-based or bank-based. In the main, the results show that while remittances have an ambiguous positive impact on stock-market development, where only two out of six specifications were significant, in bank-based financial development its positive impact is robust and unambiguous for all the specifications estimated. It is argued that this finding is not surprising given the nature of financial systems in SSA, which are largely dominated by the banking sector. On the whole, the study found that remittance inflows in SSAn countries mainly have a positive and significant impact on the bank-based financial sector. The findings of this study, therefore, emphasise the role of remittance in financial development. It is also consistent with previous studies such as that by Aggarwal *et al.* (2011), which found that remittances have the potential to influence the development of the financial sectors in recipient countries. When remittances are channelled through the banking system, some recipients may convert their remittances into deposits, which eventually results in an increase in loanable funds within the banking system – thereby leading to further development of the banking sector.

References

Adam Jr, R. H., & Page, J. 2005. Do international migration and remittance reduce poverty in developing countries? *World Development*, 33(10): pp. 1645–1669.

Adekunle, I. A., Tella, S. A., & Subair, K. 2020. Remittance and financial development in Africa. *Journal of Public Affairs*. Wiley online. http://dx.doi.org/10.1002/pa.2525.

Aggarwal, R., Demirguc-Kunt, A., & Martinez Peria, M. S. 2006. Do workers' remittances promote financial development? *World Bank Policy Research Working Paper 3957*. World Bank.

Aggarwal, R., Demirguc-Kunt, A., & Martinez Peria, M. S. 2011. Do workers' remittances promote financial development? *Journal of Development Economics*, 16: pp. 289–326.

Aslam, A. L. M., & Sivarajasigham, S. 2020. Empirical relationship between workers' remittances and financial development (an ARDL cointegration approach for Sri Lanka). *International Journal of Social Economics*, 47(1): pp. 1381–1402.

Coulibaly, D. 2015. Remittances and financial development in sub-Saharan African countries: A system approach. *Economic Modelling*, 45(C): pp. 249–258.

Demirguc-Kunt, A., & Levine, R. 2001. Bank-based and market-based financial systems: Cross-country comparisons. In: Demirguc-Kunt, A. & Levine, R. (Eds.) *Financial structure and economic growth: A cross-country comparison of banks, markets, and development.* Cambridge: MIT Press. pp. 81–140.

Giuliano, P., & Ruiz-Arranz, M. 2009. Remittances, financial development, and growth. *Journal of Development Economics*, (90): pp. 144–152. http://dx.doi.org/10.1016/j.jdeveco.2008.10.005

IMF, 2016. *Financial development in sub-Saharan Africa: Promoting inclusive and sustainable growth.* Available at https://www.imf.org/external/pubs/ft/dp/2016/afr1605. [Accessed 13 September 2021].

Jebli, M. B., Youssef, S. B. & Apergis, N. 2019. The dynamic linkage between renewable energy, tourism, CO2 emissions, economic growth, foreign direct investment, and trade. *Latin American Economic Review*, 28(2): pp. 1–19. https://latinaer.springeropen.com/track/pdf/10.1186/s40503-019-0063-7.pdf.

Kapur, D. 2004. Remittance: The new development mantra? *G24 Discussion Paper 29.*

Karikari, N. K., Mensah, S., & Harvey, S. K. 2016. *Do remittances promote financial development in Africa?* Springer Plus 5:1011. http://dx.doi.org/10.1186/s40064-015-2658-7.

Khan, Z., Rabbi, F., Ahmad, M., & Siqun, Yang. 2019. Remittances inflow and private investment: A case study of South Asian economies via panel data analysis. *Economic Research-Ekonomska Istrazivanja* 32(1): pp. 2723–2742.

Levine, R. 1997. Financial development and economic growth: Views and agenda. *Journal of Economic Literature* 35: pp. 688–726.

Lucas, R. E., & Stark, O. 1985. Motivations to remit: Evidence from Botswana. *Journal of Political Economy*, 93: pp. 901–918.

Masuduzzaman, M. 2014. Workers' remittance inflow, financial development and economic growth: A study on Bangladesh. *International Journal of Economics and Finance*, 6(8): pp. 247–267.

Migration Policy Institute, 2021. Migration Data Portal. Available at https://migrationdataportal.org. [Accessed 12 September 2021].

Misati, R. N., Kamau, A., & Nassir, H. 2019. Do migrant remittances matter for financial development in Kenya? *Financial Innovation*, 5(31). http://dx.doi.org/10.1186/s40854-019-0142-4.

Nyasha, S., & Odhiambo, N. M. 2014. Bank-based financial development and economic growth: A review of international literature. *Journal of Financial Economic Policy,* 6(2): pp. 112–132. http://dx.doi.org/10.1108/JFEP-07-2013-0031.

Nyasha, S., & Odhiambo, N. M. 2015. Economic growth and market-based financial systems: A review. *Studies in Economics and Finance*, 32(2): pp. 235–255. http://dx.doi.org/10.1108/SEF-03-2014-0053.

Olayungbo, D. O., & Quadri, A. 2019. Remittances, financial development and economic growth in sub-Saharan African countries: Evidence from a PMG-ARDL approach. *Financial Innovation,* 5(1): pp. 1–25. https//doi.org/10.1186/s40854-019-0122-8.

Persyn, D., & Westerlund, J. 2008. Error-correction–based cointegration tests for panel data. *Stata Journal, Stata Corp LP,* 8(2): pp. 232–241.

Pesaran, M. H. 2007. A simple panel unit root test in the presence of cross-section dependence. *Journal of Applied Economics,* 22(2): pp. 265–312.

Ratha, D. 2007. *Leveraging remittance for development.* Migration Policy Institute. Washington, DC: World Bank.

Ratha, D., De, S., Ju Kim, E., Plaza, S., Seshan, G., & Yameogo, N. D. 2020. *Migration and Development Brief 32: COVID-19 crisis through a migration lens.* Washington, DC: KNOMAD-World Bank.

Stark, O. 1995. *Altruism and beyond.* Oxford: Basil Blackwell.

United Nations. 2017. *International Migration Report 2017 Highlights.* Available from www.un.org. [Accessed 9 September 2021].

Westerlund, J. 2007. Testing for error correction in panel data. *Oxford Bulletin of Economics and Statistics,* 69: pp. 709–748.

Williams, K. 2016. Remittances and financial development: Evidence from sub-Saharan Africa. *African Development Review,* 28(3): pp. 357–367.

World Bank. 2019. *Migration and Development Brief 31.* [Online]. Available at https://www.knomad.org/publication/migration-and-development-brief-31. [Accessed 19 September 2021].

World Bank. 2021a. Defying predictions, remittance flows remain strong during COVID-19 crisis. Available at https://www.worldbank.org. [Accessed 4 June 2021].

World Bank. 2021b. *World Bank Development Indicators.* Available at https://0-databank-worldbank-org.ujlink.uj.ac.za/source/world-development-indicators. [Accessed 19 September 2021].

Yang, D. 2011. Migrant remittances. *Journal of Economic Perspectives,* 25(3): pp. 129–152.

Appendix

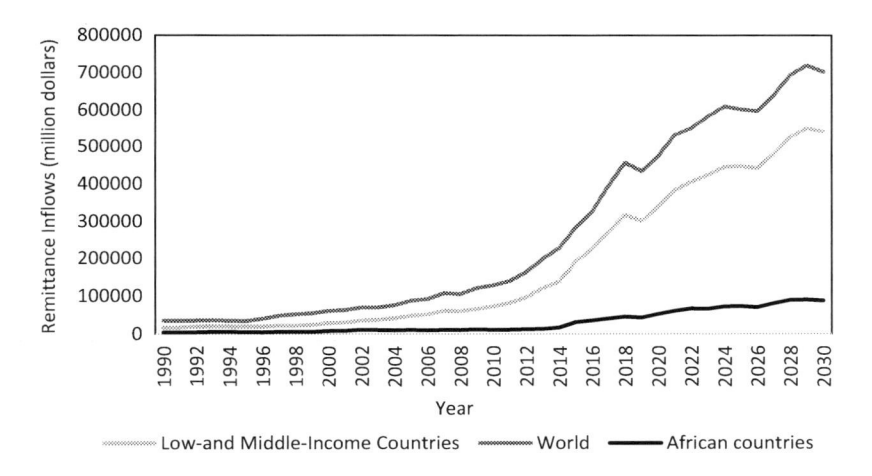

Appendix Figure 13.1 Trend in remittance inflows in Africa.
Source: Migration Policy Institute (2021).

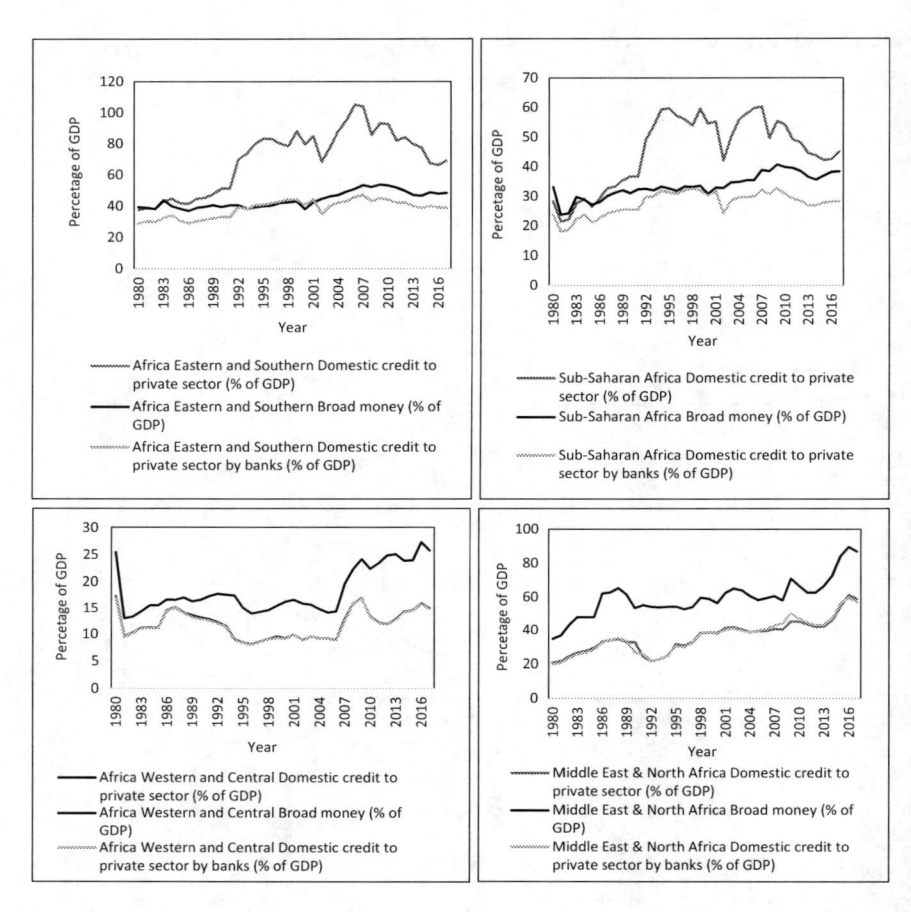

Appendix Figure 13.2 Trends in bank-based financial development indicators across regions.

Source: World Bank (2021b).

14 Financial Inclusion and Gender Inequality in African Countries

Tendai Zawaira, Carolyn Chisadza, Matthew Clance and Rangan Gupta

14.1 Introduction

Gender inequality has been marked as an impediment to growth and development (African Development Bank, 2014; Elborgh-Woytek et al., 2013). As such, it continues to be an important global development goal as noted by its historical and current inclusion in global development agendas such as the Universal Declaration of Human Rights, the Millennium Development Goals, and the Sustainable Development Goals (specifically SDG5). Women represent half of the world's population; hence, gender gaps of any form represent an under-utilisation of women's potential in the economy, which has a bearing on overall growth and development (Cuberes & Teignier, 2014). Apart from being a social or welfare concern, gender inequality is also a human capital efficiency loss concern.

The Global Gender Gap Report (2020) shows that although Africa has made significant strides in reducing gender inequality, having closed 69% of its gender gap, gaps still persist that will take 95 years to close.[1] Evidence on some of the losses due to gender inequality can be found in Cuberes and Teignier (2014) who show that due to gender gaps in the labour market, GDP per capita losses are as high as 27% in some regions of the world. Despite this understanding on the potential contribution of women in the economy, women are still marginalised in certain sectors of the economy, such as the financial sector, making up more than half of the world's unbanked population.

This paper contributes to the literature on the determinants of gender inequality, with a specific focus on understanding the underlying factors of gender gaps in financial inclusion in sub-Saharan Africa (SSA). We pay particular attention to women's financial inclusion in the credit market. This includes women's access to both formal and informal financial sources. Formal financial sources include having an account and savings at a financial institution and borrowing from a financial institution. Informal financial sources include having savings at a savings club and borrowing from friends or family.

With this background, we pose the question: has financial development been inclusive of gender? We propose that financial development

DOI: 10.4324/9781003215042-17

has contributed to decreasing gender inequality. Using financial data for 34 sub-Saharan African countries for the years 2011, 2014, and 2017, we find that firstly, women are at a disadvantage in terms of financial inclusion. On average, about 25% of the women in the sample owned accounts at a financial institution, 11% had savings at a financial institution, and 5% borrowed from a financial institution, in relation to men. Interestingly, our data highlights that women, in relation to men, appear to rely heavily on informal means of accessing credit with about 22% of the women in the sample saving at a savings club, and close to 37% borrowing from friends and family. On average, a relatively higher share of men in the sample participates in the formal financial sector (see Figure 14.1). Secondly, our results indicate that financial access to formal institutions contributes to a decrease in gender inequality in comparison with borrowing from informal sources.

The implications of our findings highlight a serious concern in the delay of women's ability to access formal financial sources. According to Kabeer (2009), women have limited access to the formal financial sector due to collateral requirements and perceived risks associated with their lack of assets. Moreover, borrowing from informal sources can leave women vulnerable to unscrupulous behaviour from loan sharks, such as unreasonable terms of payments (World Bank, 2014). To this end, policymakers may consider

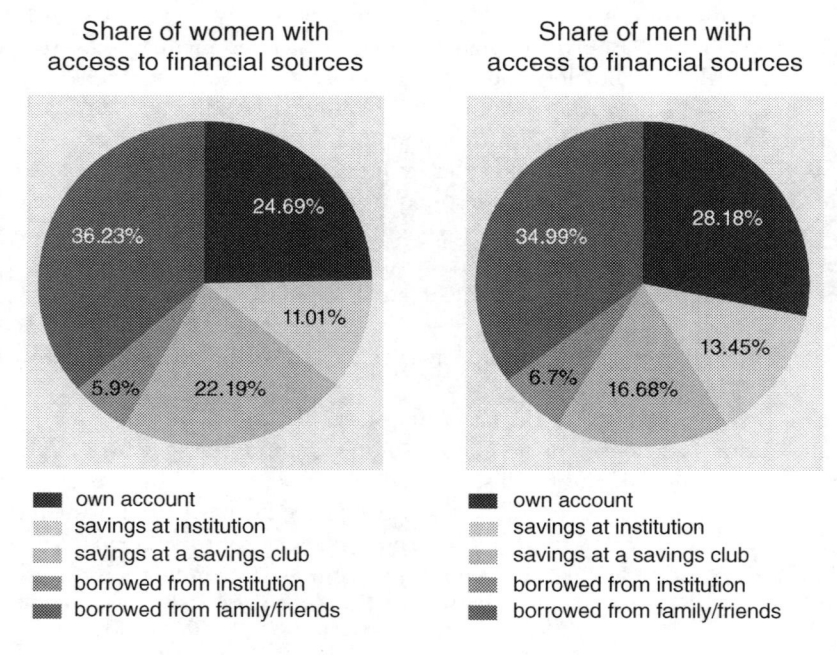

Figure 14.1 Access to financial sources by gender. Figure 14.1 shows access to formal and informal financial sources between women and men in the sample of countries.

adopting interventions that may facilitate access to finance for women with less stringent collateral requirements, whilst at the same time ensuring fair access to finance for all genders across different income levels. Evidence suggests that narrower gender gaps in financial inclusion can be associated with higher development, as well as more equitable outcomes, such as more equal income distribution between men and women (Cuberes & Teignier, 2015; Gonzales et al., 2015).

14.2 Financial Sector Development in Sub-Saharan Africa

The financial sector plays an important role in advancing economic growth and development. It promotes economic growth through capital accumulation and technological progress by increasing the savings rate, mobilising and pooling savings, producing information about investment, facilitating and encouraging the inflows of foreign capital, as well as optimising the allocation of capital (Beck, Levine, & Loayza, 2000; Levine, 1999; Levine & King, 1993). According to the World Bank (2014), financial development also reduces poverty and inequality by broadening access to finance to the poor and vulnerable groups, such as women. Financial development thus reduces dependence on personal wealth or use of unreliable and expensive sources of finance to invest in education, business ventures, or benefit from growth opportunities. It also facilitates risk management by reducing vulnerability to shocks and increasing investment and productivity that result in higher income generation. An important element of financial development is financial inclusion.

Chakrabarty (2010) defines financial inclusion as the process of ensuring access to appropriate financial products and services needed by vulnerable groups, such as low-income groups or women, at an affordable cost in a fair and transparent manner by mainstream institutional players. According to Beck, Demirgüç-Kunt, and Levine (2007), financial inclusion can contribute to reducing income inequality by raising the incomes of the poorest income quintile. Financial inclusion also reduces inequality of opportunity and mitigates the adverse effects of inequality on the level and durability of growth (IMF, 2015; Ostry, Berg, & Tsangarides, 2014; World Bank, 2014).

According to the IMF (2016), the last three decades have seen sub-Saharan Africa's financial sector development in various dimensions. For example, the region's median ratio of private sector credit to GDP doubled from its 1995 level indicating greater financial depth (IMF, 2016). The region has also led the world in innovative financial services based on mobile telephony such as M-Pesa, M-Shwari, and M-Kopa, especially in East Africa. These facilities help reduce transaction costs and facilitate personal transactions even in the absence of traditional financial infrastructure. Pan-African banks have significantly increased in most sub-Saharan African countries filling in the gaps in services left by European and U.S. banks resulting in greater economic integration and making the sector more competitive. Microfinance has also grown rapidly, making financial services available to customers at the lower end of the income distribution (Kabeer, 2009). However, access to finance is still relatively lower in sub-Saharan Africa than other developing regions in general, and women's access to formal financial services remains limited in relation to men (Kabeer, 2009). In addition, gender inequality in various aspects of financial inclusion still remains high in sub-Saharan Africa, and it is highly associated with higher income inequality (IMF, 2016); hence, the need for greater financial inclusion for women in sub-Saharan Africa cannot be overemphasised.

Generally, a number of reasons have been put forth for greater financial inclusion. At the macro level, narrower gender gaps in financial inclusion are associated with higher development, as well as more equitable outcomes. For example, women's financial inclusion is associated with more equal labour force participation rates between men and women. More equal labour force participation rates, in turn, have been previously associated with higher growth (Cuberes & Teignier, 2015) and a more equal income distribution (Gonzales et al., 2015). When women have access to individual secure (private) savings accounts, this can help foster economic resilience and increase their control over financial resources, as well as their household decision-making power (Karlan et al., 2016).

At the micro level, greater access to finance can help increase the efficiency of women's cash management and allow them to smooth consumption (Kabeer, 2009). In addition, increasing women's access to formal financial services can have benefits for women themselves and positive spillover effects for their households, such as human development outcomes through child survival, increased health and education, poverty reduction, and economic growth (Morrison, Raju, & Sinha, 2007; Schultz, 2001; Strauss et al., 1991; World Bank, 2001). When women have liquidity, they also tend to reinvest it back into their families and communities at a higher rate than men, thus contributing to the overarching goal of inclusive growth that most African countries have been pursuing for the past three decades (Esther, 2012; La Ferrara, 2016). Thus, the gender gap in access to finance can have significant impact on social and economic progress.

14.3 Data and Descriptives

In order to address our research question on whether financial development has been inclusive of gender, we conduct preliminary statistical analysis using financial data from the World Bank's Global Financial Development Index for 34 sub-Saharan African countries[2] for the years 2011, 2014, and 2017. Table 14.1 reports the sample characteristics of the data. According to the data, on average, only 26.07% of individuals above 15 years in the 34 countries have an account with a financial institution. Table 14.1 also shows that most savings and borrowing in sub-Saharan Africa generally occur outside of formal financial institutions. Average savings at formal institutions are as low as 12.08% for the whole region, whilst savings with informal institutions are slightly higher at 19.9%. On the contrary, only 6.2% of the individuals above 15 years of age borrow from financial institutions, whilst 35.03% borrow from informal sources such as family and friends.

Table 14.1 Full sample characteristics

	n	Mean	SD	Min.	Max.	Median
Gender Inequality Index	94	0.57	0.08	0.38	0.72	0.57
Account at financial institution (%)	91	26.07	18.84	1.52	89.49	20.36
Account at financial institution, male (%)	91	29.27	19.29	1.59	92.49	23.05
Account at financial institution, female (%)	91	23.00	18.72	1.45	86.64	16.88
Savings at financial institution (%)	91	12.08	8.21	1.16	35.53	9.79
Savings at financial institution, male (%)	91	13.97	8.97	1.34	36.86	11.86
Savings at financial institution, female (%)	91	10.26	7.75	.71	34.30	8.17
Savings at savings club (%)	87	19.91	10.63	1.93	46.05	19.01
Savings at savings club, male (%)	87	18.12	10.41	1.89	49.54	16.44
Savings at savings club, female (%)	87	21.63	11.49	1.97	42.97	20.11
Borrowed from financial institution (%)	91	6.20	3.65	.91	17.06	5.60
Borrowed from financial institution, male (%)	91	6.96	4.46	.87	21.81	6.05
Borrowed from financial institution, female (%)	91	5.48	3.23	.53	13.91	5.17
Borrowed from family (%)	91	35.03	12.70	3.66	71.20	32.69
Borrowed from family, male (%)	91	36.35	12.92	4.53	72.21	34.39
Borrowed from family, female (%)	91	33.76	12.81	2.85	74.44	32.98
GDP/capita	102	2088.03	2570.58	214.14	10199.50	1063.26
Urbanisation	102	38.92	17.70	10.92	88.98	39.72
Globalisation	102	51.42	7.47	37.73	72.58	51.38
Polity2	102	3.22	4.54	−4.00	10.00	5.00

Table 14.2 shows the correlations between the Gender Inequality Index (GII) and aggregated financial inclusion variables.[3] GII is the United Nations' historically extended Gender Inequality Index (Gonzales et al., 2015). The index is a composite index capturing the loss of women's achievement due to gender biases and ranges from 0 (no inequality) to 1 (complete inequality). It covers three aspects of a country's gender inequality, namely, reproductive health, empowerment, and labour market participation. GII builds on previous gender indices used in the Human Development Reports (HDRs): the gender-related development index (GDI), and the gender empowerment measure (GEM). Some of the advantages of GII over other indices are: (1) it measures inequality between genders over three dimensions, mentioned above, (2) it removes income, the most controversial component of the GDI and GEM, and (3) it does not allow for high achievement in one dimension to compensate for low achievement in another dimension (Ferrant, 2009).

From Table 14.2, having an account with a financial institution, saving at a financial institution, and borrowing from a financial institution are negatively and significantly correlated with GII. On the contrary, informal options for savings and borrowing do not show any significant correlation with GII. In Table 14.3, we show the sex-disaggregated pairwise correlations. Similar to the aggregated figures, formal financial institutions are negatively and significantly associated with GII across gender. The negative correlation is stronger when women own accounts at financial institutions.

In Table 14.4, we show some of the region-specific characteristics in our sample. East Africa has the largest percentage of individuals (an average of 23%) who are 15 years and older that have an account at a financial institution, whilst Central Africa has the lowest, at 9%. We also observe that less than 10% of the sampled individuals in all four regions save at a financial institution. However, savings with informal institutions such as savings clubs is slightly higher. This similar trend is also observed for borrowing across all regions suggesting the possibility that most individuals in the sampled countries prefer and/or are restricted to informal means of financing.

14.3.1 *Gender-Disaggregated Patterns of Financial Inclusion*

Below we show some of the gender-disaggregated patterns of financial inclusion for the sample of countries in the study. Figure 14.2 shows the number of individuals with an account at a financial institution has increased between 2011 and 2017. However, two things are apparent: (1) Men are more likely to have an account at a financial institution compared to women, and (2) the increase in account ownership at a financial institution was greater for men (14% points) compared to women (9% points).

Figure 14.3 shows that there are more savings outside the formal financial institutions. In Figure 14.3a, men generally save more at a financial institution compared to women. On the contrary, Figure 14.3b shows that women rely more on informal savings options such as savings at a club compared to men.

Table 14.2 Sample correlations: aggregated financial variables

Variables	GII	Account	SavingsFinst	SavingsClub	BorrowFinst	BorrowFamily	GDP/Capita	Urbanisation	Globalisation	Polity2
GII	1									
Account	−0.716★★★	1								
SavingsFinst	−0.677★★★	0.912★★★	1							
SavingsClub	0.019	0.252★★	0.253★★	1						
BorrowFinst	−0.509★★★	0.809★★★	0.806★★★	0.279★★★	1					
BorrowFamily	0.208★	−0.135	−0.037	0.275★★	−0.062	1				
GDP/capita	−0.545★★★	0.601★★★	0.555★★★	0.012	0.331★★★	−0.224★★	1			
Urbanisation	−0.062	0.298★★★	0.265★★	0.032	0.031	−0.183★	0.630★★★	1		
Globalisation	−0.585★★★	0.700★★★	0.623★★★	0.148	0.585★★★	−0.182★	0.623★★★	0.366★★★	1	
Polity2	−0.15	0.227★★	0.169	0.046	0.176★	−0.008	0.180★	0.02	0.474★★★	1

Table 14.3 Sample correlations: gender-disaggregated financial variables

Variables	GII	AccountM	AccountF	SaveFinstM	SaveFinstF	SaveClubM	SaveClubF	BorrowFinstM	BorrowFinstF'	BorrowFamM	BorrowFamF
GII	1										
AccountM	−0.680★★★	1									
AccountF	−0.745★★★	0.959★★★	1								
SaveFinstM	−0.667★★★	0.905★★★	0.890★★★	1							
SaveFinstF	−0.667★★★	0.855★★★	0.896★★★	0.937★★★	1						
SaveClubM	0.002	0.310★★★	0.233★★	0.316★★★	0.263★★	1					
SaveClubF	0.039	0.265★★	0.164	0.238★★	0.164	0.909★★★	1				
BorrowFinstM	−0.567★★★	0.837★★★	0.797★★★	0.824★★★	0.775★★★	0.269★★	0.240★★	1			
BorrowFinstF	−0.390★★★	0.710★★★	0.714★★★	0.712★★★	0.717★★★	0.322★★★	0.257★★	0.817★★★	1		
BorrowFamM	0.207★	−0.115	−0.106	−0.023	−0.016	0.340★★★	0.228★★	−0.059	−0.007	1	
BorrowFamF	0.204★	−0.155	−0.138	−0.049	−0.048	0.322★★★	0.219★★	−0.085	−0.057	0.959★★★	1

Table 14.4 Sample characteristics by region

Columns by: Regions	Central	East	South	West	Total	P-value
Sample size, *n* (%)	18 (17.6)	30 (29.4)	24 (23.5)	30 (29.4)	102 (100.0)	
Gender Inequality Index, mean (sd)	0.61 (0.06)	0.54 (0.08)	0.52 (0.06)	0.63 (0.05)	0.57 (0.08)	0.00
Account at financial institution (%), mean (sd)	15 (9)	32 (23)	41 (17)	17 (10)	26 (19)	0.00
Savings at financial institution (%), mean (sd)	7 (4)	15 (9)	17 (8)	8 (5)	12 (8)	0.00
Savings at savings club (%), mean (sd)	19 (9)	20 (13)	18 (8)	21 (10)	20 (11)	0.85
Borrowed from financial institution (%), mean (sd)	3 (2)	9 (4)	7 (3)	5 (2)	6 (4)	0.00
Borrowed from family or friends (%), mean (sd)	30 (8)	38 (15)	42 (14)	31 (9)	35 (13)	0.01
Number of countries	6	10	8	10	34	

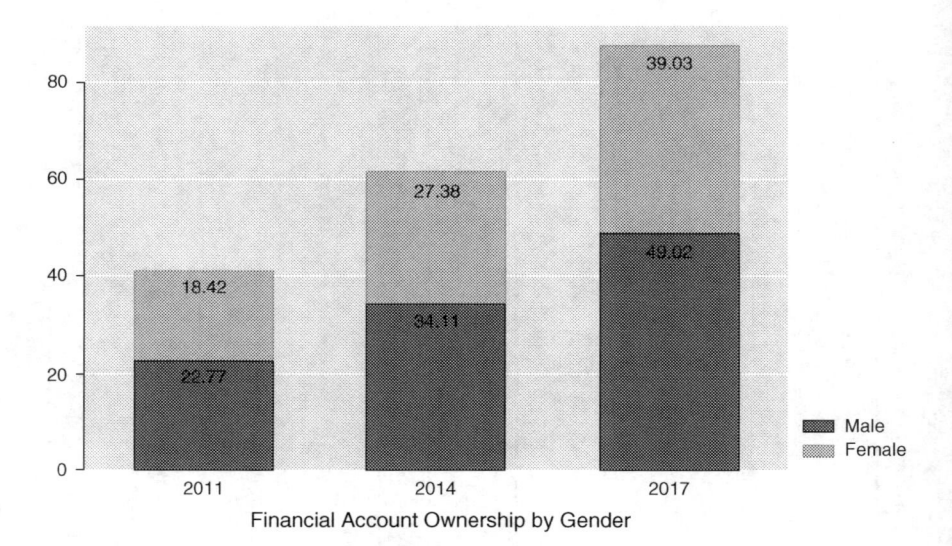

Figure 14.2 % of individuals 15 years and above that have an account at a financial institution.
Source: Global Financial Index and UNDP.

Moreover, this trend appears to have increased over the periods 2011–2017, suggesting that possibly women may still be facing some obstacles to participate in the formal financial sector.

Figure 14.4 shows the borrowing patterns of the individuals in the sample. The data shows four issues: (1) The rate at which both men and women have been borrowing from financial institutions in sub-Saharan Africa increased between 2011 and 2017. However, (2) access to formal sources of finance is generally low in sub-Saharan Africa. Across the three time points, less than 10% of all individuals in the sampled countries borrowed from financial institutions. In 2011, an average of only 5% of all individuals borrowed from a financial institution and this only increased by 2% points to 7% in 2017. This implies that (3) most individuals in sub-Saharan Africa rely on informal sources of finance such as clubs or family or friends as shown in the data. In 2011, an average of 36% individuals borrowed from family and friends.

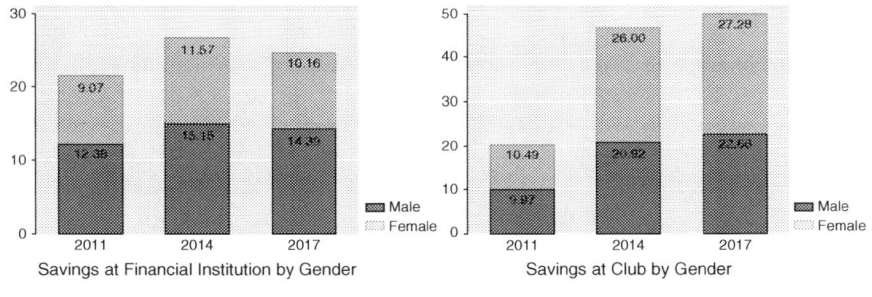

(a) Saving at Financial Institution: Formal   (b) Savings at Clubs: Informal

Figure 14.3 Savings behaviour of individuals in SSA: some evidence. (a) Saving at Financial Institution: (Formal) by Gender. (b) Savings at Clubs (Informal) by Gender.
Source: Global Financial Index and UNDP.

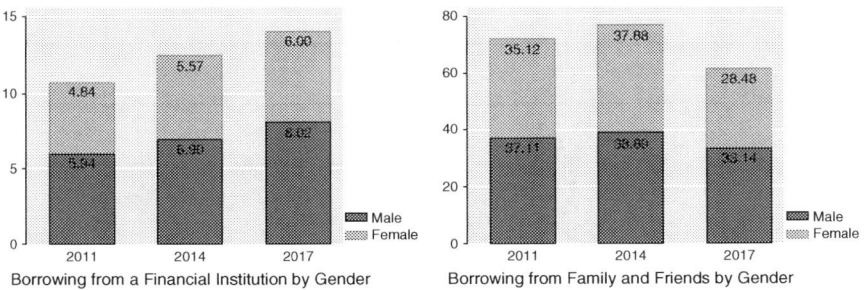

(a) Borrowing from a Financial Institution: Formal   (b) Borrowing from family and friends: Informal

Figure 14.4 Borrowing behaviour of individuals in SSA: some evidence. (a) Borrowing from a Financial Institution: formal. (b) Borrowing from family and friends: informal.
Source: Global Financial Index and UNDP.

This declined slightly to 31% in 2017. We observe that (4) men tend to have more access to both formal and informal sources of finance, compared to women.[4] In summary, the statistical evidence so far appears to highlight significant gender disparities regarding financial inclusion, more so for women accessing formal financial sources.

14.3.2 Empirical Estimation

We complement our preliminary analysis by investigating whether financial inclusion contributes to decreasing gender inequality. Given the cross-sectional dimension of the data, we use ordinary least squares (OLS) to estimate the association between financial inclusion and gender inequality. The baseline model specification is as follows:

$$GII_i = \alpha + \beta_1 F\ inancialvar_i + \beta_2 X + E_i \tag{14.1}$$

where GII_i is our proxy for gender inequality in country i, and will be estimated using the United Nations historically extended Gender Inequality Index (GII) (Gonzales et al., 2015). Figure 14.5 shows patterns in GII across regions in sub-Saharan Africa (i.e., West, East, Central and Southern Africa).[5] Gender inequality as measured by GII has been on the decline in all the regions over time. However, West Africa has consistently experienced higher levels of gender inequality averaging 0.63, whilst Southern Africa has experienced slightly lower levels, an average of 0.52 during the same period.

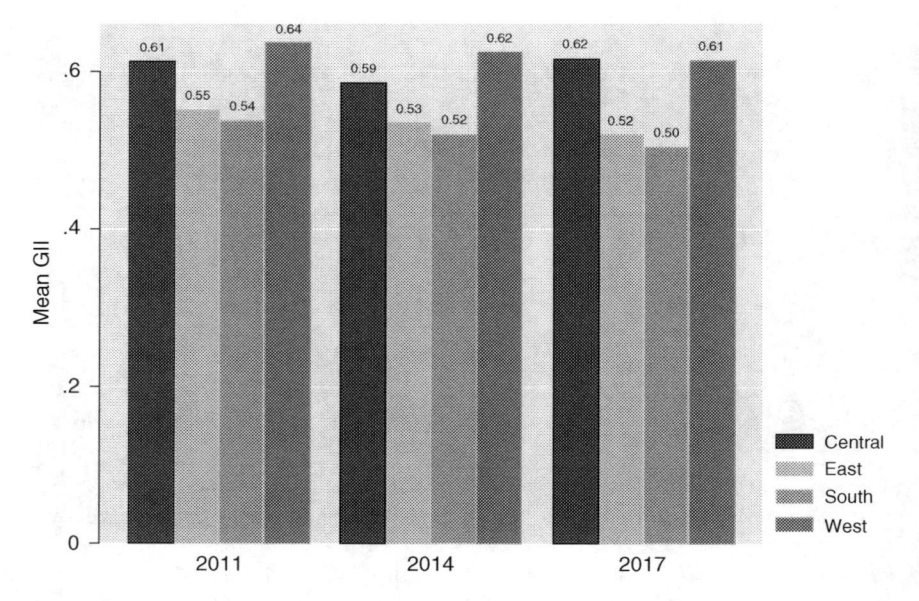

Figure 14.5 Trends in GII across regions in SSA.
Source: Global Financial Index and UNDP.

Our variables of interest are captured by *Financialvar*$_j$. These variables are measured using the World Bank's Global Financial Development Index data (Global Findex) developed by Demirguc-Kunt et al. (2018) and collected for the years 2011, 2014, and 2017. This dataset includes variables on (a) size of financial institutions and markets (financial depth), (b) degree to which individuals can and do use financial services (access), (c) efficiency of financial intermediaries and markets in intermediating resources and facilitating financial transactions (efficiency), and (d) stability of financial institutions and markets (stability). The Global Findex is a superior measure to other variables previously used in the literature such as ratio of financial institutions' assets to GDP, ratio of liquid liabilities to GDP, and ratio of deposits to GDP, which fail to capture all elements of financial inclusion.

In this paper, we will focus on access to finance and narrow down to five main variables of financial inclusion, which cover both formal (i.e., banks and credit unions) and informal (i.e., cooperatives, microfinance, family, and friends) sources. These include:(1) ownership (individual or joint) of an account at a financial institution; (2) savings at a financial institution; (3) borrowing from a financial institution; (4) saving at a savings club, and (5) borrowing from family and friends. These variables are measured in percentages. We expect the correlation between financial inclusion and gender inequality to be negative (Morrison et al., 2007; Schultz, 2001; Strauss et al., 1991; World Bank, 2001), as indicated in Figure 14.6, which shows the correlation between some of the variables of interest and gender inequality in 2017.

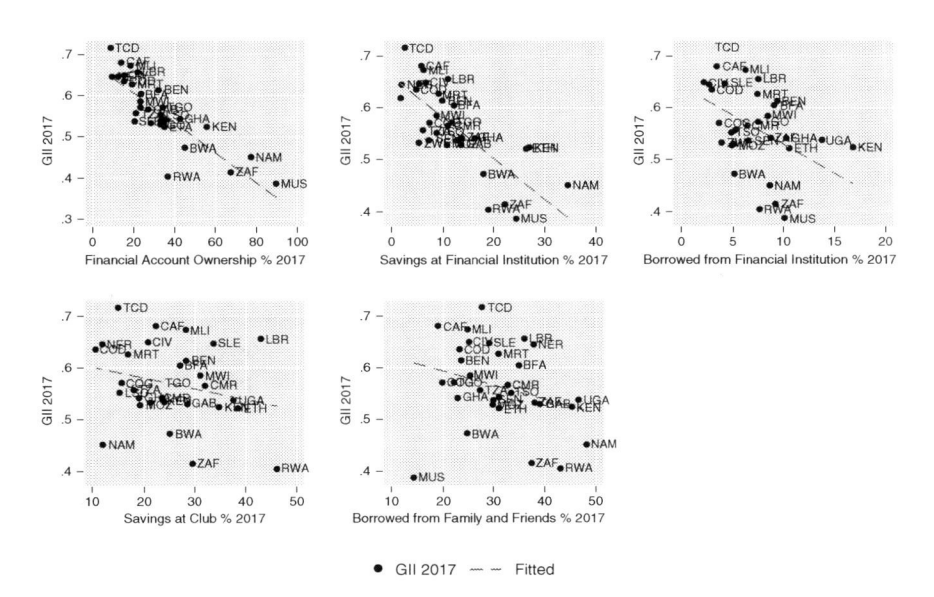

Figure 14.6 Correlation between GII and financial inclusion.
Source: Global Financial Index and UNDP.

The variable X_i is a vector of control variables that include income per capita as a proxy for modernisation (economic development), globalisation, and institutional quality (Polity2). Data on income per capita is obtained from the World Development Indicators (WDI). Income per capita is gross domestic product divided by midyear population. Data are in constant 2010 U.S. The variable globalisation is the KOF Globalisation Index which measures the economic, social, and political dimensions of globalisation and scored as a percentage. The variable Polity2 was developed by the Center for Systemic Peace, and it captures the quality of institutions. It is a score that varies between −10 and +10 and increases with the quality of institutions. The polity score is normalised to between 0 and 1.

The association between economic development and gender inequality has mixed results with one strand of literature, suggesting that as economies develop, gender inequality levels decline, whilst the other argues that it may actually worsen as women's economic opportunities trail behind men's due to educational gaps and job market skills preferences (see Boserup, 1970; Duflo, 2012; World Bank, 2011). According to the World Bank (2011), the gendered impact of globalisation largely depends on the characteristics of the society and economy that reflect existing patterns of gender inequality. These include the gender distribution of labour force by sector, areas of comparative advantage in the country, distribution of productive assets such as education, skills, property and finance – for which women generally have less access to – as well as the distribution of unpaid household labour between men and women. More democratic societies are assumed to have greater individual freedom in general, and this works to improve the conditions of previously marginalised groups, women included. As such, improved institutional quality is expected to reduce levels of gender inequality. However, the adoption and spread of new forms of institutions in society is believed to be strongly linked to and reinforcing of inherent forms of institutions in a particular area (Cooray & Potrafke, 2011; Inglehart & Norris, 2003). Except for GII and Polity2, the rest of the variables are logged.

14.3.3 Empirical Results

Table 14.5 reports on the association between account ownership at a financial institution and gender inequality. The results show a statistically significant negative correlation between account ownership at a formal financial institution and gender inequality. These results hold in general (column 1) and across gender (columns 2 and 3). These findings are consistent with the empirical evidence discussed earlier that access to finance matters for gender equality. Economic development, globalisation, and the quality of institutions are all negatively correlated with gender inequality, implying that as economic advance, open up to external values and experiences (globalisation), and the quality of institutions improve, women's outcomes in society improve.

Table 14.5 Financial institution account ownership and gender inequality SSA

	(1)	*(2)* GII	*(3)* GII
Account	−0.014★★★ (0.005)		
AccountM		−0.013★★★ (0.005)	
Acoount F			−0.013★★★ (0.005)
GDP/ capita	−0.090★★★ (0.029)	−0.090★★★ (0.029)	−0.091★★★ (0.029)
Globalisation	−0.093★ (0.053)	−0.091 (0.056)	−0.104★★ (0.050)
Polity2	−0.045 (0.028)	−0.040 (0.029)	−0.052★ (0.027)
Observations	81	81	81
R-squared	0.973	0.973	0.972
Number of *i*	31	31	31
Country FE	Yes	Yes	Yes
Year FE	Yes	Yes	Yes

Coefficients reported. Robust standard errors in parentheses. $★p < .10$, $★★p < .05$, $★★★p < .01$. Notes: Variable account captures the percentage of individual who have an account at a financial institution. AccountM is the percentage of male individuals who have an account at a financial institution, whilst AccountF is the percentage of female individuals with an account at a financial institution. GDP/capita, Urbanisation, and Polity2 are measured as described in the data section.

Table 14.6 reports on the savings and borrowing behaviour and gender inequality.[6]

In column 1, we show the aggregated associations, whilst in columns 2 and 3, we disaggregate these by gender. Column 1 shows that despite being an informal source of finance, savings at a savings club is generally negatively and significantly associated with gender inequality. On the contrary, borrowing from family and friends significantly increases gender inequality and this holds even across gender. Informal sources of finance tend to be more expensive and insecure. Moreover, because of the reliance on other people's financial capacities, this limits an individual's own capacity to make financial decisions that can benefit them at a personal or household level. This reliance on family or friends for financial support removes the autonomy individuals, particularly women's need for their emancipation. The table also shows that it matters more for gender inequality that women more than men have access to finance from formal financial institutions. Column 3 also shows that women's ability to save, even at a savings club, is negatively and significantly correlated with gender inequality.

Table 14.6 Financial institution account ownership and gender inequality SSA

	(1) GII	(2) GII	(3) GII
SavingsFinst	0.007 (0.007)		
SavingsClub	−0.014★★ (0.005)		
BorrowingFinst	−0.013 (0.008)		
BorrowingFam	0.019★★★ (0.007)		
SavingsFinstM		0.004 (0.009)	
SavingsClubM		−0.013★★ (0.006)	
BorrowingFinstM		−0.010 (0.009)	
BorrowingFamM		0.020★★ (0.008)	
SavingsFinstF			0.006 (0.005)
SavingsClubF			−0.012★★ (0.004)
BorrowingFinstF			−0.008★ (0.005)
BorrowingFamF			0.016★★ (0.007)
GDP/capita	−0.039 (0.038)	−0.035 (0.051)	−0.060★ (0.033)
Globalisation	−0.043 (0.073)	−0.066 (0.075)	−0.036 (0.070)
Polity2	−0.039 (0.025)	−0.053★★ (0.026)	−0.022 (0.029)
Observations	74	74	74
Adj. R-squared	0.973	0.971	0.973
Number of i	31	31	31
Country FE	Yes	Yes	Yes
Year FE	Yes	Yes	Yes

Coefficients reported. Robust standard errors in parentheses. ★p < .10, ★★p < .05 and ★★★p < .01.

Notes: The variable SavingsFinst shows percentage of individuals who save at a financial institution. SavingsClub is the percentage of individuals who save at a savings club, and BorrrowingFinst is the percentage of individuals who borrow from a financial institution. The variable BorrowingFam is the percentage of people who borrow from family and friends. We then separate these variables across gender to capture variable SavingsFinstM, SavingsClubM, BorrowingFinstM, and BorrowingFamM for men and SavingsFinstF, SavingsClubF, BorrowingFinstF, and BorrowingFamF for women.

In terms of controls, all three are negatively correlated with gender inequality. However, given the financial behaviour of the individuals in the sample, there is no significant correlation between globalisation and gender inequality across all the models. Economic development is only significantly associated with gender inequality when women use the formal banking systems as shown in column 3, whilst men's financial behaviour appears to matter for the impact of institutional quality reduces on inequality as shown in column 2. These results are generally consistent with the literature as discussed in the data section.

14.4 Discussion and Conclusion

The main objective in this paper was to investigate the correlation between financial inclusion and gender inequality. Our main findings suggest that access to finance is still relatively low in sub-Saharan Africa, particularly in terms of savings and borrowing from formal financial institutions. Although we find evidence of a negative correlation between owning an account at a financial institution and gender inequality across all genders, we find no effect of savings and borrowing from formal financial institutions on gender inequality for the men. Our empirical analysis, however, unearths a pattern in the savings and borrowing behaviour of women in sub-Saharan Africa that indicates a strong reliance on informal sources of finance such as savings club, family, and friends. The results showed that, for women, savings at a savings club decreased gender inequality whilst a positive correlation between borrowing from family and friends existed with gender inequality. We also find evidence in line with previous studies that women have less access to finance, especially from formal sources compared to men. This then forces women to rely on informal, less secure, and costly means of financing, which negatively affects their incomes.

These findings present opportunities for policymakers in the drive for gender equality. The most immediate recommendation should focus on improving the savings and borrowing behaviour of people in sub-Saharan Africa. This includes financial literacy education and training for all individuals. Important for this paper is the gender gap in access to finance. Improving access to finance is at the centre of improving gender equality and increasing the economic freedoms and opportunities that women have to contribute to their families and societies. Factors such as cultural norms or legal barriers are often at the root of the limited financial access and use of any type of financial service by women. Cultural norms around what is acceptable for a woman to do, where she can go alone, or with whom she can interact can all serve to limit women's access to formal financial services. Inheritance laws favour men over women, reducing women's access to family assets and in turn the need for financial services. This therefore requires policy actions from various stakeholders, especially given that some of the bottlenecks are not about financial services but more about societal norms.

Notes

1 This gap is measured in four dimensions, economic participation and opportunity, educational attainment, health and survival, and political participation.
2 The choice of countries included in the sample was largely informed by the availability of data on the Gender Inequality Index (GII).
3 These include account at financial institution, savings at financial institution, savings at savings club, borrowing from financial institutions, and borrowing from family and friends.
4 Note that the reported statistics are sample means calculated from the data. The reader can refer to the graphs to see the actual proportions between men and women.
5 Countries in Central Africa include Cameroon, Central African Republic, Chad, Congo, Congo (DRC), and Gabon. West African countries in the sample include Benin, Burkina Faso, Côte d'Ivoire, Ghana, Liberia, Mali, Niger, Senegal, Sierra Leone, and Togo. Countries in East Africa include Burundi, Ethiopia, Kenya, Mauritania, Mauritius, Rwanda, Sudan, Tanzania, and Uganda. Southern African countries included are Angola, Botswana, Lesotho, Mozambique, Namibia, South Africa, Zambia and Zimbabwe.
6 As a robustness check, we include persistence in gender inequality as an explanatory variable. The results are reported in Table Appendix 14.1A in the Appendix. Our findings remain largely consistent with those reported in Table 14.6.

References

African Development Bank. (2014). *Investing in Gender Equality for Africa's Transformation*. Available from https://www.afdb.org/fileadmin/uploads/afdb/Documents/Policy-Documents/2014-2018_-_Bank_Group_Gender_Strategy.pdf .

Bank, W. (2011). Globalization's Impact on Gender Equality: What's Happened and What's Needed. Available from https://doi.org/10.1596/9780821388105_ch6

Beck, T., Demirgüç-Kunt, A., & Levine, R. (2007). Finance, inequality, and the poor. *Journal of Economic Growth, 12* (1), 27–49.

Beck, T., Levine, R., & Loayza, N. (2000). Finance and the sources of growth. *Journal of Financial Economics, 58* (1–2), 261–300.

Boserup, E. (1970). *Women's Role in Development*. London: Earthscan.

Chakrabarty, K. (2010). Inclusive growth–role of financial sector. Address at the National Finance Conclave.

Cooray, A., & Potrafke, N. (2011). Gender inequality in education: Political institutions or culture and religion? *European Journal of Political Economy, 27* (2), 268–280.

Cuberes, D., & Teignier, M. (2014). Gender inequality and economic growth: A critical review. *Journal of International Development, 26* (2), 260–276.

Cuberes, D., & Teignier, M. (2015). How costly are labor gender gaps? Estimates for the Balkans and Turkey. *Estimates for the Balkans and Turkey (June 22, 2015)*. World Bank Policy Research Working Paper (7319).

Demirguc-Kunt, A., Klapper, L., Singer, D., Ansar, S., & Hess, J. (2018). *The Global Findex Database 2017: Measuring Financial Inclusion and the Fintech Revolution*. The World Bank.

Duflo, E. (2012). Women empowerment and economic development. *Journal of Economic Literature, 50* (4), 1051–1079.

Elborgh-Woytek, M. K., Newiak, M. M., Kochhar, M. K., Fabrizio, M. S., Kpodar, K., Wingender, M. P., ... Schwartz, M. G. (2013). *Women, Work, and the Economy: Macroeconomic Gains from Gender Equity*. International Monetary Fund.

Esther, D. (2012). Women empowerment and economic development. *Journal of Economic Literature, 50* (4), 1051–1079.

Ferrant, G. (2009). A new way to measure gender inequalities in developing countries: The gender inequalities index (GII). *CEAFE Papiers*. Available at: http://www.tn.auf.org/CEAFE/PapiersCEAFE10/MacroI/Ferrant.pdf

Gonzales, C., Jain-Chandra, S., Kochhar, K., Newiak, M., & Zeinullayev, T. (2015). *Catalyst for Change: Empowering Women and Tackling Income Inequality*. International Monetary Fund

IMF. (2015). *Financial inclusion: Can it meet multiple macroeconomic goals?* International Monetary Fund. Available from https://www.imf.org/en/Publications/Staff-Discussion Notes/Issues/2016/12/31/Financial-Inclusion-Can-it-Meet-Multiple-Macroeconomic-Goals-43163

IMF. (2016). *Financial Development in Sub-Saharan Africa: Promoting Inclusive and Sustainable Growth*. International Monetary Fund.

Inglehart, R., & Norris, P. (2003). *Rising Tide: Gender Equality and Cultural Change Around the World*. Cambridge University Press.

Kabeer, N. (2009). World survey on the role of women in development: Women's control over economic resources and access to financial resources. United Nations Entity for Gender Equality and the Empowerment of Women (UN Women). Available from https://www.unwomen.org/en/digital-library/publications/2009/1/2009-world-survey-on-the-role-of-women-in-development-women-s-control-over-economic-resources-and-access-to-financial-resources-including-microfinance

Karlan, D., Kendall, J., Mann, R., Pande, R., Suri, T., & Zinman, J. (2016). *Research and Impacts of Digital Financial Services* (Tech. Rep.). National Bureau of Economic Research.

La Ferrara, E. (2016). Mass media and social change: Can we use television to fight poverty? *Journal of the European Economic Association, 14* (4), 791–827.

Levine, R. (1999). Law, finance, and economic growth. *Journal of financial Intermediation, 8* (1–2), 8–35.

Levine, R., & King, R. G. (1993). Finance, entrepreneurship, and growth. *Journal of Monetary Economics, 32* (3), 513–542.

Morrison, A., Raju, D., & Sinha, N. (2007). *Gender Equality, Poverty, and Economic Growth*. The World Bank.

Ostry, M. J. D., Berg, M. A., & Tsangarides, M. C. G. (2014). *Redistribution, Inequality, and Growth*. International Monetary Fund.

Schultz, T. P. (2001). Women's roles in the agricultural household: Bargaining and human capital investments. *Handbook of Agricultural Economics, 1*, 383–456.

Strauss, J., Barbosa, M., Teixeira, S., Thomas, D., & Junior, R. G. (1991). Role of education and extension in the adoption of technology: A study of upland rice and soybean farmers in central-west Brazil. *Agricultural Economics, 5* (4), 341–359.

World Bank. (2001). *Engendering Development: Through Gender Equality in Rights, Re- Sources, and Voice*. The World Bank.

World Bank. (2011). *World Development Report 2012: Gender Equality and Development*. World Bank Publications.

World Bank. (2014). *Global Financial Development Report 2014: Financial Inclusion*. The World Bank.

Appendix
Robustness Check

In Table Appendix 14.1A, we perform robustness checks by including the lag of GII, the dependent variable to control for the persistence in gender inequality. Our results remain largely consistent with the findings reported in Table 14.5. Women are more likely to use informal sources of finance compared to men; informal sources of finance are generally associated with gender inequality as previously discussed.

Table Appendix 14.1 A Financial institution account ownership and gender inequality SSA robustness checks

	(1)	(2)	(3)
	GII	GII	GII
L.GII	0.132	0.170*	0.103
	(0.088)	(0.080)	(0.088)
SavingsFinst	0.010		
	(0.013)		
SavingsClub	−0.006		
	(0.009)		
BorrowingFinst	−0.011		
	(0.009)		
Borrowing Fam	0.016**		
	(0.007)		
SavingsFinstM		0.011	
		(0.016)	
SavingsClubM		0.000	
		(0.010)	
BorrowingFinstM		−0.012	
		(0.011)	
BorrowingFamM		0.010	
		(0.008)	
SavingsFinstF			0.008
			(0.007)
SavingsClubF			−0.009
			(0.008)

	(1)	(2)	(3)
BorrowingFinstF			-0.006
			(0.005)
Borrowing FamF			0.018★★
			(0.008)
Observations	44	44	44
Adj. R-squared	0.980	0.979	0.981
Number of i	31	31	31
Controls	Yes	Yes	Yes
Country FE	Yes	Yes	Yes
Year FE	Yes	Yes	Yes
F	8.398	5.151	4.785

Standard errors in parentheses. ★$p < .10$, ★★$p < .05$, and ★★★$p < .01$.

15 Financial Development and SMEs in African Countries

Joshua Akanyonge, William Obeng-Amponsah and Erasmus Larbi Owusu

15.1 Introduction

The World Bank (n.d.) defines financial development or financial sector development as occurring "when financial instruments, markets, and intermediaries ease the effects of information, enforcement, and transactions costs and therefore do a correspondingly better job at providing the key functions of the financial sector in the economy." Guru and Yadav (2019) explain financial development as "the development of the size, efficiency and stability of financial markets along with increased access to the financial markets that can have multiple advantages for the economy." Financial development empowers businesses with needed funds to develop and expand. Available research findings propose that a well-developed financial sector is the anchor to economic development. Financial development is explained as a process that

> promotes economic growth through capital accumulation and technological progress by increasing the savings rate, mobilizing and pooling savings, producing information about investment, facilitating and encouraging the inflows of foreign capital, as well as optimizing the allocation of capital.
>
> (World Bank, n.d.)

Financial development must include small- and medium-sized businesses since they are often the backbone of many economies around the globe.

Small and medium enterprises (SMEs) in the African continent have attracted the attention of governments, policymakers and implementers, development agencies including bilateral and multilateral organizations and multinational companies some of whose partners include many SMEs. Anytime and wherever this economic subsector is discussed at seminars and forums in Africa and across the world, different speakers have heralded not only the potential and successes but also the drawbacks of SMEs. Furthermore, they have highlighted both the benefits and grievances of companies who formed business relationships with SMEs. A recurring consensus has been the solid conviction that SMEs hold the key to strong growth in most African economies. This

DOI: 10.4324/9781003215042-18

economic entity is a field that holds huge resources but remains untapped and is waiting to be discovered and exploited across most African countries. In spite of their prominence in business discussions, Price Water Coopers – Ghana (2013) (PWC) observes that SMEs seem deprived of many of the opportunities that will enable them realize their potential. In African economies, that is exactly the situation of SMEs. That is precisely the circumstances of SMEs in African economies. These words echo the general sentiments of members of the academia and other research communities about SMEs.

Oftentimes, referred to as the so-called "Missing Middle", the designation emphasizes the importance of SMEs in Africa, yet they are painfully deprived of funding. Alibhai et al. (2017) stated that 5–10% medium enterprises and 20% small enterprises collectively form the missing link. They further opined that this "missing middle" forms over 95% of registered enterprises, which provide employment to over 50% of the world's working population, and contributes over 35% of the GDP of emerging market economies. However, this group of businesses have been deprived of financing over the year. Access to funding is a key strategy to SME growth across the globe. SMEs are the "missing middle" as they are unable to access bank financing and other services.

There has been a broad realization that SMEs will play a crucial role in economic growth and development, leading to robust economies. For this reason, it is imperative for willing organizations, including banks, to invest in SMEs to help propel them to greater economic heights. This financial inclusion, which is an ongoing global exercise, will help SMEs realize their full economic and developmental potential. That said, SMEs suffer a twin tragedy; they often get overlooked by banks for lacking expensive collaterals required of companies desiring to obtain bank loans and simultaneously are too large to be funded with microfinance loans and other forms of financing offered to microfinance enterprises (Abor and Quartey, 2010; Aryeetey, 1998; Quartey, 2002).

Inferring from the foregoing, this chapter sets out to analyse financing avenues for SMEs and the levels of funding attainable. The focus of this chapter is to contribute to ongoing debate in extant literature on the financial development of SMEs in Africa. The chapter reviews bottlenecks to SME financing and identifies ways to increase access for this vital economic subsector so critical for poverty alleviation and accelerated economic development. The chapter is structured as follows: Section 15.2 reviews the available literature on the subject. Section 15.3 looks at the development of SMEs on the African continent. Section 15.4 outlines SME development from selected African countries followed by the concluding section.

15.2 Literature Review

The definition of SMEs is somewhat challenging to make since there are varying opinions across the world of academics and policymakers. SMEs as economic agents are vital for economic growth and development not only in the European Union but also in other regions like the African continent, being a critical source of jobs, entrepreneurial novelty, competitiveness and livelihood. The OECD defines this economic constituency as being businesses with a workforce less than 250, a yearly revenue of 50 million euros and net assets of 43 million euros. The definition of SME is further explained in the illustration in Figure 15.1, which describes SMEs in relation to workforce, financial position and turnover. The illustration shows that annual turnover is the main variable used for categorizing SMEs.

It is worth noting that African SME growth and expansion are hampered by several causes, such as "inadequate finance, lack of managerial skills, equipment and technology and poor access to capital markets" (Quartey et al., 2017). Of these, inadequacy of funds is the factor that mainly stunts SME firm growth and development (Arthur, 2003; Aryeetey, 1994; Deakins et al., 2008; Mensah, 2004; Okpara, 2011; Parker et al., 1995; World Bank, 1994). Sowa et al. (1992) on Ghana and Daniels and Ngwira (1993) on Malawi, among several other researchers, both show a serious funding void affecting SMEs in Africa. Aryeetey (1994) specifically related that 38% SME respondents in a survey cited access to bank finance as a key setback. Osei et al. (1993), Dawson (1993), and Bani (2003) all separately reported that the vast majority of loans applied for do not get a favourable outcome.

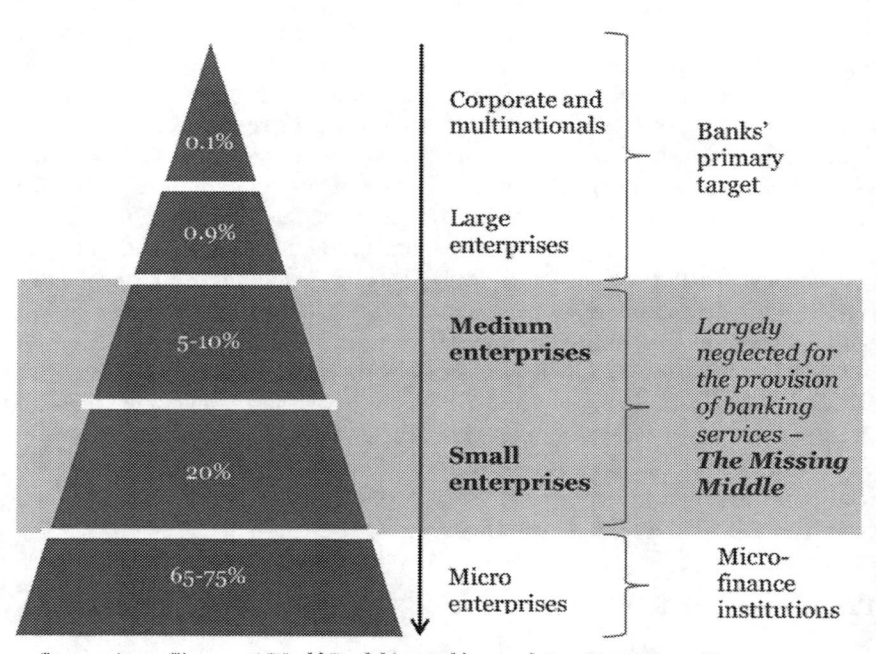

Source: AccessFinance, A World Bank bi-monthly newsletter. Issue No. 30, Jan-2010

Figure 15.1 Definition of SME.
Source: Price Water Coopers [Ghana Banking Survey (2013)].

Studies from other regions show that financial development enabled by state-sponsored competition among banks leads to funds made available for small and medium business owners. For instance, Bertrand et al. (2007) report that in the 1980s French regulators eased entry and exit criteria for banks dealing in the product markets. This resulted in increased competition among banks, thus easing up credit for businesses. Guiso et al. (2004) studied financial development among several provinces in Italy, discovering that entrepreneurship is enhanced by financially developed banks. Similarly, a study by Cetorelli and Strahan (2004) reveal that enhanced competition among banks often results in increased credit flows to businesses. Black and Strahan's (2002) earlier study finds that the number of new firms increased following competition among US banks as a consequence of deregulation. The collective import from the above findings indicates that increased bank competition arising from deregulation leads to financial development among businesses, including SMEs, as more funds are made available by the sheer number of banks.

15.3 Overview of SME Financing in Africa

SME activity is vitally important to nearly every economy in the world. They are the backbone of most developing economies, in particular, as they offer employment opportunities for the masses. An estimate by Ayyagari et al. (2011) claims that less than 5% of businesses around the globe are not SMEs and so over 95% small and medium enterprises provide employment for all but 40%. For example, in Nigeria, Ghana and South Africa, asserted by Abor and Quartey (2010) and supported by Gbandi and Amissah (2014), the majority of businesses are SMEs and PWC (2013) declares that their share of the Gross National Product (GNP) in 2012 was around 49%. West African SMEs for more than 30 years have not been able to grow and expand because they lack financial muscle to invest in the financial markets as stock or debt security holders. The cause of this has been under-developed financial markets and that inflation rates usually erode interest rates. This somewhat compels individuals to invest surplus funds into entrepreneurship. However, the entrepreneurs largely operate small shops; others invest in several small ventures, buying and selling here and there. In the end, their businesses do not grow to attract investors who could help transform the ventures into large companies. This state of affairs leaves lingering questions as to why SMEs, despite desperately in need of cash injection, often lack the ability to access credit. Collier (2009) endeavoured answering this question, citing two main reasons. First, Africa is generally perceived as a riskier place for investment than other parts of the world. Second, SMEs, no matter the region, are considered riskier investment avenues than large companies.

SME financing in sub-Saharan Africa (SSA) is the lowest along with Latin America and the Caribbean. On evidence, both bank financing and domestic credit to the private sector have been on the decline only in SSA.

15.4 Case Studies from Five African Countries

SMEs are crucial in the developmental process of a nation. Their contribution to the economy of a nation, especially, that of developing nations, is enormous. Beck and Cull (2014) opine that most businesses all over the world are SMEs, with over 95% of all them falling in this category. In poorer countries, majority of the workforce are employed in SMEs with fewer than 100 workers (Ayyagari et al., 2011). Existing literature establishes that SMEs occupy a prominent role in developing economy private sector; however, they record the highest constraints to their operations and growth than their counterpart larger enterprises (Beck et al., 2006). The main issues that constitute the bulk of the problems and constraints of micro-, small- and medium-sized enterprises (MSMEs) are centred on the following issues:

1   The availability and accessibility of affordable credit for their operations.
2   The capacity to employ the appropriate human capital.
3   The application of the right tools and resources for their operations.
4   The use of proper book keeping principles.
5   The use of appropriate technology for their operations.

However, these problems vary from one country to the other. Hence, to examine financial development and SMEs in Africa, the researchers choose five representative African countries across the length and breadth of the continent for the study. The countries studied are Ghana and Nigeria in West Africa, Tanzania in the east, South Africa in the south and Morocco in the north.

15.4.1 Ghana

The majority of Ghana's private sector enterprises fall under the informal sector. About 90% of all companies registered in Ghana are classified under MSMEs (Senzu and Ndebugri, 2018). Data from the Ministry of Trade and Industry (MOTI) show that about 80,000 registered limited liability companies and 220,000 joint ventures make up the private sector of Ghana. Generally, MSMEs in Ghana comprise three main groups defined as follows:

- Micro-enterprises: These enterprises engage a maximum of five workers with fixed assets worth less than $10,000.
- Small enterprises: These businesses engage six to 29 employees with assets valued from $10,000 to $100,000.
- Medium enterprises: These companies engage from 30 to 99 persons and have assets worth up to $1 million.

Social Security and National Insurance Trust (SSNIT) data reveals that the private sector of Ghana comprises 90% of firms engaging fewer than 20 employees, and an insignificant number of large-scale companies (Mensah, 2004).

MSMEs in Ghana typically have the following characteristics:

1   They are typically one-man businesses, which are operated as sole proprietorships, with the owner, doubling as the manager and having total control on decision making in the business.
2   The owner has little/no formal education.
3   They employ minimal application of modern technologies and market data to their operations.
4   They have limited access to credit from the banking sector.
5   They have weak managerial skills that impede their strategic developmental plans for growth that is sustainable.
6   They experience excessively high working capital instability.
7   They lack technical knowledge, and hence are unable to obtain skilled labour and contemporary technology.

Several other non-financial restrictions impede the growth of such companies in Ghana. The owners of SMEs keep their business information as confidential from the public. They operate as though they have no obligations and responsibilities towards their creditors, and have no need to search for support for improved way of doing business, say, management, accounting, marketing and strategies to position themselves to take advantage of business linkages. Such businesses perceive management and support services as unnecessary and costly, which does not add real value to production. SMEs have been slow in taking total advantage of opportunities provided by government to support businesses. The government funded support programmes for businesses, like the National Board for Small Scale Industries (NBSSI) that functions in all the 16 regional capitals under the governmental bodies such as the Ghana Regional Appropriate Technology and Industrial Service (GRATIS) – an organization that offers skill-training and initial capital for start-ups – which operates under the Ministry of Trade and Industries.

15.4.1.1 SME Funding in Ghana

Many have cited lack of capital as the single most important constraint that threatens the growth and survival of the majority of SMEs that operate in Ghana. It is widely believed that lack of finance is a major inhibiting factor that constrains the growth and development of the SME sector. However, the following underlying problems form the bedrock for this lack of finance challenge:

*   The Ghanaian financial market is an emergent sector with low levels of activities of intermediaries.
*   The SME sector of Ghana is characterized by weak institutional and legal framework that will aid in managing and mitigating SME lending risk

- High interest rates and exchange rate volatility, which translates into high cost of capital.
- Lack of proper identification and addressing system in Ghana, which makes it difficult for lenders to trace borrowers.

The above notwithstanding, government and development partners have launched many interventions to stimulate the inflow of funds to small- and medium-sized enterprises, which exceeds what exists from private sector financing firms, which will help bridge the financing gap. The Ghanaian system categorizes the prevailing SME funding interventions into the following groups:

- Official government financing schemes
- Financing made available by bank and non-bank financial institutions

15.4.1.2 Official SME Credit Schemes

Official SME financing schemes are credit schemes introduced exclusively by government, or in collaboration with donor support agencies to augment the existing financing flowing to SMEs. The government of Ghana has previously made strives at implementing some direct lending systems to SMEs, with funds either coming from government coffers or contracted from donor agencies. The Aid and Debt Management Department of the Ministry of Finance and Economic Planning usually managed these funds. A huge chunk of the funds on the official scheme is sourced under particular programmes with bilateral system of government in support of Ghana Government's Economic Recovery Program and Structural Adjustment Program. Examples are as follows:

1   Austrian Import Program (1990)
2   Japanese Non-Project Grants (1987–2000)
3   Canadian Structural Adjustment Fund and the Support for Public Expenditure Reforms (SPER)

All the programmes mentioned above are designed specifically to help importers. For instance, the Austrian Import Support Program (AIP) is specifically for importers who are interested in procuring Austrian machinery and equipment, and raw materials and related services from Austria. The funds obtained under this programme were to be used exclusively for importing Austrian products such as raw materials, machinery, equipment and associated services from Austria. The sole administrator for this facility is the Export Finance Company, which is a quasi-public institution based in Ghana. Similarly, the governments of Japan and Canada established their facilities to support and facilitate imports from their respective countries. These facilities did not target SMEs specifically; therefore, the criteria for qualification for the fund did not put constraints in relation to firm size, and clauses that favour only SMEs.

Apart from the donor-supported schemes enrolled by government to give direct loans to SMEs, government has on its own attempted to establish several lending schemes to provide lending to the sector. Such schemes include the following:

- **Business Assistance Fund**: In 1990, the Business Assistance Fund was established to directly fund the activities of SMEs operating in Ghana. These funds came in the form of microloans from the government to the SME sector. The scheme was widely perceived as being abused politically, and the loans were seen to be given to government functionaries and political activists that were sympathetic towards the government of the day.
- **Ghana Investment Fund**: The parliament of Ghana passed the Ghana investment Fund Act (Act 616) in 2002 to create a fund to be responsible for the grant of loan facilities by selected banks to businesses. However, the scheme never went to the implementation stage.
- **Export Development and Investment Fund (EDIF)**: The EDIF offered companies in the export business the opportunity to borrow up to $500,000 for a maximum period of five years at 15% Cedi interest rate. The scheme was strictly managed and controlled by the EDIF board, which was administered through the financial institutions. The board approved all the loan recommendations of the participating financial institutions.

15.4.1.3 Guarantee Facilities

The loans Act of Ghana, Act 1970 (Act 335) authorizes the Government of Ghana (GoG) in Section 13 to be the only body that provides government guarantee to any foreign financial donor who wants to transfer monies to any Ghanaian establishment. The government also has the mandate to provide guarantee for the facility as per the requirements of the terms of such a facility. Guarantee facilities are conditional liabilities of the government. The responsibility to repay the loan is on the borrower and not the government. The onus for repayment shifts to the government only if the borrower is unable to, or refuses to, repay the loan as per the agreement in which case the borrower has the obligation to recompense the government for the amount paid.

15.4.1.4 Direct Interventions from Development Partners

Several other donor programmes/schemes are channelled through both commercial banks and microcredit companies meant to provide funding for SMEs. Other government-sponsored training and support services also exist to strengthen the human capital base of MSMEs through training and business support services. Table 15.1 contains a list of some projects that may not be exhaustive.

Table 15.1 External donor activities to support MSMEs in Ghana

Donor	Title	Brief Description
CIDA	Private Sector Development Support	Assist MSMEs (deepening technological capacity)
DANIDA	Private Sector Program	Business linkages between Ghana and Denmark
DANIDA	Business Sector Development	Lending to SMEs, front-runner legal reform (pilot)
GTZ	Promotion of Private Sector	Promotes German investments in Ghana
GTZ	Promotion of Small and Micro-Enterprises	Assist MSEs (Credit Fund – Urban and Rural areas)
GTZ	Rural Financial Services Project	Capacity building to rural and community banks and informal financial sector; and to ARB Apex Bank
IFAD/AFD	Rural Enterprise Project	Enterprise development in rural areas
IFC	Africa Project Development Facility	Support the development of SMEs (training)
UNDP	African Management Services Company	Assist SMEs (training and secondment)
UNDP	EMPRETEC Ghana Foundation	Assist SMEs (entrepreneurship development)
UNDP	Micro Start Ghana Programme	Support MFIs build institutional capacity
UNDP	Promoting Private Sector Development	Capacity building of private sector interlocutors
UNIDO	Strengthening competitiveness of MSMEs	Strengthening capabilities of MSMEs
USAID	Amex International (increased private enterprise performance)	Support development of non-traditional exports
USAID	Micro enterprise Development Assistance	Assist micro- and small-scale farmers
USAID	Trade and Investment Programme	Assist SMEs in non-traditional exports (credits)
WB	Non-Bank Financial Institutions Assistance	Promote growth of non-bank financial sector

Source: Samuel et al. (2012).

Other loaning schemes carried out as partnerships between government and donors are as follows:

- Trade and Investment Program (TIP) run by the USAID and the Ministry of Finance
- The Private Enterprise and Export Development Fund (PEED) is controlled and managed by the Bank of Ghana, but administered through the commercial banks.

Several other donor-sponsored lending programmes have been instituted, where the donors work directly with the financial institutions. Examples are as follows:

- Small Business Loan Portfolio Guarantee (USAID)
- GTZ Fund for the Promotion of Micro and Small Enterprises
- European Investment Bank Facility
- FMO SME Financing Scheme
- DANIDA SME Fund
- SECO SME Financing Scheme
- Care-Technoserve Fund for Small Scale Enterprises

In addition, an international NGO called Oikocredit runs a lending scheme for SMEs via a local office by lending directly to SMEs in need of funds to capitalize their operations, or for startups in the SME sector.

However, there is no long-term funding in the form of equity capital for growth-oriented businesses in the SME sector of Ghana. There are only four viable venture capital funds in existence in Ghana. Meanwhile, the vibrancy of the business environment of Ghana energized the financial system to respond to clientele demand for more venture capitals. International bodies such as the USAID and the CDC, therefore, funded the creation of another venture capital to take care of the long-term financial needs of the ever-growing enterprises in the framework of the financial sector reform programme in 1991.

The above shows that the government of Ghana and its development partners have recognized the important and necessary role played by MSMEs in the developmental process of Ghana, and hence have accorded it the attention and focus it deserves.

15.4.2 Nigeria

The challenges of SMEs in Sub-Saharan African countries are similar across all countries in the subregion; that is, SMEs in Nigeria operate in a similar fashion and are faced with identical constraints as SMEs in Ghana, Cote d'Ivoire, Liberia, Sierra Leone and so on. The SME sector in Nigeria is under-developed and has several challenges that hinder growth and progress. Despite the financial sector liberalization to allow free flow of funds in the Nigerian business environment, there are still several challenges and constraints confronting businesses in the SME sector in relation to accessing funds. These difficulties include unavailability of reasonably priced bank loans, burdensome credit processing, demands for impracticable collateral for credit facilities and poor business record-keeping. It is also observed that financiers think through the high risk attributed to SME lending, which discourages them from lending to this sector, and this has increased the plight of SMEs in Nigeria (Ademosu and Morakinyo, 2021).

15.4.2.1 Overview of SMEs in Nigeria

The SME sector of Nigeria comprises over 90% of private sector businesses in Nigeria. This sector is considered the engine of growth for the Nigerian economy (Ademosu and Morakinyo, 2021). Productive sector analysis by NBS (2019) reveals that SMEs contribute about 50% of the GDP of Nigeria, and employs over 70% of the entire labour force of the country. However, the SME sector is bedevilled with a plethora of constraints and challenges, which hinders their growth. According to a survey conducted by the Small & Medium Enterprises Development Agency of Nigeria (SMEDAN) in 2018, 65% of new SMEs in Nigeria collapsed within the first three years of their formation due to lack of access to sustainable and adequate funding. However, commercial banks play very important roles in SME financing in Nigeria. Studies including Oke and Aluko (2015) have shown the existence of a significant positive relationship between commercial banks and SME financing in Nigeria. The Nigerian financial system is considered one of the most robust and fastest growing in Africa. The financial system consists of the money market, where organizations and individuals access short-term credit; and the capital market, where individuals and corporate bodies raise long-term facilities to capitalize their operations. The financial system of a nation exists to play an intermediary role of linking lenders to borrowers, and banks and the various stock exchanges are the main players in this market.

15.4.2.2 Interventions by Government and Stakeholders

Government interventions include a deliberate policy initiative by the Federal Government of Nigeria in 2008 to develop and advance the financial sector in order to effect change to encourage and stimulate economic growth through SMEs. The initiative is known as the Financial System Strategy (FSS) 2020, together with the Vision 2020 economic reforms and Seven – Point Agenda of the Federal Government of Nigeria, which targets aspects of society that affect Nigeria's financial institutions from the local to the state and national levels. To better ensure the safe and stable development of the Nigerian economy, the FSS 2020 places emphasis on the importance of the country's SMEs and contains an extensive framework for encouraging, supporting and promoting them in the emerging economy. As detailed in the official FSS 2020 report on SMEs, the promotional policies include the following:

- Nurturing 200 export manufacturing SMEs operating in Nigeria by 2020.
- Supporting SMEs to create jobs for the youth, which would contribute to generating more income for the nation and raise export revenues. The plan is, by 2010, manufactured exports of SMEs should increase by 10%, which is expected to see a further increase of 25% by 2015 and a further 25% by 2020.

- Creation of innovative firms that aid in the expansion of indigenous SMEs; and formalizing the operations of many informal sector enterprises.
- Designating SME groups as Priority Economic Zones (PEZs) that attract supports in relation to infrastructural development, logistics, energy, water and internet. These groups include traditional technology constellations (that is, leather works and agro-processing).
- Creating high-tech groups such as ICT clusters and specific biotechnology products to solve health and food-related glitches.
- Establishing a structure and funding schemes to advance the capacity of domestic assemblers of computer components.
- Building on prevailing organizations such as NIPRID, SHEDCO, etc. to spin-off SMEs that depend on research from these institutions.
- Developing a structure to inculcate research into marketing using SMEs (Sampath and Oyelaran-Oyeyinka, 2010).

15.4.2.3 *Other SME Funding Arrangements*

The Nigerian government with assistance from the World Bank and the African Development Bank (AfDB) previously attempted to help SMEs via several credit arrangements and loans designed to favour SMEs; such loan schemes include:

- World Bank SME loan scheme.
- African Development Bank Export Stimulation Loan scheme.
- CBN Rediscounting and Re-financing Facility.
- National Economic Reconstruction Fund.
- Bank of Industry and the Graduate Employment Loan Scheme introduced by the National Directorate of Employment.

Furthermore, SMEs have other avenues of securing loans, such as commercial banks, moneylenders, bootstrapping, grants from governmental and non-governmental institutions.

15.4.3 *Morocco*

SMEs dominate the industrial sector of Morocco, with 94% of industrial sector companies being SMEs (Amraoui et al., 2019). However, SMEs are saddled with myriad of challenges and constraints, with the main one being unavailability or limited access to finance. Majority of SMEs have yearly turnover lower than $313,000; however, the SME sector plays a very crucial role in the development of the economy and creating new job openings. Hence, the Moroccan government is prioritizing SMEs in their long-term economic planning. Morocco's extensive economic development is creating more prospects that considerably influence the expansion of the SME sector across the country. Deliberate policies by the Moroccan government to improve and modernize logistics infrastructure and transportation have eased the process of doing business for small firms. In recent years, it has become easier for smaller firms to either get large-scale projects directly or work with larger companies as subcontractors. The government's move has also enhanced transportation and telecommunications networks, which has made it easier for Moroccan firms to access target markets. Morocco's emergent systems of trade arrangements and worldwide business dealings have assisted in exposing local companies to new markets. Furthermore, Morocco's inward FDI grew by 31.3% to get to $3.6bn in 2018; the Office des Changes reported that this injected a huge sum of new capital into the economy. Although the chunk of the FDI went to insurance and financial services, other undertakings that have a direct connection to the SME sector have also profited. 14.3% of the total FDI inflows in 2018 went to the manufacturing sector, boosting the drive of domestic supply chains.

15.4.3.1 Challenges of SMEs in Morocco

The main challenges of SMEs in Morocco are lack of finance, innovation and technology, infrastructure and government support, skilled human resource insufficiency, firm characteristics and poor management. In addition, traditional loaning practices in the financial sector frequently make it problematic for smaller businesses to access funds. Besides, stringent and harsh tax and regulatory constraints impede SMEs and business owners from joining the formal sector.

In a speech by King Mohammed VI in October 2019, he indicated that economic growth is a shared responsibility; hence, government will need the support of the private sector to achieve the desired economic growth. He therefore encouraged the players in the financial sector to assist government by extending affordable loans to the private sector to boost economic growth. He specifically mentioned finance to the SME sector. The rate of SME funding in Morocco stands at 17% of GDP, which is higher than the regional average. However, majority of SMEs still have challenges with obtaining credit. The International Finance Corporation (IFC) revealed that 6% of local micro-enterprises succeeded in securing funds for their operations as of 2017. This is because of the unrealistic collateral requirement for the loan, which is very challenging for the smaller businesses to raise. Small businesses and entrepreneurs are further burdened by disbursement delays and oppressive regulatory procedures.

15.4.3.2 Reforms in SME Policies in Morocco

Several reforms have taken place in the past decade; however, there are still some remaining challenges. Industry players are optimistic that the gains from recent changes will impact the activities of the SME sector. The central bank of Morocco, Bank Al-Maghrib, established a loan scheme for commercial banks that give credit to SMEs in 2013. The government extended the period of a credit guarantee programme to assist small- and medium-sized businesses in securing credit of up to $100,000 via the Central Guarantee Fund (Caisse Centrale de Garantie (CCG)) owned by the state. Under a World Bank development programme in 2019 on policy finance valued at €611.3m, the Moroccan government sanctioned a financial inclusion and digital economic expansion strategy. The goal of the strategy is to augment financial inclusion and increase access to digital technologies for households and SMEs. It states the development of a fresh financing product and insurance policies targeting MSMEs and businesspersons. Intensifying digital access is vital to achieving growth and development in the SME sector and entrepreneurship. Digital apparatuses have made small firms to compete favourably with bigger and more reputable companies around the world, which could have a huge effect in Morocco, where household diffusion of fixed internet broadband is pegged at 22% in 2020. The World Bank predicted that about 56% of countryside households would have some kind of internet access by 2020.

15.4.3.3 Increased Competitiveness

Following the general criticism against the pricing regime in some major industries – such as, water bottling and fuel distribution – which affected the Moroccan economy in 2018. In late 2018, the government, therefore, overhauled the competition supervisory body and further relaunched the Competition Council under fresh management, with sturdier obligations. It is anticipated that the new council will assist in supervising uncompetitive practices. However, it is usually anticipated to ease blockades to entry for the country's smaller companies and businesspersons.

In addition, free enterprise is progressively being assisted by beleaguered funds and financing schemes. In October 2017, the Central Guarantee Fund pioneered the establishment of the Innov Invest Fund, an investment fund devoted to assisting inventive startups in Morocco. By March 2019, the fund had facilitated finance for 62 new businesses with over $1.3m. Similar ingenuities are anticipated to steadily develop the milieu for modernization and new business conception.

15.4.3.4 Investment Centres

The streamlining of regional investment centre networks in Morocco (Centres Régionaux d'Investissement (CRI)) tries to find assistance for indigenous enterprises from the ground up. It is worth noting that the CRIs were formed across the country in 2002 to support domestic business creation, mobilizing both local and foreign investment, and assisting businesspersons to go through the regulatory processes of starting a new business. The centres also play a major role in enticing investment regionally, distributing it across the less industrialized regions of the country.

The streamlining of the centres, which were sanctioned by Parliament in 2018, will strive to convert them into more responsive vehicles for regional development by shortening processes. It will further aim to realign CRI growth strategies with the focus on regional governance, and target the attention of these centres towards businesspersons and SME undertakings. Making the business environment more conducive for SME activities will yield far-reaching opportunities beyond employment generation. These will also have positive effects on the country's inflows from taxation in the long term, by inspiring more companies to enter the formal sector. Additionally, improving the environment for SMEs to thrive will afford the many small businesses that exist in Morocco – which are largely family businesses – with the needed prospect to develop and expand. The above will help the government's quest to fight the country's tenaciously high unemployment rates. Furthermore, it will widen the various economic sectors of the Kingdom and create several avenues and business opportunities for innovations, which will open up the economy for more enterprises and startups to operate.

15.4.4 South Africa

15.4.4.1 Core Elements of South African SME Financing

The Bureau for Economic Research (BER) (2016) estimated South African SME growth to have risen from 2.18 million in 2008 to 2.25 million in 2015. In seven years, the growth rate was 3%. In a break down, over 66% of the 2.25 SMEs were in informal retail and wholesale trade and accommodation subsectors. Reminiscent of other SSA economies, larger firms in South Africa (SA) generally grow faster than smaller ones, the key constraints being "Lack of access to markets, technology, business infrastructure, information." Statistics from the South African Reserve Bank indicate bank loans to SMEs in 2017 were 28% (ZAR 617 billion) of the total outlay to businesses. This low rate is caused by the tendency of most SMEs to seek funding sources away from the banks and other financial institutions. Instead, owner funds are the dominant capital source, supported by family members and business associates. SME loan default has progressively improved, declining from 5.2% in 2010 to 2.5% in 2017. This positive outcome is most probably caused by the rebound from the financial and economic downturn in 2009 along with discreet loan policy. The flip side on non-performing loans is the unavailability of data as some DFIs do not keep records of impaired loans using the size of firms.

The South African government funds SMEs by providing *grants* and by use of *development finance institutions* (DFIs). Straight government loans in 2017 stood at ZAR 11.48 billion, just under 2% of total SME loans. In addition, SMEs received ZAR 297 million in *credit guarantees* from IDC and SEFA, a rise from ZAR 243 million in 2016 following a dip in 2013 and 2014. The Government of South Africa has devised other ways to make bank credit accessible to SMEs. For instance, an *asset registry* for movable assets and a *credit information database* are in the process of being drafted into policy.

15.4.4.2 SME Role in the South African Economy

SMEs are critical to the growth and development of the South African economy. For this reason, over 3 million jobs were projected to have been created for the youth by 2020. In addition, another 11 million jobs should be created by 2030 and the National Development Plan (NDP) estimated that most of these openings (90%) will be contributed by growing SMEs and SME startups.

In spite of this positive development, estimates differ as to the exact number of SMEs in the country. The Bureau for Economic Research reports that the contribution of SMEs is just over 20% of the GDP before subsidy and tax deductions. A claim by the Global Entrepreneurship Monitor (2017) has it that South African SMEs support the economy with 36%. The Minister in the Presidency claims SMEs provide jobs for seven million, three hundred thousand, which is 47% of the country's working class, thus adding 42% to the GDP. South Africa ranks among the lowest in SME job creation for all the significant contribution to employment and growth. Statistics form the Small Business Development (DSBD) department portrays a bleak out for SME future: in the first year of business, most SME startups collapse (between 70% and 80%) and roughly 50% of the surviving ones die off within the ensuing five years.

National Small Business Chamber (2016) breaks down the SME sector as follows. "Micro enterprises comprise 55.6% of registered firms in the formal sector, while small and medium firms constitute 33.7% and 9.5% respectively of the South African formal economy." Of these the primary subsectors are mostly medium-sized firms, small businesses are the greater constituent of the manufacturing subsector, and micro-enterprises are the dominant component of the service businesses.

15.4.4.3 Lending to SMEs in South Africa

South African SMEs are not growing in a sustainable manner as they continue to be starved of adequate financing. The causes are non-existent finance schemes for SMEs, credit information starvation, the understood risk associated with SME financing and the unavailability of appropriate collaterals. These factors constitute SMEs as risky and hence attract high credit cost in cases where financing is accessible to them. Given the observed teething problems, most small businesses in South Africa shy away from formal financing from the banks and other institutions of finance. This results in SMEs accounting for the low support (ZAR 617 billion in 2017) in total business loans at 28%. The South African government funds SMEs using grants through development finance institutions (DFIs), including the Industrial

Development Corporation (IDC), the Small Enterprise Finance Agency (SEFA) and the National Urban Reconstruction and Housing Agency (NURCHA). Thus in 2017, DFLs outlaid a total of ZAR 11.48 billion representing 1.8% of total credit to SMEs.

The quantum SMEs receive in loans is dependent on the economic subsector. As such, service sector small businesses according to National Treasury Panel (2016) received ZAR 0 to 100,000, which is nearly 30%. Manufacturing sector loans to small enterprises stood at 20%.

15.4.4.4 Prerequisites for Credit

As seen in the first section, prerequisites for credit to SMEs in South Africa are tough, especially from the banks. A survey on bank finance of SMEs in 2015 revealed that banks are essentially a no-go place as just 2% of SME claimed banks were their main source of credit. The causes are as follows. The survey implies that SMEs are uncertain as to what sort of bank services or products are suitable for them as they are not even aware of the services and products currently not given to them. In a similar vein, a 2016 survey by National Small Business Chamber reveals a staggering 75% of SMEs never applied for a bank loan. Makina et al. (2015) findings support this statistic, showing that over 50% of small businesses are not inclined to borrow for two reasons. First, they do not really need credit financing, and second, they do not consider borrowing as a good business model. Another cause of low financing from formal banks for 30.9% of small enterprises is these firms do not either feel qualified or it is scary for them to go for loans.

15.4.5 Tanzania

The Tanzanian government has recognized the value of SMEs in three key areas. SMEs play a vital role in creating employment, generating incomes and contributing to economic growth. Mashenene and Rumanyika (2014) estimate that more than 3 million SMEs operate in varied ventures in manufacturing, retailing and trading, agriculture and services. A policy for SME growth and development was created in 2003 by the government for the purpose of reducing poverty and propping the SME subsector. Reviewed in 2013, this policy document admitted that in spite of state efforts, SMEs were still fraught with "a failure to compete in international markets, financial constraints, underproduction, poor supply chain management, technological difficulties, a lack of access to raw materials and a low business registration rate" (Badi and Ishengoma 2021). Many in academia have made concerted efforts to chronicle and report on SME challenges with hopes of finding lasting solutions. However, the constraints remain, driving the vast majority of businesses into extinction. A plausible explanation for this is that Tanzania is limited in resources and so realistically, solving all SME problems is impossible.

Table 15.2 Tanzanian SME categories

Category	Number of Employees	Capital Investment (TSHs)
Micro-enterprise	1–4	Up to 5 million
Small enterprise	5–49	Above 5–200 million
Medium enterprise	50–99	Above 200–800 million
Large enterprise	100+	Over 800 million

Source: URT Ministry of Industry and Trade (2003); 1 US$ is equivalent to Tanzanian shillings (TSHs) 2,150 in 2015

15.4.5.1 SME Definition

The definition of SMEs in the Tanzanian context is shaped by the literature. This is borne from the varied opinions across the globe as to what a small business is and what a medium business is. Definition variations seem to arise due to different strengths in economy. In the UK, an SME is a business employing below 200 workers. In the US and OECD, respectively, SME upper limit is 500 and 100 (MacGregor and Vrazalic, 2008; Mukhtar, 1998). The Tanzanian Ministry of Industry and Trade gave a contextual definition of SMEs suitable for the country's economy as seen in Table 15.2.

The SME Development Policy document of the ministry categorizes SMEs into businesses that manufacture, mine and trade, as well as those that offer services (Anderson, 2017). Generally, employee number, amount of invested capital, total assets, volume of sales and production capacity are the criteria used in SME segmentation (Anderson, 2017). Mashenene and Rumanyika (2014) disclosed that poor training, inadequate capital and disinterest in entrepreneurship are the primary factors impeding SME growth in Tanzania. Table 15.3 samples the major constraints to SME growth in Tanzania, as concluded by academics and researchers in various studies.

15.5 Conclusion

This chapter has highlighted financial development and SMEs in Africa Countries. It shows that fundamentals within the financial sector have been achieved and there has been some success in access to finance by SMEs. At the same time, the financial sectors remain poorly organized with the needs of economic transformation and this, at least partially, explains the weak relationship between financial development and growth of SMEs in many African countries compared to other regions. There is a need for further research to develop a more nuanced understanding of the relationship.

Looking ahead, financial developments need to be in consonance with the needs of inclusive SMEs and sustainable economic growth. The chapter suggests some ways in which this might be achieved. In particular, the global trend towards greener finance and socially responsible financing are significant for the continent and there is clearly an opportunity to seize a share of

Table 15.3 Selected SME studies from Tanzania

S/NO	Title	Author(s)	Major Findings (Constraints Facing SMEs)
1	Business Constraints and the Potential Growth of Small and Medium Enterprises in Tanzania: A Review	Mashenene and Rumanyika (2014)	Insufficient business training, capital constraints and an anti-entrepreneurial culture
2	The role of microfinance in promoting small and medium enterprises (SMEs) in Tanzania: empirical evidence from SME holders who have received microcredit from financial institutions in Morogoro	Makorere (2014)	Lack of capital, lock of access to finance. Inadequate business training, poor demand for products, lack of raw materials, and poor infrastructure.
3	Socio-Cultural Determinants and Enterprise Financial Sources among the Chagga and Sukuma Small and Medium Enterprises in Tanzania	Mashenene et al. (2014)	Poor partnership, capital constraints, lack of funding, lack of collateral.
4	Non-financial constraints to scaling-up Small and medium-sized energy enterprises: Findings from field research in Ghana, Senegal, Tanzania and Zambia	Haselip et al. (2014)	Inadequate human capacity.
5	Constraints of Accessing Debt Financing from Commercial Banks among Small and Medium Enterprises in Tanzania: A Literature Review	Mashenene (2015)	Poor access to debt finance, bureaucratic loan procedures, business informality, poor repayment habits and corruption.
6	Obstacles Towards Adoption of Mobile Banking in Tanzania: A Review	(Rumanyika, 2015)	Poor network coverage, lack of knowledge of m-banking users, lack of enough float of mobile money agents and ATM breakdowns, and theft.
7	The Challenges Confronting Small and Scale Businesses in Accessing Microfinance Services from MFIs Case Study: Rural Tanzania	Kimathi (2015)	Lack of access to finance.

S/NO	Title	Author(s)	Major Findings (Constraints Facing SMEs)
8	Examining the Factors Affecting Export Performance for Small and Medium Enterprises (SMEs) in Tanzania	Mpungda (2016)	Export competencies, inadequate and unstable financial capital, poor production, poor technology, ICT and information, the standard of the products produced by the SME, and complicated business laws/regulations.
9	Factors Influencing Business Succession Planning among SMEs in Tanzania	Magasi (2016)	Lack of business successors.
10	Challenges Facing Food Processing MSEs in Tanzania: A Quantitative Case Study of the Sunflower Oil Industry in Babati, Manyara	Ekblom (2016)	Lack of capital, lack of raw materials, equipment & electricity for processing, tight regulations, poor market accessibility and competition.
11	The Lack of Business Dispute Resolution in East Africa: An Unresolved Impediment to SME Development?	Tillmar (2016)	Lack of access to finance, corruption and lack of business training.
12	Challenges of Entrepreneurship Development in Tanzania	Isaga and Musabila (2017)	The motivation of the business owners.
13	Factors Affecting Small and Medium Enterprises (SMEs) Startup and Growth in Tanzania	Anderson (2017)	Inborn individual attributes, changing business environments, competitive activities and location, inadequate finance, inadequate human and social resources, and lack of technical and managerial skills.
14	Financial Barriers and how to Overcome them: The Case of Women Entrepreneurs in Tanzania	Lindvert (2017)	Lack of capital.
15	Social Capital in Selected Business Associations of Food Processing SMEs in Tanzania and Rwanda: A Synthetic Based Approach	Gamba (2017)	Lack of social capital.

(Continued)

S/NO	Title	Author(s)	Major Findings (Constraints Facing SMEs)
16	Social-Economic Constraints towards Women Business Growth in Tanzania	Nyangarika (2017)	Poor access to market information, technology and finance, poor linkages with support services, and an unfavourable policy and regulatory environment.
17	A Structuration Analysis of Small and Medium Enterprise (SME) Adoption of E-Commerce: The Case of Tanzania	Kabanda and Brown (2017)	Poor technology adoption.
18	Microfinance Traps and Relational Exchange Norms: A Field Study of Women Entrepreneurs in Tanzania	Lindvert et al. (2018)	Lack of access to capital.
19	Start-up motives and challenges facing female entrepreneurs in Tanzania	Isaga (2019)	Lack of access to finance, gender-related problems, and social and cultural commitments.

Source: Nkwabi, J.M., and Mboya, L.B. (2019). A review of factors affecting the growth of Small and Medium Enterprises (SMEs) in Tanzania. *European Journal of Business and Management*, (Online) 11 (33). www.iiste.org ISSN 2222-1905 (Paper) ISSN 2222-2839.

these markets to accelerate growth and poverty alleviation in African countries. Against this background, there are reasons for both optimism and pessimism in some countries. At the time of writing, immediate concerns relate to the COVID-19 pandemic, while the global challenges of climate change remain challenges in most African countries and across the world.

In addition, there is global political uncertainty regarding future opportunities in relation to trade and global value chains. Finally, most Africa countries face challenges, as well as opportunities, from its slow demographic transition and swelling youth unemployment. Nevertheless, there are also reasons for optimism. Young Africans have never been better educated, better connected and healthier with the wealth of talent and energy that the challenges bring. The continent is at the centre of the so-called 'fourth industrial revolution' in economic digitalization and artificial intelligent. The new African Continental Free Trade Area (AfCFTA), regional political co-operation and integration have strengthened, promising economic gains for all. All of these factors also speak to the opportunity for significant progress in SMEs and economic transformation of countries across the African Continent.

References

Abor, J., and Quartey, P. (2010). Issues in SME development in Ghana and South Africa. *International Research Journal of Finance and Economics*, 39, 218–228.

Ademosu, A. and Morakinyo, A. (2021). Financial system and SMEs access to finance: a market-oriented approach. *Studia Universitatis „Vasile Goldis" Arad–Economics Series*, *31*(3), 21–36.

Alibhai, S., Bell, S., and Conner, G. (2017). What's happening in the missing middle? Lessons from Financing SMEs.

Amraoui, B., Ouhajjou, A., Monni, S., El Idrissi, N.E.A. and Tvaronavičienė, M., (2019). Performance of clusters in Morocco in the shifting economic and industrial reforms. *Insights into Regional Development*, *1*(3), 227–243.

Anderson, W. (2017). Factors affecting Small & Medium Enterprises (SMEs) start-up and growth in Tanzania. *The Pan-African Journal of Business Management*, [online] 1 (1), 1–51.

Arthur, P. (2003). The implications of state policy for micro-enterprise development. In: Tettey, Wisdom, Puplampu, Korbla, Berman, Bruce (Eds.), *Critical Perspectives on Politics and Socio-Economic Development in Ghana*. Brill publishers, Leiden, pp. 153–175.

Aryeetey, E. (1994). Supply and demand for finance of small enterprises in Ghana. World Bank Discussion Paper 251. The World Bank, Washington, DC.

Aryeetey, E. (1998). Informal finance for private sector development in Africa. Economic Research Papers No. 41. The African Development Bank, Abidjan.

Ayyagari, M., Demirgüç,-Kunt, A., and Maksimovic, V. (2011). Small vs. young firms across the world—Contribution to employment, job creation, and growth. Policy Research Working Paper 5631. The World Bank Development Research Group.

Badi, L., and Ishengoma, E. (2021). Access to debt finance and performance of small and medium enterprises. *Journal of Financial Risk Management*, 10, 241–259. https://doi.org/10.4236/jfrm.2021.103014

Bani, R.J. (2003). *Micro Enterprise Development in Ghana*. Accra.

Beck, T., and Cull, R. (2014). Small- and medium-sized enterprise finance in Africa. Working Paper 16/July 2014. Africa Growth Initiative.

BER (2016). The small, medium and micro enterprise sector of South Africa. Research Note No 1 2016. Small Enterprise Development Agency.

Black, S.E., and Strahan, P.E. (2002). Entrepreneurship and bank credit availability. *Journal of Finance*, 57 (6), 2807–2833.

Cetorelli, N., and Strahan, P.E. (2004). Finance as a barrier to entry: Bank competition and industry structure in local US markets. NBER Working Paper No. 10832.

Collier, P. (2009). Rethinking finance for Africa's small firms in "SME Financing in SSA," Proparco Magazine on Private Sector and Development, Issue 1 May 2009.

Daniels, L., and Ngwira, A. (1993). Results of a nation-wide survey on Micro, Small and Medium Enterprises in Malawi. GEMINI Technical Report No 53. PACT Publications, New York.

Dawson, J. (1993). Impact of structural adjustment on the small enterprise sector: a comparison of the Ghanaian and Tanzanian experiences. In: Helmsing, A., Kolstee, T. (Eds.), *Small Enterprise and Changing Policies: Structural Adjustment Financial Policy and Assistance Programmes in Africa*. IT Publications, London, pp. 71–90.

Deakins, D., North, D., Baldock, R., and Whittam, G. (2008). SMEs' access to finance: Is there still a debt finance gap? *Institute for Small Business & Entrepreneurship*. 5–7 November 2008 - Belfast, N. Ireland, 1–19.

Ekblom, M., (2016). Challenges facing food processing MSEs in Tanzania: A qualitative case study of the sunflower oil industry in Babati, Manyara.

Gamba, F. (2017). Social capital in selected business associations of food processing SMEs in Tanzania and Rwanda: A synthetic based approach. *International Journal of Asian Social Science*, 7(1), 63–84.

Gbandi, E.C., and Amissah, G. (2014). Financing options for small and medium enterprises (SMEs) in Nigeria. *European Scientific Journal*, 10, 1.

Guiso, L., Sapienza, P., and Zingales, L. (2004). Does local financial development matter? *Quarterly Journal of Economics*, 119 (3), 929–969.

Guru, B.K., and Yadav, I.S. (2019). Financial development and economic growth: Panel evidence from BRICS. Journal of Economics, Finance and Administrative Science, 24 (47), 113–126. https://doi.org/10.1108/JEFAS-12-2017-0125

Haselip, J., Desgain, D., and Mackenzie, G. (2014). Financing energy SMEs in Ghana and Senegal: Outcomes, barriers and prospects. *Energy Policy*, 65, 369–376.

Isaga, N. (2019). Start-up motives and challenges facing female entrepreneurs in Tanzania. *International Journal of Gender and Entrepreneurship*, 11(2), 102–119.

Isaga, N. and Musabila, A. (2017). Challenges to Entrepreneurship Development in Tanzania. *Entreprenuership in Africa*, 15, 1–232.

Kabanda, S. and Brown, I. (2017). A structuration analysis of Small and Medium Enterprise (SME) adoption of ECommerce: The case of Tanzania. *Telematics and Informatics*, 34(4), 118–132.

Kimathi, F. (2015). The challenges confronting small scale businesses in accessing microfinance services from MFIs case study: Rural Tanzania. *International Journal of Academic Research in Business and Social Sciences*, 5(11), 299–311.

Lindvert, M. (2017). Financial Barriers and How to Overcome Them: The Case of Women Entrepreneurs in Tanzania. Entreprenuership in Africa, [online] 15. Available at: https://doi.org/10.1163/9789004351615_016 [Accessed 24 Oct. 2019].

Lindvert, M., Patel, P., Smith, C. & Wincent, J. (2018). Microfinance traps and relational exchange norms: A field study of women entrepreneurs in Tanzania. *Journal of Small Business Management,* 57(1), 230–254.

MacGregor, R., and Vrazalic, L. (2008). The role of gender in the perception of barriers to e-commerce adoption in SMEs: An Australian study.

Magasi, C. (2016). Factors influencing business succession planning among SMEs in Tanzania. *European Journal of Business and Management,* 8(3), 126–135.

Makina, D., Fanta, A.B., Mutsonziwa, K., Khumalo, J. and Maposa, O., (2015). Financial access and SME size in South Africa. *Occasional Paper,* FinMark Trust. http://www.fnmark.org.za/wp-FinMark   Trust.http://www.fnmark.org.za/ wp-content/   uploads/2016/01/Rep_Financial-Access-and-SME-Size-in-SA_ Dec2015-1.pdf, pp.001 - 2015

Makorere, R. (2014). The role of microfinance in promoting small and medium enterprises (SMEs) in Tanzania: empirical evidence from SMEs holder who have received microcredit from financial institutions in Morogoro. *Global Business and Economics Research Journal,* 3(4), 1–19.

Mashenene, R. (2015). Proceedings of the Second European Academic Research Conference on Global Business, Economics, Finance and Banking. In: EAR15Swiss Conference. Zurich-Switzerland: Global biz research.

Mashenene, R., Macha, J. & Donge, L. (2014). Socio-cultural determinants and enterprise financial sources among the Chagga and Sukuma small and medium enterprises in Tanzania. *International Review of Research in Emerging Markets and the Global Economy* (IRREM), [online] 1(5), 265–283.

Mashenene, R., and Rumanyika, J. (2014). Business constraints and potential growth of small and medium enterprises in Tanzania: A review. *European Journal of Business and Management,* [online] 6(3), 72–79.

Mensah, S. (2004). A review of SME financing schemes in Ghana. UNIDO Regional Workshop of Financing SMEs, Accra.

Mpunga, H. (2016). Examining the factors affecting export performance for Small and Medium Enterprises (SMEs) in Tanzania. *Journal of Economics and Sustainable Development,* [online] 7(6), 41–51.

Mukhtar, S.M. (1998). Business characteristics of male and female small and medium enterprises in the UK: implications for gender-based entrepreneurialism and business competence development. *British Journal of Management,* 9(1), 41–51.

National Small Business Chamber (NSBC) (2016). National Small Business Survey, 2016.

Nkwabi, J.M., and Mboya, L.B. (2019). A review of factors affecting the growth of Small and Medium Enterprises (SMEs) in Tanzania. *European Journal of Business and Management,* (Online) 11 (33). www.iiste.org ISSN 2222-1905 (Paper) ISSN 2222-2839

Nyangarika, A. (2017). Social-economic constraints towards women business growth in Tanzania. *European Journal of Business and Management,* 8(5), 130–139.

Oke, M.O. and Aluko, O.A., 2015. Impact of commercial banks on small and medium enterprises financing in Nigeria. *IOSR Journal of Business and Management,* 17(4), 23–26.

Okpara, John O. (2011). Factors constraining the growth and survival of SMEs in Nigeria: Implications for poverty alleviation. *Management Research Review*, 34 (2), 156–171.

Osei, B., Baah-Nuakoh, A., Tutu, K., and Sowa, N. (1993). Impact of structural adjustment on small-scale enterprises in Ghana. In: Helmsing, A., Kolstee, T. (Eds.), *Small Enterprise and Changing Policies: Structural Adjustment, Financial Policy and Assistance Programmes in Africa*. IT Publications, London, pp. 53–70.

Parker, R., Riopelle, R., and Steel, W. (1995). Small enterprises adjusting to liberalization in five African countries. World Bank Discussion Paper, No 271, African Technical Department Series, The World Bank, Washington DC.

PWC (2013). Ghana Banking Survey.

Quartey, P. (2002). Financing small and medium-sized enterprises in Ghana. *African Journal of. Business Management*, 4, 37–56.

Quartey, P., Turkson, E., Abor, J.Y and Iddrisu, A.M. (2017). Financing the growth of SMEs in Africa: What are the constraints to SME financing within ECOWAS? *Review of Development Finance*, 7, 18–28.

Rumanyika, J. (2015). Obstacles towards adoption of mobile banking in Tanzania: A review. *International Journal of Information Technology and Business Management*, 3(1), 1–17.

Sampath, P.G., and Oyelaran-Oyeyinka, B. (2010). Rough road to the market: Constrained biotechnology innovation and entrepreneurship in Nigeria and Ghana. *Journal of International Development*, 22 (7), 962–977.

Senzu, E.T. and Ndebugri, H., (2018). Examining business performance of micro, small and medium scale enterprise through accounting records keeping; case study in Ghana. *Munich Personal RePEc Archive Retrieved from www. mpra. ub.*

Sowa, N.K., Baah-Nuakoh, A., Tutu, K.A., and Osei, B. (1992). Small enterprise and adjustment, the impact of Ghana's Economic Recovery Programme on small-scale industrial enterprises. Research Reports, Overseas Development Institute, 111 Westminster BridgeRoad, London SE1 7JD.

Tillmar, M. (2016). *The Lack of Business Dispute Resolution in East Africa: An Unresolved Impediment to SME Development?* In: L. Achtenhagen and E. Brundin, ed., *Entrepreneurship and SME Management Across Africa*. Singapore: Springer.

World Bank (n.d.). Global Financial Development Report. https://www.worldbank. org/en/publication/gfdr/gfdr-2016/background/financial-development

16 COVID-19 Global Pandemic, Financial Development and Financial Inclusion in African Countries

Nathanael Ojong and Simplice Anutechia Asongu

16.1 Introduction

The purpose of financial inclusion is to enhance use of and access to formal financial services by individuals in order to improve economic security and opportunity to impoverished and excluded fractions of the population (Demirgüç-Kunt *et al.*, 2017; Yamada *et al.*, 2020). The concern has been of particular relevance to developing countries, especially in the light of sustainable development goals (SDGs) which are centred on, *inter alia*, consolidating the capability of financial institutions at the domestic level to expand and encourage access to financial, insurance and banking services to everyone. Yamada *et al.* (2020), however, maintain that prospects for financial services are not quite encouraging though between 2011 and 2017, those who held accounts with a mobile money provider or financial institution increased from 51% to 69%. According to the narrative, as of 2017, about 1.7 billion adults were unbanked in the world, and compared to high-income countries, a greater proportion of the unbanked are in middle- and low-income countries.

Consistent with the attendant literature (Karlan *et al.*, 2016; Demirgüç-Kunt *et al.*, 2017; Yamada *et al.*, 2020), the concept of financial inclusion can be understood as a phenomenon that enhances the availability of a plethora of financial services such as savings accounts, loans and insurance for individuals, and by extension, these individuals also benefit in terms of financial risk management, productive investment and the smoothing of consumption. Hence, the population can substantially benefit from financial inclusion if payment facilities for daily transactions, as well as pensions and wages, are switched to digital payments from cash.

Since the proclamation of SDGs, much literature has been covered on financial inclusion (Tchamyou, 2019; Tchamyou *et al.*, 2019). However, the recent outbreak of the COVID-19 pandemic has represented a serious challenge to inclusive development, especially in the light of the targeted SDGs (Asongu *et al.*, 2021; Diop & Asongu, 2021; Diop *et al.*, 2021; Ezeaku *et al.*, 2021). This chapter contributes to the extant literature on the consequences of the COVID-19 pandemic by assessing the impact and consequences of the

DOI: 10.4324/9781003215042-19

recent pandemic on financial development and financial inclusion. This is in response to both scholarly and policy concerns that across the world, financial institutions are dealing with and monitoring the impacts of the COVID-19 pandemic. Hence, this study aims to understand what immediate challenges the COVID-19 pandemic has represented to the economies and societies on the one hand and on the other, the effect of the COVID-19 on the interconnected financial systems in terms of consequences of the pandemic. The relevance of the study builds on the importance of these insights in helping both scholars and policymakers understand how the effect of the pandemic on the financial system and, by extension, the global economy can be mitigated for more financial inclusion.

The rest of the chapter is organized as follows: Section 16.2 provides insights into the impact of the COVID-19 pandemic on the financial sector with particular emphasis on digital payments, emerging risks in the financial sector and post-pandemic financial sector services. Section 16.3 focuses on the implications of the COVID-19 pandemic on the financial sector, with insights into consequences for asset management, banking and capital makers. Section 16.4 concludes with implications for SDGs and future research directions.

16.2 The Impact of COVID-19 on the Financial Sector

The COVID-19 pandemic brought uncertainties and disruptions in various sectors, including financial markets and institutions. Following the outbreak of the pandemic, there was a fall in the stock price of financials, including banking, insurance and diversified financial firms (Wójcik & Ioannou, 2020). Financial institutions experienced an increase in nonperforming loans and a drop in demand for loans (Gourinchas *et al.*, 2020; Li *et al.*, 2021; Park & Shin, 2021). Microfinance institutions (MFIs) and nonbank financial institutions were disbursing just over three quarters of pre-crisis loan volumes (IFC, 2020). Also, high nonperforming loan ratios are not good for the financial sector and the entire economy, as they are positively associated with corporate debt overhangs, which affect investment and delay economic recovery (Aiyar *et al.*, 2015; Kalemli-Özcan *et al.*, 2020). However, there is a silver lining as the disruptions caused by the pandemic also created opportunities, especially in the digital payments space.

16.2.1 Increase in Digital Payments

The pandemic has accelerated the use of digital technology to conduct financial transactions. Digital finance innovations enable marginalized communities, especially in the global South, to access financial resources (Gomber *et al.*, 2018; Bharadwaj *et al.*, 2019). Financial technology (FinTech) offers the financial industry, and consumers, innovations that render their transactions less expensive, more convenient and more secure (Chen *et al.*, 2019).

Between 2010 and 2019, over $165.5 billion was invested into FinTech firms (Imerman & Fabozzi, 2020). Financial institutions and technology firms are increasingly investing in FinTech technologies, which attracted global investments of $40 billion in 2019 (KPMG, 2019). FinTech innovations are contributing to reducing the cost of providing financial services, rendering it possible to reach more people, and reducing the need for face-to-face interactions, essential for keeping up economic activity during the pandemic.

The rise in smartphone penetration and the disruption caused by COVID-19 has contributed to a significant rise of one of the largest FinTech products – that is, digital payments. Digital payments account for about 25% of the FinTech market (Blaney, 2020). Digital payments, as used in this chapter, refer to the transfer of value from one payment account to another using a digital device such as a mobile phone or computer. According to the 2021 Digital Payments Market Report, the transaction value for the global digital payments market was $5.44 trillion in 2020, and, based on projections, will be worth $11.29 trillion by 2026. Key players in the digital payments market are Alipay, Apple Pay, Amazon Pay, Tencent, First Data, Google Pay, Paypal, Fiserv, MasterCard, and Visa Inc. In 2020, 90% of users made payments with their smartphones (Blaney, 2020).

Various factors account for the rise in digital payment in the pandemic era. First, they are regarded as playing an important role in addressing pandemic-related challenges (Remolina (2020). Digital payments enabled people to pay for goods and services while adhering to social distancing (Ziegler *et al.*, 2020). In the city of Kigali in Rwanda, taxis were directed by the regulator to acquire meters that enabled a passenger to pay for his/her ride digitally, which prevented the exchange of cash, hence contributing to the fight against COVID-19 (Ashimwe, 2020). Second, customers were attracted to digital payments due to ease and speed of transactions. In the city of Kigali, Rwanda, taxi passengers could get tickets online via the Tap & Go app or web as well as pay for tickets using cashless payment platforms (Bizimungu, 2021). Digital payment technologies are also improving the ability to provide financial assistance to vulnerable segments of the population following the outbreak of the pandemic (Agur *et al.*, 2020). Additionally, digital payment technologies enabled people to perform remittance transfers in a few minutes (Dubey *et al.*, 2020). The disruptions caused by the pandemic also required innovative and more convenient ways to send money to loved ones. Digital technology enabled people to carry out remittance transfers from the comfort of their homes without the need for physical queuing, as is the case when they use conventional remittance channels. Remittances also have a role to play in achieving the SDGs. It is precisely for this reason that one of the recommendations of the SDGs is the reduction of money transfer fees (Nurse, 2018).

In Africa, the rapid penetration of mobile phones has helped the rise of mobile payments. By mobile payments, we are referring to all purchases using mobile phones (Karsen *et al.*, 2019). PayU South Africa recorded a 35% increase in e-commerce in 2020, with most transactions completed on mobile devices (PayU, 2021). In Rwanda, the volume of mobile payment increased by 51% in the first half of 2020 following the onset of the pandemic (Bizimungu, 2021). In Kenya, use of digital payments for business transactions increased from 18% at the end of 2019 to 62% by March 2021, and there was a 58% surge in clients paying digitally during the lockdown in April–July 2020 (FSD, 2021).

The increase in digital payments is significant due to its relationship to financial inclusion, and this has implications with respect to income inequality. Studies have highlighted the role of digital financial inclusion in reducing income inequality (Asongu, 2015; Asongu & Le Roux, 2017; Tchamyou, 2020, 2021).

The importance of digital payments to financial inclusion, especially during the pandemic era, explains why governments in various African countries have provided incentives to encourage the use of digital payment platforms to pay for goods and services. For instance, the government of Uganda reduced mobile money transfer fees, while the governments of Ghana, Cameroon, the Democratic Republic of Congo, Mozambique, Kenya, Rwanda, Zambia and Senegal have cut mobile money transfer fees and raised transaction size limits (Agur *et al.*, 2020). That said, the increase in digitalization of the economy in general and the financial sector in particular, generates risks, which must be addressed. This is the focus of the next sub-section.

16.2.2 COVID-19 and Emerging Risks in the Financial Sector

The COVID-19 pandemic has increased the risks faced by financial institutions. The risks relate particularly to fraud and data security. The pandemic environment is providing conducive ground for criminals and fraudsters who are seeking to exploit the crisis. A recent survey conducted by the Association of Certified Fraud Examiners noted that 77% of fraud professionals had experienced an increase in fraud in 2020 (ACFE, 2020).

The digitalization of financial services makes financial institutions more vulnerable to cybercrime. In fact, the financial sector has been attacked by hackers relatively more than other sectors during the COVID-19 pandemic (Aldasoro *et al.*, 2021). A survey conducted among financial institutions by the Financial Services Information Sharing and Analysis Center (FS-ISAC) – an industry consortium of nearly 7,000-member financial institutions – found that COVID-19–related attacks increased with the spread of the pandemic, from less than 5,000 per week in February 2020 to over 200,000 per week towards the end of April 2020 (FS-ISAC, 2020).

Financial institutions in Africa have equally faced cyberattacks. In October 2020, about 4,000 customers of BetterSure, a South African home insurance company, experienced a phishing attack (CEIP, 2021). Still in South Africa, in August 2020, Experian South Africa, a major credit bureau, experienced a data breach that exposed personal information of millions of its South African clients (CEIP, 2021). In October 2020, the heads of MTN, Airtel and Stanbic Bank in Uganda issued a joined statement, acknowledging that hackers targeted Pegasus Technologies, a firm that processes mobile money transactions for the two telecom firms, and funds were stolen (CEIP, 2021; Signé & Signé, 2021).

Misleading information is an emerging risk which the financial sector must deal with. Social media financial bots diffuse misleading information and equally engage in speculative campaigns promoting certain stocks (Tardelli *et al.*, 2020). A recent study on the effects of fake news in financial markets found that it increases price volatility by about 40% and increases abnormal trading activity by over 50% (Kogan *et al.*, 2020). Clarke *et al.* (2020) note that fake news generates significantly more attention with respect to stock price reaction than legitimate news.

Arguably, misleading information generates negative effects because it influences sentiment. Studies have noted that sentiment is a vital driver of investment decisions in the stock market (Huang *et al.*, 2015; Deng *et al.*, 2018), and mass media plays an important role in the diffusion of sentiment (Ahern & Sosyura, 2014; Tetlock, 2015). Scholars have shown that mass media sentiment influences stock market performance (Tetlock, 2014).

In addition to addressing the emerging risks mentioned earlier, financial institutions also need to develop key priority areas in the post–COVID-19 period. We shed light on this issue in the next sub-section.

16.2.3 *Financial Services Priorities in Post–Covid-19*

The disruptions caused by COVID-19 also call on the need for financial services providers to think about major priority areas in the post–COVID-19 era. The pandemic has brought to the fore the importance of digital payments. There is a huge untapped market for digital payments in Africa, and financial services providers need to engage in digital transformation. In Africa, consumer payments are expected to top $2.1 trillion by 2025 and only about 5% of these transactions are currently digitized (UNCDF, 2021). Digital payments have the potential of improving access to other financial services, like credit, which is usually the topmost requirement of small merchants. Financial services providers in Africa need to build innovative solutions to capture this huge opportunity, especially as it affects their profit margin. For example, a study conducted in Cameroon found that SMEs using mobile payment services had higher profitability, as it provides funding opportunities (Talom & Tengeh, 2020).

To remain competitive, financial services providers would have to establish partnerships with nontraditional actors such as FinTech firms. For instance, collaboration between traditional financial institutions and FinTech firms could address payment and settlement bottlenecks (Drasch *et al.*, 2018). Such collaboration will help clients of financial services providers to access diverse financial services as well as carry out transactions remotely (Coffie *et al.*, 2021). Doing so fosters financial inclusion, as it removes some of the barriers that people often face when accessing financial services (Alfred *et al.*, 2017; Coffie *et al.*, 2020).

Additionally, the delivery of FinTech-enabled services through mobile phones overcomes the infrastructural deficiencies hindering the delivery of financial services especially to rural areas (Demirgüç-Kunt *et al.*, 2020). FinTech services also offer cost-effective platforms when compared to conventional financial services and strengthen users' experience using easy and convenient functions (Lim *et al.*, 2019), and contribute to a reduction of transaction costs and improvement of service quality (Wamba *et al.*, 2020; Aslam *et al.*, 2021). These issues have to be taken seriously if financial institutions are expect to thrive in the post–COVID-19 era.

To meet customers' needs, financial services providers need to ensure the interoperability of digital platforms, as well as deploy application programming interfaces to permit the utilization of embedded-payment systems (EIU, 2021). APIs work by establishing a mechanism for remote services to request something of the platform, loosely described as either data to be provided by the platform, or an operation to be performed by the platform (Bock, 2015). Small merchants would have to build their transaction systems to work with various payment providers (Riley, 2020).

In the post-COVID era in Africa, there will be need for services related to the fostering of digital financial literacy. Such services will be needed due to the gradual expansion of the digitalization of financial services in the continent. These services will be particularly valuable among segments of the population with low levels of formal education. Such services are needed due to the impact of FinTech developments on financial planning and financial well-being (Frame *et al.*, 2019). Researchers have noted FinTech developments may enhance financial capability, just as they may negatively affect financial well-being by setting off impulsive consumer behaviour (Panos & Wilson, 2020). Also, digital financial literacy raises awareness of digital financial risks. There is a need for users to understand the additional risks that they may encounter when using digital financial services (Morgan *et al.*, 2019). By promoting digital financial literacy, financial services providers are contributing to building inclusive and financially resilient communities.

Providing digital finance education may be one way for financial services providers to engage with the customers, as well as attract potential customers by making them aware of the existence of unconventional financial products and services provided digitally on the internet and mobile phones (Morgan *et al.*, 2019). Knowledge of products, including how they work, increases the likelihood of their usage, as customers see the value of money. Customers tend to engage with businesses that can optimize their resources and outcomes (Karpen & Conduit, 2020).

Customer engagement also entails dealing with customer complaints. Financial services providers will need to develop innovative tools aimed at dealing with customer complaints post-COVID, for instance, the use of artificial intelligence in addressing customers' complaints related to financial services. Artificial intelligence can handle large volumes of data, including unstructured inputs such as speech or images (Kietzmann *et al.*, 2018), which makes it extremely relevant to financial services providers. The use of artificial intelligence systems to address customer complaints in the financial services space is gaining in Africa. In March 2021, the African Development Bank (AfDB) approved a grant of $1.024 million for artificial intelligence–enabled systems to process customer complaints on behalf of the national banks of Ghana and Rwanda and the Competition and Consumer Protection Commission of Zambia (AfDB, 2021). The long-term goal of the project is to improve the tracking of client complaints made to financial services providers and strengthen the support for marginalized groups, which will build confidence in the use of financial services (AfDB, 2021). Consumer confidence is key to building an inclusive financial system, and the latter is linked to the SDGs. For example, according to the narrative, the UN 2030 Agenda for sustainable development acknowledges the essential role of financial inclusion in successfully implementing the SDGs.

16.3 Implications of the COVID-19 Pandemic to the Financial Sector

16.3.1 Implications for Asset, Real Estate and Private Equity Management

Consistent with the attendant literature (Giese & Haldane, 2020; KPMG, 2021), the COVID-19 pandemic also has implications for the financial sector, especially as it pertains to consequences on asset, real estate and private equity management. These are discussed in the same chronology as highlighted.

First, from the premise of asset management, *inter alia*: (i) asset management agility is needed, especially given the significant disruptions posed by the COVID-19 pandemic in the asset management industry; (ii) a perspective of asset management in the light of environmental sustainability also needs to be taken on board because environmental, social and governance issues are immense challenges for SDGs; and (iii) new tax dynamics should be considered given that the contemporary tax and investment landscape are changed in the light of those witnessed after the global financial crisis (Fabeil, 2020; KPMG, 2021).

Second, in terms of real estate management, three main insights are worthwhile, notably: (i) the capacity to effectively value real estate in the light of uncertainty in order to provide a fair assessment amid apparent volatilities; (ii) rent concessions, which are expedient for COVID-19–oriented economic operations; (iii) the real estate investment trust (REIT) industry especially as the novel coronavirus is bringing uncertainty and modifying the business environment; and (iii) leveraging on best practices that ensure the continuity of business confidence from clients amid the crisis (Fabeil, 2020; KPMG, 2021).

Third, from the perspective of private equity, due diligence is essential and six main techniques can be used by private equity investors in order to arrive at informed decisions. These include: (i) proactive portfolio management and future planning; (ii) understanding concerns surrounding private equity valuation during the COVID-19 pandemic; (iii) adopting robust strategies in trying times, especially those that are resilient, innovative and adapted to ongoing crises; and (iv) understanding private equity when times are turbulent, especially with insights from rapid capital stress testing (Giese & Haldane, 2020).

16.3.2 Implication for Banking and Capital Markets

The COVID-19 pandemic also has implications for the banking and capital markets, especially in view of the fact that banks are currently in need of resources with which to confront the current challenges and better prepare for potential challenges in the future (Berger & Demirgüç-Kunt, 2021; KPMG, 2021). It is worthwhile to articulate that with disruptions from the COVID-19 pandemic, banks of all types (e.g. small- and medium-sized banks, regional banks, large universal banks, challenger bank, FinTech banks and central banks) are being confronted with unprecedented risks and challenges (Giese & Haldane, 2020). In this context, a plethora of measures are being taken by financial institutions in order to provide the much needed support to customers and employees in view of bolstering the financial system (Berger & Demirgüç-Kunt, 2021).

In the light of the above, for financial institutions to better prepare for future pandemics, their resilience in operational efficiency in order to ensure business continuity is essential. Consistent with the relevant policy and scholarly literature (Giese & Haldane, 2020; KPMG, 2021), some relevant insights that can be considered by banks around the world in responding to the present COVID-19 challenges, as well as preparing against the unfavourable consequences of future pandemic, include: (i) forging payment deals ahead in spite of the COVID-19 pandemic, especially in view of the fact that with the global pandemic, ecosystems of payment are changing and the digital economy is growingly gaining grounds; (ii) understanding that the COVID-19 pandemic is a major catalyst in the contemporary transformation of payment operations in banks; (iii) aligning the bank strategies with SDGs; and (iv) fundamental cyber risks related to banks when banking operations are more constrained by challenges surrounding global pandemics and crises (Aldasoro et al., 2021).

16.4 Concluding Implications and Future Research Directions

This chapter examines how the COVID-19 pandemic has affected financial development and financial inclusion in African countries. The study provides both broad perspectives and country-specific frameworks based on selected country case studies. Some emphasis is placed on how the pandemic would influence the achievement of sustainable development goals (SDGs) that are related to financial inclusion. The study aims to understand what immediate challenges the COVID-19 pandemic has represented to the economies and societies on the one hand and on the other, the effect of the COVID-19 on the interconnected financial systems in terms of consequences of the pandemic. The relevance of the study builds on the importance of these insights in helping both scholars and policymakers understand how the effect of the pandemic on the financial system and, by extension, the global economy can be mitigated for more financial inclusion.

More specifically, the study has provided insights into the impact of the COVID-19 pandemic on the financial sector with particular emphasis on digital payments, emerging risks in the financial sector and post-pandemic financial sector services. The study has also focused on the implications of the COVID-19 pandemic on the financial sector with insights into consequences for asset management, banking and capital markets.

The insights provided in this chapter are relevant not least, because financial inclusion is part and parcel of economic inclusion. In addition, inclusive economic development and growth cannot be worthwhile without putting emphasis on financial inclusion. Accordingly, as recently articulated by Kasradze (2020), it is difficult to achieve most of the 17 SDGs without financial inclusion. These goals include: no poverty (Goal 1), zero hunger (Goal 2), good health and well-being (Goal 3), quality education (Goal 4), gender equality (Goal 5), economic growth and decent work (Goal 8) and reduced inequality (Goal 10).

Understanding the concern of financial inclusion in view of the insights provided in this chapter is important because during the COVID-19 pandemic, a substantial part of the global population has been out of work, and hence, there is an urgent need for governments as well as for financial institutions to provide enhanced access to financial services for poor households and individuals (Kasradze, 2020). The narratives in this chapter on the causes and consequences of the global pandemic with specific emphasis on the financial sector and financial inclusion can be leveraged by policymakers to make sure more individuals and households have access to financial services which as documented in the attendant literature are essential in supporting and ensuring their livelihoods (Eldomiaty *et al.*, 2020; Ozili, 2020).

The chapter obviously leaves room for future research, especially as it relates to empirically examining the impact of the COVID-19 crisis on financial inclusion in order to assess whether the established findings in this study withstand empirical scrutiny. In addition, more robust literature reviews as more data become available will also go long way to improving what is currently known about the causes and consequences of this major global pandemic.

Acknowledgement

The authors are indebted to the editors and referees for constructive comments.

References

African Development Bank [AfDB]. (2021). African Development Bank provides $1 million for AI-based national customer management systems in Ghana, Rwanda and Zambia. AfDB: Abidjan, press release, 10 March 2021.

Agur, I., Peria, S. M., & Rochon, C. (2020). Digital financial services and the pandemic: Opportunities and risks for emerging and developing economies. International Monetary Fund Special Issue on COVID-19, *Transactions*, 1, 1–13.

Ahern, K. R., & Sosyura, D. (2014). Who writes the news? Corporate press releases during merger negotiations. *Journal of Finance*, 69(1), 241–291.

Aiyar, S., Bergthaler, W., Garrido, J., Ilyina, A., Jobst, A., Kang, K., Kovtun, D., Liu, Y., Monaghan, D., & Moretti. M. (2015). A strategy for resolving Europe's problem loans. IMF Staff Discussion Note No. 15/19. Washington, DC.

Aldasoro, I., Frost, J., Gambacorta, L., & Whyte, D. (2021). Covid-19 and cyber risk in the financial sector. *BIS Bulletin*, no 37, January. https://www.bis.org/publ/bisbull37.pdf (Accessed: 31/10/2021).

Alfred, S., Maureen, T., & Were, M. (2017). Mobile financial services and financial inclusion: Is it a boon for savings mobilization? *Review of Development Finance*, 7(1), 29–35.

Ashimwe, E. (2020). Kigali based taxi-motos to use cashless payments from Mid-August. *The New Times*. https://www.newtimes.co.rw/news/kigali-based-taxi-motos-use-cashless-payments-mid-august (Accessed: 06/10/2021).

Aslam, J., Saleem, A., Khan, N. T., & Kim, Y. B. (2021). Factors influencing blockchain adoption in supply chain management practices: A study based on the oil industry. *Journal of Innovation & Knowledge*, 6(2), 124–134.

Asongu, S. A. (2015). The Impact of Mobile Phone Penetration on African inequality, AGDI Working Paper, No. WP/13/021, African Governance and Development Institute (AGDI), Yaoundé.

Asongu, S. A., & Le Roux, S. (2017). Enhancing ICT for inclusive human development in sub-Saharan Africa. *Technological Forecasting and Social Change*, 118, 44–54.

Asongu, S. A., Diop, S., & Nnanna, J. (2021). The geography of the effectiveness and consequences of Covid-19 measures: Global evidence. *Journal of Public Affairs*, 21(4), e2483.

Association of Certified Fraud Examiners [ACFE]. (2020). Fraud in the wake of COVID-19: Benchmarking report. ACFE: Austin, TX.

Berger, A. N., & Demirgüç-Kunt, A. (2021). Banking research in the time of COVID-19. *Journal of Financial Stability*, 57(December), 100939.

Bharadwaj, P. Jack, W. & Suri, T. (2019). *Fintech and Household Resilience to Shocks: Evidence from Digital Loans in Kenya*. National Bureau of Economic Research: Cambridge, MA.

Bizimungu, J. (2021). How Covid-19 pandemic triggered surge in cashless payments. *The New Times*. https://www.newtimes.co.rw/news/how-covid-19-pandemic-triggered-surge-cashless-payments (Accessed: 06/10/2021).

Blaney, B., (2020). Chart-topping fintech stats for 2020. https://tipalti.com/fintech-stats-for-2020/. https://tipalti.com/ (Accessed: 06/10/2021).

Bock, M. (2015). WTF is an API? How the internet works behind the scenes. Hackernoon, January 20. https://hackernoon.com/apis-how-the-internet-works-behind-the-scenes-690288634c32 (Accessed: 06/10/2021).

Carnegie Endowment for International Peace [CEIP]. (2021). Timeline of cyber incidents involving financial institutions. https://carnegieendowment.org/special-projects/protectingfinancialstability/timeline (Accessed: 06/10/2021).

Chen, M.A., Wu, Q., & Yang, B. (2019). How valuable is FinTech innovation? *Review of Financial Studies*, 32(5), 2062–2106.

Clarke, J., Chen, H., Du, D., & Hu, Y. (2020). Fake news, investor attention, and market reaction. *Information Systems Research*, 32(1), 35–52

Coffie, C. P. K., Zhao, H., & Mensah, I. A. (2020). Panel econometric analysis on mobile payment transactions and traditional banks effort toward financial accessibility in sub-Sahara Africa. *Sustainability*, 12(3), 895.

Coffie, C., Hongjiang, Z., Mensah, I., Kiconco, R., & Simon, A. (2021). Determinants of FinTech payment services diffusion by SMEs in sub-Saharan Africa: Evidence from Ghana. *Information Technology for Development*, 27(3), 539–560.

Demirgüç-Kunt, A., Klapper, L., & Singer, D. (2017). Financial inclusion and inclusive growth: A review of recent empirical evidence, Policy Research Working Paper 8040. World Bank: Washington, DC.

Demirgüç-Kunt, A., Klapper, L., Singer, D., Ansar, S., & Hess, J. (2020). The global Findex Database 2017: Measuring financial inclusion and opportunities to expand access to and use of financial services. *The World Bank Economic Review*. https://doi.org/10.1093/wber/lhz013 (Accessed: 06/10/2021).

Deng, S., Huang, Z. J., Sinha, A. P., & Zhao, H. (2018). The interaction between microblog sentiment and stock returns: An empirical examination. *MIS Quarterly*, 42(3), 895–918.

Diop, S., & Asongu, S. A. (2021). The Covid-19 pandemic and the new poor in Africa: The straw that broke the camel's back. *Forum for Social Economics*. https://doi.org/10.1080/07360932.2021.1884583

Diop, S., Asongu, S. A., & Nnanna, J. (2021). COVID-19 economic vulnerability and resilience indexes: Global evidence. *International Social Science Journal*, 71(S1), 37–50.

Drasch, B. J., Schweizer, A., & Urbach, N. (2018). Integrating the 'troublemakers': A taxonomy for cooperation between banks and Fintechs. *Journal of Economics and Business*, 100, 26–42.

Dubey, V., Sonar, R., & Mohanty, A. (2020). FinTech, RegTech and contactless payments through the lens of COVID 19 times. *Money*, 29(6), 3727–3734.

Economist Intelligence Unit [eiu]. (2021). *Going Digital: Payments in the Post-Covid World*. EIU: London.

Eldomiaty, T., Hammam, R., & El Bakry, R. (2020). Institutional determinants of financial inclusion: Evidence from world economies. *International Journal of Development Issues*, 19(2), 217–228.

Ezeaku, H., Asongu, S. A., & Nnanna, J. (2021). Volatility of international commodity prices in times of COVID-19: Effects of oil supply and global demand shocks. *The Extractive Industries and Society*, 8(1), 257–270.

Fabeil, N. F., Pazim, K. H., & Langgat, J. (2020). The impact of covid-19 pandemic crisis on MicroEnterprises: Entrepreneurs' perspective on business continuity and recovery strategy. *Journal of Economics and Business*, 3(2). https://papers.ssrn.com/sol3/papers.cfm?abstract_id=3612830 (Accessed: 31/10/2021).

Financial Sector Deepening [FSD]. (2021). Annual Report 2020. https://www.fsdkenya.org/wp-content/uploads/2021/06/FSDK-Annual-Report-2020-Web.pdf (Accessed: 06/10/2021).

Financial Services Information Sharing and Analysis Center [FS-ISAC]. (2020). COVID-19 effects on cyber security survey, July.

Frame, W. S., Wall, L., & White, L. J. (2019). Technological change and financial innovation in banking: Some implications for Fintech. In *Oxford Handbook of Banking*, 3rd ed., edited by A. Berger, P. Molyneux, and J. O. S. Wilson, 262–284. Oxford University Press: Oxford.

Giese, J., & Haldane, A. (2020). COVID-19 and the financial system: A tale of two crises. *Oxford Review of Economic Policy*, 36(S1), S200–S214.

Gomber, P., Kauffman, R. J., Parker, C., & Weber, B. W. (2018). On the Fintech revolution: Interpreting the forces of innovation, disruption, and transformation in financial services. *Journal of Management Information Systems*, 35(1), 220–265.

Gourinchas, P. O., Kalemli-Özcan, S., Penciakova, V., & Sander, N. (2020). Covid-19 and SME failures. NBER Working Paper Series. https://doi.org/10.3386/w27877

Huang, D., Jiang, F., Tu, J., & Zhou, G. (2015). Investor sentiment aligned: A powerful predictor of stock returns. *Review of Financial Studies*, 28(3), 791–837.

IFC. (2020). *The Early Impact of COVID-19 on Financial Institutions*. IFC: Washington, DC.

Imerman, M. B., & Fabozzi, F. J. (2020). Cashing in on innovation: A taxonomy of FinTech. *Journal of Asset Management*, 21, 167–177.

Kalemli-Özcan, S., Laeven, L., & Moreno, D. (2020). Debt overhang, rollover risk, and corporate investment: Evidence from the European crisis. NBER Working Paper Series. https://doi.org/10.3386/w24555.

Karlan, D., Kendall, J. Mann, R., Pande, R., Suri, T., & Zinman, J. (2016). Research and impacts of digital financial services, NBER Working Paper No. 22633, Cambridge.

Karpen, I. O., & Conduit, J. (2020). Engaging in times of COVID-19 and beyond: theorizing customer engagement through different paradigmatic lenses. *Journal of Service Management*, 31(6), 1163–1174.

Karsen, M., Chandra, Y. U., & Juwitasary, H. (2019). Technological factors of mobile payment: A systematic literature review. *Procedia Computer Science*, 157, 489–498.

Kasradze, T. (2020). Challenges facing financial inclusion due to the COVID-19 pandemic. *European Journal of Marketing and Economics*, 3(2), 50–63.

Kietzmann, J. H., Paschen, J., & Treen, E. (2018). Artificial intelligence in advertising: How marketers can leverage artificial intelligence along the consumer journey. *Journal of Advertising Research*, 58(3), 263–267.

Kogan, S., Moskowitz, T. J., & Niessner, M. (2020). Fake news: Evidence from financial markets. https://papers.ssrn.com/sol3/papers.cfm?abstract_id=3237763 (Accessed: 06/10/2021).

KPMG. (2019). *The Pulse of Fintech 2019—Biannual Global Analysis of Investment in Fintech*. KPMG: Zurich.

KPMG. (2021). Implications of COVID-19 for Asset Management. *KPMG International Entities*. https://home.kpmg/xx/en/home/insights/2020/04/covid-19-impact-and-implications-to-asset-management.html (Accessed: 31/10/2021).

Li, X., Feng, H., Zhao, S., & Carter, D. (2021). The effect of revenue diversification on bank profitability and risk during the COVID-19 pandemic. *Finance Research Letters*, 101957

Lim, S. H., Kim, D. J., Hur, Y., & Park, K. (2019). An study of the impacts of perceived security and knowledge on continuous intention to use mobile Fintech payment services. *International Journal of Human–Computer Interaction*, 35(10), 886–898.

Morgan, P. J., Huang, B., & Trinh, L. Q. (2019). The need to promote digital financial literacy for the digital age. In *Realizing Education for All: In the Digital Age*, edited by P. Morgan, and N. Kayashima, 40–46. JICA and ADBI: Tokyo.

Nurse, K. (2018). Migration, diasporas, remittances and the sustainable development goals in least developed countries. *Journal of Globalization and Development*, 9(2), 1–13.

Ozili, P. K. (2020). Financial inclusion and Fintech during COVID-19 Crisis: Policy solutions. *SSRN Electronic Journal*. https://doi.org/10.2139/ssrn.3585662

Panos, G., & Wilson, J. O. S. (2020). Financial literacy and responsible finance in the FinTech era: Capabilities and challenges. *The European Journal of Finance*, 26(4–5), 297–301.

Park, C-Y., & Shin, K. (2021). COVID-19, nonperforming loans, and cross-border bank lending. *Journal of Banking & Finance*, 106233.

PayU (2021). *The Next Frontier: The Most Promising Markets for Emerging E-Commerce Leaders in 2021 and Beyond*. PayU: Bucharest.

Remolina, N. (2020). Towards a data-driven financial system: The impact of COVID-19. SMU Centre for AI & Data Governance, *Research Paper* (08).

Riley, C. (2020). Unpacking interoperability in competition. *Journal of Cyber Policy*, 5(1), 94–106.

Signé, L., & Signé, K. (2021). How African states can improve their cybersecurity. March 16, 2021, Brookings. https://www.brookings.edu/techstream/how-african-states-can-improve-their-cybersecurity/ (Accessed: 08/10/2021).

Talom, F. S. G., & Tengeh, R. K. (2020). The impact of mobile money on the financial performance of the SMEs in Douala, Cameroon. *Sustainability*, 12(1), 183.

Tardelli, S., Avvenuti, M., Tesconi, M., & Cresci, S. (2020). Characterizing social bots spreading financial disinformation. In *Social Computing and Social Media: Design, Ethics, user Behavior, and Social Network Analysis Lecture Notes in Computer Science*, edited by G. Meiselwitz, 376–392. Springer: Cham.

Tchamyou, V. S. (2019). The role of information sharing in modulating the effect of financial access on inequality. *Journal of African Business*, 20(3), 317–338.

Tchamyou, V. S. (2020). Education, lifelong learning, inequality and financial access: Evidence from African countries. *Contemporary Social Science*, 15(1), 7–25.

Tchamyou, V. S. (2021). Financial access, governance and the persistence of inequality in Africa: Mechanisms and policy instruments. *Public Affairs*, 21(2), e2201.

Tchamyou, V.S., Erreygers, G., & Cassimon, D. (2019). Inequality, ICT and financial access in Africa. *Technological Forecasting and Social Change*, 139(February), 169–184.

Tetlock, P. C. (2014). Information transmission in finance. *Annual Review of Financial Economics*, 6(1), 365–384.

Tetlock, P. C. (2015). The role of media in finance. In *Handbook of Media Economics* (Vol. 1), edited by S.P. Anderson, J. Waldfogel, and D. Strömberg, 701–721. Elsevier: Amsterdam.

UNCDF. (2021). *Research on Small and Micro Merchants Payments Digitization in Africa.* UNCDF: Brussel

Wamba, F., S., Kamdjoug, K., Bawack, E., & Keogh, J. G. (2020). Bitcoin, Blockchain and Fintech: A systematic review and case studies in the supply chain. *Production Planning & Control*, 31(2–3), 115–142.

Wójcik, D., & Ioannou, S. (2020). COVID-19 and Finance: Market developments so far and potential impacts on the financial sector and centre. *Tijdschriftvoor Economischeen Sociale Geografie*, 111(3), 387–400.

Yamada, E., Shimizutani, S., & Murakami, E. (2020). The COVID-19 pandemic, remittances and financial inclusion in the Philippines. *The Philippine Review of Economics*, 57(1), 18–41.

Ziegler, T., Zhang, B. Z., Carvajal, A., Barton, M. E., Smit, H., Wenzlaff, K., Natarajan, H., et al. (2020). *Global COVID-19 FinTech Market Rapid Assessment Study – CCAF Publications.* University of Cambridge Alternative Finance Center. https://www.jbs.cam.ac.uk/faculty-research/centres/alternative-finance/publications/2020-global-covid-19-fintech-market-rapid-assessment-study/

17 Financial Institutions, Poverty and Severity of Poverty in African Countries

Simplice Anutechia Asongu, Valentine B. Soumtang and Ofeh M. Edoh

17.1 Introduction

The purpose of this study is to assess how financial institutions in terms of depth, access and efficiency have affected poverty and the severity of poverty in Sub-Saharan Africa (SSA). The premise of the study builds on two fundamental foundations in the policy and scholarly literature, notably, (i) the importance of addressing the poverty concern in SSA in the light of the post-2015 global development agenda related to sustainable development goals (SDGs) and (ii) gaps in the literature. These two underlying premises are expanded in turn.

First, the policy syndrome of poverty is as old as humanity and policy concerns surrounding how the underlying policy syndrome can be addressed have been central in economic, social and political discussions, especially in the light of achieving most SDGs (Nwani & Osuji, 2020). The high poverty rate in SSA has left millions of people in the region without decent avenues for livelihood given the apparent unequal distribution of the fruits of economic growth, poor economic governance and entrenched inequality (Asongu & Nwachukwu, 2016; Tchamyou, 2019). In spite of some efforts that have been made in the direction of addressing poverty in SSA, the number of poor is growing in absolute terms owing to the population rising at a faster rate than the rate of poverty reduction (Asongu & le Roux, 2017). With the contemporary poverty line of 1.90 USD per person per day, in 2019, SSA edged Asia to become the region hosting the highest number of the world's poorest population (Nwani & Osuji, 2020). It is therefore of policy relevance to assess how various financial and economic outcomes affect poverty reduction in SSA, not least, because poverty eradication or SDG1 is the first bold goal of the United Nation's sustainable development agenda. A complementary motivation for the study is an apparent gap in the scholarly literature.

Second, as discussed in Section 2.2, the contemporary literature has not assessed the importance of financial development in reducing poverty as considered within the framework of this study. The closest study in the literature to the present research is by Ofori et al. (2021) who have assessed the effectiveness of financial development and information and communication

DOI: 10.4324/9781003215042-20

technology (ICT) in mitigating the intensity and severity of poverty in SSA. The empirical evidence is based on panel corrected standard errors estimation and generalized method of moments (GMM) estimation techniques. The finding shows that while ICT skills mitigate poverty, the incidence is more apparent when financial development is pronounced.

The present study departs from Ofori et al. (2021) by directly assessing the nexus between financial institutions and poverty and putting into perspective the conditional distribution of poverty and the severity of poverty. Hence, the adopted estimation strategy takes into account the conditional distribution of poverty and the severity of poverty. Accordingly, it is argued in this study that the effect of financial institutional dynamics on poverty dynamics can be contingent on initial levels of poverty dynamics, such that the effect differs when initial levels of poverty are high compared to when initial levels of poverty are low. It follows that blanket finance-poverty policies are unlikely to succeed unless they are tailored towards existing poverty levels. The quantile regression strategy adopted in the present study takes into account initial levels of poverty in the finance-poverty nexus.

The rest of the study is structured as follows. The theoretical underpinnings and literature review are covered in Section 17.2, while the data and methodology are discussed in Section 17.3. Section 17.4 presents the findings, while Section 17.5 concludes with implications and future research directions.

17.2 Theoretical Underpinnings and Literature Review

17.2.1 Theoretical Underpinnings

The investigated nexus between financial institutions and poverty is informed by theoretical strands in the inclusive development literature which posit for the importance of financial development in reducing inequality and alleviating poverty (Tchamyou et al., 2019). Consistent with the corresponding literature, poverty reduction is possible if and when citizens are provided with financial access opportunities, especially when the poorest fraction of the population lacks basic access to commodities that enhance well-being owing to limited or no financial access (Beck et al., 2007; Tchamyou & Asongu, 2017a; Asongu & Odhiambo, 2018). These more contemporary perspectives are consistent with less contemporary scholarly views supporting the importance of enhanced financial access opportunities as a means of promoting inclusive development outcomes, *inter alia*: Greenwood and Jovanovic (1990), Galor and Zeira (1993), Galor and Moav (2004) and Aghion and Bolton (2005).

In accordance with Tchamyou et al. (2019), the relationship between financial development and poverty alleviation can be theoretically substantiated with two main underpinnings: the intensive and extensive margin theories. First, in the light of the intensive margin theory, financial development can reduce poverty when existing bank customers are provided enhanced financial access services, especially when these existing customers entail a significant proportion of the poor population (Chipote et al., 2014). Second, when the attendant financial services are extended to people who did not previously have access to financial services by means of bank accounts, the extensive margin theory applies (Odhiambo, 2014; Orji et al., 2015; Chiwira et al., 2016). The extensive margin theory is even more feasible and apparent when and/or if majority of the people without bank accounts are from the poor fraction of the population such that improved financial access opportunities for poverty reduction are associated with extension of bank services to those who hitherto did not have access to formal bank accounts (Evans & Jovanovic, 1989; Holtz-Eakin et al., 1994; Black & Lynch, 1996; Bae et al., 2012; Batabyal & Chowdhury, 2015).

17.2.2 Literature Review

Relative to extant literature on the dynamics of financial sector activities on poverty, a number of studies have revealed different results from different regions in the world. Although there has been a mix (some results show a positive relationship, while others show a negative relationship) in the results obtained concerning the influence of financial development on poverty, the majority of the extant literature records a positive influence. Tsaurai (2020) studied the financial development-poverty nexus in BRICS (Brazil, Russia, India, China and South Africa) by using the pooled ordinary least squares, fixed effects and fully modified ordinary least squares for the period 1994–2013. Results from the study showed that financial development and foreign direct investments jointly influence poverty reduction.

Majid et al. (2019) carried out a study to investigate whether financial development reduces poverty in Indonesia. Data was employed from the year 1980 to 2014, and the Autoregressive Distributed Lag (ARDL) method was used to capture the long-run relationship between financial development and poverty. They equally made use of the Vector Error Correction Model (VECM) to demystify the direction of influence (the causal relationship) between financial development and poverty in Indonesia. As results, the study found that there exists a long-run relationship between financial development and poverty and that there equally exists a bi-directional relationship between financial development and poverty. Equally, Keho (2017) examined the relationship between financial development, economic growth and poverty reduction in selected African countries from the period 1970 to 2013. The study used the ARDL method. Results proved a long-run relationship among the variables, and financial deepening was found to have a positive effect on poverty reduction in some of the countries.

Rashid and Intartaglia (2017) examined the impact of financial development on poverty reduction in developing countries for the period 1985–2008. Their empirical evidence was backed by the use of the two-step system GMM estimator, and consequently, results revealed that financial development significantly reduces absolute poverty, but no significant results were recorded in terms of the influence of financial development on relative poverty. The findings went ahead to show that financial sector development impacts the reduction of poverty to a greater extent when there is high economic growth. Thus, a mix of measures and policies should be put in place that will enhance the reduction of both absolute and relative poverty in developing countries.

Zahonogo (2016) investigated how financial development affects poverty indicators in 42 SSA countries from the year 1980 to 2012 by using the GMM estimator, which is particularly appropriate when controlling for endogeneity and country-specific problems. The results revealed that there exists a financial development threshold above which financial development could be associated with lower levels of poverty and below which financial development will greatly deteriorate conditions for the poor. It concludes on the premise that the relationship between financial development and poverty reduction is not the same for countries in SSA. Abosedra et al. (2016) carried out a study on the linkages between financial development and poverty in Egypt. Quarterly data was used from 1975Q1 to 2011Q4. For empirical evidence, they used the structural break autoregressive distributed lag-bounds approach and the results showed that financial development proxied by domestic credit to the private sector reduces poverty. This therefore means that financial sector development is a direct channel which eases and broadens access to financial services by the poor. Their results equally showed that financial development reduces poverty through economic growth in Egypt. This translates the existence of an indirect channel in the financial development-poverty relationship.

A study carried out by Danduame (2014) on financial sector development, economic growth and poverty reduction in Nigeria made use of times series data covering the period 1970–2011 to empirically investigate the relationship between the said variables. He adopted the ARDL model alongside the Toda and Yamamoto causality test and the results revealed that financial sector development does not lead to poverty reduction in Nigeria. He concludes on the term that financial development although being important, is not sufficient for poverty reduction. Chemli (2014) examined the relationship between financial development and poverty reduction in eight MENA countries, notably, Algeria, Egypt, Iran, Jordan, Mauritania, Morocco, Tunisia and Yemen. She employed data from 1990 to 2012 and made use of the ARDL model method of analysis. The empirical results showed that financial development works for the betterment of the poor although access to credit remains a major problem for the poor.

Uddin et al. (2014) investigated the relationship between financial development, economic growth and poverty reduction in Bangladesh. The study employed quarterly data for the period 1975–2011. They used a number of regression methods, among which were the ARDL, ordinary least squares (OLS), Error Correction Model (ECM) and VECM. Results showed that there is a long-run relationship between financial development, economic growth and poverty reduction in Bangladesh. Fowowe and Abidoye (2013) in examining the effect of financial development on poverty and inequality in African countries found that financial development does not influence poverty and inequality in African countries in any significant way. The results were achieved by the use of the system GMM estimator after careful consideration to mark out possible data-related errors.

Odhiambo (2010) in his study on financial development and poverty in Kenya studied to find out if financial development in Kenya is a spur to poverty reduction by using the cointegration and error correction mechanism methods in a trivariate causality model. He finds a distinct causal flow from financial development to poverty reduction. Another interesting finding from his study was a bi-directional causality between savings and poverty reduction in Kenya. To close up, Jalilian and Kirkpatrick (2005) equally carried out a study on the contribution of financial development to poverty reduction in developing countries by employing a panel data analysis for the period 1960–1995. They studied and tested for the causal relationship between financial sector development and poverty reduction, and it was established that financial development leads to poverty reduction through enhanced economic growth.

17.3 Data and Methodology

17.3.1 Data

The study focuses on 42 countries in SSA for which data is available at the time of the study for the period 1980–2019.[1] As apparent in Appendix 17.1, the data comes from two main sources, namely the Global Findex database and World Development Indicators (WDI) of the World Bank. Consistent with Ofori et al. (2021), two main poverty indicators are employed: (i) the poverty headcount ratio at national poverty lines (% of population) to proxy for poverty and (ii) the severity of poverty generated as the squared of poverty gap index.

Three main financial institution variables are adopted, namely financial institutions depth (FID) index, financial institutions access (FIA) index and financial institutions efficiency (FIE) index. This is consistent with financial development literature on the need to improve policy relevance by taking into account dynamics of depth, access and efficiency (Asongu & Nting, 2021). In order to control for variable omission bias, seven control variables are adopted in accordance with recent inclusive development literature (Tchamyou et al., 2019; Asongu & Nting, 2021; Ofori et al., 2021), namely inflation, foreign aid, government expenditure, gross domestic product (GDP) growth, foreign direct investment, inequality and remittances. While inflation, foreign aid and inequality are expected to increase poverty, the expected signs from the other control variables are contingent on initial levels of poverty and the severity of poverty. What is quite evident is that the adopted control variables have been documented to influence inclusive development. Hence, we should be confident that they would display some significant nexuses, irrespective of signs.

Appendix 17.1 provides the definitions and sources of the variables, while the Appendix 17.2 discloses the corresponding summary statistics. A correlation matrix, which is provided in Appendix 17.3, enables to study to avoid concerns of multicollinearity that can severely affect the expected signs of the investigated nexuses (see Asongu et al., 2020, 2021).

17.3.1.1 Methodology

In accordance with the motivation of the research, which is to assess how financial institutions affect poverty dynamics throughout the conditional distribution of poverty dynamics, a quantile regression (QR) methodology is adopted because it is consistent with the problem statement being examined. Accordingly, with the QR technique, low, intermediate and high initial levels of the outcome variable are articulated (Billger & Goel, 2009; Asongu, 2013; Tchamyou & Asongu, 2017b; Boateng et al. 2018; Asongu et al., 2021).

It is also important to emphasize that relative to the OLS technique in which the error terms are assumed to be distributed normally, with the QR approach, the residuals are not assumed to be distributed normally. Furthermore, with the QR technique, estimated parameters are obtained from various points of the conditional distribution of the dependent variable (Koenker & Bassett, 1978; Keonker & Hallock, 2001).Accordingly, the θ th quantile estimator of poverty is derived by solving for the optimization problem in Equation (17.1), which is disclosed without subscripts for simplicity in presentation.

$$\min_{\beta \in R^k} \left[\sum_{i \in \{i: yi \geq xi'\beta\}} \theta \left| yi - xi'\beta \right| + \sum_{i \in \{i: yi < xi'\beta\}} (1-\theta) \left| yi - xi'\beta \right| \right], \tag{17.1}$$

where $\theta \in (0,1)$. Relative to OLS that is predominantly based on minimizing the sum of squared residuals, multiple quantiles are considered with the QR approach that is based on the sum of absolute deviations for all quantiles. For instance, in the technique, multiple quantiles such as 10th and 90th quantiles (with $\theta = 0.10$ or 0.90, respectively) are minimized by weighing approximately the residuals. The conditional quantile of poverty or yi given xi is

$$Q_Y(\theta \, / \, xi) = xi'\beta\theta \tag{17.2}$$

where for the respective θ, the determined quantile, unique slope parameters are estimated. This formulation is parallel to $E(y \, / \, x) = xi'\beta$ in the OLS slope in which parameters are assessed purely at the average of the conditional distribution of poverty. For the model in Eq. (17.2), the dependent variable y_i is the poverty or severity of poverty indicator, while x_i contains a constant term, financial institutions depth, financial institutions access, financial institutions efficiency, inflation, foreign aid, government expenditure, gross domestic product (GDP) growth, foreign direct investment, inequality and remittances.

17.4 Empirical Results

Tables 17.1 and 17.2 provide the empirical findings in this section. Table 17.1 is focused on the nexus between financial institutions and poverty headcount, while Table 17.2 is concerned with the relationship between financial institutions and the severity of poverty. From the findings, it is apparent that the motivation for adopting the QR strategy is justified because compared to the OLS results, the QR findings are distinct in terms of significance and magnitude of significance. In other words, the responses of poverty dynamics to financial institutions dynamics differ with initial level of poverty headcount and the severity of poverty. The results as provided in Tables 17.1 and 17.2 are reported in terms of: (i) S–shape, (ii) U–shape, (iii) thresholds and (iv) estimated coefficients that do not belong to the first two categories.

Prior to presenting the findings, it is worthwhile to clarify the notion of thresholds as employed in this study. Such a notion of threshold is consistent with Asongu (2014, 2017) when the responses of the outcome variable to the independent variable of interest are assessed throughout the conditional distribution of the outcome variable. A positive threshold is employed when estimated coefficients reflect either an increasing positive or increasing negative tendency from bottom to top quantiles. In the same vein, a negative threshold is used when estimated coefficients reflect a decreasing positive or decreasing negative tendency throughout the conditional distribution of the attendant poverty distribution. Conversely, an S–shape is apparent when throughout the conditional distribution of poverty: (i) the effects of estimated coefficients decrease and then increase before decreasing again throughout the poverty distribution and (ii) the impacts of estimated coefficients increase and then decrease before increasing again throughout the poverty distribution. U–shapes and inverted U–shapes are by definition apparent in an S–shaped tendency.

The following findings are apparent in Table 17.1 on the nexus between financial institutions and poverty headcount: (i) financial institutions depth increases poverty, with an inverted U–shape tendency from the median to the 90th quantile of the poverty distribution; (ii) financial institutional access decreases poverty, with a positive threshold from the median to the 90th quantile of the poverty distribution; and (iii) financial institutions efficiency decreases poverty with an S–shape tendency throughout the conditional distribution of poverty.

Table 17.1 Financial institutions and poverty headcount

	Dependent Variable: Poverty Headcount					
	OLS	Q.10	Q.25	Q.50	Q.75	Q.90
Constant	54.703★★★	38.758★★★	43.726★★★	49.833★★★	63.257★★★	75.995★★★
	(0.000)	(0.000)	(0.000)	(0.000)	(0.000)	(0.000)
Financial institutions depth	17.047★★★	15.978★★★	−5.333	22.956★★★	31.845★★★	18.275★★★
	(0.000)	(0.000)	(0.127)	(0.000)	(0.004)	(0.000)
Financial institutions access	−16.088★★★	−60.879★★★	−4.407	−6.246★	−13.278★★★	−20.024★★★
	(0.000)	(0.000)	(0.297)	(0.052)	(0.004)	(0.000)
Financial institutions efficiency	−18.386★★★	−11.897★★★	−9.957★★★	−18.843★★★	−27.994★★★	−18.262★★★
	(0.000)	(0.000)	(0.000)	(0.000)	(0.000)	(0.000)
Inflation	0.001★★★	0.001★★	0.001★	0.001★	0.0009	0.0003
	(0.000)	(0.031)	(0.088)	(0.040)	(0.254)	(0.634)
Foreign aid	0.380★★★	0.381★★★	0.481★★★	0.399★★★	0.341★★★	0.191★★★
	(0.000)	(0.000)	(0.000)	(0.000)	(0.000)	(0.000)
Government expenditure	0.010	0.012	0.008	0.008	−0.002	−0.0008
	(0.322)	(0.450)	(0.647)	(0.520)	(0.915)	(0.963)
GDP growth	−0.222★★★	−0.298★★★	−0.293★★★	−0.208★★★	−0.119	−0.146
	(0.004)	(0.000)	(0.001)	(0.002)	(0.210)	(0.114)
Foreign direct investment	0.121★★	0.104	0.189★★	0.048	−0.015	0.168★★
	(0.020)	(0.130)	(0.010)	(0.383)	(0.848)	(0.032)
Inequality (Gini)	0.036★★	0.074★★★	0.039★	0.051★★★	0.014	−0.040★
	(0.023)	(0.001)	(0.086)	(0.003)	(0.565)	(0.096)
Remittances	0.063★★★	0.100★★★	0.095★★★	0.013	−0.043	−0.036
	(0.000)	(0.000)	(0.000)	(0.500)	(0.137)	(0.202)
Trade	−0.059★★★	−0.075★★★	−0.074★★★	−0.009	0.010	−0.045★★★
	(0.000)	(0.000)	(0.000)	(0.408)	(0.531)	(0.004)
R^2/Pseudo-R^2	0.278	0.245	0.153	0.188	0.182	0.095
Fisher	65.54★★★					
Observations	1680	1680	1680	1680	1680	1680

★,★★ and ★★★indicate significance levels of 10%, 5% and 1%, respectively. OLS: ordinary least squares. R^2 for OLS and Pseudo-R^2 for quantile regression. Lower quantiles (e.g., Q 0.1) signify nations where poverty headcount is least.

Table 17.2 Financial institutions and severity of poverty

	OLS	Q.10	Q.25	Q.50	Q.75	Q.90
	\multicolumn{6}{l}{Dependent Variable: Severity of Poverty}					
Constant	13.396★★★	−1.425★★	−1.778★	4.605★★	15.495★★★	33.381★★★
	(0.000)	(0.023)	(0.079)	(0.016)	(0.000)	(0.000)
Financial institutions depth	−16.635★★★	1.380	−3.214★	−10.949★★★	−16.477★★★	−31.151★★
	(0.000)	(0.192)	(0.060)	(0.001)	(0.008)	(0.038)
Financial institutions access	−42.995★★★	−10.327★★★	−17.062★★★	−22.523★★★	−34.263★★★	−69.390★★★
	(0.000)	(0.000)	(0.000)	(0.000)	(0.000)	(0.000)
Financial institutions efficiency	−3.859	3.960★★★	9.432★★★	12.203★★★	5.684	−20.408★
	(0.325)	(0.000)	(0.000)	(0.000)	(0.193)	(0.054)
Inflation	0.002★★★	0.002★★★	0.002★★★	0.001★★★	0.008★★★	0.0005
	(0.000)	(0.000)	(0.000)	(0.006)	(0.000)	(0.859)
Foreign aid	0.012	0.032★★	0.096★★★	0.155★★★	0.305★★★	−0.112
	(0.781)	(0.010)	(0.000)	(0.000)	(0.000)	(0.524)
Government expenditure	−0.005	0.010★	0.017★★	0.030★	−0.006	0.029
	(0.729)	(0.057)	(0.044)	(0.059)	(0.823)	(0.698)
GDP growth	−0.112	−0.022	−0.125★★★	−0.136★	−0.300★	−0.250
	(0.324)	(0.390)	(0.003)	(0.090)	(0.052)	(0.504)
Foreign direct investment	−0.047	0.045★★	0.052	0.069	−0.082	−0.339
	(0.539)	(0.042)	(0.142)	(0.308)	(0.528)	(0.283)
Inequality (Gini)	0.119★★★	−0.0007	0.024★★	0.045★★	0.078★	0.299★★★
	(0.000)	(0.919)	(0.028)	(0.030)	(0.053)	(0.002)
Remittances	−0.092★★★	0.031★★★	0.022★	0.031	−0.048	−0.285★★
	(0.000)	(0.000)	(0.080)	(0.204)	(0.302)	(0.013)
Trade	0.064★★	0.009★★	0.004	−0.033★★	0.009	0.265★★★
	(0.015)	(0.032)	(0542)	(0.017)	(0.711)	(0.000)
R^2/Pseudo-R^2	0.116	0.026	0.073	0.090	0.097	0.142
Fisher	35.31★★★					
Observations	1680	1680	1680	1680	1680	1680

★, ★★and ★★★significance levels of 10%, 5% and 1%, respectively. OLS: ordinary least squares. R^2 for OLS and Pseudo-R^2 for quantile regression. Lower quantiles (e.g., Q 0.1) signify nations where severity of poverty is least.

The following findings are apparent in Table 17.2 on the nexus between financial institutions and the severity of poverty: (i) financial institutions depth decrease the severity of poverty with a positive threshold from the 25th to the 90th quantile; (ii) financial institutions access decreases poverty with a positive threshold throughout the conditional distribution of the severity of poverty; and (iii) financial institutional efficiency increases poverty in the bottom quantiles, the effect is negative in the top quantile of the severity of poverty distribution. Most of the control variables are significant.

Overall, the main differences between Tables 17.1 and 17.2 are that (i) while financial institutions depth increases poverty headcount in the top quantiles, it decreases the severity of poverty from the 25th to the 90th quantile and (ii) financial institutions efficiency, which previously decreased poverty headcount throughout the conditional distribution, now only decreases the severity of poverty in the top quantile, with the effect positive in the bottom quantile of the same distribution. What is also apparent is that financial access consistently decreases both poverty headcount and the severity of poverty and the decreasing effect increases with increasing levels of poverty headcount in the top quantile and throughout the distribution of the severity of poverty. It follows that at least for the top quantile of poverty distribution and throughout the conditional distribution of the severity of poverty, the decreasing response of poverty to financial institutions access is an increasing function of the levels of poverty. In other words, the effect of financial institutions access in decreasing poverty is consistently higher with increasing levels of poverty.

17.5 Concluding Implications and Future Research Directions

The study has assessed how financial institutions dynamics have affected poverty and the severity of poverty in Africa using data from 1980 to 2019 from 42 sub-Saharan African countries. In order to increase for policy relevance of the study, three financial development indicators have been used, namely financial institutions depth, financial institutions access and financial institutions efficiency. The adopted empirical strategy is a quantile regression approach, which has enabled the study to assess how financial institutions dynamics affect poverty and the severity of poverty throughout the conditional distribution of poverty and the severity of poverty. The findings provided show various U-shape, S-shape, inverted U-shape and threshold tendencies; notably, financial institutions depth (efficiency) consistently decreases the severity of poverty (poverty headcount), while financial institutions access consistently decreases both poverty headcount and the severity of poverty, and the decreasing effect increases with increasing levels of poverty headcount in the top quantiles and throughout the distribution of the severity of poverty. It follows that at least for the top quantiles of poverty and throughout the conditional distribution of the severity of poverty, the decreasing response of poverty to financial institutions access is an increasing function of the levels of poverty. In other words, the effect of financial access in decreasing poverty is consistently higher with increasing levels of poverty and the severity of poverty.

The findings above clearly show that blanket financial development policies designed to reduce poverty are unlikely to be effective unless these policies are contingent on initial levels of poverty and tailored towards different initial levels of poverty. The policies should also be contingent on the financial policy instruments being leveraged upon. For instance, we have shown that the financial institutions access mechanism is the most effective financial instrument in reducing poverty and the severity of poverty. Moreover, the financial institution access should be considered by policymakers with specific knowledge of the fact that its effect in decreasing poverty consistently increases with increasing levels of poverty. The findings obviously have policy implications in terms of SDG1 on poverty reduction.

Poverty reduction is an issue everywhere in the world and in all its forms. Moreover, it is the first bold initiative of the SDG agenda or SDG1 of ending poverty. In SSA where the concern is most apparent in the light of the narrative in the introduction, financial institutions (especially the financial access channel) should be improved in the sub-region as a means to reducing poverty and the severity of poverty. When such financial access resources are being mobilized, policymakers should also bear in mind the fact that for similar cross-country financial access resources, the effect on reducing poverty is higher in countries where poverty is comparatively higher and vice versa.

The findings in this study obviously leave room for further research, especially as it pertains to considering other poverty measurements and mechanisms by which such poverty proxies can be addressed. Moreover, it would be interesting to provide policymakers and scholars with insights into whether the findings established in this study withstand empirical scrutiny within the framework of other regions in the world.

Note

1 The 42 countries are:

Angola; Benin; Botswana; Burkina Faso; Burundi; Cabo Verde; Cameroon; Central African Republic; Chad; Comoros; Congo Democratic Republic; Congo Republic; Cote d'Ivoire; Ethiopia; Gabon; Gambia, The; Ghana; Guinea; Guinea-Bissau; Kenya; Lesotho; Liberia; Madagascar; Malawi; Mali; Mauritania; Mauritius; Mozambique; Namibia; Niger; Nigeria ; Rwanda; Sao Tome and Principe; Senegal; Seychelles; Sierra Leone; South Africa; Sudan; Tanzania; Togo; Uganda and Zambia.

References

Abosedra, S., Shahbaz, M., & Nawaz, K. (2016). "Modeling causality between financial deepening and poverty reduction in Egypt", *Social Indicators Research*, 126(3), pp. 955–969.

Aghion, P., & Bolton, P. (2005). "A theory on trickle-down growth and development", *Review of Economic Studies*, 64(2), pp. 151–172.

Asongu, S. A. (2013). "Fighting corruption in Africa: Do existing corruption-control levels matter?" *International Journal of Development Issues*, 12(1), pp. 36–52.

Asongu, S. A. (2014). "Financial development dynamic thresholds of financial globalization: Evidence from Africa", *Journal of Economic Studies*, 41(2), pp. 166–195.

Asongu, S. A. (2017). "Assessing marginal, threshold, and net effects of financial globalisation on financial development in Africa", *Journal of Multinational Financial Management*, 40(June), pp. 103–114.

Asongu, S. A., Biekpe, N., & Cassimon, D. (2020). "Understanding the greater diffusion of mobile money innovations in Africa", *Telecommunications Policy,* 44(8), 102000.

Asongu, S. A., Biekpe, N., & Cassimon, D. (2021). "On the diffusion of mobile phone innovations for financial inclusion", *Technology in Society*, 65(May), 101542.

Asongu, S. A., & le Roux, S. (2019). "Understanding sub–Saharan Africa's extreme poverty tragedy", *International Journal of Public Administration*, 42(6), pp. 457–467.

Asongu, S. A., & Nting, R. T. (2021). "The role of finance in inclusive human development in Africa revisited", *Journal of Economic and Administrative Sciences*. DOI: 10.1108/JEAS-07-2020-0138

Asongu, S. A., & Nwachukwu, J. (2016). "Rational asymmetric development, Piketty and poverty in Africa", *The European Journal of Comparative Economics,* 13(2), pp. 221–246.

Asongu, S. A., & Odhiambo, N. M. (2018). "Information asymmetry, financialization, and financial access", *International Finance*, 21(3), pp. 297–315.

Asongu, S. A., Soumtang, V. B., & Edoh, O. M. (2021). "Financial determinants of informal financial development in Sub-Saharan Africa", *African Governance and Development Institute Working Paper* No. 077, Yaoundé.

Bae, K., Han, D., & Sohn, H. (2012). "Importance of access to finance in reducing income inequality and poverty level", *International Review of Public Administration,* 17(1), pp. 1–24.

Batabyal, S., & Chowdhury, A. (2015). "Curbing corruption, financial development and income inequality", *Progress in Development Studies,* 15(1), pp. 49–72.

Beck, T., Demirgüç-Kunt, A., & Levine, R. (2007). "Finance, inequality and the poor", *Journal of Economic Growth*, 12(1), pp. 27–49.

Billger, S. M., & Goel, R. K. (2009), "Do existing corruption levels matter in controlling corruption? Cross-country quantile regression estimates", *Journal of Development Economics*, 90(2), pp. 299–305.

Black, S. E., & Lynch, L. M. (1996). "Human-capital investments and productivity", *American Economic Review*, 86(2), pp. 263–267.

Boateng, A., Asongu, S. A., Akamavi, R., & Tchamyou, V. S. (2018). "Information Asymmetry and market power in the African banking industry", *Journal of Multinational Financial Management*, 44(March), pp. 69–83.

Chemli, L. (2014). "The nexus among financial development and poverty reduction: An application of ARDL approach from the MENA region", *Journal of Life Economics*, 1(2), pp. 133–148.